VERNACULAR POETICS IN THE MIDDLE AGES

EDITED BY LOIS EBIN

STUDIES IN MEDIEVAL CULTURE, XVI

MEDIEVAL INSTITUTE PUBLICATIONS
WESTERN MICHIGAN UNIVERSITY, KALAMAZOO, MICHIGAN——1984

Vernacular Poetics in the Middle Ages.

   (Studies in medieval culture; 16)
   Includes bibiographical references.
   1. Poetics—Addresses, essays, lectures. 2. Poetry, Medieval—History
and criticism—Addresses, essays, lectures. I. Ebin, Lois. II. Series.
CB351.S83   vol. 16 [PN1041]   940.17s [809.1]   83-23606
ISBN 0-918720-22-2
ISBN 0-918720-19-2 (pbk.)

Cover and book design by FAIRFAX, Clair Dunn, designer.
Printed in the United States of America.

VERNACULAR POETICS IN THE MIDDLE AGES

Contents

Abbreviations
Used in Notes

AM JNL SOC	American Journal of Sociology
ANM	Annuale Mediaevale
ATHENAEUM	Athenaeum: Studi Periodici di Letteratura e Storia dell' Antichità (Pavia, Italy)
BBSIA	Bulletin Bibliographique de la Société Internationale Arthurienne
BGDSL (HALLE)	Beiträge zur Geschichte der Deutschen Sprache und Literatur
BJRL	Bulletin of the John Rylands University Library of Manchester
CFMA	Classiques Français du Moyen Âge
CHAUR	The Chaucer Review

CL	Comparative Literature (Eugene, OR)
CLASSQ	Classical Quarterly
CN	Cultura Neolatina
DSARDS	Dante Studies, with the Annual Report of the Dante Society
ECR	L'Esprit Créateur (Lawrence, KS)
EIC	Essays in Criticism: A Quarterly Journal of Literary Criticism (Oxford, England)
ELH	Journal of English Literary History
ELR	English Literary Renaissance
FEW	Französisches Etymologisches Wörterbuch
GL & L	German Life and Letters
GRLMA	Grundriss der Romanischen Literaturen des Mittelalters
JEGP	Journal of English and Germanic Philology
JPC	Journal of Popular Culture
LR	Lettres Les Romanes
M & H	Medievalia et Humanistica
MÆ	Medium Ævum
MEDR	Medioevo Romanzo

SATF	Société des Anciens Textes Français
SMED	Studi Medievali
SP	Studies in Philology
SSL	Studies in Scottish Literature
TC	Troilus and Criseyde
TLF	Textes Littéraires Français
UTQ	University of Toronto Quarterly: A Canadian Journal of the Humanities
VR	Vox Romanica: Annales Helvetici Explorandis Linguis Romanicis Destinati
YFS	Yale French Studies
ZDA	Zeitschrift für Deutsches Altertum und Deutsche Literatur
ZRP	Zeitschrift für Romanische Philologie

INTRODUCTION

THE PRESENT VOLUME deals with the attitudes and assumptions about poetry of vernacular writers from the eleventh to the fifteenth century. In contrast to most previous studies, the essays consider not only the formal poetics, but, more importantly, the self-conscious examination of poetry which is increasingly evident in the poems themselves in this period as writers turn from Latin to the imperfect, mutable language of the vernacular. From different perspectives, the essays explore the poets' changing conceptions of their roles and their efforts to develop an effective medium in the vernacular. In the largely neglected dialogue between poets which underlies many medieval poems, the essays reveal an important reassessment of the value and effect of poetry.

In defining the vernacular poets' attitudes toward poetry, the contributors address among other issues three significant groups of problems. In part, the concerns of the medieval poets are an extension of the debate, inherited from Plato and Aristotle and reiterated in different form in the writing of the Church fathers, about the truthfulness of poetry and the role of the poet as an enlightener or a deceiver of men. In this context, the essays consider the vernacular poets' changing notions of the value of poetry as a vehicle of truth and their responses to the problems inherent in the poet's craft—particularly their awareness of the limits of mortal man as artist, their uneasiness about the motives of his rhetoric and eloquence, and their debate about the effectiveness of poetic language as a signifier of meaning.

From these concerns, the essays turn to the medieval poets' effort to create a poetic medium in the vernacular. In the process of developing new literary languages, these poets redefine the qualities of poetic excellence, articulating, by means of the critical vocabularies which they introduce in their poems, the ideals which underlie their changing conceptions of good poetry. Similarly, the vernacular poets' reassessment of their craft finds form in their attempts to develop effective formal and metrical structures to deal with the changed demands of their art. Even more conspicuously, their poetics are embodied in the striking self-images of the poet which appear in their poems—Dante's pilgrim, Chaucer's ingenuous narrator, and Langland's minstrel among others.

Finally, the essays consider the new relations among poet, text, and audience which result in this literature and the relation of the text to its changing social, historical, and political contexts. In the literary dialectics of vernacular poetics, the conspicuous response of poem to poem in this period in examining its own art, one finds a significant redefinition of the poetic process. By this means, rather than by formal criticism, which, for the most part, does not appear in the vernacular until the end of the Middle Ages, authors attune their audiences to the literary concerns they are grappling with.

The organization of the volume provides for a consideration of the major European vernaculars and of many of the texts central to the development of vernacular poetics. The essays are extremely disparate in nature and range from broad surveys of the changing conceptions of poetry to close studies of the emerging literary languages in France, Germany, Italy, England, and Scotland and the significant contributions of individual poets. Robert Hanning's essay, "Poetic Emblems in Medieval Narrative Texts," which opens the volume, draws our attention to the unique emblems of the poetic process which authors from the eighth to the fifteenth centuries introduce in their works to define their craft. These emblems—symbols or characters within the work that transcend their role as elements of the fiction to comment on the artistic practices of their creators—not only reflect the poet's view of his craft and mission, but also represent the changing function of art within medieval culture. Turning in more detail to one area of the terrain the first essay surveys, Douglas Kelly, in his essay, "Obscurity and Memory: Sources for Invention in Medieval French Literature," considers the medieval French poets' methods of invention, particularly the processes by which they render the past significant by transforming their sources. Beginning with Priscian, Kelly traces a view of the fictioning process and the role of memory in mediating between the obscurity of sources and the contemporary world of the poet which underlies the practices of the twelfth-century writers, Marie de France and Chrétien de Troyes. From the perspective of language and figure rather than matter, Frederick Goldin reconsiders the poetic dispute between Walther and Reinmar as a redefinition of the role of poetic language and the emergence of a new kind of poetry in Middle High German literature. Similarly, in examining the craft of the early Trobador poets, Joan Ferrante draws attention to the ways in which these poets created a new medium as they were working in it, a medium which is distinct from the Latin poetics of their predecessors in its unusual technical innovations.

The next three essays move from the poetics of Dante, the concluding point of Professor Ferrante's essay, to the practices of the fourteenth-century poets, Chaucer and Langland. Eugene Vance's essay, "The Differing Seed: Dante's Brunetto Latini," reconsiders Dante's vision of the poet as a maker of signs in terms of the clustering of concerns found in Canto XV of the *Inferno*—those of erotic desire, rhetoric, and text. Vance argues that in situating Brunetto in this canto as poet and rhetorician in a perspective that is both explicitly political and sexual, he is asking us to consider the role of the poet in engendering truth by language and also the boundaries that prevail in the relation between the individual and society. Winthrop Wetherbee turns to Dante's conception of himself as poet, using Dante's encounter with Statius as a key to his self-definition as a Christian poet of a new epic poetry, and, in the second part of the essay, he contrasts Dante's conception with the more ambivalent formulation articulated in Chaucer's

Troilus. Finally, George Economou distinguishes Dante's self-evaluation as a poet who attempts to come to terms with the meaning and design of his career within the tradition of poetry from Langland's justification of his role as part of a special class of minstrels, a role in which his salvation lies and which he is both compelled to hide and to reveal. While Dante translates the meaning of his experience as poet to a context under the aspect of eternity, Langland presents his "making" as the seeking of the field in the parable of Matthew, for which he, like the Merchant, has invested all that he has.

Linking early and late medieval visions of the poet, Judson Allen, in his essay,"Grammar, Poetic Form, and the Lyric Ego: A Medieval *A Priori*," offers a definition of the lyric "I" which underlies medieval poetry. Distinguishing between "clear" and "difficult" poems, he argues that most medieval lyrics are clear poems which invite the reader not to decode them by evoking an "other," but to displace oneself, as particular ego, into the ideal monologue or dialogue of the poem, to perfect or universalize oneself by "plagarizing" or occupying the language of the poem as one's own. Such a displacement is the central mode of the medieval lyric.

The last three essays turn specifically to late medieval poetics. Glending Olson's study, "Toward a Poetics of the Late Medieval Court Lyric," provides a counterpart to Judson Allen's in its consideration of the culture and aesthetic context of the lyric at the end of the Middle Ages. Approaching this lyric from the theoretical perspective of Brunetto Latini and Deschamps, Olson describes a vision of poetry as performance, refreshment, conversation, and personal expression which underlies the late medieval lyric. Robert Payne, in his essay, "Late Medieval Images and Self-Images of the Poet," returns to the issue of the poet's self-definition through his persona, arguing that late medieval poetry is characterized by a conspicuous effort on the part of poets to present themselves as fallible men speaking. Rejecting the historical view of medieval poetry as language decorously embodying ideas, Payne demonstrates that the late medieval poets regularly image forth themselves as part of the process of their craft in their attempt to define and come to terms with the role of the poetry they create. Finally, my essay, "Poetics and Style in Late Medieval Literature," considers the relation between the late medieval poets' use of high style and their redefinition of their roles as poets. Arguing that the preoccupation with high style in the late Middle Ages is an important indication of a changed conception of poetry, the study demonstrates that the late medieval poets' style is linked to ideals and assumptions about poetry which differ from their so-called masters'.

The approaches of the contributors to this volume, thus, represent a variety of methodologies and points of view, valid in their own right, and complementary in their visions. The conclusions, in many cases, qualify our assumptions about the body of vernacular literature and draw attention to issues which we must now begin to address. In completing this project, I would like to give particular acknowledgment to Otto Gründler, Director, and to Thomas Seiler of the Medieval Institute where the volume first was conceived as a special session for the 1977 International Congress and included the papers of Professors Hanning, Kelly, Allen, and Payne. In response to the considerable interest in the subject after this session, I have expanded the volume to its present form.

Lois Ebin

POETIC EMBLEMS
IN MEDIEVAL NARRATIVE TEXTS
ROBERT W. HANNING

ONE OF THE MAJOR critical preoccupations of recent years has been
to explore and demonstrate the extent to which the subject of all art
is art itself. The means chosen by verbal artists to express their self-
consciousness are as varied as the forms that consciousness may
take. An especially interesting manifestation of self-consciousness is
the poetic emblem—a symbolic artifact or character within a
narrative that transcends its role as an element of the fiction in
which it appears and becomes a powerful comment on the artistic
enterprise of its creator. Poetic emblems are an important part of
the poet's communication with his or her audience, supplementing
the narrative, descriptive, and sincere or ironic hortatory modes of
address. This essay attempts a preliminary survey of the evolution of
poetic emblems in medieval narrative by offering a brief examination of examples from different stages of medieval culture. I hope
thereby to support the contention that poetic emblems are valuable
indices not only of the medieval artist's understanding of his task,
but also of the changing functions of art in society during our
period.

Poetic emblems already function in the western world's oldest
extant poetry. Speaking of the presence and import of emblems in
the Homeric epics, James Nohrnberg has recently declared, "the art

1

of the *Iliad* observes aesthetic criteria analogous to the unifying shield of Achilles"—an image of the poem as universe and of Homer as Hephaistos, its divine craftsman—while "the art of the Odyssey resembles the over-elaborated, repeatedly woven shroud of Laertes"—an art, that is, of highly colorful, varied episodes laid end to end in a sequence reflecting the crafty resources of Homer as well as of Penelope.[1] Ovid, most self-conscious of Roman poets, created many emblems of his peculiarly complex and polyvalent art, including the figure of Daedalus in *Ars amatoria* ii and *Metamorphoses* viii, and especially the tapestry woven (with consequences disastrous to herself) by Arachne in her contest with Minerva in *Metamorphoses* vi. The complexly interwoven patterns of the tapestry, portraying the loves of the gods for mortals, obviously reflect the equally virtuosic verbal and rhetorical strategies that link the myriad stories comprising the Ovidian epic of change as the basic principle of life.[2] Some poetic emblems, originally classical, have had a long, useful cultural life: for example, A. Bartlett Giamatti has traced the emblem of the horse and rider from Vergil through the Middle Ages, and into the Renaissance epics of Pulci, Boiardo, and Ariosto. In the *Georgics* and the *Aeneid*, he notes, the horse managed by its rider already denoted the poetic activity of "disciplining the imagination in order to shape a work of art," and, he continues, "there is no figure more central to the chivalric epic than the checked or unchecked horse and its rider; nor is there a more apt image for the effort the epic poet is engaged in."[3]

In every age, in every genre, poetic emblems, once perceived, invite us to share the artist's sense of his enterprise, expressed now in earnest, now in game. Even a hard-boiled detective novel like Raymond Chandler's *The Big Sleep* opens with its hero, Philip Marlowe, staring up at a stained-glass transom, over the front door of the Sternwood mansion, that depicts a knight attempting to untie a naked damsel from a tree, but being distracted from his task by her charms.[4] The tableau is an emblem not only of the dangers posed to Marlowe's latter-day, fallen chivalry by the depraved Sternwood sisters, but of Chandler's own, ironic, twentieth-century relationship to the chivalric tradition, a legacy at once seductive and potentially destructive to a writer in an industrial democracy. In Chandler's emblem, as in that of Homer's *Iliad* mentioned above, we see the artist taking account of, and confirming, his audience's expectation about his narrative endeavor: Homer chooses a shield for his extended, encyclopedic ekphrasis, thereby suggesting the

continued hold of the heroic tradition on his audience and present-
ing the epic as an encompassing record of his culture's legacy and
values; Chandler opts for a purely decorative medium—the stained
glass window—and an archaic one at that, suggesting that the
"legacy" he is ironically exploiting has been domesticated, and
reduced by *his* culture to the level of a fragile, escapist fantasy.

——— I ———

From these preliminary remarks let us turn now to medieval
literature. Here, as we consider nearly one thousand years of poetic
narrative, we begin to notice an evolution, within the period, in the
type of image or artifact used by poets to encapsulate their self-
awareness: there would seem to be some congruence between the
emblem and the function of poetry in the culture for which the poem
and emblem were created. *Beowulf* provides an ideal starting point
for such an investigation. In an earlier essay, I singled out two poetic
emblems in the Old English epic: the necklace Wealhtheow gives
Beowulf after he has slain Grendel (ll. 1195 f.), and the sword hilt
Beowulf brings back from Grendel's underwater hall, after killing
the monster's mother, and gives to Hrothgar (ll. 1677 f.).[5] Both these
artifacts are works of art in their own right, and both function as
mnemonic devices, prompting the characters who see them and the
poet who describes them to recall and link together various stages of
the Germanic past. The necklace reminds the poet of the age of
Hama and Eormenric, anterior to that of Beowulf, but also of the
subsequent event of Hygelac's last raid, on which the Geatish king
wore the necklace passed on to him by Beowulf. The hilt, with its
inscriptions of ancient battles between God and the giants before the
Flood, will become for Hrothgar a reminder of Beowulf's own
monster-killing deeds, and seems, as well, to prompt the old Danish
king to look ahead to imagine the sad end that may await the
Geatish hero. Like the poem, the necklace and the hilt make the past
live and suggest the transitoriness of all life. In addition, the hilt and
necklace, like all other artifacts in the epic, Heorot alone excluded,
were fashioned in generations preceding that of the poem's main
action, even as *Beowulf*, whatever its actual textual history, presents
itself to its audience as the remembered (not newly created) record
of famous deeds done *in geardagum*, in days long past (l. 1).[6]

To the extent that such "artifacts of inheritance"—i.e., cultural
implements produced by an earlier stage of civilization, then passed
on to succeeding ages—point outward beyond themselves and their

immediate function to the poem that contains them and to its cultural status, they take on important resonances not, perhaps, noticed at first reading (or hearing). The sword hilt that Beowulf gives to Hrothgar, for example, having lost its blade in the course of the hero's underwater exploits, has become a diminished thing, to be admired, certainly, but now useful only for purposes other than those for which it was originally designed. Hrothgar can hold it and utter kingly commonplaces to the warrior who has saved the Danes when he, the king, could not; but no warrior can use it (either literally or metaphorically) to get a grip on elemental heroic action. The bladeless hilt, I would suggest, represents the whole heroic tradition in an age no longer fully heroic in values and outlook; it is the heroic poem which (like *Beowulf* itself) has ceased to be the cutting edge of its post-conversion culture, and is on the way to becoming a nostalgic memorial of days gone by and values irretrievably lost—a monument of the Heroic Age threatening only to a zealous Alcuin.

Each poetic emblem in *Beowulf* can variously manifest emblematic significance as mnemonic device, prized treasure, hortatory heirloom, or surviving remnant inspiring nostalgia, and even pathos, because of its now fragmentary state. Such a spectrum of meaning and effect testifies to the epic's complexity and to the ambivalence with which it was received in Anglo-Saxon England. The heroic poem's multiple function can perhaps best be characterized using a word that is applied to several emblematic artifacts in *Beowulf*, and which, as a constituent part of the name of an emblematic character in the poem, helps us to understand that character's role, and the meaning of the poem's ending as well. That word is *laf*. The two basic meanings of *laf* are: (a) a survivor or survival, what is *left* from a once larger group or artifact, a fragment or relic; and (b) an heirloom, legacy, or inheritance, something bequeathed or *left* by one generation to another.[7] The first of these meanings often carries the implication of sadness or negativity; as the poem *Wanderer* graphically demonstrates, there is a particular pathos attached in Anglo-Saxon society to being alone—cut off from one's lord, fellow hall-thanes, and the social rituals that define identity and security in the politically unstable world of early medieval Europe—and the *laf*, or survivor, of an otherwise extinct kin-group or annihilated *comitatus* has been reduced by time and circumstances to a state of radical, irreversible aloneness. By contrast, in a profoundly conservative and oral-based culture like that which produced *Beowulf*, the *laf*-as-heirloom, putting people of one generation in touch with the achievements of their predecessors, played an important and highly honored role. To own a sword or piece of jewelry that had been passed down from father to son across generations testified to the continuities of human civilization in the face of an environment usually perceived as hostile, and helped one to call to mind the brave deeds of one's ancestors—those deeds, real or mythical, which define exemplary virtue in a traditional culture lacking elaborate written laws or ethical codes.

As a relic of the past, the heroic poem earns the special honors accorded to an heirloom because it carries to each new audience a priceless legacy of the heroic actions of former days; it becomes, in this way, as much a treasure as any of the treasures it ekphrastically "contains." But as a record of an age now gone—an oral society succeeded by a literate one, a pagan by a Christian—the epic is also a melancholy survivor, recalling past glories, and thereby signalling the transitoriness of things, the passing of heroes and of whole civilizations. Just as the cross in *The Dream of the Rood* wavers between the states of jeweled and bleeding relic—between triumphant ornament and grim reminder of the Passion—so the secular heroic artifacts of *Beowulf*, and the poem of which they are emblems, alternate between being testaments of the triumph of civilization (which produces artifacts and poem alike) and testaments of its limits, its futility, and also of its burdens. This latter characteristic assumes special importance in the heroic tradition. The memories attached to the *laf* are rarely neutral; they impose on the possessor, and even on the audience or viewer, crucial obligations, either general (with respect to the recognized norms of heroic behavior) or, in some cases, agonizingly specific. By its very presence, the *laf* makes demands, bespeaks responsibilities, and consequently creates responses which may reaffirm the values embodied by the artifact, thereby validating its heirloom status in a vital and continuous civilization. But responses to the *laf*, or to the situation in which it exists and functions, may also reveal conflicts and contradictions in heroic society and thus underscore the pathetic, limited nature of human action; even worse, circumstances may give the *laf* its other meaning, making of it a survivor, a testimony to life's transitoriness. How *Beowulf* illustrates the related, yet fundamentally opposed, significances of a heroic *laf* will emerge with sufficient clarity from two more emblematic examples from the poem.

The first of these occurs in Beowulf's "prophetic" account of the dissolution of the shaky alliance arranged by Hrothgar between

5

the Danes and Heathobards (ll. 2024 f). Freawaru, Hrothgar's daughter, has married Ingeld, prince of the Heathobards, and Beowulf imagines (or predicts) a situation in which a member of the band of Danish retainers accompanying the new queen at her husband's court appears in Ingeld's mead hall wearing

> gomelra lafe,
> heard ond hringmael   Heaða-Bear[d]na gestreon,
> þenden hie ðam wæpnum   wealdan moston,
> oð ðæt hie forlæddan   to ðam lindplegan
> swæse gesiþas   ond hyra sylfra feorh.   (ll. 2036–40)
> (the *laf* of ancestors, hard and ring-marked [?] treasure of the Heathobards, as long as they could possess the weapon, until they sacrificed their own lives and their retainers in battle.)

The sword here described is a Heathobardic heirloom now, through the vicissitudes of battle, the property of a Dane, who wears it in public, presumably as a sign of prowess and personal worth. (One thinks of the sword, *Hreðles lafe*, that Hygelac ceremonially girds on Beowulf [*on . . . bearm alegde*] as a sign of the latter's exploits, and perhaps coming of age, only 150 lines later in the poem.)[8] But to an old Heathobard warrior who sees the treasure of his people adorning a traditional enemy, the *laf* becomes an inducer of bitter memories, which, when articulated, impose the burden of revenge on the next generation, with results disastrous to Hrothgar's diplomacy:

> eald aescwiga,   se ðe eall gem(an),
> garcwealm gumena   —him bið grim sefa—
> onginne geomormod   geong(um) cempan
> þurh hreðra gehygd   higes cunnian,
> wigbealu weccean. . . .   (ll. 2042–46)
> (the old warrior, who remembered it all, the falling of men in battle—his spirit is angry—begins, sad of mind, to provoke the thoughts of a young champion by laying bare his own heart, [and thus] to instigate war. . . .)

The half line, *se ðe eall geman*, describing either the old warrior's particular memories of the battle in the course of which the *laf* he now sees changed hands (and sides), or his more general abilities of recollection, points up the close relationship between the *laf* and focussing of heroic memory so that the latter, too, becomes a kind of weapon—an instrument of instruction, exhortation, and ultimately aggression. The locution, moreover, recalls Hrothgar's

6

words as he looks at the sword hilt Beowulf has brought back from Grendel's swamp:

Þæt, la, mæg secgan   se þe soð ond riht
fremeð on folce,   feor eal gemon,
eald eþelweard,   þæt ðes eorl wære
geboren betera!   (ll. 1700–04; emphases mine)

(That, indeed, may he say, he who performs truth and justice among his people, remembers all the distant past, the old guardian of his homeland; that this warrior was born superior!)

Here again, a *laf* seems to serve as a midwife of wide-ranging heroic memory, this time to deliver an accurate assessment of a "modern' hero within the context of past achievements.[9]

An even more instructive antecedent of the Heathobard warrior's power of recall comes after the fight between Grendel and Beowulf in Heorot. While the Danes celebrate their liberation from the oppressor by racing their horses, a *cyninges þegn* puts Beowulf's exploits into song, and compares them to Sigemund's brave deeds, on the one hand, and Heremod's follies, on the other (ll. 867–915).[10] The *þegn* is described as

guma gilphlaeden,   gidda gemyndig,
se ðe ealfela   ealdgesegena
worn *gemunde*. . . .   (ll. 868–70; emphases mine)

(a man well-stocked with praises, mindful of songs, he who recalled such a large number of old stories. . . .)

The skilled singer has his stock of tales ready to press into service to embellish and interpret a great deed of his own time. In effect, the old Heathobard inspired by the sight of the *laf* to incite his youthful companion to a deed of heroic kin-revenge fulfills an office equivalent to that of heroic poet, and the old heirloom that inspires him stands as emblem of the *ealfela ealdgesegena worn* the poet must control if he is to fulfill his social function.

The older man asks the younger if he recognizes the sword his father wore to his last, fatal battle; now, he says, see how one of the band of his killers, exulting in the treasure which the young man by right should possess, struts in the hall (ll. 2047–56)! The instigator *manað swa ond myndgað* (l. 2057) by his words that finally the son avenges his father by killing the Dane who wears the *laf*; thereafter, Beowulf says, both sides break the peace agreement, and Ingeld's love for his Danish wife inevitably cools. The key actions of the whole sequence are summed up in *manað* and *myndgað*: the old

7

warrior urges on and calls to mind. We may safely assume, given what we know about heroic culture, and from the evidence of the poem, that despite the double verb, only a single process is being described; to remember is, ultimately, to act. The *laf* carried into Ingeld's hall by the Danish warrior is a real sword, but a metaphorical time-bomb, triggering explosive memories that result not only in the death of its wearer, but in the destruction of peace between two nations, as well. This powerful parable of the burden of the past in a heroic culture becomes an emblem of the potential power of the heroic poem because of its organization around an heirloom-artifact that embodies and stimulates memories crucial not just to individuals, but to the societies within which they live, recall, and act on their recollections.

To complement this emblem of the strength of the poem-as-*laf,* *Beowulf* offers the figure of Wiglaf, a character whose very name ("battle-survivor"), as well as his function, alerts us to his importance for any attempt to derive from the poem an understanding of its peculiar cultural role. As the only member of Beowulf's band of retainers who does not run away in fear when his lord enters into mortal combat with the dragon, Wiglaf exemplifies the loyalty and courage on which heroic society must depend for its survival. His words of rebuke to his cowardly companions possess similarly normative force as a statement of cultural, rather than individual, condemnation. Many modern readers of the poem have seen in Wiglaf's aid to the aged Beowulf a parallel to Beowulf's earlier rescue of the aged Hrothgar from the depredations of Grendel, and in the young prince's assumption of rulership over the Geats at the dying Beowulf's request an affirmation of heroic continuity. But the context in which Wiglaf appears at least complicates, if it does not negate, such a straightforwardly optimistic reading.

Beowulf challenges the dragon in single combat in order to obtain the latter's treasure hoard, the decaying *laf* of a once-great civilization. The lament uttered by the last human *laf* of that civilization as he consigns the treasure, useless now as heirloom or incentive to those who gathered it, to the earth ranks as one of the most affecting passages in the epic (ll. 2247–66). When Wiglaf undertakes to help his lord, disabled now by the dragon's fiery breath, he does so as a *laf*, the only warrior in the comitatus not to have abandoned the wounded king and run to the woods, and thus the sole survivor, in behavioral terms, of the heroic band. In fact, before we learn Wiglaf's name, he is defined for us by his isolation from his peers:

8

> Hiora [i.e., the retainers] *in anum* weoll
> sefa wið sorgum. . . .   (ll. 2599-2600; my emphasis)
> (In one of them the spirit surged with grief. . . .)

Only then are we told he is Wiglaf, son of Weohstan (l. 2602). The young warrior sees his lord's danger, and recalls (*gemunde*, l. 2606) the gifts he has received from Beowulf. As recollection again prompts action, he grips his sword—and there follows a digression on the sword, *Eanmundes laf* (l. 2611), which Weohstan won when he killed Eanmund at the request of Onela, King of the Swedes and Eanmund's uncle, against whom Eanmund was rebelling. Weohstan possessed the sword for many years and passed it on to Wiglaf when he died, so that with it his son might emulate his prowess. Now Wiglaf will use the sword for the first time; he and it will perform equally well, says the poet:

> Ne gemealt him se modsefa,   ne his mæges laf
> gewac at wige. . . .   (ll. 2628-29; I follow Klaeber's
> emendation of *mægnes* to *mæges*)
> (His courage did not melt, nor did the *laf* of his kinsman
> weaken in battle. . . .)

Wiglaf's sword encapsulates in its peregrinations from father to son and nation to nation all the continuities and traumas of heroic society. It reminds the poet of war between kinsmen (Onela and Eanmund), which subverts the basic obligation of kin revenge by absolving the survivor (or *laf*)—Onela in this case—from avenging his nephew on the latter's *bana*.[11] But it also typifies the orderly passing on of heirlooms (and the valor they represent) from one generation to the next, within which continuity a father can legitimately hope that

> . . . his byre mihte
> eorlscipe efnan   swa his ærfæder. . . . (ll. 2621-22)
> (his son might perform brave deeds like his father before
> him. . . .)

Wiglaf, using *Eanmundes laf* (which is also *his maeges laf*), is himself his father's *laf*, the *laf* of his comitatus, and indeed the last of his royal line. The dying Beowulf tells him:

> Þu eart *endelaf*   usses cynnes,
> Wægmundinga;   ealle wyrd forsweop
> mine magas   to metodsceafte,
> eorlas on elne. . . .   (ll. 2813-16; emphasis mine)

9

(You are the last survivor of our kindred, the Wægmundings;
fate has swept away all my kinsmen by its decrees, the heroes in
all their valor. . . .)

Wiglaf's position as *endelaf* cannot but remind us of the last
survivor of the race whose treasure has lured Beowulf to his doom.
Now, as the only *laf* of the fight between two old "kings," Beowulf
and the dragon, the young hero carries into the closing lines of the
epic the entire weight of all the meanings of *laf* operative in its latter
part. He is a precious heirloom, a testimony that the heroic spirit
has not died with Beowulf; but as a last survivor of the battle and of
his race, he cannot avenge his lord—the dragon, after all, is itself an
isolate, and those who cursed the treasure hoard have long since
died—nor can he protect his new people, the Geats, from the enmity
of the many nations encircling them. These hostile neighbors,
enumerated (along with the historic circumstances of their feuds
with the Geats) by the messenger Wiglaf dispatches from the
dragon's barrow to inform the Geats of their lord's death (ll.
2900–3027), stand ready to destroy the Geats, and whether or not
the poem actually predicts the doom of Beowulf's people, it
certainly suggests the precariousness of social and political stability,
and thereby raises the possibility of future wars and their inevitable
concomitant, pathetic survivors.[12] Indeed, with Beowulf gone, not
only Wiglaf but all the Geats are cast in the role of *laf*, epic
survivals.

Finally, when the mourning Geats arrive at the barrow, Wiglaf
gives them a more circumstantial account of the hero's last fight and
instructs them in preparing the funeral rites, which he also super-
vises. Here again, he mirrors the poem's status as repository of
information about the glorious yet sad deaths of heroes and about
the observances appropriate to commemorate their passing. In
effect, all of Wiglaf's functions as Beowulf's *laf* find correlations
with functions of the heroic poem as *laf*; there is no place left for
heroic action per se after the death of the hero. As a later poet would
say, all the rest is literature, and Wiglaf acts out and emblematizes
the essential nature of heroic literature in early medieval culture,
incorporating in his identity the affectively opposed yet inextricably
linked elements of the heroic *laf* as pride-inspiring heirloom and
pathos-inspiring survivor.

——— II ———

In the next poetic corpus to claim our attention, the courtly French
narrative poems of the twelfth century, emblems of the artist's task

and of the standing his work achieves reveal a markedly different set of aesthetic and social attitudes. They betray the poet's delight in the clever, even outrageous, inventiveness of his art, but also his concern with its subversive, amoral qualities. Whichever perspective a particular emblem offers on the artist, there can be no doubt that it presents him, for the first time in medieval Europe, as a creator, rather than as the recapitulator or disseminator of a traditional, shared body of stories bequeathed by past generations. This crucial change in society's perception of its poets—to see them as fabricators of the new and surprising, rather than as guardians of the old, the understood, and the cherished—freed them of their hitherto inextricable linkage to the career of a particular nation or group of nations, and gave them license instead to inhabit, via their imaginations, a world of their own creation. Guillaume IX of Aquitaine, the first troubadour, whose highly original lyric poems are discussed by Professor Ferrante elsewhere in this volume,[13] expressed the partly serious, partly ironic consciousness of his age's courtly narrative poets as well when he began one of his songs, "Farai un vers de dreyt nien" (I will make a song [of or from] absolutely nothing). This literature, cut off from the safe haven of a corpus of received "historical" matter, veered toward the complete frivolity of fantasy and make-believe, on the one hand, but demanded respect—indeed wonder—as a new *creatio ex nihilo*, on the other. The problem of creation loomed large in twelfth-century philosophy and philosophical poetry, particularly that associated with the school of Chartres; that courtly clerics trained at the same schools where Plato's *Timaeus* and the Genesis creation accounts were harmonized (or, in some cases, kept rigorously apart) should have echoed these learned concerns in their own, less scientific way—and with an emphasis on the problems inherent in human creatures undertaking to imitate their Creator precisely as creators—need not surprise us.[14] Such a radically new way of looking at the artist simultaneously invited praise for its audacity (and for the virtuosity with which the creator-artist showed his skill), laughter at its absurdity, and worry at its potential for blasphemy in usurping a divine function for human talent.

The age which saw the rise of romance was, as we all know, a time of innovation in every sphere of European culture—political, educational, ecclesiastical, philosophical—as well as in the arts. The courtly poet, writing for a self-consciously elite society, participated in this climate of innovation by redefining the poetic act as the fresh application of intelligence and sensitivity—of *ingenium*, or *engin*, to use twelfth-century terms[15]—to large preoccupations of the moment, under the guise of tales and adventure. The mixture of shrewd social commentary, psychological analysis of the individual, and detached, ironic awareness of art's fictive freedom—its status as a new creation related to, yet separate from reality—is the hallmark of the courtly narrative, and of its poetic emblems.

Even the *romans antiques*, ostensibly rooted in history via the Latin classics of which they are free adaptations, acknowledge their commitment to the new, creative view of literature in emblematic passages. In the *Roman d'Eneas*, for example, a tent painted to look like a castle is erected overnight by the Trojans and thoroughly cows their enemies, who awaken to find outside their city walls what seems to be a stone keep that should have taken three years to build (ll. 7281–356).[16] The tent, the poet tells us, had been built only for its beauty and *richece*: "ne fu pas forz, mes molt fu biaus" (l. 7330; it wasn't strong, but it was very beautiful). By means of this creation, and the perplexity it causes, the Trojans—and the poet—inject flagrant make-believe into a Vergilian battle for national survival, thereby affirming the legitimacy, even primacy, of the creative impulse in the treatment of inherited material, but also managing to suggest that the products of this impulse lack something of reality, though they may be confused with it. By calling attention to the power and illusoriness of a newly created artifact, the tent in *Eneas* becomes an emblem for the poem that offers to its sophisticated audience the simultaneous pleasures of partisan involvement and amused detachment: we applaud the Trojans' resourcefulness in an hour of need, but laugh at the gullibility of the Laurentians, taken in by such a fraud, and at ourselves, who are being similarly manipulated by the trickster-poet playing Creator with his invented and inherited materials.

Elsewhere in the *Roman d'Eneas*, we find another emblematic artifact in the tomb built to house the remains of the Amazon Camilla (ll. 7531–718). This marvel is built in stages with each one larger than the one below, giving the effect of an inverted pyramid. The text's explicit comment on the wonder aroused by this method of construction (quite beyond the capacity of medieval engineering) calls attention to the art of the impossible—the creation of an imaginary universe—by which the poet makes us participants in his world of mingled classical and chivalric fantasy: "Grant mervoille sanbloit a toz / que graindre ert desus que desoz" (ll. 7629–30; it seemed to everyone a great marvel that [the tomb] was larger above than below). The entire *Roman*, reality-defying artifact that it is, coerces its audience into esteeming its maker for the very brazenness of his imagination, and the inverted pyramidal tomb functions as an emblem of this feat.

In certain courtly texts, the poet's self-consciousness, his or her new role as creator (we must include Marie de France's *Lais* among those twelfth-century works most keenly manifesting such self-awareness),[17] assumes more complex dimensions, raising questions about the relationship between art and magic, the morality of the illusions practiced by the artist, and (the ultimate question) the diabolic or blasphemous potential inherent in imitating the creative power of the Deity. These problematic assessments of art's power and limits find embodiment in equally problematic, morally ambiguous, even terrifying poetic emblems. Consider, for example, the tower that Jehan the serf constructs in Chrétien de Troyes' *Cligès*, where Cligès and Fénice live in secrecy after the latter has escaped from her loveless marriage to Cligès' uncle by means of a potion that induces a deathlike trance. The *engin* with which the tower is constructed (see ll. 5487 f.)[18] calls attention to Chrétien's own *engin* in creating a rival to the Tristan legend, not from the mists of Celtic saga, but from a mixture of epic Arthuriana à la Geoffrey of Monmouth and thinly disguised details from contemporary Byzantine and European politics. The tower is beautiful and full of works of art that give pleasure to the visitor (l. 5491 f.); but it also contains secret chambers, known only to its maker, that give it greater significance, as a safe hideaway for Fénice, when they are revealed to Cligès by Jehan (l. 5508 f.; they are reachable only by a hidden door which Jehan alone, "qui avoit fet l'uevre"[5545; who had made the artifact], can open.) Jehan has provided these innermost chambers with every modern comfort, including hot running water (ll. 5562–63), and it is here that he himself stays when indulging in artistic creation:

> Par mi un estage vostiz,
> Ou Jeanz ses oevres feisoit,
> Quant riens a faire li pleisoit.   (ll. 5550–52)
> (In the middle of a vaulted room, where Jehan created his works, when it pleased him to make something.)

The secret, as it were thematic, dimension of the tower buttresses the parallel between Jehan and Chrétien who can, by his art, endow beautiful courtly narratives with higher, metaphorical significance. Furthermore, the image of Jehan creating, as the spirit moves him, in his vaulted (church-like?) chamber completely isolated from the world outside by its secret door, yet possessed of

13

every convenience, constitutes a splendid, arguably tongue-in-cheek portrait of the artist at court: a fully domesticated courtier, yet also a kind of magician, living in his own, somewhat mysterious and unreachable creative world.

Perhaps the most striking aspect of Jehan's tower as an emblem of Chrétien's art is its negative element. The tower fails to do what its creator promises it can, namely provide permanent security and secrecy for the love affair of Cligès and Fénice. It fails because, marvelous artifact that it is, it is also completely unnatural. No sunlight can penetrate its recesses, and it becomes in fact a living tomb for the lovers (a cause of further irony in this most ironic of Chrétien's romances; Fénice, we recall, is ostensibly dead, "killed" by a potion administered by the romance's other artist-figure, Thessala, and, true to her name, she has "risen" to live with Cligès— but only a life akin to death in its removal from nature and human society). Finally, after fifteen months of enclosure, Fénice, prompted by hearing the song of a nightingale (l. 6267), asks Cligès for a return to the living world:

> Biax amis chiers,
> Grant bien me feïst uns vergiers,
> Ou je me poïsse deduire.
> Ne vi lune ne soloil luire
> Plus a de quinze mois antiers.
> S'estre poïst, molt volentiers
> M'an istroie la fors au jor,
> Qu'anclose sui an ceste tor. . . .   (ll. 6271–78)

(Dear, fair beloved, a garden where I could enjoy myself would do me a lot of good. I haven't seen the sun or moon for fifteen whole months. If it were possible, I would gladly go out there into the daylight, because I'm [too?] cooped up in this tower.)

The limits of the world created by art are as clearly articulated here as in Chaucer's glass temple of Venus, set in the middle of a desert, that appears in *The House of Fame* some two hundred years later. The odd relationship between this world and that of experience and nature is further clarified when Cligès asks Jehan's help in satisfying Fénice's desire. The artist-serf opens a door and lets them into a garden; the door is

> Tel qui je ne sai, ne ne puis
> La façon dire ne retraire.
> Nus fors Jehan nel poïst faire.
> Ne ja nus dire ne seüst

14

> Que huis ne fenestre i eüst,
> Tant con li huis ne fust overz,
> Si estoit celez et coverz.   (ll. 6298–304)
>
> (Of a kind that I don't know how to tell or describe. No one
> except Jehan could make it. Nor could anyone tell that there
> was a door or window there, as long as the door wasn't
> open, it was so well hidden and covered.)

There *is* a connection between Jehan's art and the real world, but
again only he knows where (or what) it is. The hidden door provides
another ambiguous emblem, both of the poet's complete control
over his enterprise, and of his and its isolation from our perception
unless he opens his work to the light of understanding. (We would
do well here to recall the *trobar clus*, the deliberately difficult or
"closed" poetic language of Provençal lyricists, which similarly
created an inaccessible world of language within which the poet and
his created lovers "live.")

Once the lovers venture out of the tower into the adjoining
garden, they find abundant evidence of Jehan's art, cultivating the
garden. The imposition of his art on nature finds its emblem in the
grafted tree (l. 6314) in the midst of the garden. There the lovers are
discovered by a knight who happens upon them while chasing his
hunting bird, and they must flee for their lives.[19] The creator-artist
cannot finally co-opt nature in constructing his imagined world:
dabbling with reality will only demonstrate the indisputable fragility
of fantasies of love exempt from responsibility to the fallen world.

Not only does Jehan's creation point to troublesome aspects of
the twelfth century's assessment of artistic excellence; Jehan himself,
the great artist, suggests ambiguities of an emblematic nature. When
Cligès first refers to him, his description is honorific, not to say
hyperbolic:

> Un mestre ai . . .
> Qui mervoilles taille et deboisse:
> N'est terre ou l'en ne le conoisse
> Par les oevres que il a feites,
> Et deboissiees, et portreites. . . .   (ll. 5314–18)
>
> (I have a master who carves and sculpts marvels: There isn't
> anywhere that he isn't known by the works he has made,
> sculpted, and portrayed. . . .)

Jehan is a *magister*—a title originally reserved for highly trained
scholars, and only gradually in the Middle Ages bestowed also on
master masons and other artists. Fénice has already referred to her

15

nurse Thessala (she of the magic potions) as a *mestre* (l. 5303), so both protagonists cast themselves, in effect, in the role of students of an artist-figure. But Cligès adds one crucial line to his description of Jehan: "Jehanz a non, et s'est mes sers" (l. 5319; His name is Jehan, and he is my serf). The great artist is not free; Cligès promises to free him and his heirs (l. 5332) if Jehan will help him in his hour of need with a place to hide Fénice. Jehan buys his liberty by turning his great creation over to the lovers for illicit purposes, only to have them discover that they cannot stay enclosed in it forever. Can this be our first recorded emblem of the Daedalan artist, seeking to free himself from all obligation to the inherited codes and norms of the traditional art of early medieval Europe? If so, Chrétien shows his awareness of the acute limits reality places on his newly perceived status as a creator.

Still, Jehan remains loyal to Cligès even under threat of the emperor Alis' displeasure and defends his actions by saying that he and his tower in fact belong to Cligès. This assertion of serfdom, even after Cligès has freed Jehan (an apparent inconsistency which may have prompted Guiot to omit the passage from his copy of the romance),[20] can perhaps be clarified by a passage in Boethius' *De musica*, ii.34 comparing "the practical execution of a work of art to a slave, the science that should guide such work to a ruler."[21] In Chrétien's case, the "bondage" is not to *scientia* or *theoria* conceived abstractly, but, I believe, to the ideals of personal autonomy and the quest for self-fulfillment articulated for the new courtly elite by its sophisticated poets. These artists developed (none more spectacularly than Chrétien) a set of chivalric and love conventions to which we can say they were in some sense bound—perhaps by the very success of their narratives with their patrons and audiences.[22] Yet they also evolved an ironic technique that constantly verged on burlesquing, or at least questioning, the very conventions they had evolved.[23] The basic situation of *Cligès*—a parody of the Tristan story in which the protagonists, cast in the artist-hero mold of Tristan and Isolde, create the impossible situation from which their "masters," Thessala and Jehan, attempt to save them—shows Chrétien maintaining his artistic freedom by playing generic conventions of romance, love-tragedy, and historiography against each other, creating a play-world as unique as Jehan's tower, and as inevitably flawed, given its insulation from reality.

Jehan the master-servant stands, then, as an ironic, possibly bitter emblem of Chrétien and his class of courtly makers, while Jehan's tower and garden manifest an analogous relationship to the

16

marvelous, complex creations that revolutionized European narrative in the twelfth century, established poetic individuality and autonomy for the authors of verbal fictions (now first perceived as fictions, not the record of ancient truths), but could not, in my reading, ever quite accord them complete freedom from the constraints of reality. In other words, the new understanding of the artist as creator had to confront, and live in tension with, the fact (or, as we might say, the belief) that there was already a Creator whose work, fallen though it was, could be neither ignored nor challenged with impunity. New conceptions of artistic power created a revolution of rising expectations in the twelfth century, the frustration of which, by the nagging realization of art's limits in the face of both natural and supernatural reality, led to the presence of ambiguous "artifacts (and artificers) of creation," like Jehan and his tower, as powerful poetic emblems in courtly and chivalric narratives.

Jehan's tower is far from being the only marvelous poetic emblem of problematic import in twelfth-century chilvalric romance. Perhaps the most complex and revealing such emblem, or more precisely, network of interconnected emblems, occurs in the anonymous romance, *Partonopeu de Blois*.[24] This network merits special attention not only because of its complexity, but because of the thoroughness with which it explores the extraordinary power of human creativity and the extraordinary problems, moral and psychological, inherent in such a cultural perception of the artist as creator.

At the center of *Partonopeu de Blois'* emblematic network is an artifact comprising several spatial units of progressively diminishing size, the smaller fitted within the larger. At its outermost extent, the emblem is an entire city—Chief d'Oire, capital of the empire of Besance (Byzantium). The city encloses a main palace, the most beautiful of its myriad beautiful structures; and within the palace lies a *chambre*, a bedroom furnished with articles of an excellence even more hyperbolic than that of the rest of the palace. The protagonist of the romance, the thirteen-year-old Partonopeu, experiences these progressively diminishing spaces (and artifacts) in succession and with a heightened sense of wonder and fear that we are invited, nay coerced, to share with him. This dynamic aspect of the emblem—its ever-increasing hold on our faculties of wonder, mystery, and willing-unwilling involvement in a world of created beauty—effectively represents a significant part of the aesthetic

17

appeal of twelfth-century romance as a genre, vis-a-vis the traditional narratives of early medieval culture, in which the use of widely known stories and a technique of moving backward and forward freely in narrative time for didactic purposes tend to diminish the possibilities for suspense and mystery.[25] The audience of romance, in contrast, like its surrogate Partonopeu at Chief d'Oire, can be led episode by mysterious episode deeper into the dark forest of adventure, toward a sudden, climactic moment of epiphany or confrontation.

Partonopeu is brought to Chief d'Oire by a mysterious boat he finds at the seashore after becoming lost in the forest while hunting near his natal home in France. The boat, "tant bele com s'el fust faee" (l. 702; as beautiful as if it were enchanted), has no visible crew, yet it sails with Partonopeu straight toward a great light, "com s'on le conduisist par art" (l. 770; as if someone were guiding it artfully). It is itself an emblem, of the unique propulsive power of the romance plot controlled by the artist's invisible hand and directed toward climaxes we cannot perceive as we set out on the narrative journey (again in contrast to epic narratives dealing with events known to their audiences or at least anticipated for them by the narrator).

The *clarté* at the end of Partonopeu's journey is a city of marvellous beauty—the possibility of enchantment is again raised (l. 807 f.)—full of polished marble palaces in complementary colors, constructed with great expertise ("grant savoir," l. 838), and adorned with gilded images of beasts which, despite their obvious artificiality, still "sanblent vives par nature" (l. 844; seem naturally alive). No one familiar with twelfth-century courtly narratives—in which extravagant poetic fantasy and mimetic renderings of experience in time and space coexist in delightful tension—will, I believe, disagree that this ekphrasis of a whole city as an autonomous work of art (it is completely protected from the outside world by towered walls, and need fear no assault, l. 820), full of self-consciously balanced beauty at once fairy-tale-like and natural, constitutes an admirable emblem for the literary genre in which it appears. Any doubts as to Chief d'Oire's function as an image of the courtly artist's re-created universe vanish when the narrator, addressing us directly, says of the decorated palace facades,

> La veriés les elements,
> Et ciel et terre et mer et vens,
> Solel et lune et ans et jors
> . . . .

> Les estoires des tans antis,
> Et les guerres et les estris.   (ll. 853–58)
>
> (There you could see the elements, heaven and earth and sea
> and winds, sun and moon and years and days . . . stories of
> ancient times, and of wars and battles.)

Here is an art that encompasses in its imaginings the cosmos, nature, and history. Partonopeu thinks he has entered paradise (l. 874), yet we are immediately told he is hungry and thirsty (l. 882 f.), a reminder of the limits of even the most enchanting artifice. A final noteworthy characterizing feature of the emblematic city is that Partonopeu sees no other living creature in it. He exists alone in a beautiful world of art, not knowing if he wakes or sleeps (l. 908 f.). Consciously or unconsciously, the chivalric poet calls our attention to an important change in the relationship between audience and narrative when the latter no longer recapitulates (or ostensibly recapitulates) stories which are the legacy of an entire social group. The poet-reciter in an archaic culture summons his audience to a communal, identity-confirming event: "Listen! *we* have heard of the great deeds of kings of the Danes in years gone by," or "Charles the king, *our* great emperor, has been in Spain for seven years " (emphases mine). In romance, we are invited singly, via our surrogate the lone hero, into the world of chance and adventure, to venture we know not where. The literary experience of romance is isolating and often dream-like in its vividness, yet foreignness to our normal world of activity; we, too, as we read or listen, do not know if we are awake or dreaming, or partaking in the dream-creation of another, the poet.[26]

Chef d'Oire as a whole, then, stands for the world created for and around us by chivalric romance. When Partonopeu enters the finest palace and eats, served by invisible hands, he ceases to be a mere observer of this world, becoming instead a participant nourished by its mysterious processes. He is still surrounded by artful beauty, and drinks from a cup made of a sapphire with a ruby lid

> Qui a la coupe se joint si
> Que bien i pert a sa mesure
> Que hom ne le fist fors nature.   (ll. 1028–30)
>
> (which is so joined to the cup that in its exactness it seems
> that nature, not man, made it.)

The fantastic cup, flaunting yet hiding its artifice, comments yet again on the impossible, yet mimetic art of the poet. The total effect on the protagonist reminds us of one of the problems of mimetic art in a society that worships a divine Creator: Partonopeu

> ... crient molt que diables
> Li ait tot fait cel bel sanblant
> Por lui del tot trair avant.   (ll. 1054–56)
> (fears greatly that the devil has created this beautiful appearance in order to betray him completely.)

"Cel bel sanblant"—a phrase here applied loosely to all that the young hero has seen—serves admirably to characterize the whole world of courtly imagining.

Finally, compelled by another physical need—to sleep— Partonopeu enters a *chambre*, the innermost space of the emblem here under discussion, in search of a bed. The richness of the *chambre* defies description (ll. 1102–03), but we are told that it is furnished with artifacts made from the skins of exotic beasts, and a carpet of phoenix feathers! (ll. 1075–90). Since the bed beside which the carpet lies will shortly become for Partonopeu a place of rebirth, where he has his first sexual encounter, the symbolism is internally apposite, but it also looks beyond the confines of the *chambre* to serve as an emblem of the metamorphosis of experience into fantastic adventure fiction, where even the commonplace act of getting into bed becomes an event of great significance.

Once Partonopeu has entered the bed, the candles that have led him into the *chambre* go out. In short order, he is joined in bed by a woman whom he cannot see, whom he begs to allow him to remain when she angrily threatens to expel him (it is *her* bed)—and whom he then rapes. This astonishing turn of events gives way to the even more astonishing revelation that his victim, whom he cannot see in the dark, is Mélior, the empress of Byzantium, a woman of extraordinary powers of art and magic, who has fallen in love with him and has used her *engin* to bring him from France to her city, palace, and bed. In effect, Mélior reveals the hand of the artist behind all the mysterious events so far; the adventures of Partonopeu, so surprising to him (and to us) as they unfolded, are her carefully executed plot. The young man, in effect, discovers that he is now, willy nilly, the hero of a romance created by Mélior. Chief d'Oire is her city, and by a further exercise of her art she has made all its inhabitants and Partonopeu mutually invisible. Now she explains her scenario for the rest of the story: if Partonopeu will live with her at Chief d'Oire for two and one-half years, having no human companionship but Mélior and never trying to see his beloved's face when she comes to him at night, at the end of his period of probation she will make him visible to her vassals (whose desire that she marry has led her to select Partonopeu as her ideal mate), and take him as her lord and emperor.

From this scant summary, it should be evident that Mélior is as much an emblem of the courtly poet as Chrétien's Jehan, and an even more compelling one, at that. The contrast between her status as empress and Jehan's as serf might seem to suggest that in Mélior we have a wholly positive view of the artist as creator-controller of an imagined universe. But closer inspection disputes such an assumption. Her control over Partonopeu and his new environment involves first tricking him, then revealing that his experiences (even his act of sexual mastery, presumably) have been planned for him. She requires absolute obedience and isolation of him; to win her love he must forego human society and live in a world artifically emptied of all other mortals. In fact, they are still there, but her art, in the service of her fear of discovery by her vassals, has rendered them invisible and unobtainable to Partonopeu. Mélior's city is an emblem of a world totally transformed and controlled by the power of art to make it the setting of an ideal love match, a place where an adolescent's dream-quest of love and worldly fortune can come true—provided it holds itself completely apart from the threatening world of reality.

In short, Chief d'Oire, its palace and *chambre*, are the world of romance imagination, an alternative creation fabricated according to principles of selection, truncation, and desocialization that enlist art in the service of wish-fulfillment. Mélior's powerful, all-encompassing artfulness retains its force only as long as Partonopeu (the hero, but also the audience of Mélior's romance-making) acquiesces completely in its absolute demands. But such acquiescence in effect makes of Mélior Partonopeu's creator, and involves her in the risk of blasphemous rebellion against nature's Creator. Throughout the first part of *Partonopeu de Blois*, there are suggestions that Mélior's art is in fact diabolical. I have quoted one passage to that effect; and Partonopeu's concern lest his beloved turn out to be a fiend finds its echo in the worries of his mother, when he twice returns to France during his probationary period. Furthermore, the world of Chief d'Oire offers Partonopeu (and us) support for the dread conjecture: when Partonopeu elects to go riding in the countryside around the transfigured city the morning after his encounter with Mélior, she supplies him with clothes, richer than those in which he arrived (a sign that he has been transformed into part of Mélior's romance world), and a fine horse:

> Mais tant est noirs que il le crient
> Et a mal cose le tient. . . .   (ll. 1617–18)

21

> (But it is so black that he is afraid of it, and considers it a
> bad omen. . . .)

And the next day, when he goes hunting, she supplies dogs,

> Mais molt par sont noir tot li chien;
> Partonopeu nel tient a bien.   (ll. 1831–32)
> (But the dogs are all equally black; Partonopeu doesn't
> think it's a good sign. . . .)

Finally, when he arrives back in France for an interlude of martial
adventures to increase his worth, Mélior sends him much wealth,
carried by twelve black mules.

Clearly, the poet plays in these passages on his audience's
worries about the strange, potentially destructive power of the
mimetic artist.[27] And so, when Partonopeu, egged on by his mother
and the Bishop of Paris and convinced that Mélior is a devil, breaks
her commandment and, using a smuggled lantern, sees her when she
comes to him in bed one night, we are horrified at his disobedience,
which will cost him the wish-fulfillment romance offers its audience,
and become his accomplices in the rebellion against an art which
makes such demands on us in defiance of reality. And, with
Partonopeu's sin against his (re-)creator, Mélior's magic is broken.
Chief d'Oire becomes once again a city of real people who see and
are seen by Partonopeu, and the love affair of the protagonists
moves into a period of crisis which can only be resolved by the very
different, non-magical, and compassionate art of Mélior's sister,
Urraque.[28]

Chief d'Oire provides us with an audacious emblem of the
created fiction's fragile tyranny over its audience. Mélior's radical
transformation of society into a magic world of exotic beauty sums
up all the appeal of "escapist" fiction, but also, like Jehan's tower in
Cligès, reveals the poet's (and his culture's) apprehension of the
dangers in the artist's dream of total control over reality. That
Mélior can justly be seen as an emblem of the new courtly poet
receives definitive confirmation in her description to Partonopeu of
her early training by her father in all the arts and sciences (ll.
4573 f.).[29] After she had mastered all the disciplines, she turned
secretly to the highest study of all—*nigremance et enchantement* (l.
4612). Aided by a chosen few tutors, she learned the arts by which
Mohammed performed the feats for which he was held to be a god
(ll. 4621–22). She continues:

> Quant nos estions a sejor
> Et plaisoit a l'empereor

Que li feïsse aucun deduit,
Si me mandoit a mïenuit
Et mes maistres ensanble moi
En ses chambres tot a secroi.
La faisions par mon savoir
La chambre croistre et grant paroir;
Tant par ert grans, ce lor ert vis,
Que tot porprenoit le païs.
Dedens faisoie tel clarté,
Com el plus bel des jors d'esté,
Et puis faisoie cheveliers
Venir armés sor les destriers,
Mil ou deus mil a mon plaisir,
Et entr'iaus meller et ferir;
Ja ne verrés plus dur estor
Ne plus mellé qu'estoit le jor.
Tant com moi plaisoit se melloient
Et puis a nïent repairoient. . . .
Je ravoie tel poësté,
Par le sens que Dex m'ot doné,
Que d'un chastel u d'une vile
S'il i eüst homes cent mile,
Ja li uns l'autre ne verroit
Ne de son estre ne savroit;
Par cest savoir vos ai celé
A tos ciax de ceste cité.
Or m'avés si tolu mon sens,
Por moi vëir sor mon deffens,
Que jamais nul jor de ma vie
Par moi n'en iert ouvre bastie.   (ll. 4629–64)

(When we were at home and it pleased the emperor that I perform to entertain him, he would summon me and my masters [tutors] secretly to his chamber at midnight. There, by my knowledge, we would make the chamber expand and appear large—so large, it seemed to them, that it encompassed the entire countryside. Within it I would create light like that of the finest summer's day, and then I would make knights appear, armed, on their chargers, a thousand or two at my choice, and fight and joust; you never saw a harder, more layabout battle than occurred that day. For as long as I pleased they fought it out, and then they vanished completely. . . . Again, I had such power, by the skill God had given me, that if a castle or a town had a hundred thousand inhabitants, I could bring it about that one never saw the other, nor even knew of his existence; by this skill I hid you from everyone in this city. Now you have so robbed me of my power, by seeing me despite my prohibition, that never

23

again for the rest of my life will such deeds be performed by me.)

What can one call this striking passage but a metaphoric representation of the creative imagination at work, "stretching the walls" of the narrow chamber of reality into a wider world of fantasy, and specifically a world of chivalric combat?[30] Allied to this power of Mélior's is her ability to prevent people from perceiving each other's presence—to create private, fictional worlds in which the imagination can move unhindered. Yet, if this is art, it is tinged with magic; it must be performed in secret, as it makes the artist seem like a god—and perhaps (as the reference to Mahomet, arch heretic for the Middle Ages suggests), like an agent of the devil, as well. In this latter perspective, Mélior represents the artist as elitist, practitioner of a discipline above all other learned sciences, the property of only a few. But the danger of this view of art is that it makes of reality—daylight, the ability to see and understand as well as to be transported and amazed, the possibility of communication between social beings—its enemy, that which will ruin it, "tolir son sens." Chief d'Oire in its transformed state is a tenuous monument to this elitist, antinomian view of the creative artist and his private world. The poet of *Partonopeu*, by having his hero destroy this world and, after despair and near death, finally win Mélior in a socially as well as personally satisfying manner, pleads for a fiction that presents a mimesis of reality accepted, rather than escaped, in the quest for personal happiness.[31] The creation and destruction of Mélior's magic city should be taken as an emblem of a rite de passage for the new European poet of the twelfth century. By his ability to confront the dangers inherent in a personal and imaginative, rather than communal and commemorative, art, the courtly poet demonstrates that he is neither dangerous magician nor silly escapist, but a valuable spokesman of a vital, creative, self-consciously modern culture.

——— III ———

If the twelfth century sees narrative poetry come of age as a creative discipline within European culture, the late fourteenth century in England—the period John Burrow has recently dubbed Ricardian—manifests a glorious, if brief, efflorescence of that creativity. During the last quarter of the century, Chaucer, Langland, Gower, and the anonymous poet of *Sir Gawain and the Green Knight*, *Pearl*, *Patience*, and *Cleanness* expanded the poetic re-

24

sources of the English language and the imaginative capabilities of medieval poetry. These great poets built on the achievement of twelfth-century French courtly art (as Charles Muscatine, in a deservedly famous study, has demonstrated with respect to Chaucer), but also ranged eclectically through other ancient and modern, learned and popular, religious and secular (not to say profane) material in the service of their powers of invention. In fact, their eclecticism, and their sense of debt to a wide variety of poetic and intellectual traditions, informs their poetry in many defining ways. The self-consciousness of Ricardian poets is less that of an artist creating something new—outrageous in its reality-defying fantasy and marvellous in its ingenuity—than it is of an older, less naive practitioner who has come to take a serio-comic, ironic, slightly detached view of his labors. Chaucer and his contemporaries saw themselves as inheritors of a multiform poetic tradition which they were trying to live up to, continue, transform, reinvigorate, and above all *interpret* by means of their own imagination and of the culture in which they had their experiential roots.

Evidence for the complex attitudes toward poetry that I have just sketched in oversimplified fashion has been adduced by Burrow in his comparative study of the major fourteenth-century English poets, *Ricardian Poetry*; and Robert Payne, in *The Key of Remembrance*, provides corroborative analysis of Chaucer's evolving concern with the relationship of books, dreams, and experience (i.e., of poetic tradition, imagination, and the pressures of reality) in his own poetry. But the poetry itself contains emblems which can be characterized neither as "artifacts of inheritance" nor as "artifacts of creativity, ingenuity, or deceit," requiring instead that we understand them as artifacts of metamorphosis, of process, and (in consequence of these two) of ambiguity; these emblems demand for themselves and their contextual narratives not pride, not pathos, not wonder or worry, but above all interpretation—without, however, offering the satisfaction of being susceptible of a single, consistent, unchanging interpretation. As a result, Ricardian poetic emblems highlight the changing processes of reality that require constant re-estimation and approximate, rather than definite, evaluation. They reveal the poet's self-consciousness as above all the awareness of his dilemma: how to make a statement at once true to reality and tradition by its inclusiveness, yet open to the audience's understanding by its vividness and distinctness.

Within available space, I can refer to only a few Ricardian emblems, and those briefly. (I hope in future essays to do more justice to this segment of my subject.) The only one I shall consider in any detail occurs in the second fitt of *Sir Gawain and the Green Knight*. Gawain has arrived, unexpectedly, at Bercilak's castle on Christmas Eve, badly in need of shelter and a place to celebrate the feast with appropriate solemnity. After his initial warm welcome, he is led to dinner, and served a bounteous repast of varied, well-seasoned stews and many kinds of fish, diversely prepared (ll. 884 f.); of these latter, the poet adds, "And ay sawes so sle3e that the segge lyked" (l. 893; and always in such cunning [or artful] sauces as pleased the man). The adjective *sle3e*, in its nominal form, *sle3tes*, is used by the castle's inhabitants to describe Gawain's own super-courtly behavior a few lines later; it is clearly a value-laden, and positive, term in this society. The point about the slyly-sauced fish is that they are served to Gawain as part of what should be a penitential repast appropriate to the fast day that precedes a major liturgical feast. When Gawain repeatedly calls the meal a feast, his hosts courteously reply, "this penaunce now 3e take, / And eft hit schal amende" (ll. 897–98)—a remark whose playfulness Gawain clearly appreciates. But behind the joking, this passage and the image of the well-sauced penitential fish at its center raises most of the main questions that inhere in this most enigmatic of medieval romances. Bercilak's court (and his cooks) are making a game of penance, demonstrating their skill at covering the facts of nature with the ornaments of art, for the sake of human pleasure—and in the process are recapitulating the Green Knight's concealment of his deadly challenge to Arthur's court, and particularly to Gawain, in the guise of a Christmas game. The sauced fish also looks forward to the elaborate rituals with which Bercilak and his retainers will decorate the bloody violence of the hunt on three successive days, and, with its reference to "taking penance," even anticipates the final meeting of Gawain and the Green Knight, which, as Burrow suggests, turns into an outdoor, ad hoc administration of penance by the marvelous green man to Gawain as a result of the latter's "fall" during his last bedroom tete-a-tete with Bercilak's wife. Indeed, we learn after the fact at the Green Chapel of yet another sauced-fish analogue: although the bedroom scenes had appeared to be a serio-comic interlude in which a young woman who had read one romance too many attempted to seduce a visiting knight in the best literary fashion, they were in fact the main test Gawain had journeyed from Arthur's court to undergo.

Everywhere one looks in *Sir Gawain and the Green Knight*, facts and significances are hidden under misleading appearances, behind the colorful façades of courtly routines and games. We are left perpetually uncertain how to interpret key aspects and figures of the romance: is the Green Knight a wild man or a supercivilized evil genius? Does Bercilak hide the Green Knight's true identity or vice versa? Is Morgan La Fay the real instigator of the action, or a blind behind whom the Green Knight hides his own intentions? Is Arthur's court silly, corrupt, merely young—or finally wiser than the overwrought Gawain in treating his adventure as a cause for celebration instead of breast-beating when he returns wearing the green girdle?[32] The relationship between the penitential fish and its sly sauce stands as an adequate, nay superb, emblem for the problematic relationship between appearance and reality, or act and interpretation, throughout *Sir Gawain and the Green Knight*. Does the disguising of the fish constitute a subversion of the Christian impulse toward penance by the principle of deceit and the yearning for pleasure so deeply ingrained in fallen human nature? Or is the creation of the sauce a more neutral, or even positive, tribute to human artfulness, like the adornment of Bercilak's rugged castle with pinnacles and turrets that make it seem more like a paper cutout than an outpost of civilization standing firm against the onslaughts of hostile nature (ll. 763 f., esp. 785–802)?

The poem never answers these questions directly, but delights in raising them, and in giving hints that seem to lead to mutually contradictory solutions. This is the poet's high art: he, too, can sauce the fish of problematic, potentially tragic moral and social realities with the sly games of his literary imagination, well-stocked as it is with the romance conventions and conceits of two centuries.[33]

If Beowulf's necklace and sword hilt are artifacts of inheritance, and the tent castle of *Eneas* or Jehan's tower in *Cligès* are artifacts of ingenuity and deceit, the sauced fish of *Sir Gawain and the Green Knight* is an artifact of transformation and process. Several stages are implied in the emblem: the subduing of nature (catching the fish), its disguise and sophistication by cooking and saucing, and its endowment with moral and social ambivalence by being served as part of a penitential meal on Christmas Eve. (The fact that the fish is a traditional Christian symbol only complicates the possible meaning even further.) This multi-staged, transformational quality reappears in several of Chaucer's poetic emblems. For example, the lists built by Theseus in the "Knight's Tale," which starts out as a great *teatrum mundi* where Theseus' ordering power is exercised to settle the dispute between Palamon and Arcite over Emelye, with no "destruccion of blood." Suddenly, however, it becomes the stage on which the gods show their power over the fates of men—a tragic stage on which Arcite, in the moment of his victory, meets his doom. And finally, it gives way to the funeral pyre on which Arcite's body is burned—a pyre constructed on the same site where Palamon and Arcite first fought in the woods over Emelye—the site on which Theseus first constructed the lists, and then the pyre.

Perhaps the most provocative Chaucerian emblem of transformation is the figure of Alceste in the F Prologue of the *Legend of Good Women*. As Alceste shifts through her many guises—she is the daisy, the day's eye or Sun, the wife who sought her husband in hell, the *marguerite* or pearl, the consort of the god of Love, the savior of the poet who has offended the god—our sense of her significance for the narrator and for his poetic enterprise (which, as Professor Payne has taught us, is the real subject of the prologue) must constantly grow in subtlety and sophistication or be false to the emblem and the poem. The metamorphic, polysemous figure of Alceste is an emblem for the shifting, developing view of meaning in all of Chaucer's major poetry, and especially in the *Canterbury Tales*, where each successive tale or encounter between pilgrims enriches, and is enriched by, all that has gone before.

To judge a Ricardian emblem—or poem—by merely seizing on one part of its existence as process is potentially to misjudge it badly. The sauced fish and Alceste challenge and perplex us, by showing us that art constantly shifts its form in order adequately to reflect and define protean reality but, paradoxically, in doing so becomes, like Proteus himself, a great disguiser of reality.

Thus, in every phase of the medieval world, poetic emblems reflect the artist's view of his gift and mission and also the function of art within the culture of the day. In explicating medieval poetry, the discovery and interpretation of poetic emblems should, I believe, be as important a part of the critic's task as source study, linguistic analysis, or doctrinal exegesis. Certainly no aspect of medieval narrative offers such aesthetic satisfaction to the critic, even as it challenges his or her interpretive ingenuity.

——— NOTES ———

[1] *The Analogy of the Faerie Queene* (Princeton, 1976), p. 11.

[2] On Daedalus see Valerie M. Wise, "Flight Myths in Ovid's *Metamorphoses*: An Interpretation of Phaethon and Daedalus," *Ramus*, 6 (1977), 53–58; on Arachne, Eleanor W. Leach, "Ekphrasis and the Theme of Artistic Failure in Ovid's *Metamorphoses*," *Ramus*, 3 (1974), 102 f.

³"Headlong Horses, Headless Horsemen: An Essay on the Chivalric Epics of Pulci, Boiardo, and Ariosto," in *Italian Literature, Roots and Branches*, ed. Giose Rimanelli and Kenneth John Atchity (New Haven and London, 1976), pp. 267, 270.

⁴*The Big Sleep* (1971; rpt. New York, 1973), p. 1.

⁵"*Beowulf* as Heroic History," *M & H*, n.s., 5 (1974), 94–96. In the present essay, all quotations from the poem follow the edition of F. Klaeber, 3rd ed., rev., with suppl. (Boston, 1950). All translations are my own.

⁶Heorot's exceptional status is interesting, because as soon as it is built by Hrothgar, it is invaded and rendered half-useless by the demonic figure, Grendel. The poet links Grendel's first approach to Heorot to a creation song sung within by a *scop*, ll. 86 f. Do these facts point to a Christian sense of danger involved in new creation, in a society which defined the good as the customary and received?

⁷See Bosworth-Toller's Anglo-Saxon Dictionary, s.v. *laf*, I and III.

⁸See lines 2190–96, and, on the significance of the scene, Eric John, "*Beowulf* and the Margins of Literacy," *BJRL*, 56 (1974), 409–11.

⁹Hrothgar goes on to recall the career of the negative exemplary king, Heremod, as a foil and warning to Beowulf.

¹⁰On this passage see Jeff Opland, "*Beowulf* on the Poet," *MS*, 38 (1976), 457–58.

¹¹We are told (ll. 2618 f.) that Onela did not dwell on Weohstan's hostile act, even though he had killed Onela's nephew. Earlier (ll. 2435 f.) Beowulf says that Hrethel did nothing to revenge the death of his eldest son, Herebeald, who was slain by his own brother in a hunting accident, because an accidental death could not be so avenged, even though the lack of vengeance was a cause of grief and disgrace to the father. At this point (ll. 2444 f.) reference is also made to the hypothetical case of a father who cannot avenge his son because the latter has been hung as a criminal. In both cases, the father is left as the unnatural and helpless *laf* of his son, and the pathos of the situations contributes to the general darkening of tone toward the end of *Beowulf*.

¹²For a vigorous statement about the poem's meaning with respect to the survival of the Geats as a nation, with a summary of opposing views, see Kenneth Sisam, *The Structure of Beowulf* (Oxford, 1965), ch. 4: "Fiction and History: The Geats after Beowulf's Death." Beowulf himself says (ll. 2732 f.) that he has kept hostile nations at bay during his long kingship, which may suggest that his death will unleash the long-checked fury of the Geats' neighbors.

¹³See pp. 96–99 below.

¹⁴For one aspect of the relationship between chivalric romance texts and Chartrian philosophy, see Claude Luttrell, *The Creation of the First Arthurian Romance* (London, 1974), ch. 1, "Nature." See also M. Stevens,

"The Performing Self in Twelfth-Century Culture," *Viator* 9 (1978), esp. 207–12.

[15]See R. W. Hanning, "*Engin* in Twelfth-Century Romance: An Examination of the *Roman d'Eneas* and Hue de Rotelande's *Ipomedon*," *YFS*, 51 (1974), 82–101; and *The Individual in Twelfth-Century Romance* (New Haven and London, 1977), ch. 3.

[16]I follow the edition of J. -J. Salverda de Grave (Paris, 1929). Translations are my own.

[17]See the Introduction to *The Lais of Marie de France*, trans. J. M. Ferrante and R. W. Hanning (New York, 1978).

[18]I follow the edition of A. Micha (Paris, 1957). Translations are my own.

[19]On the absurdity of the conditions of their discovery, see P. Haidu, *Aesthetic Distance in Chrétien de Troyes: Irony and Comedy in Cligès and Perceval* (Geneva, 1968), pp. 102–04. Note also the ancient metaphoric and emblematic opposition between the activities of hunting and love, as well as their symbolic equivalence.

[20]Micha's edition, based on Guiot's copy, omits thirty-four lines present in the other manuscripts, and printed in Förster's edition as ll. 6559–82, but includes these lines in the "Notes critiques et variantes," pp. 215–16, from which I have taken them. Jehan says, "Ce set an bien certainement / Que je sui suans et la tor soe."

[21]Quoted from Otto von Simson, *The Gothic Cathedral* (New York, 1956, rev. ed., 1962, rpt., 1964), p. 31 and n. 27.

[22]Chrétien suggests in the opening lines of his romance, *Le chevalier de la charette*, that his patroness, Marie de Champagne, has given him the material for his story of Lancelot and Guinevere, and many scholars have speculated that Chrétien wrote the romance against his will, since its content is very different from his others in some respects, and he did not complete it, leaving that chore to Godefroi de Leigny.

[23]See especially P. Haidu, *Lion-queue-coupée* (Geneva, 1972) for a lively appreciation of this aspect of the courtly poets' art. See also Hanning, *Individual*, pp. 135–38

[24]I follow the edition of Joseph Gildea (Villanova, 1967). Translations are my own. I have found the section on Mélior in J. M. Ferrante, *Woman as Image in Medieval Literature* (New York, 1975), pp. 84–87, particularly useful and have more recently profited greatly from work on the romance done by Dr. Sandra P. Prior. For a different perspective on *Partonopeu*, see Hanning, *Individual*, pp. 80–102, 213–18.

[25]On this point see John Burrow, *A Reading of Sir Gawain and the Green Knight* (London, 1966), pp. 1–3.

[26]In the lyric by Guillaume IX, "Farai un vers de dreyt nien," to which I have already referred, the poet says he has created his song while sleeping on his horse (ll. 5–6).

ROBERT W. HANNING

[27]For an interesting, latter-day confirmation of this worry, see *The New York Times*, 18 March 1977, which contains a story of a Bedouin tribesman who began to carve human heads in stone although his tribe has no tradition of figural art, and was accused of "defying a Moslem injunction against the worship [!] of graven images." The Bedouin is quoted as saying, "It sometimes happens I create a thing and I get a sudden fear I am going to make something that is evil, as if a devilish force is overtaking me."

[28]On Urraque, see Hanning, *Individual*, pp. 80–102.

[29]See Ferrante, *Woman as Image*, p. 86 and n. 20, and, on the significance of the fact that Mélior is the only child of the emperor, see Ferrante, "The Education of Women in the Middle Ages in Theory, Fact, and Fantasy," in Patricia H. Labalme, ed., *Beyond Their Sex: Learned Women of the European Past* (New York, 1980).

[30]The sudden appearance and disappearance of the knights in the magically-expanded room cannot but recall the passage in Chaucer's "Franklin's Tale," ll. 1139 f., where the cleric-magician of Orleans treats Aurelius and his brother to a series of outdoor panoramas of action (including knights jousting, l. 1198) without their ever leaving the magician's book-lined study.

[31]There is a fascinating parallel between the claim I am making here for the *Partonopeu* poet as the exponent of a mimetic, rather than escapist, art and an analogous claim made for Charles Dickens in John Romano, *Dickens and Reality* (New York, 1978). Romano uses the famous mirror scene at the beginning of *Our Mutual Friend* as a poetic emblem of Dickens' sense of the limits of art in a manner that closely parallels the argument of this essay.

[32]Gawain's "fall"—and therefore, the significance of the girdle—is the subject of interpretation and disagreement among Gawain, the Green Knight, Arthur's court, and the poem's many critics. Surely this is part of the point: experience cries out for interpretation to give it meaning, but no two observers (or participants) seem able to arrive at the same interpretation. Art can therefore only approximate truth or the constantly shifting face of reality. Interestingly enough, the green girdle becomes for Gawain a *laf* of his adventure, and, as donned sympathetically by all members of the Round Table, a *laf* for them as well. But the disagreement over its meaning, the result of subjective interpretations of experience, is a far cry from the ambivalence of the heroic *laf* in *Beowulf*, which varies from heirloom to survivor—from triumphant to pathetic artifact—as a function of objective social circumstances, not individual points of view.

[33]The *Gawain* poet alludes pointedly to his use of romance tradition more than once in the course of the poem: Bercilak's wife, seeking to seduce Gawain, prompts him to behave amorously by noting that knights in romances always devote themselves to love; "Hit is þe tytelet token, and tyxt of her werkke" (l. 1515; it is the title page and text of their deeds). Even the metaphor is bookish. And the inhabitants of Bercilak's court, when they

31

learn that their guest is Gawain of Round Table fame, accord him a reputation for fine manners and love dalliance that belongs to Gawain's character in French romances, rather than to our hero (ll. 916–27). The whole question of literary reputation vs. experiential reality constitutes one of the poem's most persistent jokes—and most serious concerns. Subsequent to writing these lines on *Gawain*, I have offered a fuller discussion of the issues raised here: "Sir Gawain and the Red Herring: The Perils of Interpretation," in *Acts of Interpretation: The Text and its Contexts, 700–1600*, ed. Mary J. Carruthers and Elizabeth D. Kirk (Norman, OK, 1982), pp. 5–23.

OBSCURITY AND MEMORY:
SOURCES FOR INVENTION
IN MEDIEVAL FRENCH LITERATURE
DOUGLAS KELLY

In diverse wise and oon entente. Chaucer

CURTIUS' ATTACK on the autonomous study of European national literatures introduced a dramatic swing in scholarship towards Latin rhetoric and poetics, especially within the framework of historical topics. Current authoritative statements tend towards a balance between the prepotency of Latin and vernacular norms in literary history, both synchronic and diachronic, allowing for independent differentiation and mutual influences. Jean Frappier rightly distinguishes between the process of composition learned from Latin tradition and the subject matter such techniques were applied to and by which they underwent further elaboration.[1] The dichotomy is especially remarkable in courtly literature, a set of writings in which the interaction of Latin and vernacular traditions was most fruitful and complex.

In the second half of the twelfth century, writers in French and Provençal began to make more precise terminological distinctions as *roman* replaced *estoire* and *canso* supplanted *vers*.[2] This suggests that they were beginning to ponder and conceptualize the material

33

handed down to them through diverse literary, oral, and social traditions. These traditions needed to be understood, evaluated, and adapted, if the society receiving and continuing the line of transmission was to take a meaningful place in the world and in history. But the memory of the past carried by the diverse traditions was often perplexing and obscure. How was the past to become meaningful for the present? The answer was to be found in the careful study of sources.

A source may be either material or mental (*status sensilis* or *status archetypus* [= actual and archetypal states]).[3] This differentiates between the source as an antecedent version of the work the author proposes to write, and a conception of the work that springs from the *ingenium*, a mental construct or imagination, drawn up in and visible, as it were, to the mind's eye. The source of such imaginations is the memory. Memory is both the faculty for mental recall and the record of past thoughts and actions.[4] Both of these senses are implied in Marie de France's allusions to Breton lais and the adventures they relate:

> De l'aventure de ces treis
> Li auncïen Bretun curteis
> Firent le lai pur remembrer,
> Qu'hum nel deüst pas oblier.   (El 1181–84)[5]
> (The ancient and courteous Bretons composed the lai, recounting what happened to these three in order to preserve the memory of their adventure, for it should not be forgotten.)

But the lais Marie used as sources were not always readily comprehensible—they required some interpretation, some effort on her part to probe their mysteries and elucidate what seemed obscure or unclear.

> Le cunte e tute la reisun
> Vus dirai, si cum jeo entent
> La verité.   (El 2–4)
> (I shall tell you the story and the entire narrative, as I understand it to be true.)

For example, Marie points out, the original title of the *Eliduc* was changed to "*Guildeluëc ha Guilliadun*" (El 22) because they are the persons the adventure happened to, and it is their truth that Marie proposes to relate (El 21–28).

The problem and the evaluation of antecedent sources is clearly and succinctly set forth in the Prologue to Marie de France's *Lais*.

Marie emphasizes the advantages of learning and eloquence (Pro 1–2) in extracting and propagating the works handed down from the Ancients:

> Custume fu as ancïens,
> Ceo testimoine Precïens,
> Es livres ke jadis feseient,
> Assez oscurement diseient
> Pur ceus ki a venir esteient
> E ki aprendre les deveient,
> K'i peüssent gloser la lettre
> E de lur sen le surplus mettre.   (Pro 9–16)
>
> (The Ancients were wont, so says Priscian, in the books they wrote to express themselves somewhat obscurely so that future writers who would learn from them might explicate their words and complete the meaning of what they had said.[6])

There have been numerous attempts to interpret these lines. Notably, Mortimer J. Donovan analyzed them in relation to a passage in Priscian usually believed to have inspired Marie's words.[7] Donovan argues that Marie did not view the Ancients as deliberately obscure; the Moderns, standing on their giant shoulders, penetrate further into their writings than even they could, and thus elicit meanings not yet revealed in the past. However, Marie's words suggest that the Ancients did know what they were obscuring, both by the intentionality expressed in the preposition of purpose *Pur* in v. 13, and by the sense of vv. 21–22, not considered by Donovan: "E plus se savreient garder / De ceo k'i ert a trespasser" (And they would be better equipped to avoid passing over what was contained in them). In his suggested translation of vv. 9–16, Donovan follows A. Ewert, although the latter's version allows for deliberate obscurity in the sources: "the Ancients . . . put their thoughts somewhat obscurely, *so that* [emphasis mine] those who were to come after them and were to learn them, might construe their writing and add to it from their own ingenuity."[8] Jean Rychner, in his edition of the *Lais*, follows Gaston Paris' more literal version of these lines: the Ancients

> s'exprimaient assez obscurément, *en vue de* [emphasis mine] ceux qui devaient venir après eux et qui devaient apprendre ces livres, afin qu'ils pussent ajouter des gloses au texte, et y mettre ce qu'ils auraient de sens de plus que leurs prédécesseurs.[9]

That such "glosses" elucidate what is contained "obscurely" in the old works is made even more explicit by vv. 21–22. Ewert renders these lines: "and know better how to avoid the transgression of that (i.e. the teaching) which was contained therein." G. Paris is less helpful here: "et mieux ils se sauraient garder des choses dont on doit s'abstenir," and is therefore corrected by Rychner to: "et mieux ils se sauraient garder de négliger *ce qui était déposé dans leurs livres* [emphasis mine]."[10]

From the practical point of view of modern criticism, it does not perhaps matter too much whether Marie de France saw the obscurity of the Ancients as deliberate on their part or not. It is however important if we want to understand how Marie envisioned her art in relation to that of her alleged forebears. If the first inventors of the lais Marie de France collected left their productions "obscure," she has the *escience* to uncover what had been hidden in that obscurity, that is, "ceo k'i ert." Her evaluation amounts to the archeological reconstruction of past monuments from extant remains. The qualities perceived in the sources will, ultimately, depend upon authorial acuity, artistry, and genius, and thus the presumed pristine or "archetypal" work itself. Marie's sources are at one and the same time "material" and "mental"—simply summed up in her phrase: "Des lais pensai, k'oïz aveie" (I thought on the lais which I had heard [Pro 33]). As time passed, one could expect a gradual unveiling of hidden significations aiming at a totality. Marie herself felt that the possibilities inherent in Latin literature had been exhausted, and that is why she turned to the lais in other languages.

Towards the end of the thirteenth century, the anonymous author of *Claris et Laris* would boast that romances contained the sum total of learning handed down from the past:

> Et qui vos verroit demander,
> S'en puet riens en romanz aprendre,
> Et je diroie sanz mesprendre,
> Qu'il i gist tout li sens du monde,
> Tant come il dure a la roonde,
> Car se les estoires ne fussent,
> Les genz de droit riens ne seussent;
> Li philosophe les escrisent,
> Qui tout le sens du monde lisent,
> Qu'en Ebreu furent premier fetes
> Et de l'Ebreu en Latin tretes,
> Ou molt bien furent translatees,
> De Latin en Romanz portees
> Fors que li sacres de la loy.   (vv. 29623–36)[11]

(And, should anyone desire to ask whether anything can be learned from romance, I would rightly respond that it contains all the wide world's learning. For, were it not for stories, people would possess no certain knowledge. Philosophers wrote them, they who read all the world's learning. They first wrote them in Hebrew, and they were then translated from Hebrew into Latin, and very well indeed, then from Latin into French—with the exception of the mysteries of faith.)

Estoires in v. 29628 shows that *romanz* (v. 29624) is romance narrative; in v. 29635, however, *romanz* refers only to the vernacular language. The *Claris* passage makes translation coincide with transmission. But elucidation is the discovery of hidden meaning. How did Marie de France, the *Claris* author, and their peers comprehend such discovery, or more accurately, invention of past records and their obscurities? How did they pass from *matiere* and *sens* to the new, finished work, itself described as a faithful, clear record transmitting the past to the present?

The technique learned in the schools, and for which Priscian supplied authoritative instruction for the Middle Ages, was topical invention.[12] It is, briefly, the technique for identifying "places" or topoi in a given *matiere*, and amplifying them in a manner consonant with authorial conception of the work. It therefore expresses authorial intention. Such investigation of the *matiere* construes source both as mental and material and seeks the elucidation of obscurity through patterns of events that express context. This is the technique Marie refers to in her Prologue. It discloses the full import of her reference to Priscian.

Marie, like the troubadours, trouvères, and romancers of the twelfth and thirteenth centuries, wrote what is today termed courtly literature. Judgements regarding that literature have varied, both in modern and medieval times. For example, Jehan Bodel pronounced "British," that is, Arthurian literature "vain," as opposed to the more profitable and truthful writings on "Roman" and "French" subjects.[13] The diverse evaluations of medieval romance raise two questions regarding topical invention. First, how was the technique applied in romance? Second, what determines the validity of topical invention in a given work?

The Technique of Topical Invention.

The romances *Amadas et Ydoine* and *Flamenca*, together with Marie de France's *Guigemar*, will illustrate the application of topical invention as a *surplus de sen*.[14] Each work depicts two idealized figures, both of whom stand as exemplars of aristocratic perfection, save for one defect: initially, none of them loves. And each romance complicates the situation by a marriage triangle, including corollary developments on attraction and separation familiar from the troubadour and trouvère chanson. Each romance can be distinguished from the others by topical adaptations of the theme of extramarital love leading to marriage.

In the *Amadas*, Amadas loves Ydoine, at first in vain; his suit is received with harshness, cruelty, and moral outrage because he is of lower birth than his lady. But when on one occasion he faints before Ydoine, her pity is aroused. *Pité* in Old French is also "sympathy," and an Ovidian amplification effects her swift transition to love. While Amadas loved in vain, Ydoine's cruelty and his own love sickness stopped him from exercising prowess. This is bad love. The advent of happy love restored his prowess. Inspired by Ydoine's love, Amadas successfully completes a great round of tournaments.

In *Flamenca*, Guilhem is a consummate exemplar of noble humanity, except that he too does not love. His own awareness of the defect inspires a decision to love, followed by the choice of Flamenca for her noble excellence and sorry plight in unhappy marriage to the jealous Archambault (vv. 1761–81). The consummation of their love is brought about gradually in amplifications on the words hastily exchanged in church, as well as by subsidiary activities that further the realization of love. Here too the climax is followed by the knight's departure for tournaments.

Finally, in the *Guigemar*, the hero's perfection is flawed by his failure to love. Marie's lai abbreviates what in *Amadas* and *Flamenca* is retarded by topical obstacles (Ydoine's cruelty) or topical amplifications (Guilhem's and Flamenca's monologues analyzing their loves and relations). Instead, Marie puts into Guigemar's mouth a topical justification for haste which convinces his lady. They enjoy their love for a year and a half, confirmation of Guigemar's argument that by skipping courtship "avrunt il mut de lur pru fait" (they will have profited considerably v. 525). But they are discovered by the jealous husband, and Guigemar is forced to leave. He goes on to take part in tournaments and finally a siege which restores his lady to him.

Each romance varies the characterization of the adultery by topical adaptation. Marie de France exemplifies the advantages of haste, *Flamenca* those of patience. *Amadas* separates declaration and response into two amplificatory narrative sequences on, first, despairing love and, second, mutual love. Ydoine's change is

38

analogous to Archambault's, both by its suddenness and by its topical adaptation of descriptive features that are retailored to fit the new role assigned to each personage.

The husbands are therefore a source of topical complexity and divergent adaptation. Ydoine's marriage to the Count of Nevers is imposed on her after she begins to love Amadas; and the Count is, by and large, a good match. Guigemar's lady is already espoused to a jealous and impotent old man. Archambault is a jealous, suspicious villain for most of *Flamenca*, with some extant sections that portray him as a model fiancé and model husband, not dissimilar in type to the Count of Nevers, except that the marriage, initially happy, preceded Guilhem's intervention, and indeed had to turn bad for Guilhem even to choose to love Flamenca. The Count takes a second wife. Archambault's imagination arouses jealousy when he perceives the friendly but innocent rapport between Flamenca and the King of France. His subsequent transition from jealous to model husband (part of which is missing in the manuscript) is descriptive adaptation of one type to another, whereby jealous defects give way to corresponding positive qualities lost during jealousy:

> ques a perdut
> Sos mals aips e sa vilanía
> Et a cobrada cortesía.   (vv. 6776–78)

(For he has lost his bad ways and his villainy, and recovered courtesy.)

The old man in *Guigemar* hardly appears, and then only as a foil consistent with his age, marital state, and impotence.

The topical features provide descriptive quality, context, motivation, and exemplary character. In the narrative they mesh with the *aventures merveilleuses* drawn from the sources. Ydoine resorts to witches and a *fausse mort*; Marie de France uses a white doe that bears antlers and talks; and the consummation of the love between Flamenca and Guilhem takes place in a marvelous bathhouse with locked entrances and a secret underground passageway—an analogue to Jehan's tower in *Cligès*.

Topical developments from commonplaces or topics can support striking or even contrastive juxtapositions. For example, there is a conventional antifeminist diatribe in *Amadas et Ydoine* that begins:

> Ha! feme, com es enginneuse
> Et decevans et artilleuse,

39

> D'engin trouver puissans et sage,
> De bastir mal a grant damage!   (vv. 7037–40)

(Ah! woman, how cunning, deceitful, and slippery you are—skilled
and able in inventing schemes and contriving devastating evil!)

This continues until v. 7067, whereupon the narrator stops short: his
patrons are women, yet they are not deceptive! Obviously then,
engin trouver,[15] among women, may be good or bad.

> Mais qui ira par mi le voir,
> S'eles ont engin et savoir
> De mal querre, por voir le di
> Qu'eles resevent autresi
> Le bien, la francise et l'ounour.   (vv. 7985–89)

(But, to be correct, although they have cunning and knowledge enough
to pursue evil, I protest that they also know what is good, noble, and
honorable.)

Rupprecht Rohr has demonstrated that the combination of abstract
words determines their semantic range and affective value in both
romance and the chanson.[16] Topical statements, and especially
topical abstractions, are neutral outside of context. They are thus
susceptible of antithetical interpretation, as in the *Amadas* evaluation of *engin*. Affective differentiation allows elsewhere in the
romance for the argument that a good woman is better than a
hundred men (vv. 3643–56). In each case the appropriateness of the
commonplace condemnation or praise depends on authorial intention in depicting the quality of the figure represented.

  Gautier d'Arras skillfully combines antifeminism in the *Eracle*
with characteristics that undercut it and show how "complexes" of
abstractions can produce a reasonably subtle ideal representation.[17]
Facile resolution of oppositions is no more unusual than, and often
just as compelling as, the accommodation of man's fallen state with
the virtues that may inhere in him to lift him up to a greater or lesser
degree, as the *Queste del saint graal* shows. From the point of view
of historical topics, the arguments in *Amadas* and *Eracle* recall
other striking developments on the theme of woman's goodness:
Jean de Meun's artful denial that there are any good women,
Chaucer's hyperbolic assertion in the *Legend of Good Women* that
for every bad woman there are a hundred good ones, the capacity
for moral decisiveness equally shared by both sexes as proclaimed in
Partonopeu de Blois.[18] These works appeal to ancient authority.
Such appeals, as topical invention, are just as valid and convincing
as would be mine if I were to argue, in separate but appropriate

40

contexts, that rich men are generous and that rich men are misers. The *Amadas* author extols Ydoine's *engin* or cunning because it combines with her loyalty, love, and reasonableness. Cunning may indeed be deceit, and Eve deceived Adam, Delilah deceived Samson. But then, on the credit side, Judith deceived Holophernes, Rahab deceived the city of Jericho, and Esther deceived or at least "led on" Ahasueres. Solomon's wife in the *Queste del saint graal*, whose *engin* circumvents all her husband's wisdom, invents the ship of Solomon.[19] Viewed in this light, the commonplace of woman's *engin* opens interesting and intriguing possibilities to the author possessed of the *ingenium* requisite for the adaptation and arrangement of sources.

Amadas' prowess equals Ydoine's *engin*. Love enhances prowess and *engin* so that, despite vicissitudes and sudden, unexpected changes in fortune, the two lovers achieve exemplary status. By staggering the falling in love, the *Amadas* romancer sets a pattern for alternately bringing Amadas' prowess and Ydoine's *engin* to the fore in succeeding narrative sequences. Thus the marriage of Ydoine to the Count of Nevers parallels a *maufé*'s attempted seduction of Ydoine; Ydoine deals with the former, Amadas with the latter interference. Similarly, the marriage of Ydoine to the Count causes Amadas' madness and temporary loss to Ydoine. Amadas' failure to function as an active agent is followed by Ydoine's temporary abduction as a *fausse morte*. Ydoine's *engin* assists her in discovering and healing Amadas, just as Amadas' prowess twice frees Ydoine from the *maufé*. The crowning achievement is Ydoine's. Inspired by her *engin*, she produces three witches who convince the Count of Nevers that they are the Fates or "Destinees," and that he will die if he consummates the marriage with Ydoine. The ploy is repeated to convince her father and his counsellors to annul the marriage. And there are interesting topical developments on the Count of Nevers, whose sense of honor and courage almost aborts her plans. In any case, he is convinced because, with an abruptness recalling Archambault's change from jealously to courtesy, we learn that the Count actually loved the daughter of the Count of Poitou all along and would happily accept her free hand! Marriage and love may or may not go together.

It is not unusual to find disparate material made whole by topical amplifications. In Chrétien's *Erec*, Enide's beauty unites the hunt for the white stag and the sparrowhawk contest to make the first part of Chrétien's romance. Chrétien drew from his sources this credible and coherent *conjointure*, thereby eliminating the lacunae and dispersion he found in them.[20] In this and the works discussed above, the meaning of the romance is the expression of what seems credible in the *matiere* as the romancer perceives it. This is the topical invention that, for Marie de France, allowed the Moderns to find the truth the Ancients had buried in their works under obscure surfaces. Topical invention springs in the last analysis from the author's *ingenium*, whether after immediate reflection upon the *matiere*, or whether as intelligent borrowing of commonplaces adapted from extant works which turn the source's patterns, formulae, and topics to the interpretation of new *matiere*. Ovidian borrowings and imitations are the most obvious and widespread kind of such topical adaptation. However, direct borrowing from secondary sources does not preclude giving them new signification or affective value. Ovidian developments in Guillaume de Lorris[21] do not serve the same purpose as in Jean de Meun, any more than the figure of Lancelot is the same in Chrétien's *Charrette*, the prose *Lancelot*, or the *Queste del saint graal*.

Cristal et Clarie[22] offers an instructive example of the blend of the topical and the disparate, and thus unexpected, as sources. The anonymous author, like Guillaume de Lorris in the *Rose*, intends his romance to be an art of love, that is, a combination of discursive and narrative statements depicting love's progress. The romance begins with a 396 line prologue on love; and the narrative is interspersed with topical developments pertinent to Cristal's progress towards Clarie, her love, and marriage. To set the narrative in motion, Cristal is made to dream of Clarie, whom he has never seen or heard of; filled with longing, he sets out on the quest for her. The separate adventures show different features of Cristal's love and worth. The quest lasts ten years. In spite of considerable narrative diversity in the discrete adventures, numerical diminution in the number of feminine protagonists coupled with a gradual approximation to Clarie in excellence among the women encountered provides, through gradation, for growing concentration on and elaboration of the character and qualities of Clarie. Topical amplification achieves this purpose. The conclusion, at Clarie's castle, alternates Cristal's attempts to draw nearer to Clarie with monologues during sleepless nights—"adventures" reminiscent of alternate proximity and separation of the lover and his lady as described by the god of Love in Guillaume de Lorris.[23] And a dream inspired the lovers in both romances.

This is not to say that the *Cristal* author used Guillaume's poem, tempting as it may be to discover a work influenced by the

Rose prior to Jean de Meun's adaptation. Although the quest for the lady in a castle is frequent in romance, Breuer is no doubt correct in affirming that the basic plot of *Cristal* was the anonymous author's own achievement.[24] This suggests that the *Cristal* author, like Chrétien, combined his sources into a meaningful *conjointure*. The emphasis in descriptive and digressive passages, as well as in monologues and dialogues, on problems of love brings forth Ovidian topics adapted to *fin'amours*. The stay at Clarie's castle only accelerates the *gradus amoris* adumbrated in Cristal's dream and quest.

A second, more compelling argument against the *Rose*'s influence on *Cristal* is the absence of any plagiary from Guillaume de Lorris, despite the author's demonstrable willingness to expropriate large segments from other works and incorporate them verbatim into his own narrative. This is not occasional borrowing, but wholesale expropriation. Breuer has demonstrated that nearly twenty percent at least of *Cristal et Clarie* is out and out plagiary![25] Undaunted by considerations like Horace's warning against mindless use of source and topical material, he strove to make foreign wine domestic. However, he was not merely putting new labels on old bottles, nor is he really guilty of the faults Horace castigates.

> Publica materies privati iuris erit, si
> Non circa vilem patulumque moraberis orbem,
> Nec verbo verbum curabis reddere fidus
> Interpres, nec desilies imitator in artum,
> Unde pedem proferre pudor vetet aut operis lex.
> (vv. 131–35)[26]

(Common subject matter will become original if one does not linger in a trite, broad circle, nor strive faithfully to render word for word, nor slip into such close imitation that fear or poetic constraints prevent overstepping the imposed limits.)

Horace and medieval interpretation of him allowed imitation and even plagiary. But the new work had to be coherent and congruant. Thus, as the Vienna scholiast read Horace, there would be no discrepencies, no indiscriminate sewing together of patches purple or otherwise.

> Si quis profitetur se describere magna ut res bellicas et postea omisso incepto transferat se ad aliquam materiam describendam, ubi valeat extollere ingenium suum, tamquam si scriberet de amore aut de quolibet huiusmodi, ubi bene

43

exercitatus fuerit: ille similis est alicui assuenti novum panniculum veteri panno.[27]

(Should anyone boast that he will set forth great matters, like warfare, and then, abandoning what he began, should turn to some other subject—say love or something similar he was accustomed to treating—in order to show off his genius, such a person would resemble a tailor sewing a new patch onto old cloth.)

Rather the whole work should be conjoined so that all parts are consistent and coherent (p. 13, ll. 26–27). Breuer recognized that *Cristal* fits these requirements.[28] The interpolations coalesce easily and appropriately with passages that are only loosely imitated from sources and those that appear to be original with the romance's author.

Of more significance than the fact of borrowing is the kind of material borrowed. Generally speaking, it is topical; that is, the author extracted from his sources commonplaces, or passages "quae transferri in multas causas possunt"[29] (which can be used in many different cases.) Two kinds predominate: Ovidian love themes and scenes of knightly adventure and festivity. The extensive use of the *Lai de Narcisse* explains the resemblance to Guillaume de Lorris,[30] who, besides borrowing from Ovid, applies the story of Narcissus to the exemplification of good and bad love. The whole is a *bele conjointure*, using Cristal and Clarie as exemplary lovers to combine diverse adventures and topical themes and motifs, including the amplifications expropriated from various sources, that depict the nature and progress of love.

Another instance of topical amplification is suggested by the Cligès analogue in *Marques de Rome*, the second book in the thirteenth-century prose cycle the *Sept sages de Rome*.[31] Chrétien, in the Prologue to his own *Cligès*, says that he discovered the source as a *conte* in a library in Beauvais. What relation may one reasonably postulate among Chrétien's romance, the Beauvais *conte*, and the *Marques de Rome* analogue? The brevity of the *Marques* version, and especially its vilification of Cligès' affair with the Empress and limitation of the narrative to the *fausse mort* episode, have inclined scholars to regard Chrétien's romance and the *Marques* analogue as independent of one another, although deriving from a common source identifiable with or related to the Beauvais *conte*. How may the three relate to one another in the perspective of topical invention?

Topical invention allows for extensive modification and ampli-fication in conformity with authorial intention and interpretation. For example, *Cassidorus*, the fourth book of the Seven Sages cycle, combines in an exemplary tale some topical features found in both *Erec* and *Yvain* to illustrate the antithetical vices of uxoriousness and excessive devotion to knighthood as they succeed one another in the same marriage,[32] like the change from model to jealous and then back to model husband in *Flamenca*. Just as the *Cassidorus* author amalgamated features no doubt taken from *Erec* and *Yvain*, Chrétien de Troyes combined material from the Beauvais *conte*, some or all of which is present in the *Marques* analogue, with features of the Tristan and Iseut legend and their adulterous love. The Tristan legend accounts for the narrative addition of the love of Alexandre and Soredamors and perhaps the Arthurian setting.[33] The fact that Cligès is the Emperor's (Alis in Chrétien) nephew in both Chrétien and the *Marques* analogue fits the Tristan circum-stances and allows for narrative and topical linking of the two parts of the romance. Topical reinterpretation explains Chrétien's cele-bration of fidelity in spite of the marriage bed as opposed to the condemnation of the lovers in the *Marques*. The divergent inten-tions lead to praise of the protagonists in Chrétien, blame in the analogue. Chrétien's romance is largely an amplification of these features, especially in monologues, festivities, tournaments, com-bats, siege, and other descriptions. He even foreshadows the sub-stance and method of topical amplification in *Amadas et Ydoine*, which may have been influenced by *Cligès*.[34] The *Amadas* also makes use of the *fausse mort*, a duped husband, Tristan and Iseut as contrast to its idealization of love, and extensive topical amplifi-cations founded on prowess and cunning at the service of *fin'amours*. These are not so much sources as topics that amplify and structure different romances. Even if they are direct sources, the demonstration is still valid, as *Cristal et Clarie* shows.

In the *De inventione* Cicero gives a description of *narratio* that was widely known in the Middle Ages and that fits the stress in medieval romance on both diversity of *matiere* and topical uni-formity as a source of coherence.

> Illa autem narratio, quae versatur in personis, eiusmodi est, ut in ea simul cum rebus ipsis personarum sermones et animi perspici possint. . . . Hoc in genere narrationis multa debet inesse festivitas, confecta ex rerum varietate, animorum dissimilitudine, gravitate, lenitate, spe, metu, suspicione,

desiderio, dissimulatione, errore, misericordia, fortunae commutatione, insperato incommodo, subita laetitia, iucundo exitu rerum. (I.xix.27)[35]

(However, that narrative which treats of persons is of the same kind: one may recognize in it the words and sentiments of the personages together with actions. . . . In this kind of narrative there should be considerable diversion composed of variety, differing characters, seriousness and levity, hope and fear, suspicion, desire, dissimulation, error, pity, change in fortune, unexpected discomfiture, sudden happiness, and a happy end).

Cicero's emphasis requires careful topical articulation of the narrative variety. The Vienna Scholiast expresses this by his interpretation of Horace's use of *vices* and *operum colores*. The latter are the formulae for topical invention, the former cover narrative diversity.[36]

Topical invention is not inconsistent with sudden reversals like those anticipated in these descriptions of *narratio*. Therefore, the madness of Amadas and Cristal's doubts on the value of pursuing an apparently impossible love are credible responses to unexpected diversity; that is, respectively, the apparent loss of Ydoine by marriage to the Count of Nevers, and the difficulties encountered in quest of an *amor de lonh*. The same principles permit the author of *Amadas* to restore to *engin* its universality and neutrality before assigning new, positive affective value to it. The rapidity with which Ydoine falls in love with Amadas when she believes him dead parallels the even more striking changes in Archambault from jealous husband to distinguished courtier. Abrupt change is also evident in Lancelot's return to sin at the beginning of the *Mort Artu*.[37] Such extraordinary shifts in character and role are typical *merveilles* that combine "unmotivated concrete detail and genetic questioning."[38]

Invention of topoi, as distinguished from Curtius' conception of historical topics,[39] reveals source, structure, and psychology in medieval romance and lyric; and it does so in terms demonstrably peculiar to medieval literary language and practice. The extensive scholarship devoted to sources and analogues over the last century facilitates the investigation of how and to what extent borrowing and imitation were carried on. We are often in a position even to gauge a work's originality and meaning. But awareness of topical invention also helps evade the wrongheaded critical judgments many source investigators ventured into without proper appreciation of the importance and nature of adaptation in the Middle Ages. The art of medieval romance and lyric is very much an art of adaptation. The extensive topical elaboration illustrated in *Amadas* and the wholesale plagiarism so skillfully employed in *Cristal* mark the range of romance adaptation. Its origins, in the generic sense, are to be found in Priscian and the other rhetoricians that Marie de France chose as guides to vernacular composition. In exemplary tales like the *Marques* "Cliges," a truth coalesces with a *conte* to produce an example. The possibilities for amplification and interpretation, variety and consistency, are limited only by the romancer's art, *ingenium*, and intention.

The Validity of Topical Invention.

Solomon's wisdom availed him nothing against the wit of his wife in the *Queste*. It also stumbled before the self-confidence of the emerging aristocratic civilization as early as Alberic de Pisançon, who in the 1130's could top Solomon's wisdom by the example of the very Ancients who inspired Marie de France's own confidence, and whose *sens* even Jehan Bodel admired.

> Dit Salomon, al primier pas,
> Quant de son libre mot lo clas:
> "Est vanitatum vanitas
> Et universa vanitas."
> Poyst lou me fay m'enfirmitas,
> Toylle s'en otiositas!
> Solaz nos faz' antiquitas
> Que tot non sie vanitas!   (vv. 1–8)[40]

> (Solomon exclaims mournfully at the outset of his book: "Vanity of vanities, all is vanity." Since my illness makes me weak, away with idleness! Antiquity console us in the certainty that all is not vanity.)

Marie de France even turned from Rome (and presumably Charlemagne) to Britain and the Bretons.

> ... començai a penser
> D'aukune bone estoire faire
> E de latin en romaunz traire;
> Mais ne me fust guaires de pris:
> Itant s'en sunt altre entremis!   (Pro 28–32)

> (I began to contemplate writing some good story, turning it from Latin into Romance. But I would hardly have gained

any credit from that, since so many others have done the same!)

Tout est dit, et l'on vient trop tard depuis plus de sept mille ans?
Yet Jehan Bodel pronounced "British"—and thus, by extension, Arthurian—*matiere* "vain," as opposed to more instructive writings on "French" and "Roman" subjects. Had Arthur's knight become "L'homme esgaré qui ne scet ou il va"?[41] Vanity was in fact attributed to various writings in the Middle Ages, notably: the productions of jongleurs; fabliaux and *risees*; Arthurian romance, including those about Cligès and Perceval, and thus the grail; Roland and Olivier; and history as such.[42] Vanity of vanities, all is vanity?

To be sure, *vain* may connote "marvellous," "ornamental," even "surrealistic": Arthurian romance is both "vain *et plaisant*" (emphasis mine).[43] In fact, Jehan Bodel's distinction is based on the topical, not the historical validity of "French" *matiere*. In his eyes, the French crown held a preeminence, especially in the person of Charlemagne,[44] that elevated narrative about its past glories above other real or imaginary monarchs.

Solomon did say that to revere the ruler is not vanity (*Eccl.* 8.12-17). Despite criticism, Arthurian romance enjoyed esteem among many precisely because of its conception of prowess and love as dominants in a good society.This is apparent in the hierarchical distinctions and the Arthurian examples in Andreas Capellanus, and still holds in the *Echecs amoureux* and its Commentary at the end of the Middle Ages.[45] There are, therefore, distinctions to be made among romances and lyrics, and they were made. The medieval writers were not of one mind on the ideals of prowess, love, and moral strength. And they tried to make sense of them in and for the sources that they inherited from the past and tried to elucidate. Marie de France emphasized love in the *Lais*. She saw each lai as a case study. The topical elaboration as such is not necessarily consistent from lai to lai. Thus, the entire collection provides interest in diverse situations convincingly elucidated. The reader is free to accept or reject. "Ceste parole n'est pas mienne, / Car onques n'amai par tel art" (Those words don't fit me, for I never loved in that way), comments a lady in Froissart's *Meliador*.[46] This does not mean she did not find the poem interesting.

"Tout li sens du monde" of *Claris et Laris* now appears as the manifold representation of prowess, love, and moral strength in the diverse personages and situations of romance and lyric. *Claris* itself is structured as a series of ever more complex and numerous quests that show knights of different kinds and degrees of excellence.

One of those knights, Dodinel, is an analogue to Dinadan in the prose *Tristan*.[47] Vinaver has shown that Dinadan sought and failed to find the very universal *sens* that the *Claris* author says that romance reveals. The specific passages in the prose *Tristan* in which Dinadan ventilates his despair have to do with prowess in arms, love, and moral courage.[48] Dodinel, although a more farcical figure than Dinadan, takes these ideals lightly in *Claris* (vv. 26750–952). This puts him on a par with the Beau Mauvais: he is cowardly, pretentious in love, and deceptive; and he even declines from his class to become a minstrel, or more correctly, a jongleur who relates "ses aviax" (v. 26947) for the entertainment of knights and ladies. Although Dodinel lacks Dinadan's insight into the uncertainty of noble ideals and chivalric accomplishments, he does illuminate the incongruous, even humorous side of Dinadan. Neither knight evokes hate or disgust among his peers, who obviously see more *sens* in the world than they do; rather, their companions are moved either to laughter or tears at these two knights.

Dinadan and Dodinel raise questions about the realization of knightly ideals. The problems of realizing topical idealizations had existed since the first romances and chansons, as Erich Köhler has demonstrated;[49] the desolation illustrated in the *romans d'antiquité* adumbrates Salisbury Plains and the end of the Arthurian world. The conflict between reality and the world of topical inventions on prowess, love, and moral fortitude continued down to the fifteenth century, to Jean le Séneschal's *Cent Ballades*, Chartier, René d'Anjou's *Livre du cuer d'amours espris*, and *Jehan de Saintré*. Chaucer's *Troilus and Criseyde* itself asks the same compelling questions raised by all these authors and works about the agonizing subject of love. The author of *Claris et Laris* was still striving for Marie de France's accommodation of good and bad love in the uncertain, obscure matter of Celtic and other sources. This is true for Jehan Bodel as well. All of them find good, evil, and doubts, a plethora of hierarchies and options to amplify in romance and lai.

Love idealized was rarely defined in the Middle Ages. It was a topical subject open to understanding and elucidation: *hoc genus omne*. Marie de France's *Lais* are again a good illustration. Love was an idea, an obscure idea latent in her *matiere*, and thus part of a dim memory handed down from the past. The author's task was to elucidate that idea in conformity with authorial *engin* and *sens* and the data available in the *matiere*. The subject of love was obviously disturbing, in ways more acute than is imaginable today, at least in the Occident. In the genus of *homo sapiens*, vernacular writers recognized the same diversity in sex, class, habit, occupation, age, etc., that their Latin predecessors had, and those *loci* served as sources of invention. In the context of love, Andreas Capellanus borrowed topical invention from *eloquentia*—as did Marie—to characterize *amor sapiens* and its practitioners, the *sapientes*, the *docti*, the *prudentes*. Such persons evince intellectual and social differences, and Andreas therefore envisages love under diverse circumstances in the dialogues to Book I and the judgments in Book II.[50] That diversity is readily assimilable to the extraordinary events and complex narrative of romance *conjointure*. It is also integral to the postures and attitudes expressed in courtly lyric.

Elaboration by topical invention allowed for what such invention had always intended in rhetoric: the accommodation of understanding to data and the advancement of a credible hypothesis or proposition.[51] The audience was free to recognize itself in or be swayed by such propositions, or not. But it was most assuredly offered the memory of a past alive with the truths it understood or accepted. Literature kept the memory of those past deeds and past loves, adapting them to new audiences and more profound and original understanding. The critical basis is not anachronistic.

> The only access we have to the writer's *voluntas* is through his *scripta*, which must be interpreted . . . by an act of the historical imagination and the disciplines at its command. That act starts with the text itself as all investigation starts with the present reality to be understood. We "analyze" it backward in time until the writer's meaning becomes apparent as a beginning, and then, following the laws of the historical elenchus, we come forward again in synthesis to the present. Only if no contradictions emerge to refute our assumption about its original meaning can we understand it in relation to ourselves—that is, understand how the author might explain his words to us were he living today.[52]

These words are consistent with Marie de France's notion of interpretation. They describe a conception of invention that has prevailed for centuries, and which still has a certain hold on interpretation through literary history, psychocriticism, and the sociology of literature. Priscian was one of its traditional proponents. Marie de France learned from him how to pierce the obscurity of her sources and bring back past memory in language meaningful to her contemporaries. Hence, the Prologue to the *Lais* expresses a historical consciousness and the art which made it practicable in vernacular literature.

When all is said and done, there always remained a potential, an ineffable in romance and lyric. Ineffable *merveilles* whether construed as "dark holes" or authorial "blind spots" survive in each new adaptation of a *matiere*. The ineffable or partial character of medieval romance and lyric has not escaped modern critics either.[53] That *clairobscur* in the new adaptation points to the very obscurity that Marie de France saw in the Ancients. The *antiqui* are any authors, including medieval ones, whose work precedes the present adaptation.[54] Thus, the *moderni* are themselves contributing to, but not exhausting the great *merveilles* of romance and lyric. "Meravilh me com posc durar . . . !" (I marvel at my perseverance!)[55] Yet they did endure. For if one adaptor did not see all that the archetypal conception of the work might offer, that conception still existed. And, from that point of view, it is quite correct that, "si l'auteur pouvait ne pas comprendre très bien ce qu'il était en train d'écrire, le conte, lui, le savait."[56] The topical amplification of *matiere* persisted until, in fact, a new criticism regarded the predecessors not as sources of inquiry and invention, but as giant, unified constructions that could be studied, but never surpassed. By then, Marie de France's conception of tradition had given way to La Bruyère's.

NOTES

[1]"Littérature médiévale et littérature comparée," *GRLMA*, I, 148.

[2]J. H. Marshall, "Le *Vers* au XIIᵉ siècle: genre poétique?" *Actes et Mémoires du IIIᵉ Congrès International de Langue et Littérature d'Oc* (Bordeaux, 3–8 Septembre 1961), 2 vols. (Bordeaux, 1964–65), II, pp. 55–63; see also Erich Köhler, "Die Sirventes-Kanzone: 'genre bâtard' oder legitime Gattung?" *Mélanges Rita Lejeune*, 2 vols. (Gembloux, 1969), I, pp. 159–83; and Hans Robert Jauß, "Theorie der Gattungen und Literatur des Mittelalters," *GRLMA*, I, 122. Tobler-Lommatzsch, VIII, 1441–43, and *FEW*, X, 453 and 455, show *roman* to take on the sense of romance in Chrétien, although earlier examples exist that are ambiguous enough to include the generic sense (Wace, Guernes de Pont-Sainte-Maxence, Benoît de Sainte-Maure); see also P. Voelker, "Die Bedeutungsentwicklung des Wortes Roman," *ZRP*, 10 (1886), 485–525.

[3]See Geoffrey of Vinsauf, *Poetria nova*, vv. 47–48, in Edmond Faral, *Les Arts poétiques du XIIᵉ et du XIIIᵉ siècle* (Paris, 1924, 1958), p. 198. See also Marjorie C. Woods, "The *In principio huius libri* Type A Commentary on Geoffrey of Vinsauf's *Poetria Nova*: Text and Analysis," Diss. Toronto 1977, pp. 23–26.

[4]See Winthrop Wetherbee, "The Theme of Imagination in Medieval Poetry and the Allegorical Figure 'Genius'," *M & H*, 7 (1976), 45–64; Daniel Poirion, "The Imaginary Universe of Guillaume de Machaut," in *Machaut's World: Science and Art in the Fourteenth Century*, Annals of the New York Academy of Sciences, 314 (New York, 1978), pp. 199–206; Douglas Kelly, *Medieval Imagination: Rhetoric and the Poetry of Courtly Love* (Madison, 1978).

[5]Marie de France, *Les Lais*, ed. Jean Rychner, CFMA (Paris, 1968). See Rychner's Introduction, p. xiii.

[6]Translation from Alfred Foulet and Karl D. Uitti, "The Prologue to the *Lais* of Marie de France: Towards an Interpretation," to appear in the August 1981 number of *RPh*. Professors Foulet and Uitti kindly provided me with a typescript of their important article. Their reading of Marie's Prologue agrees with mine, while offering more evidence for what must now be considered the definitive reading of the text.

[7]"Priscian and the Obscurity of the Ancients," *Speculum*, 36 (1961), 75–80; see also Donovan's *The Breton Lay: A Guide to Varieties* (Notre Dame, London, 1969), pp. 13–25. For an up-to-date bibliography on interpretations of the Prologue, see Glyn S. Burgess, *Marie de France: An Analytical Bibliography*, Research Bibliographies and Checklists, 21 (London, 1977), p. 115; see also Rychner, *Lais*, pp. 236–37; and Rupert T. Pickens, "La Poétique de Marie de France d'après les prologues des *Lais*," *LR*, 32 (1978), 367–84.

[8]Marie de France, *Lais* (Oxford, 1947, 1958), p. 163.

[9]*Romania*, 14 (1885), 602.

[10]*Lais*, p. 236.

[11]*Li Romans de Claris et Laris*, ed. Johann Alton, Bibliothek des litterarischen Vereins in Stuttgart, 169 (Tübingen, 1884).

[12]See Kelly, "Topical Invention in Medieval French Literature," in *Medieval Eloquence: Studies in the Theory and Practice of Medieval Rhetoric*, ed. James J. Murphy (Berkeley, Los Angeles, London, 1978), pp. 231–51; see in the same volume Michael C. Leff, "Boethius' *De differentiis topicis*, Book IV," pp. 3–24. For the best recent discussion of topical invention, see Lothar Bornscheuer, *Topik: zur Struktur der gesellschaftlichen Einbildungskraft* (Frankfurt, 1976).

[13]See his *Saisnes*, vv. 1–44, in *Saxenlied*, eds. F. Menzel and E. Stengel, Ausgaben und Abhandlungen aus dem Gebiete der romanischen Philologie, 99–100 (Marburg, 1906–09). See Kelly, "Topical Invention," pp. 237–39. On the adaptation of art to audience—a feature of topical invention—see Frederick Goldin, "The Array of Perspectives in the Early Courtly Love Lyric," in *In Pursuit of Perfection: Courtly Love in Medieval Literature*, eds. Joan M. Ferrante and George Economou (Port Washington, London, 1975), pp. 51–100; Jauß, *GRLMA*, I, 109–10, 119; and Karl D. Uitti, "The Clerkly Narrator Figure in Old French Hagiography and Romance," *Med R*, 2 (1975), 394–408.

[14] On the adaptation of Marie's poetics in the composition of *Guigemar*, see Kristine Brightenback, "Remarks on the 'Prologue' to Marie de France's *Lais*," *RPh*, 30 (1976-77), 168-77. Citations are from *Amadas et Ydoine*, ed. John R. Reinhard, CFMA (Paris, 1974); from *Flamenca* in René Lavaud and René Nelli, *Les Troubadours*, Bibliothèque Européenne, 2 vols. (Bruges, 1960-66), I, pp. 644-1063; and from *Guigemar* in Rychner's *Lais*; Pickens, *LR*, 32 (1978), 367-78.

[15] On *engin*, see Robert W. Hanning, "*Engin* in Twelfth-Century Romance: An Examination of the *Roman d'Enéas* and Hue de Rotelande's *Ipomedon*," *YFS*, 51 (1974), 82-101. These two romances show that both men and women may have *engin*.

[16] "Zur Skala der ritterlichen Tugenden in der altprovenzalischen und altfranzösischen höfischen Dichtung," *ZRP*, 78 (1962), 292-325; see also Richard Glasser, "Abstractum agens und Allegorie im älteren Französisch," *ZRP*, 69 (1953), 63-68; and Rohr's *Matière, sens, conjointure: methodologische Einführung in die französische und provenzalische Literatur des Mittelalters* (Darmstadt, 1978), pp. 18-29.

[17] Franz Rauhut, "Das Psychologische in den Romanen Gautiers von Arras," *Wissenschaftliche Zeitschrift der Friedrich-Schiller-Universität Jena. 5: Gesellschafts- und Sprachwissenschaftliche Reihe*, 2-3 (1955-56), 343-45; repr. in *Der altfranzösische höfische Roman*, ed. Erich Köhler (Darmstadt, 1978), pp. 142-49.

[18] See Guillaume de Lorris and Jean de Meun, *Le Roman de la Rose*, ed. Félix Lecoy, 3 vols. (Paris, 1965-70), vv. 15165-212; Geoffrey Chaucer, *The Works*, ed. F. N. Robinson, 2nd ed. (Boston, 1957), *LGW* Pro G (only) 267-310; *Partonopeu de Blois*, ed. Joseph Gildea, 2 vols. (Villanova, 1967-70), vv. 5507-34.

[19] *La Queste del saint graal*, ed. Albert Pauphilet, CFMA (Paris, 1949), pp. 220, 1.7-226, 1. 3.

[20] See Kelly, "The Source and Meaning of *conjointure* in Chrétien's *Erec* 14," *Viator*, 1 (1970), 195-97.

[21] See the illuminating study of such adaptation by Michelle A. Freeman, "Problems in Romance Composition: Ovid, Chrétien de Troyes, and the *Romance of the Rose*," *RPh*, 30 (1976-77), 158-68.

[22] Ed. Hermann Breuer, Gesellschaft für romanische Literatur, 36 (Dresden, 1915); see also Kelly, *Medieval Imagination*, pp. 99-100.

[23] Kelly, "'Li Chastius ... Qu'Amors prist puis par ses esforz': The Conclusion of Guillaume de Lorris' *Rose*," in *A Medieval French Miscellany*, ed. Norris J. Lacy, University of Kansas Humanistic Studies, 42 (Lawrence, 1972), pp. 62-63.

[24] *Cristal*, pp. xlix-l.

[25] *Cristal*, pp. l-lix; see also the Notes to the edition. My calculations based on pp. lvii-lix. Breuer's statement that the romance is composed *mostly* of borrowings is inaccurate (p. xlviii).

[26]*Ars poetica*, in Horace, *Opera*, eds. Edward C. Wickham and H. W. Garrod, 2nd ed. (Oxford, 1901, 1959)

[27]*Scholia Vindobonensia ad Horatii Artem poeticam*, ed. Joseph Zechmeister (Vienna, 1877), p. 2, ll. 40–45; on the extension to topical invention: "in scriptura vero tunc res prodigialiter variatur, quando alterius rei naturam ad aliam rem attrahimus; veluti cum quis debet scribere leonem fortem et iracundum, describat eum mitem et placidum" (p. 4, ll. 5–8). [A subject is altered in an unnatural way when we attribute the nature of one thing to another, as when one describes the lion, a strong, irascible beast, as being gentle and peaceful.] Unless, of course, the change can be supported by allegory or special circumstances, as with the lion in the *Queste* or in Chrétien's *Yvain*. The *Scholia* are an important link in the medieval poetic tradition deriving from Horace; see Franz Quadlbauer, *Die antike Theorie der genera dicendi im lateinischen Mittelalter*, Österreichische Akademie der Wissenschaften: Philosophisch-historische Klasse, Sitzungsberichte 241.2 (Vienna, 1962), § 25 et passim.

[28]*Cristal*, p. xlviii.

[29]Cicero, *De inventione*, ed. E. Stroebel (Leipzig, 1915), II.15.48.

[30]*Cristal*, pp. liii–liv.

[31]References to *Marques de Rome*, ed. Johann Alton, Bibliothek des litterarischen Vereins in Stuttgart, 187 (Tübingen, 1889), pp. 135–36; and Chrétien de Troyes, *Cligés*, ed. Alexandre Micha, CFMA (Paris, 1957).

[32]*Le Roman de Cassidorus*, ed. Joseph Palermo, 2 vols., SATF (Paris, 1963–64), especially § 173.

[33]See (although I cannot agree with the reading of Thomas' *Tristan* as "uncourtly") Hubert Weber, *Chrestien und die Tristanforschung*, Europäische Hochschulschriften, ser. 13, vol. 32 (Bern, Frankfurt, 1976).

[34]On *Amadas'* sources, see Reinhard, *The Old French Romance of 'Amadas et Ydoine': An Historical Study* (Durham, 1927), pp. 18–44.

[35]On this passage, see Kelly, "Motif and Structure as Amplification of Topoi in the *Sept Sages de Rome* Prose Cycle," in *Studies on the Seven Sages of Rome and Other Essays in Medieval Literature*, eds. H. Niedzielski [at alii] (Honolulu, 1978), pp. 134–35.

[36]See the *Ars poetica*, v. 86; and the *Scholia*, pp. 9, l. 30–10, l. 1.

[37]*La Mort le Roi Artu*, ed. Jean Frappier, TLF, 3rd ed. (Geneva, Paris, 1964), § 4; see also Frappier, *Etude sur 'La Mort le Roi Artu'*, 2nd ed. (Geneva, 1968), pp. 229–46.

[38]Peter Haidu, "Realism, Convention, Fictionality and the Theory of Genres in *Le Bel Inconnu*," *ECr*, 12 (1972), 41. Haidu's notion of "genetic questions" is analogous to topical invention, and indeed the medieval notion of *genera dicendi* as Material Style; see Erich Kleinschmidt, *Herrscherdarstellung: zur Disposition mittelalterlichen Aussageverhaltens, untersucht an Texten über Rudolf I. von Habsburg*, Bibliotheca Germanica, 17 (Bern, Munich, 1974), pp. 14–18; Kelly, "Topical Invention," pp. 236–40; and, especially, Bornscheuer, *Topik*.

[39]See Peter Jehn, ed. *Toposforschung: eine Dokumentation* (Frankfurt, 1972).

[40]Ed. Alfred Foulet, "Alberic's *Alexandre*," in *The Medieval French 'Roman d'Alexandre*,' Elliott Monographs in the Romance Languages and Literatures, 38 (1949; rpt. New York, 1965), pp. 37-38. On these lines, see Wolfgang Fischer, *Die Alexanderliedkonzeption des Pfaffen Lambreht*, Medium Aevum, 2 (Munich, 1964), pp. 32-49.

[41]Charles d'Orléans, *Poésies*, ed. Pierre Champion, CFMA, 2 vols. (Paris, 1966), Bal. 63.8.

[42]For convenience and general reference, see Faral, *Les Jongleurs en France au moyen âge* (Paris, 1910); Ulrich Mölk, ed. *Französische Literarästhetik* des 12. und 13. Jahrhunderts, Sammlung romanischer Übungstexte, 54 (Tübingen, 1969), especially §§ 51, 64, 74-75; on history, see Benoît Lacroix, *L'Historien au moyen âge* (Montreal, Paris, 1971), pp. 229-30.

[43]Robert Guiette, "'Li Conte de Bretaigne sont si vain et plaisant'," *Romania*, 88 (1967), 1-12.

[44]Cf. Ernst Robert Curtius, "Über die altfranzösische Epik IV," *RF*, 62 (1950), 306-08; rpt. in his *Gesammelte Aufsätze zur romanischen Philologie* (Bern, Munich, 1960), pp. 245-46.

[45]See Frappier, "Le Concept de l'amour dans les romans arthuriens," *BBSIA*, 22 (1970), 119-36; Kelly, *Medieval Imagination*, pp. 14-22.

[46]Ed. Auguste Longnon, SATF, 3 vols. (Paris, 1895-99), vv. 20353-54.

[47]Eugène Vinaver, "Un Chevalier errant à la recherche du sens du monde," in *Mélanges Maurice Delbouille*, 2 vols. (Gembloux, 1964), II, pp. 677-86; rpt. in his *A la recherche d'une poétique médiévale* (Paris, 1970), pp. 163-77. See also Alfred Adler, "Dinadan, inquiétant ou rassurant?" in *Mélanges Rita Lejeune*, II, pp. 935-43; and Köhler, *Ideal und Wirklichkeit in der höfischen Epik: Studien zur Form der frühen Artus- und Graldichtung*, Beihefte zur ZRP, 97, 2nd ed. (Tübingen, 1970), pp. 82-83.

[48]Vinaver, *Etudes sur le 'Tristan' en prose* (Paris, 1925), p. 29; texts on pp. 93-98.

[49]*Ideal*, especially chapters V and VI on, respectively, love and the grail. It was a persistent problem; see Kelly, *Medieval Imagination*, pp. 177-203; and Maurice Keen, "Huizinga, Kilgour and the Decline of Chivalry," *M & H*, 8 (1977), 1-20.

[50]Kelly, "Courtly Love in Perspective: The Hierarchy of Love in Andreas Capellanus," *Traditio*, 24 (1968), 119-47; see also the pertinent discussion of Andreas by Wesley Trimpi, "The Quality of Fiction: The Rhetorical Transmission of Literary Theory," *Traditio*, 30 (1974), 81-89.

[51]Trimpi, "The Ancient Hypothesis of Fiction: An Essay on the Origins of Literary Theory," *Traditio*, 27 (1971), 1-78; and his "Quality," pp. 1-118.

[52]Trimpi, "Quality," p. 36, n. 43 (on p. 37); see also Kleinschmidt, *Herrscherdarstellung*, pp. 9-10.

⁵³Vinaver, *A la recherche*, pp. 159–61; Paul Zumthor, "De la chanson au récit: *La Chastelaine de Vergi*," *VR*, 27 (1968), 89–95; [rpt. in *Langue, texte, énigme* (Paris, 1975), pp. 232–36; and in Köhler, *Altfranzösischer Roman*, pp. 246–53]; Sandra Ihle, "The Style of Partiality: Gothic Architecture and the Vulgate Cycle of Arthurian Romances," *Genre*, 6 (1973), 376–87.

⁵⁴Curtius, *Europäische Literatur und lateinisches Mittelalter*, 2nd ed. (Bern, 1954), pp. 256–61; R. W. Hunt, "Studies on Priscian in the Eleventh and Twelfth Centuries," *Mediaeval and Renaissance Studies*, 1 (1941–43), 200–01 (with additional bibliography).

⁵⁵Bernart de Ventadorn, *Seine Lieder*, ed. Carl Appel (Halle, 1915), 39.17.

⁵⁶Tzvetan Todorov, "La Quête du récit," *Critique*, no. 262 (1969), 214.

WALTHER VERSUS REINMAR:
THE REGENERATION OF POETIC LANGUAGE
IN MEDIEVAL GERMAN LITERATURE
FREDERICK GOLDIN

THE "FEUD" BETWEEN Reinmar and Walther will always be a
fascinating and tantalizing subject for students of the Minnesang.
What could be more fascinating in the history of literature than a
feud between two great poets—an older poet composing in a traditional vein and a younger poet hungry for distinction? And what
could be more tantalizing than a feud between two giants, when no
one can say for sure what it was about or prove that it even existed?
Talk of a "feud" began with scholars who thought they found traces
of mutual hostility in numerous passages in the songs of the two
poets. But nowadays, after a hard look, it is clear that most of these
passages contain ordinary Minnesang formulas that any non-
feuding courtly poet might have used.[1] Take these passages away,
and all that remain are a few derogatory references clearly aimed by
one poet at the other—hardly enough to demonstrate the sustained
and systematic aggression of a feud. Still and all, these few
exchanges, though they might have been only passing shots to them,
are very important to us; and the impulse to dramatize a disagreement between the two poets is a natural response to the great
difference in their styles: they really had different ideas about
composing songs, and we long to have those ideas spelled out. Even
if their little assaults upon each other were not as pervasive or as

acrimonious as some have believed, the things that annoyed them and the things they were proud of may be precious clues to their thoughts about their craft and their position in the world—all the more precious since we have no vernacular poetics, no manuals of composition, dating from one of the greatest periods of German lyric poetry.

Though there is an occasional reference to music in the lyrics that belong to the "feud"—which might better have been called a rivalry—it was only the other poet's *words* that moved Reinmar and Walther to their ingenious attacks and defenses: when they have each other in mind, their ultimate concern is the nature of poetic language. Our study of the feud must therefore be limited to the one subject they both addressed. Can we deduce from their aggressive and playful references to each other's words what Reinmar and Walther thought poetic language was, what distinguished it from ordinary language, what problems had to be solved in order to compose a worthy song?

These are broad and sweeping questions, and this is a single chapter in a wide-ranging book. I have to leave out many things that would belong to a full-scale study of the feud; I intend to deal with them in the future. To begin with, I must exclude all questions pertaining to the establishment of the text. Except in one instance, I use the latest edition of *Des Minnesangs Frühling* for Reinmar, and both the Lachmann-Kraus and Maurer editions for Walther, and I hold fast to these texts even in those passages where I would prefer another reading.[2] I wish I could have used Alfred Kracher's forthcoming edition of Walther, which will surely be the definitive one for our time. At any rate, I am confident that with one exception the following study rests on passages in which the establishment of the text is not a crucial issue.

For the same reasons I must forego extensive references to previous studies, even though the feud has inspired some splendid works of scholarship and literary criticism. I can only cite certain studies concerned specifically with the texts and issues discussed in this chapter. Though the notes must necessarily be brief and few, I am fully conscious of my dependence on the work of those who have written before.

If it began as most scholars believe, then Reinmar started it by poking fun at a verse of Walther's. Walther was at the beginning of his career, at a stage when he was still writing in the old style, before he found the voice that would distinguish him from all others. He had composed a strophe on an old familiar theme, older than courtly lyric itself; it had been used a number of times by Heinrich von Morungen, a poet whom Walther greatly admired. Walther's quite ordinary strophe reads as follows:

> Als ich under wîlen zir gesitze,
> sô si mich mit ir reden lât,
> sô benimt si mir sô gar di witze,
> daz mir der lîp alumme gât.
> Swenne ich iezuo wunder rede kan,
> gesihet si mich einest an,
> sô hân ich es vergezzen,
> waz wolde ich dar gesezzen.   (L.-K. 115,22 ff.; M.33)

(Sometimes, when I sit in her presence—those times when she allows me to speak with her—she robs me of my wits so completely that I start going in circles. It happens every time: just when I have so many marvelous things to say, let her look at me just once and then I have forgotten everything that I had in mind when I sat down with her.)

Now Reinmar, apparently, decided to have some fun with this.[3] He alludes to these lines in his song *Ich wil allez gâhen* (MF 170, 1–35), which begins, typically enough, with a complaint: he longs continually to make his way to his love, but his *wân*, his dream of requital, is no closer to fulfillment (strophe i). He was moved to love her by the talk that he had heard about her courtly bearing, and all that talk was true. He has tested it out: no woman can compare with her (strophe ii). The last three strophes are as follows:

> iii. Swaz in allen landen
>   mir ze liebe mac beschehen,
>   daz stât in ir handen:
>   anders nieman wil ichs verjehen.
>   5.   Si ist mîn ôsterlîcher tac,
>   und hân si in mînem herzen liep:
>   daz weiz er wol, dem ich niht geliegen mac.
> iv. Si hât leider selten
>   mîne klagende rede vernomen.
>   des muoz ich engelten.
>   nie kunde ich ir nâher komen.
>   5.   Maniger zuo den vrouwen gât
>   und swîget allen einen tac
>   und anders niemen sînen willen reden lât.
> v. Niemen im ez vervienge
>   zeiner grôzen missetât,

ob er dannen gienge,
   dâ er niht ze tuonne hât;
5.   Spraeche als ein gewizzen man
    "gebietet ir an mîne stat!",
daz waere ein zuht und stüende im lobelîchen an.

(Whatever joy and pleasure may come my way wherever I
go—it all lies in her hands: that is something I would say of
no one else. She is my Easter Day, and I hold her dear in my
heart: He knows this, to Whom I may not lie.
Sad to say, she has rarely heard my songs of complaint; I
have to pay for that. I never could get closer to her. Many a
man makes his way to ladies and keeps silent the whole day
long and never lets anyone else say what is in his heart.
No one would consider it one of his great misdeeds if he
should go away from there where he has no business; and if
he should speak like a sensible man and say, "Come and
take my place!"—now that would be a piece of good
breeding and something to praise him for.)

Now no one knew better than Reinmar that this old motif was a
good courtly formula: he himself uses it in one of his most
interesting songs (*Wie ist ime ze muote*, MF 153,14, str. ii). There
are, in fact, classical precedents for this motif; but it is particularly
appropriate in a courtly song, where, because of the unique position
of the singer, it takes on a complex meaning and exerts an
integrative force. It is, to begin with, an expression of the lover's
passion and earnestness: his unaccountable muteness testifies to his
adoration of the beloved as the *summum bonum*, the highest earthly
good, the most exalted human figure whose favor he could ever
hope to win. But the greatest effect of this formula lay in its power
to call attention to the song itself: the motif of his muteness *then*
contrasts with the reality of his eloquence *now*—as he sings. In the
performance of his song he is supremely articulate about his
inarticulateness, and all those wonderful things get said after all,
before this audience, the object of his true allegiance. Thus the real
proof of his devotion is not to be found in anything he may have
said or failed to say in the past—his success or failure *then* being
represented as accidental and incomprehensible—but in this moment, when he tells us the meaning of what happened, in his
eloquence about his silence in this composed and deliberate song of
recollection.

The theme of his muteness is a poetic fiction available to
everyone who cares to adopt it, but the song is a present *fact*, a

unique reality witnessed by an attending audience. For the literary theme precedes the poet and has no real existence except as a possibility that he—or anyone else—may choose to realize. It is always there, a universal possibility and therefore (like an infinitive) incapable of conveying the experience of an individual subject; it, too, is mute until it is chosen. Only when it appears in a song does it tell us something; but then its critical message is not that the "I" was once unable to speak in the presence of his beloved—it said all that when it was still only one of many possible themes for a real song and could not speak for anyone in particular. What it proclaims, once it is realized in rhythm, image, and phrase, is that it has been *chosen*. In its realized state it bears witness to the will that picked it out and embodied it in a song composed with great care. The poet who chose to make this theme expressive must have been moved by something other than the theme itself, something outside of every literary convention; he must have been impelled by things really existing in his world and in himself: the goodness and beauty of that which he praises, the strength and constancy of his love. Here he is in the present telling us about a vivid moment in the past; the past event is a fiction universally recognized as such, but his song is a fact in the world of his audience, a truth that he creates, impelled by his allegiance. He proves the genuineness of his motive—his deep, abiding devotion—when he transforms a common theme into his intricate and elegant song. The lover's silence belongs to the theme and tells us nothing in particular. Only the formal perfection of the song gives that silence a concrete meaning and enables it to express the truth that lies in a single heart.[4]

Reinmar mischievously pretends that he has never heard the like of this common theme. He takes up Walther's poetic statement with aggressive literal-mindedness, draws out its spatial and temporal consequences, plots it out on a finite ground. All of a sudden we are faced with a problem in logistics: that man sits there dumb the whole day long so that no one else gets a chance—he takes up space, holds up the line, so that no other man can speak *sinen willen*. Here we can see Reinmar playing one of his brilliant games with the audience. The first part of the strophe (the *Aufgesang*, here the first four lines), in which he voices his complaint, deliberately arouses certain expectations. For when a courtly poet complains that his lady does not hear his lamenting song and grieves that he cannot get close to her, that is a standard ploy, a time-honored method of representing the glory and the necessary cruelty of one who is beyond the lover's reach, separated from him by a distance that expresses her ideal being; at the same time, it demonstrates the lover's loyalty in the absence of all requital. And this ploy can be followed by one of several possible moves expressing hope or dread regarding the future, in any case by a confirmation of his vow to unconditional service. But now, contrary to every conceivable expectation, we suddenly learn (in the remaining three lines, the *Abgesang*) that the reason he cannot get close to her has nothing to do with her perfection or his sense of unworthiness; it is only that some incompetent young man is blocking the way.

A poetic statement—one that makes sense only as a figure of speech, as an imaginative representation of a truth that cannot be directly expressed—is now treated as literal statement. The image of the man tongue-tied by love is wrenched out of its true context and ceases to be an image: it no longer evokes the sense of a devoted heart and a being whose goodness lies beyond the reach of language. The mute figure of the lover is no longer referred to our imagination, the meaning of his silence no longer situated in the realm of represented truth. The words that describe him are now understood as a report from ordinary life; their literal meaning becomes their only meaning. Thus the theme of the man who keeps silent changes from image to event; it tells us of something now that literally *takes place*—and in a quite limited space, inevitably causing a traffic problem. When a figurative statement is stuck in an unpoetic context and reduced to its denotation, the result is bound to be comic and absurd. The lover struck dumb with admiration is here treated with the same literalizing vaudeville technique that has elsewhere made such a mess of the roses and lilies in a glorious face and produced a nauseous hero on the billows of the Euxin.

I believe that it was Reinmar, both here and in many other songs, who showed Walther the way to a new kind of poetic language— a de-poeticized poetic language, in which only the base meaning of words is allowed any currency. At any rate, considering his trick of literalizing poetic language, Reinmar exposes himself to similar treatment when he speaks of his lady as his *ôsterlicher tac*, his Easter Day—he is asking for it there, and he is going to get it.

It was this song, apparently, that started the fireworks and taught Walther a lesson that he would never forget. But it was another song of Reinmar's that gave Walther most of his ammunition when he counter-attacked. The first strophe of Reinmar's song reads as follows:

Ich wirbe umbe allez, daz ein man
ze weltlîchen vröiden iemer haben sol.

daz ist ein wîp, der ich enkan
  nâch ir vil grôzem werde niht gesprechen wol.
  Lobe ich si, sô man ander vrouwen tuot,
  daz engenimet si niemer tac von mir vür guot.
  doch swer ich des, si ist an der stat,
  dâs ûz wîplîchen tugenden ni vuoz getrat.
  daz ist in mat!   (MF 159, 1–9)

(I strive for everything that a man needs for joy in this
world: I mean a certain woman, of whom all the good that I
can speak would fall short of her great worth. If I praise her
as they praise other women, she will never take pleasure in
that—not coming from me. But this I swear: she abides in
that place where she never strayed the width of a foot from
the virtues of woman. That checkmates them!)

    Reinmar explains his problem with apparent forthrightness
and clarity. It is, he tells us, two-fold: he must find words of praise
commensurate with her worth and at the same time unlike those of
any other poet; for if he praises her as others praise their ladies, his
song will fail. Now here is the essential Reinmar; this is where he
lives, in this brilliant formulation of an insoluble problem—insoluble by its very terms. One could not ask for a clearer statement
of the courtly singer's difficult position.

    For the only language that could be adequate to her indefinable
worth is the one language that Reinmar must avoid: the language of
Minnesang. The language that the lady has forbidden him consists
of traditional formulas of praise dedicated to one whose worth
surpasses the reach of all ordinary utterance, venerable phrases,
universally accredited, that exalt the beloved far above all those
whose qualities are adequately defined by the chance expressions of
everyday speech. The very quality that makes the courtly lyric seem
at first so alien to modern readers, the fixed and formulary nature of
its language, is the source of its greatest effect and the means by
which it accomplishes its purpose. For only these prescribed and
abstract phrases are fit for the praise of a being whose virtues are
not to be *represented* but rather *celebrated*. The Minnesänger
praises his beloved lady for her grace, her beauty, her understanding, her imperious concern. But, with rare exceptions, he never
shows her living out these splendid qualities; they are never realized
by her deportment in concrete experience. Apart from certain highly
stylized gestures, we see nothing of her in the songs her lover sings;
she has a deeply felt presence, but no real appearance. The language
of the Minnesang is based on the assumption of her status as the

fulfillment and the judge of all that is good and valuable in the world; it does not establish her in that role—she is already there.

That is why the hardly varying phrases of courtly language are the essence of its dignity. The beloved is not to be praised in any style that any man thinks fit, for the individuality of such praise would belie the universality and absoluteness of her virtues. Instead, the Minnesang reserved for her, as their exclusive object, certain fixed strategies of praise, a repertory of themes and procedures which, by their prescriptive nature, take on something of the quality of ritual language. Her perfection is an article of faith preserved by custom, and every authorized statement concerning her is intended either to praise her or to affirm the devotion of the one who loves her. For any concrete *representation* of her worth would inevitably limit it—she would be kind, and beautiful, and redemptive only in one specific way. But the *celebration* of her worth in customary phrases leaves it essentially undefined, preserves its majesty, allows the imagination to glorify her as beyond its furthest reach. Every poet of the Minnesang, including Walther at the beginning of his career, entered the realm of poetry speaking the language of celebration; it was the confrontation with his great rival that impelled him to use the language of representation.

Now Reinmar, the master of the Minnesang's traditional language, immediately deprives himself of its resources: he must not praise her as others praise. But how can he do otherwise? Here he faces one of the most formidable problems of the courtly poet, one that he inherits with the peculiar nature of his language. Since all courtly poets share in a common heritage of fixed poetic themes and constructions, how can he, using the same formulas, sound different from them—or at least different enough so that his words about love appear to reflect individual experience? For traditional language is the natural prey of hypocrites. Courtly poets, beginning with the earliest Occitan lyrics, are haunted by this problem, and they bring it up continually in their songs, each voicing either his hope that the beloved one will be able to tell that he really means the things he says, in contrast to the others who merely mouth the words; or his dread that she will take the words of others as true avowals of devotion, whereas only his arise from the heart. But how can the lady distinguish one from another, when they all say the same things? And how can he say something different, when he is obliged to use the one dedicated language of praise? This is the great problem that Reinmar's lady sets him: he has to praise her in a new or at least different way. She demands this of him for the same reason that the poets have demanded it of themselves: the distinctiveness of his praise is to be valued not because of its unprecedented brilliance but because, bound as he is to a language that makes everyone sound the same, sounding different is the only way he has to prove his sincerity. She does not tell him: "Make it new," for she could not dream of demanding such a thing—and would not even if she could, for that would be much too easy, and his praise would lack all the authority and the glory of the Minnesang. What she demands is far more difficult: Make it *yours*.

The courtly poet had to find a nexus between the formulary language of celebration and the immediate reality of individual experience. He had to find a way of making standard phrases and familiar themes express a unique truth, the *singer's* truth here and now—the things he feels as he sings, the inspiring image in his heart, his struggle to keep his lust from subverting his devotion—at the same time preserving the vague, ritual universality of the language that exalts the beloved. In the early courtly lyric there were two ways in which the singer could tie that soaring language down to his particular moment. One of these was followed, in varying degrees, by all the poets; the other was explored only by the troubadours and the Minnesänger.

The first way, the one that everyone followed, lay in difficulty. Difficulty is an essential poetic sign of the speaker's profound commitment. "Improvise, rhapsodize," Roxanne demands of her lover, and, considering that they both equate simplicity with emptiness, she is right to do so. For the *meaning* of words that express love is no evidence of the lover's sincerity; but in the extraordinary pains that he takes in putting the words together he enacts his devotion. All the things that distinguish his words from ordinary statement must have their motive in his inner life. The grand obstacles of rhythm and rhyme, the constrictions of the strophic form, the ramifying paths of metaphor, all of the formal demands that make poetic expression more difficult than ordinary speech would silence him if he lacked nobility, ardor, and discipline, and were not inspired by the longing to serve. Many readers today mistake these formal elements for "mere" ornamentation, rhetorical devices tacked on to an essentially prosaic statement, as though it all boiled down to "I love you." But they do not realize that the bare assertion is utterly valueless and unreliable because the moral condition of the speaker remains untested and unrepresented. On the other hand, one can believe that the lover's dedication is enacted in his triple rimes and intricate conceits. That is why courtly poets

65

from the very beginning have equated their skill in composition with their capacity as lovers.

When one calls such highly formalistic poetry "artificial," he is judging the lyrics of the past by the conditions in which poetic language is engendered today, for we consider plain but unexampled phrasing and a casual style hallmarks of genuineness. But the poets of the past had to erect obstacles that they could overcome precisely in order to avoid "artificiality"—if by that word we mean the use of poetic devices that have no necessary relation to the message. In their poetry, only part of the message was conveyed by the literal and even the figurative sense of the expression: the urgency and the genuineness of the message was conveyed by the *difficulty* of the expression. This can be seen as well in many poets of the Renaissance—in the sonnets of Sir Philip Sidney, for example, whose conceits would convey only truisms if they were not difficult; their intricacy is the unmistakable sign of his passionate dedication and his courtier's restraint and self-mastery. It is the necessity of difficulty that accounts, at least in part, for the development of many new trends in courtly poetry. It is one of the basic causes of *troubar clus*. Though scholarly discussion of this poetry usually associates it with the question of the poets' class allegiance and their attitude toward the audience, the primary reason for the development of this difficult style is clearly its difficulty—for difficulty proves the moral validity and the personal reference of figurative expressions. It is true that hypocritical poets can use many intricate devices in order to fake a love that they do not feel—these are *die falschen*, the *fals amador*, the false lovers so bitterly denounced in the courtly lyric. However, the poetry of these hypocrites does not prove, as our modern prejudice assumes, that formal elaborateness is cultivated alone by the insincere; it is rather that, being hypocrites—and very clever ones—the false poets put on what they and all their rivals regard as the most convincing sign of sincerity.

This same complex formality is also a sign that the speaker's words mean something different from what they usually mean. The words we exchange when we are involved in an experience have a different reference—an immediate, urgent, verifiable reference— from the words we search for when we try to express the meaning of that experience, or to represent its essence. The meaning is not a part of the experience, and when we want to designate an enduring reality beyond the accidents that we encounter, all that we can do is point toward it. The formal elements of poetry, therefore, signify that every statement points beyond its denotation. This aspect of poetic language has been dealt with many times before and need not be dwelt upon here except for this one point: the reason why certain formal patterns are a sign of poetic utterance is—once again—that difficulty functions as a test of moral commitment. The formal elements of the lyric signify that now, as he speaks, the poet is far beyond the machinations and concerns of ordinary speech (in which he sounds like everyone else), that his words at this moment are inspired by a disinterested vision and prophetic earnestness and therefore bear a message that cannot be accurately expressed in the language with which we handle our affairs and come to terms with friends and enemies. Thus difficulty is a sign, an assurance; through it the speaker signifies that he is exercising a sacred moral privilege, and it is not too much to say that the abuse of this sign—even if the consequences are unimportant—is a betrayal of the bonds of community.

The troubadours and the Minnesänger had still another way of bringing the universal language of celebration down to the level of specific experience. Their way began with the performance situation. I have written on this subject before and can give only the briefest account here.[5]

The principle of coherence and unity in the Occitan and early Middle High German lyric (apart from the formal patterns just mentioned) is a certain construct of the audience: the singer's image of those who listen to his song. In his eyes the audience is divided into various sectors, ranging from the sympathetic friends to the determined enemies of his song. Among these enemies are the spies and slanderers who search his words for hints of scandal; the vulgar ones who understand nothing but the literal meaning of words and are convinced that his words are lies; and the false lovers, the hypocrites who share the poet's language but have none of his inner truth. Every conceivable attitude is represented in the singer's vision of his audience, and he takes note of every sector in his song, for this array of perspectives is the ethical scale upon which he plays—from the high level of the friends to the low of the enemies. This broad representaton is absolutely necessary, for it provides the singer with the form and the object of his performance: he must resolve the conflicting attitudes of the audience in the harmony and integrity of his song, bringing friends and enemies together in a vision that surpasses them both. For they are the elements of his total message. If the audience consisted only of the friends, the singer would face few challenges and his song would have little worth, for the friends want nothing better than the same song endlessly repeated, a song of praise and joy celebrating love. The other members of the lyric audience are the saving thorn in his flesh; they are there to goad him.

In the course of the song we can follow the performer's eye as it passes through these various sectors of the audience: now he sings for the friends, now for the enemies. In each instance he represents the attitude that he perceives. When his eye dwells on the vulgar ones, he sees things as they see them: the lady is subtly—or not so subtly—denigrated in his song; the language of Minnesang is treated as literal statement and shown to be, when so regarded, mendacious and absurd. When his eye returns to the friends, his song is an anthem of courtliness, a representation of the great virtues that distinguish the courtly class—the moral aspiration, the dedication to service, the courteous deportment, the great capacity for devotion, renunciation, and loyalty. This is the technique of "the array of perspectives": the singer gives his words of praise an immediate and genuine content by subjecting poetic language to the mockery and derision of common sense and unexalted vision.

In one way or another poetic language had to be continually challenged and re-established. If it were always naïvely summoned for the values that tradition had bestowed upon it, it would have lost its nature as a language of individual performance: there would have been no identifiable "I" to speak it. Here it is not a question of "poetic individuality" as we use that term today. It is rather that this language, if its traditional value had remained fixed and unquestioningly accepted, would have lacked the power to create the illusion of personal experience, to represent the here-and-now, the secular coordinates that locate the speaker in our realm confronting us. It would have become a ritual language, one in which the performer is merely the agent of formulas and gestures, which alone produce the effect of the performance. The poets had to tie this language down, for the lyrics of the Minnesang refer to individual experience and can have no meaning unless there is someone—some one—who experiences, an agent endowed with the faculties of experience, with memory, intelligence, will, and five discerning senses; a speaker bearing witness on a specific occasion, proving that traditional language can truly describe his own reality. To establish this "I-effect"—the effect of a real person speaking from the heart—the singer must show that he chooses his words: he can use poetic language only if he shows that he is free to reject it.

Ritual language—language already phrased, unmediated by

individual experience, transcending every unique instance, preserving its efficacy regardless of the subjective state of the performer—is the purest form of the language of celebration. It has a single reference, a being whose character and value are established for all time. It makes no difference who speaks the solemn phrases that name this being's attributes. The celebrant must, on occasion, be authorized as the performer of a ritual utterance; but he is so ordained by an authority that lies outside that language: his right to speak these words is conferred upon him before he ever speaks. But when a courtly singer declares that he would rather serve one supreme woman without requital and suffer in vain hope than find pleasure and recognition with another, and speaks these words not as a universal formula of adoration but as a reflection of his own experience, he must *earn* the right to say these things. His language must bear the proof of its authenticity; he must speak as an experiencing agent, as an individual. The poet represents the "I" as a sentient and responsible person by showing that he exercises a choice—here and now, before us—a choice of language.

The singer's alternatives are represented by the various sectors of the audience. When he speaks of the service that brings joy even in the absence of reward, he uses the image of the audience to represent the different ways in which his words can be understood. The friends of his song understand his words as figurative statement, the language of celebration, which is alone appropriate to the figure of all their aspirations; and their understanding is correct. The vulgar people, the *ungefüege liute*, understand his words as literal statement, too ridiculous to be true, and they accuse him of lying; and, as he makes clear when he sees things from their point of view, they are right too. At these moments the singer must display his gift for self-mockery, and here no one surpasses Reinmar. He always presents these conflicting attitudes in his songs, and always for the same reason: to win the freedom to choose.

That is how he overcomes the prescriptiveness, the formalism, and the non-specific reference of traditional poetic language. Once he proves that he can see the beloved as the enemies of poetry see her, as the unenhanced and unsignifying creature that ordinary language denotes, he proves that he uses the language of celebration *by choice*: for now we know that he is free to speak of her in other ways. His songs continually dramatize his commitment to poetry and to the noble values represented by figurative language—the values of the noble class. In this way, by freely choosing among a range of alternatives, he makes the language of celebration *his*

69

language and uses it to describe the decisive events of his inner life and of his life in the world. In making this choice, in confirming his vocation as poet, and reclaiming poetic-language, he confirms his allegiance to the courtly class. The warring elements of the audience are harmonized in the song: language and class are now twin expressions of the same ethical ideal. This was the great achievement and the great power of the poetic language of the Minnesang: formulas that solemnize the attributes of a transcendent being—many of them adapted without any change from songs addressed to the Virgin—are brought down to human beings, and then, once subjected to mockery and derision, they take on a new validity and express a new revelation for a certain time and a certain place, shedding their glory on the little world of the court. The man who sings discovers, in the presence of his audience and through its influence, that the old words tell the exact truth about his love.

But Reinmar's lady has placed a great restriction on his use of these honored commonplaces: he must find a way of praising her without saying the same things that all his rivals say. That is the impossible trick he announces, and now we can watch the master performer at work.

For it is through the strategy of performance that Reinmar slides out of his predicament—the same sleight-of-hand by which he triumphs in many another song. He takes six lines to set up this devastating problem and then, before our eyes, only three to disarm it:

> doch swer ich des, si ist an der stat,
> dâs ûz wîplîchen tugenden ni vuoz getrat.
> daz ist in mat!
>
> (But this I swear: she abides in that place where she never
> strayed the width of one foot from the virtues of woman.
> That checkmates them!)

A great bone of contention among many scholars is the reference of the little word *in*: who, exactly, is "checkmated," one wants to know—Reinmar's competitors, or the women they praise? But that question is all wrong; it does not present true alternatives. To begin with, the *ander vrouwen*, as poetic figures, only exist in the songs that celebrate their virtues: the subject of these lines is not "other women" but the *praise* of other women. It therefore does violence to Reinmar's text to force a decision regarding *in*, since the very ambiguousness of this reference is a part of his meaning. If, for example, we insist that *in* must refer to the other Minnesänger, then we hear Reinmar claiming victory in the game: he checkmates all the others who praise great ladies; he, Reinmar, wins the competition with *his* praise. If, on the other hand, we say that *in* refers to "other women," the meaning of Reinmar's statement is still the same: for how his beloved surpass the women praised by his rivals except in the manner in which she is evoked? She whom he praises surpasses all others who have been praised; *his* lady—the lady whose majesty is celebrated in his songs—is greater than all the ladies brought forth in the praise of other poets. The pronoun *in* must refer at once both to his competitors and to the things they create.

Manuscript A, incidentally, has *iu*, suggesting that Reinmar has a particular adversary (Walther?) in mind, whom he addresses directly. At any rate, the only ones he wants to "checkmate" are the ones he must surpass: his lady has forbidden him to praise her *so man ander vrouwen tuot*, as they praise other women.[6] The vague reference of *in* reflects the equally vague reference in *man*.

But when do we hear this praise that is better than everyone else's, where is it? Now here is where we have to tip our hats to the old magician. That magnificent praise that makes him the king of poets—is not there. He never lets us hear it, we shall not find one word of it. He only tells us the *result* of his long career of praising her: *si ist an der stat. . . .* Considered as praise, this is less than mediocre and could never win the match, and it would be a grave misreading of these lines to take them as such, for he has told us that he has been denied the very language of praise. These spare lines, lacking all the elaboration of sincerity, cannot be an example of how his song surpasses all others. But if this is the result of his praise— that she abides alone in perfection—how great that unheard song must be.

Her virtues remain an article of faith: they are not represented, they are not even named—for only the old phrases, now forbidden, could name them; they are simply posited, their existence made necessary, by the logic of Reinmar's rhetoric. The effect of his maneuver is not to define her excellence but to affirm it: the queen of all women is endowed with existence as the object of her lover's praise. She is made real by virtue of the position to which his songs have exalted her. She alone is in that glory because of his praise, and never in all his songs has she come forth as less than perfect in courtly virtue: that checkmates them.

And all this without one word of praise directly spoken—the strophe begins by renouncing the language of praise. That is his

71

victory, a victory on many fronts, for the advantages of his silence are numerous. His silence magnifies the effect of his song, for praise unheard surpasses all utterance. No one can conceive the greatness of that which never comes forth, and only that praise which is greater than any that can be conceived is commensurate with her merit; the others who sing can never equal it. Furthermore, by guarding his silence at this moment, he refers unmistakably to all the songs that he *has* sung in her honor: it is not through some occasional formula, but through a lifetime of praise devoted to her that he triumphs now. One can marvel at all the virtues of these lines, and they all come from necessity; he has to praise her without actually praising her, because she has forbidden him to use the only language he knows, the one he shares with those whom he must outperform.

It is in the word *mat* that his victorious maneuver is finally accomplished. The strophe begins with an apparent account of his relation with his lady, but at the end it is focused upon Reinmar's competition with his rivals and the game he plays with them. He wins by calling attention to his own brilliant move, showing us how he escapes from the rules that tie down his competitors: they cannot play the game as well as he. There is his sleight-of-hand: he switches subjects, and we never realize it until we hear him call "Mate!" The speed with which he moves is amazing. He begins with what seems to be a declaration of his love for "a certain woman," but before we know it he is all wrapped up in the problem of surpassing his rivals, the other poets of the court. We learn this only at the end, for it is the word *mat* that changes the focus from the apparently auto-biograpical content of the song to the play element of the performance. That last little word suddenly reveals that he has been engaged in a poetic strategy, that this is *poetry*, and that the ultimate object of his praise is his humble self. It is this last word that tells the secret of his beloved: she is a poetic creation set against the competing works of others. That one word is a sign that *all* his words are composed; that he is not speaking, but singing; that the lady and her impossible demand are gorgeous problems of his own creation, and that he created them in order to execute his grand and masterly maneuver.

The word *mat* gives an unexpected retroactive value to the word it rimes with, *stat*. At the last moment of the strophe all the meanings change: *stat* has had a secret context all the time, signifying not only the ideal precincts of virtue but also *the square of a chessboard*.[7] She is in a certain "square" from which she has never moved, and her position there checkmates "them" all, every adversary. His triumph is established by a kind of rhetorical ontological proof: if his praise does not surpass all others, how could she occupy that position, how could she abide alone in perfection? While everyone waits for the performer to exalt his lady above all others, he eludes their attention, produces his game-boards, and all at once reveals that she is *already there*. By the time we are aware of the chessboard, she already occupies the Queen's square. When he sings that final word, his victory is complete, for only then does he reveal the key to every line: this strophe contains, not an account of some actual experience (though it deliberately aroused this false expectation in the beginning), but the master's offering in a rivalry of song; so that, in a wonderful way, the very declaration that the others are checkmated makes the statement true. Everyone who studies Reinmar's songs will recognize here a kind of strategy of which he is the supreme master and which is uniquely his—so that, after all, he has praised her as no one else can.

In another strophe in this song (MF 159,37 ff.), Reinmar has a charming and witty surprise for his audience, a really clever turn that Walther will, naturally, try to outdo:

> Unde ist, daz mirs mîn saelde gan,
>   daz ich abe ir wol redendem munde ein küssen mac versteln,
> gît got, daz ich ez bringe dan,
>   sô wil ich ez tougenlîchen tragen und iemer heln.
>   Und ist, daz sîz vür grôze swaere hât
>   und vêhet mich durch mîne missetât,
> waz tuon ich danne, unsaelic man?
> dâ nim eht ichz und trage ez hin wider, dâ ichz dâ nan,
> als ich wol kan.
>
> (And if my blessed good luck should grant me this: that I
> can steal a kiss from her sweetly speaking mouth—then, if
> God grants that I bring it away, I shall bear it in secret and
> always keep it hidden. But what if she thinks it a great
> offense and attacks me for my misdeed—what do I, unlucky
> man, do then? Why, then I'll take it up again and put it back,
> as best I can, exactly where I took it from.)

The idea of stealing a kiss has a long history; Reinmar probably inherited it directly from Heinrich von Morungen.[8] But the ingenious idea of promising to return it seems to be all Reinmar's own—and so here again he goes beyond the others. The strategy of the self-serving proviso, whereby Reinmar increases his ill-gotten gains by promising to restore them, is a hallmark of this master.[9]

The first song in which Walther turns Reinmar's own trick against him is L.-K. 111,22 ff.; M. 38. The text of the first strophe in the edition of Helmut Birkhan is as follows:[10]

111,22. In dem dône Ich wirbe umb allez daz ein man
Ein man verbiutet âne pfliht
ein spil des ime nieman wol gevolgen mac:
25. er gihet swenne sîn ouge ersiht
ein wîp si sî sîn ôsterlîcher tac.
wie waere uns andern liuten sô geschehen?!
suln wir im alle sînes willen jehen?
ich bin derz ime versprechen muoz:
30. bezzer waere mîner frouwen senfter gruoz
dâst mates buoz.
(To the tune of *Ich wirbe umb allez daz ein man.* A man makes a bid / *or:* a move / *or:* calls checkmate, without really being bound / *or:* without the concurrence of the others in the game, or of the referee / *or:* without anyone's having a chance to test his bid—so that no one can go along with him / *or:* so that no one can do anything against his move: he says, every time his eye catches sight of a woman, that she is his Easter Day. Now what would that mean for the rest of us? Should we go along with what he wants? Well, I for one have to tell him no: the gentle greeting of my lady would be far better. There's the defense against his "mate.")

As the translation shows, the exact sense of certain passages in this lyric is uncertain, owing to the garbled text in the manuscript. But the general sense is clear enough: a "man" makes a bid or a move that is unacceptable because it is spurious for one reason or another, and the *ich* will not allow it. The singer explains how this man *verbiutet âne pfliht*: whenever his eye spots some woman, he says she is his Easter Day. Can we allow this man to play "the game" like this? No! for I say my lady's simple greeting would be a better move. If Walther's words are understood according to the play-context of this lyric—and of the entire "feud"—this is what they mean: it would be better to represent my lady as greeting me gently—better, when I sing of her, to show that she *greets* me, that we meet face-to-face on a common ground, than to try that spurious maneuver of exalting her to heaven till she becomes my Easter, my redeemer, whom I can only catch sight of and praise from far below. That is not the way to make your praise surpass all others; in this *spil*, the lady who shares our common life is more valuable. The word *senfter* ("friendly," "gentle," "responsive") establishes the level movement of her *gruoz*, represents her as engaged with *us*. She is "better," more genuine, rated more highly by the rules of the game, than a woman who is falsely enhanced so that no human praise seems adequate to her untested worth. And so that man's praise has no worth, it does not win the game: his false "checkmate" is reversed.

Here Walther shows that he knows a trick or two himself. He could not in a million years find any reply to Reinmar's masterly checkmate: who could rebuke any man for saying that his lady never departed from virtue? But Walther will not be checkmated either, and so, in order to trip up the master, he combines passages from two of Reinmar's songs in his reply—the checkmate-passage from one, the Easter-passage from another—as though the Easter-Day image had been the move for which Reinmar claimed the victory. This little trick of Walther's tells us a great deal about how to read these lines, because it shows that he needs to find something spurious in Reinmar's words. That is his strategy: he wants to show that his rival's purported checkmate is no good because the move is unacceptable. Walther is not counter-attacking with a move of his own (that will come, but not in this strophe); he is not saying that *his* lady is better than Reinmar's, so much better that her simple greeting is worth more than anything Reinmar receives from his Easter Day. Such a reply would be irrelevant since the burning issue between them is how to praise the beloved in an acceptable way, not whether one poet's lady is better than the other's—a stupid and impossible question to boot. Besides, such a reading would not only add things to the text but do violence to it: Walther says *bezzer waere*—it would be, or would have been, better—and the subjunctive rules out any possibility that he is asserting something positive about his own lady. He is speaking of something that never came to pass, a rejected alternative, another way that Reinmar could have chosen in singing his praise: it would have been better to say that she gives me her sweet and friendly greeting—that is a move that all the other players could have accepted. What Reinmar did instead is no good; that is why there is no checkmate.

Wapnewski has suggested another way of reading 111,30, a line he finds too commonplace as it is generally construed.[11] He takes *miner frouwen* as dative: a simple greeting to my lady is better (or, a simple greeting is better for my lady) than hailing her as one's Easter Day. His reading is grammatically possible, though some consider it far-fetched. At any rate it fits the context perfectly and has the merit of accurately rendering the sense of the possessive in *miner frouwen*:

not *my* lady (as opposed to Reinmar's—the sense ruled out by the subjunctive), but "milady," "madame," the possessive forming part of an honorific term.

Walther's argument is not—cannot be—merely that if we grant Reinmar his image ("Easter Day") we would have to acknowledge that the object of Reinmar's praise is superior to all other women—to "our" ladies. Reinmar simply said, she is *my* Easter, at least implicitly acknowledging that others may have theirs. "So seine Dame zu preisen . . ." says Kralik, "war doch gewiss auch Reinmars gutes Recht." Walther is addressing the same question that occupies Reinmar: how does one find the language to praise justly? how does one overcome the blind generality of traditional language so that its phrases can perceive the unique and local person? That *osterlicher tac* can have no value because it rises in its glory for *everyone* and cannot be pinned down, at least not by the simple use of the possessive adjective. It is too grand and too available, its borrowed splendor obliterates all distinction among the men who praise and the women who are thus uniformly exalted: any man can proclaim, any woman can be, an Easter Day.[12]

In this song we see the beginning of Walther's poetic program. He rejects the technique of the "array of perspectives." No one can be allowed henceforth to use the language of Easter Day in the play of song, for if we allow it, what shall we put in to match it? If we compete with that "man" by putting up the same pre-composed and hyperbolic formulas, we would be committing ourselves anew to a language whose ritual formality can never truly represent individual experience, to figures of speech that blindly exalt the beloved and automatically degrade the lover. Its manner of praise can only be appropriate in a relation between unequals, based on the unverifiability of the beloved. Walther demands a poetic language of immediate reference: let us now compose songs about unmetaphorical ladies—ladies who simply greet us courteously (or, if Wapnewski is correct, ladies whom we greet). Let us keep out of the game all language oriented to one who is pre-established as a poetic figure, who appears invested with extraordinary meaning and redemptive power. Let us sing a love song about a woman who does not "mean" anything before the song is composed, whose meaning is engendered each time—and for the first and only time—by our words. Let us return to the base value of language and use words that signify unenhanced things, things as they are—or as they were before an old tradition laid extra meanings over them. It was Reinmar who showed him the way, and now Walther goes further than his great rival had ever imagined: let us re-literalize poetic language.[13] The new rules that Walther lays down begin as a countermove against Reinmar; but the consequences of this strategy are enormous, and Walther will follow them through. What is at stake in this "game" is an attack on poetic language as such, the language of celebration, the whole tradition of Minnesang, its rhetoric, its imagery, its realm of discourse.

It has long been said that Walther broke with the old Minnesang conception of love and, while still confining himself to traditional forms of versification, sang of a new kind of love, reciprocal love, one that was free of the old sickness of solitary longing. In this new relation between man and woman, the beloved is depicted as accessible, unexalted, involved, no longer a tutelary figure beyond the reach of praise. There is a good deal of truth to this assessment, but in depicting Walther's poetic career as a kind of ethical pilgrimage it is apt to obscure the nature of Walther's poetic thought, and of poetic thought in general. For what may have ended in a new moral vision actually began as a dispute about language; and Walther's great ethical innovation, the representation of mutual love between two equals, was the consequence of his response to Reinmar's provocation—of the play that Reinmar began and that Walther continued, in which traditional poetic language was shorn of its non-objective reference.[14] This new, strictly denotative language could now do little more than name things, describe actions, and combine these non-connoting, first-intentional things and actions in a certain spatial and temporal relation. Any such relation between human beings would necessarily be a relation between equals, since the vocabulary of exaltation has been excluded from the language that describes them. One person could, of course, be ranked more highly on a scale of secular values, could be more highly born or command greater power, but no moral superiority could ever be implied by the facts of rank and power. For in this language, every single fact is a raw fact. Reciprocal love is the only kind of love-relation this language can define, since neither partner could ever appear already endowed with wisdom and redemptive force—for wisdom must be represented, and the longing for redemption cannot be fulfilled in this new realm of poetic discourse, which is strictly limited to the concrete objects of experience. If the beloved withholds her love, her cruelty could never be a metaphor revealing, to the dedicated aspirant, her glorious station; if she withholds her love and demands service without requital, she is claiming more authority than any fact can warrant, and she herself

77

must be rejected as spurious. Walther depicted a new kind of love—new to the Minnesang tradition—one that was in many ways more true, more in the realm of human possibility, than the service-reward relation of the high Minnesang. He taught poetry a new truth, but we need not assume that he found it by observation, in the facts of human nature; he could have found it where every poet (and every artist) finds his truth: in the astonishing nature of his medium, in language.

Walther found the role he now plays already defined, to a great extent, in the Minnesang tradition. The earlier poets would, in the course of their performance, sing for and even impersonate "the vulgar ones": that was their way of grounding the exalted praise they addressed to the "friends." Walther now takes up the position of these *ungefüege liute*, literal-minded hecklers who are blind to figurative meaning, and composes songs for the world that they inhabit. What poetry can be found outside the old poetic circle, in literal discourse? How can one make poetry naming objects that are not automatically "poetic," whose "meaning" and affective power are not already established by a glorious tradition? Distinguishing himself in every way from his great rival, the supreme exponent of the language of celebration, he now looks for a new source of poetry in the language of the "enemies"—"enemies" in quotation marks, for one must never forget that they are characters created by the poets themselves. Around this time Walther composes *Si wundervol gemachet wîp* (L. -K. 53,25; M66), in which he first systematically demetaphorizes a traditionally poetic figure and then invests it in a new significance.

The song begins with a challenge, aimed no doubt at Reinmar:[15]

> I. Si wunderwol gemachet wîp,
>   daz mir noch werde ir habedanc!
>   ich setze ir minneclîchen lîp
>   vil werde in mînen hôhen sanc.
> 5. Gern ich in allen dienen sol,
>   doch hân ich mir dise ûz erkorn.
>   ein ander weiz die sînen wol,
>   die lob er âne mînen zorn.
>   hab ime wîs unde wort
> 10. mit mir gemeine: lob ich hie, sô lob er dort.

> (She, a woman created miraculously beautiful, may her thanks and requital yet be mine. In my song of praise I set her beauty in the place of honor. I would gladly serve them all,

but I have chosen this one out for myself. Another knows his own beloved well enough: let him praise her, I do not object to that. Let him have words and melody in common with me: if I sing my praises here, let him sing his there.)

The issue on which he challenges this "other man" is clearly drawn: how shall one praise the beloved?

The following strophes contain a description of the lady's body, proceeding according to the prescription of the Latin rhetorics: that is, beginning at the top with the lady's *houbet* and moving down to each foot, *ietweder fuoz*, lingering occasionally on the way. As the description progresses down from the head, however, it departs more and more from the traditional Minnesang language of celebration.

> II. Ir houbet ist sô wünnenrîch,
>   als ez mîn himel welle sîn.
>   wem solde ez anders sîn gelîch?
>   ez hât ouch himeleschen schîn.
> 5. Dâ liuhtent zwêne sternen abe,
>   dâ müeze ich mich noch inne ersehen,
>   daz si mirs alsô nâhen habe!
>   sô mac ein wunder wol geschehen.
>   ich junge, und tuot si daz,
> 10. und wirt mir gernden siechen seneder sühte baz.
>
> (Her head is so beautiful, a source of delight, as though it would be my heaven. To what else can it be compared? It has a heavenly light. There two stars shine down; if only I could see myself in them, if only she would hold me so close! A miracle can take place then. I become young if she does that, and I, a man sick with longing, find my longing healed.)[16]

In the following strophe, Walther gives us a virtuoso example of the Minnesang technique of patterning audience perspectives. The performer's eye is still on the "friends" when the strophe begins; but at a certain unmistakable point his eye comes to rest on another sector of the audience, and the level of his song abruptly changes:

> III. Got hât ir wengel hôhen flîz,
>   er streich sô tiure varwe dar,
>   sô reine rôt, sô reine wîz,
>   hie roeseloht, dort liljenvar.
> 5. Ob ichz vor sünden tar gesagen,
>   sô saehe ichs iemer gerner an

79

dan himel oder himelwagen.
owê, waz lob ich tumber man?
mach ich si mir ze hêr,
10. vil lihte wirt mîns mundes lop mîns herzen sêr.

> (God put all his care in the creation of her cheeks, painted such precious colors there—that pure red, that white so pure!—the red of roses here, the white of lilies there! If I dare say it, fearing sin—I'd rather gaze on her than behold heaven, or heaven's wagon [The Great Bear]. Ach, what am I doing, praising her like this, fool that I am? If I put her so lordly high above me, how easily the praise on my lips can become the pain in my heart.)

"I'd rather gaze on her than on heaven—or heaven's wagon": the perfect inanity of these lines is an achievement of Walther's great art. That little phrase *vor sünden*—"were it not for my fear of sin"—does all the damage here. It determines the meaning of *himel* when we first hear that word: the Kingdom of Heaven, not the sky we all can see, for there could not be any danger of sin in preferring to gaze on her than on the stars at night.[17] The singer suggests that he is afraid of committing idolatry—that is the "sin" that her divinely created beauty puts him in danger of, if he desires the sight of her more than paradise. But then this rapturous praise is nullified by something that Walther adds in his apparent enthusiasm, something joined to "heaven" by a coordinating conjunction, *oder*, leading us to expect a parallel image of divinity. Instead, we get more vaudeville—more literalization—and that slapstick descent from Paradise to the Big Dipper (or The Great Bear, to be exact).

The difference between *himel* and *himelwagen* here is something like that between lightning and the lightning bug, the images that Mark Twain uses in order to represent the difference between talent and genius. Only Walther's joke is utterly pointless, and that is just why it is there: this nonsense aborts his praise. What begins as a significant statement ends in a completely unedifying play on words; the net effect is that of total self-repudiation. The presence of the word *himel* suddenly has nothing more to do with its meaning: it is there because of its accidental relation to another word, both words no longer referring to anything but themselves, and only reflecting each other. The sudden shift from heaven—the image of his idolatrous love—to that devastating alternative is a sign that the sector of influence in the audience is changing. In the rest of this strophe—"What am I doing, praising her so highly?"—and in the next, the singer adopts the perspective of the *ungefüege liute*, who are lustful and literal-minded, and the beloved is quickly hauled down to earth. For that is the serious and deliberate purpose of all this play: no poetic figure may be seated any longer in heaven; words sung in praise of another human being may not soar beyond the sublunary sky; poetic language must stop at The Great Bear, which marks the furthest point at which it can have any meaning. Henceforth the objects of poetry must be concrete, verifiable things, which exist as things and are inherently unsignifying—the language of celebration is banished from courtly song.

The strophe that follows consists almost entirely of Walther's response to Reinmar's joke about the stolen kiss, even borrowing Reinmar's brilliant proviso at the end. Walther's joke consists of a play on the word *küssen*, meaning "cushion" when one first hears it and then suggesting "kiss" as well:

IV. Si hât ein küssen, daz ist rôt,
    gewünne ich daz für mînen munt,
    sô stüende ich ûf von dirre nôt
    und waere ouch iemer mê gesunt.
 5. Swâ si daz an ir wengel legt,
    dâ waere ich gerne nâhen bî:
    ez smecket, sô manz iender regt,
    alsam ez vollez balsmen sî.
    daz sol si lîhen mir.
10. swie dicke sô siz wider wil, sô gibe ichz ir.

(She has a *küssen*, a red *küssen*: if I could win that for my lips, I would stand up free of all my pain and be a well man forever. When she lays it against her soft cheek, how gladly would I be there, close by. If one touches it at all, it exhales a fragrance as though it were full of balsam. Let her lend it to me: whenever she wants it back again, no matter how often, I'll give it to her.)

This little joke has generally been taken as a corrective rejoinder to Reinmar: one should get himself a kiss not by stealing it but by borrowing it with the lady's willing cooperation.[18] There may be something to that—though I doubt it. The clear intention of this strophe lies in its contrast with that rapturous praise at the beginning of the song. This trivializing pun conveys absolutely nothing about the nature of the beloved, but it tells a great deal about the way in which she is regarded. For this is how he keeps from exalting her *ze hêr*.

This strophe follows his sudden awakening—"*What am I doing . . . ?*" It is the one strophe in which he expresses his desire to touch her, expressing it, through the pun and the shy indirection of his lust, in a way intended to provoke laughter. For the lower down her body the description moves, the lower the level and the more ambiguous his praise. Her eyes inspired him by their rejuvenating light; her cheeks first moved him to the thought of God the Creator, then—with his eye on another part of the audience—to the pun that nullified his praise. Now her lips bring on this other pun. In both cases the effect of the singer's empty play on words is the same: the lady is replaced as the object to which the words refer. These statements reveal nothing but the singer's ingenuity and his absolute freedom in the choice of language: he can praise to the skies and then take it all away. Now it becomes clear that everything we have heard about so far, including the heavenly light of her eyes, is the product of that same unbounded skill, the showpiece of a master who can work his will with words.

For this pun, too—the one about the cushion—is focused upon an accidental similarity between two words, not on any essential relation between the things they signify. Sometimes, when we come across a pun, we suddenly realize that of the two meanings in play the unexpected one conveys a deeper truth than the one that more obviously fits the context, and then, very quickly, our attention arcs back from the signifier to the things signified. But here, in Walther's song, the pun points to nothing beyond itself, and our attention rests immobile in the mere sound of the word. Comparing the beloved to heaven seems to reveal something about her nature and the singer's attitude; but all that talk about her cushion tells us nothing except that the thought of her inflames the speaker and that her body is capable of arousing such thoughts. The words no longer pertain to her, and the only thing we contemplate is the performer's clever turn, his way with words, and the inspiring energy that brings this trick to pass—namely, his lust, no longer controlled by the thought of her virtue, since the pun has no significance with respect to her. The effect of his play on words is to curtail the objective reference of poetic language to the point where it is practically no longer referential. The words point only to the speaker, and not even directly to him, only casually reflecting his immediate mood and thoroughly obliterating the image of the beloved. His enthusiastic celebration of her divine beauty is completely undone: his praise amounts to nothing, because his language has ceased to signify. His words function, with complete indifference to their meaning, as mirrors of his faculties and his momentary state—his skill, his lust, both careless of their object. This is all a performer's

trick, a sure-fire way to arouse the audience's laughter, and Walther
could not have learned it from a greater master than his rival,
Reinmar.

We can understand the purpose of this strophe in the entire
scheme only if we bear in mind what inspired it: Reinmar's own play
with words. Walther is competing with Reinmar, trying to surpass
him. He, like Reinmar, departs from the language of celebration—
but not, like Reinmar, in order to reclaim it. Reinmar's own silly
joke enables him to *return* to the level he abandoned, and that
return is an act of his will, the nexus between celebration and
experience, transforming that platitudinous language into the true
and considered expression of his longing and devotion here and
now. And so, Reinmar's song follows the traditional pattern of the
Minnesang: after a departure, a return.[19] In Walther's song, one
more strophe follows the one in which he evokes our laughter, and
that one should contain the lines of reaffirmation, redeeming poetic
language with the dignity of choice. Or it could simply go on
degrading her. But what actually happens is altogether different—a
wonder, a new way of creating poetry:

V. Ir kel, ir hende, ietweder fuoz,
daz ist ze wunsche wol getân.
ob ich da enzwischen loben muoz,
sô waene ich mê beschouwet hân.
5. Ich hete ungerne "decke blôz!"
gerüefet, do ich si nacket sach.
si sach mich niht, dô si mich schôz,
daz mich noch sticht als ez dô stach,
swann ich der lieben stat
10. gedenke, dâ si reine ûz einem bade trat.
(Her neck, her hands, each foot—all beautiful, formed as
one can only wish. If I may praise what lies between, then I
imagine I've seen more. How unwilling I'd have been to
shout "Take cover!" when I saw her naked. She did not see
me as she struck me; that shot pierces me still, as it pierced
me then, whenever I think of that dear place where she
stepped, all pure, out of her bath.)

A man, hiding, sees the beloved naked in her bath—and keeps
his distance. At first her nakedness is a sign of her vulnerability—
she can be spied upon all unawares—her undefended presence, her
loss of authority. She appears now bare of the influence that she
wielded from the center of her remoteness, bare of the power to

signify. Her nakedness figures forth her subjection to the laws that govern us all, her creatureliness, her simplicity, her pathetic visibility. But once divested by the man's clear vision of all that old significance, she is reinvested in a new poetic status by the distance that he maintains.

Those lines about his "imagining" that he must have seen "more" are intended to suggest intimate physical experience—in order to make the surprise at the end all the more effective. It turns out, after all, that he really did only *see* her—the idea of "seeing" appears three times in this strophe, once in a rhyme-word. The vision of her beauty was such that it kept him rooted where he was, separated from her. The distance between the *stat* where she bathes and the position from which he observes her is the distance traversed by her effect on him, the "shot" that pierced him and pierces him still. In contrast to the meaning of separation in the classic Minnesang, the distance depicted here does not derive from, or represent, those virtues that tradition attributed to the beloved. He does not stay away for reasons that he can name—and that the others have so readily named—awed by that familiar list of courtly graces. Nor does she, in her presumed perfection, ordain that distance; she does not even see him. Unlike Artemis, she is aware of nothing, least of all her own value in relation to his. She is naked, divested of the robes of her authority, unsignifying, so that this separation between them now cannot express the relation between ideal and aspirant, as it did even in the second strophe of this song, when he longed to see himself reflected in her eyes—when she still appeared as the embodiment of an ideal. The effect of the singer's reductive praise is that she appears naked, diminished, simply a woman in her bath, a figure washed clean of all the old accretions; and the distance depicted here is the necessary condition of desire, the separation without which desire is impossible, which alone prevents desire from dying in fulfillment. But the fact that he *preserves* that distance gives it a new poetic resonance.

In this last strophe she is enhanced, not by her association with heaven and the Creator's hand or by the moral authority in which she was clothed by tradition—the forces of belief that made the beloved the source of all the truths that courtly experience could teach—but only by his desire. She is made remote, and thus exalted, by the very effect that she evoked in him, by the longing that still pains him, the longing to traverse that distance—the longing that in the performance of the song *establishes* that distance. It is this separation that re-defines, and re-poeticizes, the unadorned woman:

she is someone to be gazed upon from a distance and therefore, after all, something more than a beautiful body. She is made significant by the frame of time and space that separates her from the one who desires her. Her new-born status as poetic image, as representation and bearer of meaning, is revealed entirely by the attitude and the condition of the one who watches her without moving forward to tread on the ground she occupies, who establishes the defining context of memory, distance, and longing from which she emerges *reine*. This context is reinforced by the versification of the last two lines: by the rime that stresses *stat*, by the enjambement that stresses *gedenke*, by the elision of the final vowel in *reine*, which causes the root vowel to be stretched out in compensation. She is *reine* in body as she steps out of her bath; and *reine*, too, as representation, as *word*, as non-secular and impalpable figure of a reality that eludes the language of ordinary discourse. *Reine* is Walther's cry of triumph at the end, the mark of his achievement: he has made the language of poetry *rein*.

This song begins with recollections of the beloved's traditional rôle: the rejuvenating mirror of her eyes, the face adored as the countenance of an authority as great—*vor sünden!*—as heaven's. But that rôle is introduced only to be relinquished (. . . *oder himelwagen!*). Her nakedness is a sign of her role-less, undefined reality: the walls of the court do not enclose her. There is no background against which the elements of this song are situated. There is nothing but these three things: her born beauty, the man who sees and remembers, and the distance that relates them— without any familiar context to determine their relation. Her nakedness here, as poetic sign, means that she comes forth devoid of all unearned and automatic values.[20] The process of divesting the image of such accretions begins with the praise of the parts of her body below the eyes, and it is paralleled by Walther's treatment of certain key words, which appeared as poetic terms in Reinmar's song. The *stat*, the "place" that in Reinmar's song signified the precincts of virtue and appeared as part of a poetic figure (the metaphor of the chessboard), is here the place where she takes a bath. The "foot" and the "step," which represented the idea of the slightest conceivable departure from perfection, are here a real foot ("each foot" as real as her neck and her hands) and a real step out of the water. The concretization of these words, their application to the creature, epitomizes Walther's attack on poetic language. And yet all these things—her bathing, her foot, her emergence—along with every aspect of her creatural existence, are framed by the observer's admiring distance and transformed into imagery: that step she takes at the end marks her emergence as a new poetic word.

This newly created poetic image contains no trace of the doctrinaire element that characterized the role that she has shed. The song ends with everyday reality transfigured by memory, distance, and longing, but the "meaning" of this new image cannot be defined as readily as the old one, for this one has limitless possibilities of meaning. She is now an image that can be evoked as the *word*—the all-encompassing representation—of a host of experiences, not just the specific experience of courtly life. This is so because of the unclouded, non-tendentious gaze of the *ich* and the mute concreteness of the one that he observes. The three preceding strophes have made it impossible to read the old meanings into the figure of the beloved, and his reductive description of her no longer reflects the attitude of one inclined to look for such meanings, the loving servant aspiring to courtly recognition. Until the very end of the song we never know exactly what his attitude is, because, until then, he does not have one. He does not see in her a fixed sign whose meaning is definite and universally recognized: he sees a woman in her bath, and at the end he is astounded by her significance. Then she is transfigured by his gaze and his unexpected response, his awed immobility. In the final lines we hear that the memory still sticks in his heart, and so, through his remembering, she is framed by the distance of time as well as of space. Since, apart from his gaze, she is inherently unsignifying, there is no limit to what she can eventually signify: it all depends on what she is related to (in this case, a remembering observer singing to us of the beloved's permanent effect) and on the character of that relation (in this case, that of a discoverer to an unexpected revelation). Her meaning, at the end, is indefinable, her potential relatedness infinite. When he has sung his song we know that she is radiant with meaning, and we know it because of his reaction to her. His behavior reveals that he is in the presence of something that cannot be possessed as ordinary things are possessed, that she is a figure to which the proper reaction is contemplation, and recollection—note the emphatic position of *gedenke* at the end. Insofar as the singer strips words and images of their traditional connotations, he shares the viewpoint of the old enemies of the song. But his gaze is itself transfigured by distance, for distance invests his vision with another value, with admiration; and this capacity to engender, or to recognize, poetic meaning in the thing he contemplates finally distinguishes his attitude from the obliterating lust of the *ungefüege liute*.

The limitless possibilities of meaning in this new poetic image are what most profoundly distinguish it from the old. One can never spell out the meaning of the new figure, as one could with the old. The lady who appears in the traditional song is immediately and entirely readable; she is valued for the specific things she stands for—witness the vagueness and sameness of the women praised in so many different songs. But the new figure is valued as a signifying and transfigured image, rather than for some specific doctrine or defined experience that the public has already associated with her. Because of her objective concreteness and the observer's free and neutral vision, the signifying range, the compass and variety of the poetic context, transcends the narrow courtly world of the classic Minnesang.

In the songs of Walther's predecessors, the established meaning of the beloved necessitated the distance that separated her from those who admired and contemplated her. But in this song she first appears as unenhanced creature, and it is her distance from the *ich* that *reveals* her essential status as representation, as the singer's *word* for beauty—that transforms her from natural object to poetic image. A new kind of poetry is in the making here. Considering the background of the feud, we should hear this song as Walther's reply to Reinmar, as a poem about the making of poetry. Henceforth, to the end of his life, Walther will follow the path he has marked out here. As the beloved is here transfigured through her relation to the one who gazes on her, so will every object appear first in all its concrete, unsignifying physicality, and then, no longer inherently poetic, will take on significance through its relation to another equally mute object: the poetry will lie no longer in the objects but in their *relation*.[21] The beloved will be re-secularized and then transformed into a poetic figure by being related to something else. She will come forth no longer as a fixed metaphor, and she will be free now to become one of the *elements* of a metaphor.

—— NOTES ——

[1]See Burghart Wachinger, *Sängerkrieg: Untersuchungen zur Spruchdichtung des 13. Jahrhunderts* (Munich, 1973), pp. 95-105.

[2]*Des Minnesangs Frühling*, ed. Hugo Moser and Helmut Tervooren, 36th ed., 2 vols. (Stuttgart, 1977); referred to here as MF. *Die Gedichte Walthers von der Vogelweide*, ed. Karl Lachmann, newly ed. by Carl von Kraus, 13th ed. (Berlin, 1965); referred to here as L. -K. *Die Lieder Walthers von der Vogelweide*, ed. Friedrich Maurer (Tübingen, 1967/1969); referred to as M.

[3]Assuming that the strophes attributed to him are genuine. Their authenticity has been called into question chiefly by Henry W. Nordmeyer in *JEGP*, 28 (1929), 203–14; *ibid.*, 29 (1930), 18–40; *ibid.*, 31 (1932), 360–94; and *PMLA*, 45 (1930), 629–83. Carl von Kraus, who readily accepted the last two strophes in his study and edition of Reinmar—*Die Lieder Reinmars des Alten*, Abhandlungen der Bayerischen Akademie der Wissenschaften, philosoph. -philolog. und hist. Klasse, Vol. 30, Nos. 4, 6, and 8 (Munich, 1919); see esp. III, pp. 5 ff.—later rejected them in response to Nordmeyer's work: *Walther von der Vogelweide, Untersuchungen* (Berlin and Leipzig, 1935), pp. 396 ff., 416; cf. *Des Minnesangs Frühling, Untersuchungen* (Leipzig, 1939). He has been followed by many others. The question is too complex to discuss here. Suffice it to say that Nordmeyer's objections rest on an assumption that has been seriously doubted and often discredited by modern editors of medieval texts: namely, that there is a single authentic "original" version which either is contained in one or more of the manuscripts or else needs to be "reconstructed"; and on the basis of the supposed "original" all variant readings must be rejected as emendations by another hand. This assumption arbitrarily—and often unjustifiably—excludes the possibility that the variations were composed by the poet. The unquestioning acceptance of this assumption mars nearly all of the textual criticism in Dietrich Kralik's otherwise valuable study, *Walther gegen Reinmar* (Vienna, 1955).

[4]This is especially clear in the examples from Heinrich von Morungen, where every occurrence of the *Verstummen* motif is associated with another equally venerable theme, the service of song; see, for example, MF 136, 15; 141, 26. See also Wiebke Schmaltz, *Reinmar der Alte: Beiträge zur poetischen Technik* (Göppingen, 1975), p. 201. This work is an important and exhaustive study of Reinmar's rhetorical devices.

[5]"The Array of Perspectives in the Early Courtly Love Lyric," in *In Pursuit of Perfection*, ed. Joan M. Ferrante and George D. Economou (Port Washington, N.Y. and London, 1975), pp. 51–100. See also the introductory essays to Guillaume IX, Bernart de Ventadorn, and Thibaut de Champagne in *Lyrics of the Troubadours and Trouvères* (Garden City, N.Y., 1973); and to Heinrich von Morungen and Reinmar in *German and Italian Lyrics of the Middle Ages* (Garden City, N.Y., 1973).

[6]Kralik is thus simply wrong when he says (p. 11) that Reinmar does not refer to the lovers of other ladies.

[7]See Peter Wapnewski, "Der Sänger und die Dame: zu Walthers Schachlied (111, 23)," *Euphorion*, 60 (1966), 1–29, esp. 17 ff.

[8]MF 141, 37. See Kurt Herbert Halbach, *Walther von der Vogelweide und die Dichter von Minnesangs Frühling* (Stuttgart, 1927), pp. 57 f.; Carl von Kraus, *Reinmar*, III, p. 10.

[9]See, for example, MF 166, 16; see also Goldin, "The Array of Perspectives," pp. 78 ff.

[10]"Reinmar, Walther und die Minne," *BGDSL*(Halle), 93 (1971), 168–212; text on p. 211.

[11]"Der Sänger," pp. 9–14. See also his article "Reinmars Recht-fertigung," in *Medieval German Studies Presented to Frederick Norman* (London, 1965), pp. 71–83.

[12]See Birkhan, pp. 186 ff.; and Karl Korn, *Studien über "Freude und Trûren" bei mittelhochdeutschen Dichtern* (Leipzig, 1932), pp. 62 ff. It should be noted that Walther's attack on Reinmar's Easter Day is an attack on traditional poetic language; Heinrich von Morungen, for example, uses this venerable image (MF 140, 15 f.); see Kralik, pp. 16, 64.

[13]He gives us some idea of what he means in the second strophe of this *Schachlied*, where the motif of the stolen kiss is treated, not as a poetic expression of the aspirant's desire and the moral distance that prevents him from ever *deserving* the favor of one so exalted, but as an event that takes place, as a narrative rather than a lyrical motif; and where the lady speaks with the indignation of one who has really been taken advantage of.

[14]See Wolfgang Bachofer, "Zur Wandlung des Minne-Bergriffs bei Walther," in *Festgabe für Ulrich Pretzel* (Berlin, 1963), pp. 139–49, who arrives at the following conclusion from a completely different approach: "Ohne den 'Stachel' Reinmar wäre Walther diesen Weg vermutlich nicht gegangen" (p. 149).

[15]See von Kraus, *Walther, Untersuchungen*, pp. 196 ff.; and Kurt Herbert Halbach, "'Humanitäts-Klassik' des Stauferzeitalters in der Lyrik Walthers von der Vogelweide," in *Festschrift für Klaus Ziegler*, ed. E. Catholy and W. Hellmann (Tübingen, 1968), pp. 25 ff. Halbach also discusses the tradition and the contemporary use of the head-to-foot description.

[16]On the mirror-image see F. Goldin, *The Mirror of Narcissus* (Ithaca, N.Y., 1967).

[17]See Halbach, "'Humanitäts-Klassik,'" p. 29. Anton Schönbach (*ZDA*, 39 [1895], 352) remarked that *himelwagen* was a well-established symbol signifying the community of the saints, the Heavenly Kingdom, eternal blessedness. If these meanings are at play here—Schönbach himself doubts that they are—then the singer really is guilty of the "sin" he so fears to commit. And even if we believe that Walther intended this blasphemy, we are still left with the critical question: why did he choose this particular constellation? For all of the signs of heaven stood for the same essential truth: this is a cardinal point in one of the sources that Schönbach cites, the *De Universo*, Book IX, of Rabanus Maurus. In Chapter iii, for example, *De coelo* (PL 111, cols. 263–65), the figure of heaven is said to stand for the prophets, the apostles, and the saints; sometimes, as well, for the contemplation of supernal beings, for divine justice, for Holy Scripture, for the angels who are above the firmament (which stands for the law). The East and the West are the Gates of Heaven (Chap. v. col. 265). They stand for the

two Testaments; the clouds, for the preachers. The light of heaven (Chapter vii, cols. 265–67) stands variously for God the Trinity, the Son of God, the Saints, Holy Scripture, the message of the Gospels, the Church, the illumination of faith, the elect, divine justice. The sun (Chapter ix, cols. 267 f.) stands in different contexts for the Redeemer, the glory of His saints, the splendor of wisdom, the beauty of virtue and good works, the fiery turmoil of persecution, and the tribulation of this present life. The moon (Chapter x, cols. 268–71), though it sometimes stands for the misery of this life, also signifies the Church, the passion of the martyrs, the Savior incarnate and His Resurrection, among other things. The constellations (Chapter xi, cols. 271 f.) signify many things, among them the saints, the elect, and Christ. Arcturus (Chapter xiii, cols. 272 f.—apparently a mistake for Arctus: see Boethius, *Cons. Phil.* 4, 5 and Otto Sigfrid Reuter, *Germanische Himmelskunde* [Munich, 1934], pp. 250–54), aside from the meanings cited by Schönbach, also signifies the Law; the Pleiades, the grace of the New Testament. Orion and the Hyades (Chapter xiv, cols. 273 f.), signify, respectively, the martyrs and the doctors of the Church. Lucifer (Chapter xv, col. 274), understood *in bonam partem*, signifies God the Savior and the light of wisdom.

Any one of these—with a less ambiguous name for Lucifer—and all the other splendid figures of the sky would have been as appropriate in Walther's song as *himelwagen*—if the passage were meant to be understood *per allegoriam*. But in that case we would be at an even greater loss to understand Walther's choice. For if all the figures of heaven have an equally well-established and vital religious significance, then the religious significance cannot be the decisive reason why Walther chose this particular one. Clearly it is a mistake to look for such meanings here, all the more so as the text explicitly excludes them. The very clause that gives a false signal of danger—*ob ichz vor sünden tar gesagen*—simultaneously arrests that danger by shutting out all religious associations: he will *not* commit blasphemy. The message that that phrase conveys is this: I am going to come as close to blasphemy as one can without actually committing it, and watch for the brilliant maneuver by which I extricate myself and preserve my innocence. That maneuver consists in first introducing *himel* under a false sign, and then revealing the sign as false. The phrase *oder himelwagen* announces, at the last moment, that *himel* only means the stars in the sky after all—*per litteram*, and nothing else. The neutralizing function of *himelwagen* also explains why it is a rime-word: its choice is determined primarily by the accidental exigencies of rime, meter, and sound—least of all by its meaning, as any other figure would have done as well. There is no blasphemy in this song, but there is plenty of emulation: the role of the creator—announced in the first line by *gemachet* and developed by the statuary appearance of the created lady and by the figure of God—is proudly assumed by the poet.

[18]For example, von Kraus, *Reinmar*, III, p. 10; Kralik, p. 40; Wapnewski, "Rechtfertigung"; Halbach, "'Humanitäts-Klassik,'" p. 30.

[19]That is why the strophic order of Reinmar's song in the current edition of MF is to be preferred to that in previous editions.

[20]See L. -K. 62,6; M. 84 (*Ob ich mich selben rüemen sol*): the lady's *reiner lîp* is *ein vil werdez tach*. See also D. R. McLintock, "Walther's *Mädchenlieder*," *OGS*, 3 (1968), 30–43, esp. p. 37.

[21]I can do little more here than suggest how Walther continued to "de-poeticize" traditional poetic language and to create a poetry of relations in some of his other songs. In several lyrics, including the *Mädchenlieder*, the beloved is brought into a signifying relation with a being other than the singer or observer: with nature. In L. -K. 51,13; M. 42 (*Muget ir schowen was dem meien*) the beloved, removed from the context of the court, is redefined by the realm she now inhabits: she is informed by her analogous relation to May, revivifying nature. The singer says to her: *ir sît doch genâden rîche* (V,6), but the meaning and effect of *genâde* are to be sought not in her being but in the character and works of May. Here she is transformed from source to recipient of meaning.

In L. -K. 49,25; M. 62 (*Herzeliebez frouwelîn*) the poetic reduction of the beloved is reflected in the impoverishment of her ornament or gift. The accusation of the others that he pitches his song too "low" refers ultimately to Walther's language, its strict denotativeness, its suppression of all celebrated associations. The girl appears in fact unrelated to anything else—and that is why the song ends with the singer's uncertainty regarding her steadfastness. She is completely isolated in the singer's reductive gaze, and the process of re-investment so powerfully carried through in *Si wunderwol gemachet wîp* is completely missing here.

In L. -K. 74,20; M. 65 ("*Nemt frouwe, disen kranz*") the implicit lesson of *Herzeliebez frouwelîn* is fully realized. He offers her the garland, she receives it in a certain way; and the way in which she receives it is his *lôn*, something given to him in return. The bonding energy of the relation arcs back and forth continually between the two (the word *lôn* has been completely emptied of its feudal meaning and its connotation of a relation between unequals). Both giver and receiver come forth without the traditional repertory of qualities; there are no diamonds to be given or received. Each of the two human figures acts the roles of giver and recipient at once, each needy, requiring definition, and reciprocally establishing their natures through their essential acts of giving and receiving. Nature is here represented as a realm, three-dimensional, inhabitable (*in jener heide*). It replaces the court setting as the realm of significance—in great contrast to *Herzeliebez frouwelîn* and its realmless, unsituated, unsignifying figure of the beloved. Finally, the encounter is revealed as a dream. But its effect is real; and the song that conveys the effect—and is part of the effect—actually takes place in performance. The dream finally desecularizes the beloved and frames her as a poetic figure.

The basic attitude which calls forth the new language can be observed in L. -K. 47,36; M. 72 (*Zwô fuoge hân ich doch*). When Walther asserts that not every *frouwe* is good, that only the good ones deserve to be loved, and

91

that he can tell the difference, he effectively removes the basis of traditional language in the courtly lyric. For in the traditional lyric all extremes were united in the figure of the beloved—concern and indifference, consolation and cruelty. The courtly ideal and its insubstantiality were mirrored in her: she was the image of all of the possibilities of courtly life and the object of every attitude that could be taken toward it. (This theme is beautifully developed in Reinmar's *Wiest im ze muote*). But when Walther says that there are both good and bad ladies and that they must be distinguished, the figure of the beloved becomes fixed as a character, immutable and readable, which we must judge. It is no longer possible to create a song by unraveling the reflections she contains, for she no longer reflects, and her attributes are unilateral, determined, no different from those of the other ladies who are either good or bad. Similarly, the singer's attitude is determined completely and precisely by the condition of the object that he contemplates.

The distance that Walther puts between himself and Reinmar can be measured by his use of the word *maere* in L. -K. 56,14; M. 49 (*Ir sult sprechen willekomen*), his apparent answer to Reinmar's Preislied (von Kraus, no. 16). In Reinmar, *maere* refers to the "latest news" in his relation to the beloved, therefore to the theme of his song. For Walther, *maere* means real news, facts, confirmed by a diligent, world-wide, comparative study.

In L. -K. 15,30; M. 57 (*Mich nimt iemer wunder*), the reduction of both figures is carefully worked out: the woman's *zauber* turns out to be no mystery at all, and the singer's primary trait is his plainness.

These and many other examples of the new kind of poetic language that Walther pursued throughout his life are the subject of a study now in progress.

FARAI UN VERS DE DREYT NIEN
THE CRAFT OF THE EARLY TROBADORS
JOAN M. FERRANTE

PROVENÇAL POETRY is the first body of lyric poetry in a romance language. This means that the trobadors who wrote the first lyrics had no native literary tradition to draw on—they had to create their medium as they were working in it. Because they were composing in a language which differed in important ways from that of the dominant written culture, Latin, they had to develop new forms. They could look to Latin poetry and rhetoric for images and allusions, but they had to find the rhyme-schemes, sound effects, and word-plays which would be appropriate to Provençal for themselves.[1] They had to create a literary language and a poetic tradition. This led, on the one hand, to a heavy reliance on conventional material which is common to much early Provençal poetry—the spring opening, the yearning and suffering of the lover, the powers of the lady—and, on the other, to a pursuit of unusual and distinctive technical devices which mark the individuality of the poets. The early trobadors take particular pride in their technical achievements, and it is this aspect of their poetry that will be investigated here.

The trobadors of the first century of Provençal poetry are quite self-conscious about their role as poets. Whether they are nobles playing at it to amuse or to preen, or professionals who make their living by it, they lose no opportunity to make the audience aware of their technique. They can be obvious or subtle about it: by announcing that they are about to "make a poem" or try a new style; by witty and pointed self-parody, which calls attention to their other works; and by frequent references to the text and the music, and the relation of one to the other. It seems highly probable, from the frequency of technical allusions in the poems and from the number of aristocratic poets whose work survives, that a good proportion of a Provençal court audience dabbled in poetry and might be expected to appreciate technical skill and virtuosity. The poems suggest a rapport between poet and audience that is rare outside literary circles. The poets anticipate and respond to audience reaction. They seem often to speak for the audience, expressing its ideals and desires, as well as their own, offering models to imitate and identify with, and sometimes to laugh at.

The traditions developed by the trobadors in this sympathetic setting gave shape to many of the major medieval lyric traditions. The subject matter, poetic postures, stanzaic forms, rhyme schemes, and word-plays can be traced through medieval poetry, particularly in French, German, and Italian. I shall attempt no more here than a review of representative poets from the first century of Provençal lyric, and a brief look at one of the last medieval poets who consciously wrote in their tradition, Dante. The six Provençal poets whose work will be discussed span four generations and represent a balance between the complex style (*trobar clus*) and the simple (*trobar leu* or *plan*), as well as between the aristocratic amateur and the professional poet: Guillem IX (1071–1127), Count of Poitiers and Duke of Aquitaine; Marcabru and Jaufré Rudel, prince of Blaye, from the second quarter of the twelfth century; Bernart de Ventadorn and Raimbaut, Count of Orange, from the third quarter of the twelfth century; and Arnaut Daniel (fl. 1180–1200).[2] Whether Guillem is actually the first to compose poetry in Provençal or not, he is the first whose work we have, and his poems display a variety of tones and moods, though all essentially in a simple style. Jaufré and Bernart illustrate the simple style for their respective periods, Marcabru and Raimbaut, the complex style. Jaufré and Bernart write mostly love poems, while Marcabru is given to moral allegory and social satire, Raimbaut to obstruse eccentricity and idio-syncratic wit. Jaufré and Raimbaut were amateur poets who could please themselves first, Marcabru and Bernart professionals who made a living from their compositions. Arnaut, a professional poet possibly of good birth,[3] and a self-styled craftsman, writes his love

94

poems with obvious delight in his own virtuosity. Dante, like the early trobadors, was conscious of giving new structures to poetry and to his language; his poetry shares many characteristics and techniques with theirs, though it was written over a century later and in a different social setting. He acknowledges their primacy in the vernacular lyric, singling Arnaut out for particular praise in *De vulgari eloquentia* and, in the *Comedy*, tracing the heritage of Italian lyric poetry back to Arnaut. Aware of the lack of order in Italian—the variety of forms and constructions in the numerous dialects—Dante consciously attempted to offer a model in his own poetry.[4] His work, therefore, seems a fitting place to end this study.

Although modern readers tend to concentrate on the words and the poetic structure of the lyrics, music was a very important element in the earliest periods of vernacular poetry: lyrics were sung, not recited, and many poets took particular care over the melodies. Of the six to be discussed here, two, Jaufré and Bernart, were particularly noted for their music; they allude frequently to the music within the poems, and their melodies have survived in greater number, proportionally, testifying to the relative importance of the music for them and their audiences.[5] The increasing importance of the words as the lyric tradition develops is reflected in the use of the terms *vers* and *chans(o)* by the six trobadors. Originally, *vers* is the word for a poem, *chans* for the music, the "song." As a vida of Marcabru explains: "en aqel temps non appellava hom cansson, mas tot qant hom cantava eron vers" (at that time, one did not call them *cansson*, but whatever was sung was a *vers*).[6] Eventually *chanso* comes to mean a poem in the light style, while *vers* deals with more complicated or serious matter. Finally, with Arnaut, *chanso* becomes the generic name for the love lyric, even when the emphasis is on the words; the musical aspect of the word is virtually lost.[7] *Chanso* later becomes a specific poetic form in French (the *chanson*) and in Italian (the *canzone*). One can deduce a good deal about an early poet's attitude towards his poetry from his use of the terms *vers* and *chanso*, whether he thinks of a particular piece as light or serious, whether he is more concerned with the words or the music or the overall effect.

As the poet's attitude focuses more and more on the words, the technical aspect of the poetry becomes more important and more complex. The rhyme schemes develop from simple patterns and repeated sounds (often the same sounds repeated like the melody, in each stanza), to more complex schemes and a greater variety of sounds, to rhymes which are not answered within the stanza (dissolute rhymes). Since dissolute rhymes must be answered in other stanzas, they have a double effect of leaving individual stanzas suspended, apparently incomplete, and at the same time, drawing the entire poem together. The more dissolute rhymes per stanza, the more the audience is likely to perceive the entire poem as one large pattern, rather than as a series of self-contained stanzas, with the same pattern repeated any number of times. Guillem, Jaufré, and Marcabru work with fairly simple rhyme schemes, although Marcabru is partial to unusual words. Bernart has a relatively small vocabulary, but he plays with the ambiguities inherent in the language, compelling the audience to concentrate more on the words in order not to miss his meaning. Raimbaut goes even further than Marcabru in the use of odd words, sounds, and rhyme-schemes; he extends the use of dissolute rhymes so that they dominate many of his poems. Arnaut goes further still—perhaps as far as one can go—with dissolute rhymes and odd sounds, using longer stanzas and increasing the number of unanswered rhymes and sounds. The display of technical virtuosity, already an important element of Raimbaut's poetry, becomes Arnaut's chief reason for writing, and the aspect of his poetry which particularly attracted Dante.

Guillem IX, the earliest poet we know in a romance vernacular, displays a fairly simple technical apparatus—in his ten (or eleven) poems, there are never more than three rhyme sounds per stanza, usually only two[8]—within a wide variety of literary moods—courtly, bawdy, boasting, and mocking.[9] But whatever the mood, Guillem rarely lets us forget that he is a poet creating a poem. Guillem calls attention to his work in the most straightforward manner: "farai un vers" (I shall make a poem), he announces towards the beginning of four (or five) of the poems, with occasional variations, such as at the end of a poem, "fait ai lo vers" (I have made the poem). And in three others, he boasts directly about his poetic ability. It may well be that Guillem's position as ruling lord has something to do with his assertiveness; whether he is talking about poetry, sex, gambling, or wisdom, he speaks as a "master" (*maistre certa*, 6.36), and yet he is able to make fun of himself, as a poet and a lover. He is capable even, in what appear in the light of later poets to be more conventional love poems, to adopt the posture of the humble lover.

In the more courtly poems, Guillem plays the adoring, obedient lover (see *Pus vezem, Mout jauzens*, perhaps *Farai chansoneta*); even in *Ab la dolchor*, where he is a satisfied lover, he does not preen. But he does not let us forget that he is also a poet. In *Pus vezem*, Guillem devotes a whole stanza to praising the technical success of the poem:

> Del vers vos dic que mais ne vau
> qui be l'enten e n'a plus lau:
> que·ls motz son faitz tug per egau
> comunalmens,
> e·l son et ieu meteus m'en lau,
> bo's e valens   (7.37–42)

(About the verse, I tell you that it is worth more if one understands it, and it receives more praise, for the words are all equal and the same [perhaps a reference to the syllable count] and the melody, if I say so myself, good and worthy.)

One could read the first two lines to mean: "About the verse . . . *he* is worth more / who understands it and *he* receives more praise"; this would imply a challenge to the audience, in that one who understands and responds to the poem is thereby worth more (see "Companho, farai un vers . . . e tenhatz lo per vilan qui no l'enten," 1.1–4).

In *Mout jauzens*, in contrast, Guillem plays down his poetic abilities: he says he is afraid to tell the lady about his love or even send her a message. And in *Ab la dolchor*, the poem which describes a happy, mutual love, only the birds sing ("li aucel / chanton chascus en lor lati / segon lo vers del novel chan" 10.2–4), a conventional motif not otherwise found in Guillem's extant poems. Human speech for these lovers is either dangerous ("qu'eu non ai soing d'estraing lati / que'm parta de mon Bon Vezi" I have no care for strange tongues that might part me from my Good Neighbor, 10.25–26), or superfluous ("qu'eu sai de paraulas com van . . ." for I know how it is with words . . . some boast of love, while we have the bread and the knife, 10.27–30). The rhyme scheme of this poem is one of the more interesting in Guillem's repertoire: the sounds remain the same, but the arrangement differs, aabcbc in one pair of stanzas, bbcaca in the next three, offering both variety and unity within the harmony of the repeated sounds, echoing the love they describe.

If he is distrustful of speech in *Mout jauzens*, Guillem actually mocks the poet's reliance on language in *Farai un vers pos mi sonelh*. He describes an encounter between himself, in the guise of a pilgrim, and two women who keep him imprisoned for eight days to service them. He achieves this infernal paradise by pretending to be mute—a poet who obtains without words, or with non-words (*barbariol, barbarian* 5.29–30), what others cannot achieve with them. The women test his disguise by drawing a cat's claws along his body, but he says nothing; finally, however, he has the last word, because he describes the whole event in his poem. And perhaps in the rather involved and asymmetrical patterns of his rhyme words, he is also asserting the poet's power to order, as well as to confuse, through language.[10]

In *Ben vuelh que sapchon li plusor*, Guillem begins with boasts of prowess in various areas, poetry, dice, and by implication love, but he ends the poem with a stunning failure. The first stanza establishes Guillem's "mastery" as a poet who forms and binds the *vers* in his workshop, with the skills of rhetoric (implied by the words *color*, 6.2, and *flor*, 6.4); the second proclaims his cleverness at debate ("I know what folly and wisdom are . . . and if you propose a game of love—*joc d'amor*, which suggests a *joc partit*, a debate—to me, I can choose the best part"). There is some ambiguity in the *joc d'amor*, which is increased when Guillem shifts to the game of dice, the *joc dousa* ("sweet game"), at which he is equally skilled, and prepared to advise others ("none will be sent away uncounseled" 6.34–35). As he describes the play, it becomes clear that dice is a euphemism for the sexual act. The surprise, however, is that after all the claims of skill—that he is a *maistre certa*, 6.36, a claim both reinforced and undercut by the puns in *mester* "profession," 6.4, 23, 39, and "use," 48—when he finds himself in a particularly heavy game (*un joc grosser*, 6.45), he cannot meet the woman's challenge and he fails. If sex, like dice, is a game of chance as well as skill, where one can fail no matter how experienced,[11] and if poetry is also a game, then perhaps the master poet can occasionally fail there too.

Not, however, in the "nonsense" poem, *Farai un vers de dreyt nien*, which is a highly successful parody of literary conventions. At the same time, Guillem begs the question of why one writes poetry, if one can write a perfectly good poem about "absolutely nothing." Certainly the creation *ex nihilo* has other connotations—only God (and I) can make something of nothing—as does the reference to the *contraclau*, the key which will explain it all, perhaps a crack at the traditions of biblical and literary exegesis[12]—the author pretends to have no idea what it all means, but there is someone else who does. The poem is a series of negatives—it is not about me or anyone else, not about love or youth or anything else—and parodies of love cliches—I am sick and trembling with death; I have a friend I have never seen, but I love her fiercely. Since *Companho, farai un vers* purports to be about love and youth but in fact talks only about sex, it may be that this poem, which pretends *not* to be about love or youth, is meant to be about "courtly love." In that case, it may be telling us that there is no such thing. The poem ends, "I've made the poem, I don't know about what and I'll send it to the one who will send me, through another . . . the key from his case." The only really positive statements in the poem are "Farai un vers" and "fait ai lo vers," but if the *vers* is about nothing and makes no sense to the poet, what do these phrases mean? Is poetry simply a game which any clever, literate person can play? Is a poem nothing more than an arrangement of words in a proper metre and rhyme scheme, with some sort of tune, and a content determined by the preconceptions of the audience which automatically supplies the "key"? Guillem's poetry raises, but does not answer such questions.

The fact that Guillem is a lord, a poet by choice not profession, may well affect his attitude towards poetry. Marcabru's view is quite different. He does not make fun of poetry because to him it is a serious matter, both a source of income and a tool for reform; he is intent on selling himself as a poet and on putting a message across. Marcabru is primarily a social critic. Although he writes occasional love poems, he devotes most of his attention to the corruption of the world around him. Thus he is far more concerned with the content of his poems than with their sound, more boastful of his ability to observe and describe, than of his talent in turning a phrase; in fact he refers to his own style as *trobar naturau*, "natural," although it is usually thought of as a forerunner of *trobar clus*. The words are important because of the message. It is Marcabru's wisdom and understanding that make him better than other poets, who have the minds of children (37.7, 25.42) but who nevertheless ridicule his efforts (33.7–12).

Marcabru's view of himself as teacher and social critic often leads him to adopt an aggressively assertive stance: "Sap Marcabrus qui son" (M. knows who they are 2.21);[13] "lo ditz Marcabrus" (M. says so 12.35); "Totz vostres us / sap Marcabrus" (M. knows all your ways 20.bis 19–20); "Hoc / si cum Marcabrus declina" (Yes, just as M. declares 31.53–54); "Lai penaran, ditz Marcabrus" (There they will hang, says M. 40.32). He names himself in half of his poems, either to remind the audience of his identity and keep his name before the public, or to make certain that no other poet could claim his work, or both. Sometimes he praises his own poetic skills:

E Marcabrus, segon s'entensa pura,
sap la razon e'l vers lassar e faire
si que autr'om no l'en pot un mot traire   (9.2–4).

(And M., according to his pure understanding knows how to
make and bind the argument and the words, so that noone
can take a word out of it.)

Marcabrus ditz que noil l'en cau
qui quer ben l vers e'l foill
que no'i pot hom trobar a frau
mot de roill   (33.49–52).

(M. says that he doesn't care if someone investigates and
ransacks his poem, for he cannot secretly find a rusty word
in it.)

Once, at least, Marcabru presents himself as a debater and a clever
user of words, perhaps to mock such a character, since he is
normally distrustful of rhetoric:[14]

om non es de major albir
qu'ieu sui . . .
. . . . . .
De gignos sens
sui si manens
que mout sui greus ad escarnir   (16.3–4, 13–15).

(there is noone with better judgment than I have
. . . . . .
in cleverness I am so rich that I am very hard to mock.)

Only infrequently does he engage in self-mockery, as in the following examples, at the end of *Contra l'ivern que s'enansa*:

Selh qui fes lo vers e'l tresc
no sap don si mou la tresca.

Marcabrus a fag lo tresc
e no sap don mou la tresca   (14.49–52).

(He who made the verse and the song (dance?) doesn't know
where the dance began.

M. made the song and doesn't know where it began);

and at the beginning of

Pax in nomine Domini!
Fetz Marcabrus los motz e'l so   (35.1–2).

(*Pax in nomine Domini*! M. made the words and the melody),

where the only words so far heard are certainly not his.

Like Guillem, he has virtually no interest in the music, to the extent that he is content to use a borrowed tune: "Al son desviat, chantaire, / veirai si puosc un vers faire" (Singing to a borrowed melody, I shall see if I can make a poem, 5.1–2); "Lo vers comenssa / a son veil, sen antic" (the poem begins with an old melody, and ancient wisdom, 32.1–2). It is not surprising that only four of his melodies have survived. Even the music of nature seems to be strident to Marcabru's ear; he talks about the cries and shrieks of birds, owls, and woodpeckers, and the song of frogs: "Bel m'es quan la rana chanta . . . e'l rossinhols crid' e brama" (11.1–5); cf. 3.5 and 21.7–12. When Marcabru sings, his song has the same quality: his lady likes to hear him *cridar e braire* (9.8).

Marcabru's preference for harsh sounds may well be, as Paterson suggests, a rejection of the smooth language of flatterers or of less socially committed poets.[15] In his own poetry, he seems to maintain a clear distinction between *chan* (song) and *vers* (poem); when he talks about his own feelings of love and joy, or their absence, he "sings" (see 7, 13, 14, 28, and 26, where his messenger, the starling, "sings" for him); when he acts the social critic, he "makes a *vers*" (see 3, 5, 15, 18, 32, 33). The *vers* is filled with virtues—*Jovens, Proeza,* and *Joi*—usually in decline, and vices—*Malvestatz, Avoleza, Escarsetatz, Fals' Amor*—on the rise. Sometimes, moved by spring or love, Marcabru begins a *chant*, but as he proceeds, unable to forget the corruption which obsesses him, he turns it into a *vers* (see 37 and 40). Only once does he begin a *chan* about joy and spring and end with a moral fable without calling it a *vers*, but he does comment: "e dic ver, segon mon albir," (I tell the truth as I see it, 39.20), with a pun in *ver*, "truth" and "poem." The same pun occurs in "Dirai vos senes duptansa / d'aquest vers la comensansa; / li mot fan de ver semblansa" (I shall tell you without any doubt the beginning of this poem; the words produce the image of truth 18.1–3).[16] *Chan* seems to be associated with nature, with animal impulses, while *vers* implies reason and wisdom and truth.

As one would expect, Marcabru's rhyme schemes are not elaborate; roughly half of his poems are *unissonans* and limited to two or three rhymes per stanza. Several are *coblas doblas* (about nine), several *singolars* (about fourteen), but often with at least one dissolute rhyme, which must be repeated, thereby connecting the

stanzas. The few poems with more than three rhymes per stanza—
there are seven with four rhymes, two with five, one with six—also
usually include at least one dissolute rhyme. There is a certain
amount of variety even within the conventional patterns; the
strophes are often divided, part *unissonans*, the rest *singolars* or
doblas; and occasionally the order of the rhymes is inverted. Most
of the variety, however, is in the vocabulary.[17] Marcabru personifies
virtues and vices, sometimes giving them family relationships: "Tant
cant bos Jovens fon paire / del segle e fin'Amors maire, / fon
Proeza mantenguda" (As long as Youth was the father of the world,
and true Love its mother, Worth was maintained 5.37–39). He
makes up compound words: *corna-vi, coita-disnar, bufa-tizo, crup-
en-cami* (35.46–48); and he varies the nature opening with specific
names of birds and other wild-life, woodpeckers, nightingales, jays,
orioles, toads, serpents, flies, beetles, gnats (see 38). The effect of the
large cast of personifications and of animal species is to reinforce
Marcabru's presentation of the extent and variety of corruption in
the world, both natural and man-made, which dominates his poems.

Jaufré Rudel, Marcabru's contemporary and friend or patron—
one of Marcabru's poems is dedicated to him—is virtually his
antithesis. For Jaufré, nature and the birds are sophisticated
teachers of music and love, and music is apparently more important
to him than words. Like Guillem, he seems to write to please
himself, a luxury a noble poet can afford, and like Guillem, he can
make fun of himself. The poem which Marcabru addressed to
Jaufré is unusual for its author, better suited to the recipient than to
the donor, and as such, may serve as an introduction to Jaufré's
poetry. It begins "cortesamen" and deals graciously with Cortezia
and Mesura; it is both a *vers* and a *chans* because, on the one hand,
it is concerned with abstract qualities and behavior, and on the
other, the poet has taken greater care than usual with the music, in
deference, presumably, to Jaufré's taste: "Lo vers e'l son vuoill
enviar / a'n Jaufré Rudel" (I wish to send the words and the music
to sir Jaufré Rudel, 15.37–38). Jaufré's *vida* alludes to his preference
for music, but less tactfully: "e fez . . . mains vers ab bons sons ab
paubres motz" (he made many poems . . . with good melodies and
poor words).[18] Jaufré himself speaks of his verse as *plan et en lenga
romana* (simple and in a romance tongue, 2.31)[19] and suggests that
the words are unimportant:

> Senes breu de pargamina
> tramet lo vers en chantan
> plan et en lenga romana (2.29–31)

102

(Without a parchment I send the poem in song, simple and
in a romance tongue.)

In other words, the poem does not have to be written down; the
music will carry it. Even in the nonsense poem, where the content
matters if only in a negative sense, the music comes first: "No sap
chantar qui so non di" (he doesn't know how to sing who can't say
the melody 6.1).

Jaufré has learned his music from the birds who take pains over
their songs: "e'l rossinholet el ram / volv e refrainh e aplana / son
douz chantar e afina" (the nightingale on the branch turns and
modulates and smoothes his sweet song and refines it 2.4–6); and
who sing in a variety of forms, *voutas, lays, critz* (3.1–4). Jaufré
speaks of his poems as *chans* (3.1, 4.52, 6.5 and, by implication, 2.7),
and even in the words he is preoccupied with sounds. The "j" sound,
particularly in *joy* and *jauzen*, dominates *Quan lo rossinhols: jauzen
joios,* 1.3, *grans jois jacer,* 1.7, *joia,* 1.9, *joy meravelhos / per qu'ieu
la jau ab joy jauzen* 1.17–18 (versions 3 and 3a), *mon cor jauzen,*
1.32; in the last stanza, where the tone changes suddenly to a
religious mood, the "j" sound is echoed in *ja mais* (1.38) and *ja* (1.39,
how can one *ever* be saved?) and culminates in Jhesus, 1.41, who
teaches the one sure lesson (versions 2 and 3). The connection of
sound suggests that earthly and heavenly love (*joy* and Jhesus) are
not opposed but are degrees of a similar feeling. One wonders if the
frequent repetition of *jauzen* does not also suggest the poet's name;
if so, it is the only self-reference in the poems. The repetition of the
word *loing* as the *b* rhyme in *Lanquan li jorn* (5), twice in each
stanza, and the repetition of the whole *amor de loing* phrase once in
all but one stanza and twice in two, creates not only a harmony of
sound, but a growing intensity of emotion. The rhyme schemes are
all *unissonans*, but occasionally there is a change in the order (as in
2 and 4), and there is at least one dissolute rhyme in all but the
nonsense poem, creating some suspence within the otherwise overwhelming harmony. The use of dissolute rhymes is a technique that
will be developed to an extreme by Raimbaut and Arnaut.

The harmony of Jaufré's poems is a reflection of his own sense of
harmony with nature, particularly with the birds who inspire his
song (see *Quan lo rius, Pro ai del chan, Lanquan li jorn*). Even in
Belhs m'es l'estius, where he claims to prefer winter because he has
experienced the greatest joy then, he wants his song to be heard in
April when the birds sing; in other words, it partakes of a spring
mood, even though it was written in winter. Of the outside world
apart from nature, very little intrudes on him; Jaufré is an in-

troverted poet, concerned with his love, which is often far away and inaccessible (see 2, second stanza; 3.17–18; and 5) or accessible only in dreams (see 3.35; 4, third stanza, which describes a nightmare apparently caused by a real event; and 1, third and fourth stanzas [versions 3 and 3a] which describe both the joy he finds in his sleep and the frustration—"as I run towards her, she seems to move backwards . . . and my horse moves so slowly, it will never reach her").[20]

Jaufré is aware of the ridiculous aspect of the love posture he assumes, the hopeless yearning for the distant object, and he makes fun of it in *No sap chantar*; when he sleeps, his spirit goes immediately to the lady, but when he wakes in the morning, all his pleasure departs: "Ben sai c'anc de lei no'm jauzi" (I know I've never enjoyed her 6.25, version 2). Like Guillem, he says he is in love with someone he has never seen, but in Jaufré's case, one has to see this as a reference to the far-off love he speaks of so frequently, which adds a level of self-parody. At the same time, he justifies what others see as folly: noone should be surprised if I love what I have never seen, he tells us, because the heart has joy from no other love (6.7–10); this suggests that, foolish as it may sound, the love imagined and nourished in the imagination is in fact the only really satisfying love. The whole poem teases the audience with lines which seem sense and nonsense at the same time. Unlike Guillem, however, Jaufré does not claim to make something of nothing; even in this poem, he is aware of the need for technical skill:

> No sap chantar qui so non di
> ni vers trobar qui motz no fa
> ni connoys de rima quo's va
> si razos non enten en si   (6.1–4).
> (He doesn't know how to sing who doesn't say the melody, or compose a poem, who doesn't make the words, nor does he know how rhyme works if he doesn't understand the meaning within himself.)

The vaunted rhymes are, in fact, all vowels, an unusual and comic effect, enhanced by the gratuitous repetition of "a, a" at the end of each stanza. In his other poems, Jaufré uses vowel-rhyme sparingly: as a dissolute feminine rhyme in 1; as the couplet *c* rhyme in 3; as the *a* rhyme in 5, where it is always followed, and thus anchored, by the *b* rhyme word, *lonh*. Only in 2, which is unusual for several reasons—three dissolute rhymes per stanza and a change in the order of rhymes after the first two stanzas—are there as many as three vowel rhymes, all feminine. But in *No sap chantar*, where all are vowel-rhymes, Jaufré praises his technique: "Bos es lo vers, qu'anc no'l falhi, / si tot so que'i es ben esta" (The verse is good, because I never made a mistake in it, and everything that's there sits well, 6.31–32, version 2). Furthermore, he wants any who would learn the poem to be careful not to spoil it (6.33–34).[21]

Jaufré, like Guillem, wrote primarily for his own satisfaction, and probably for the amusement of his friends; he was therefore capable of the detachment which allowed him to mock his own postures as a poet. Marcabru, who wrote for a living, and had the serious purpose of moral instruction, rarely made fun of himself or his medium. In the next generation of poets, Bernart de Ventadorn, a professional poet like Marcabru, is able to adopt a much more sophisticated attitude towards his work, in part, perhaps, because he is composing for a more sophisticated audience. Although, like Jaufré, he writes mostly about the joys and pains of love and analyzes his own feelings and moods, he seems to expect at least a part of his audience to identify with him.[22] Like Marcabru, Bernart teaches about *fin'amor*, but he emphasizes the joy and pain of love rather than the corruption in the world which interferes with it and seeks to further his own cause in love or encourage other lovers rather more than to correct the mores of society.

When he does talk about the troubles of the world, as in 21 and 13,[23] Bernart calls his poem a *vers* as Marcabru does. "I am so troubled by what I see, I no longer feel like singing," he says, "because worth and courtesy and love-service (which give rise to pleasure and song) have fallen into disuse" (21.1–2, 7–8, 26–28); the poem is therefore not a *chans* but a *vers* (21.57). Similarly, in *Be'm cuidei de chantar sofrir*, Bernart says he intended to stop singing until the spring, but since he sees that no one is rejoicing and worth and generosity are dying, he cannot help setting about a *vers novel* to comfort others (13.1–7). Those who slander love—he uses the verb *deschanton*, "abuse in song"—act against nature in their speech ("a lor parladura . . . renhon mal, contra natura," 13.50–51). Recognizing his own responsibility, he promises not to leave Ventadorn without a singer any longer ("Ventadorn er greu mais ses chantador" 13.55), that is, he will begin to sing once more, but *this* poem is not yet a song.

For the most part, Bernart does not make a sharp distinction between *chans* and *vers*; his poems are usually "songs," the expression of his feelings about love, and the *vers*, the words, are an integral part of the song.[24] One poem which begins with *chantars* and *chans* and repeats the words three more times in the first five lines, comments at the end that *lo vers es fis e naturaus* (15.50), that is, the words suit the mood of the song. Bernart's *chans* is the result of inspiration, the *vers* of technique; when love deserts him, he has difficulty singing, but the ability to make a *vers* never fails. In 29, he wants to sing when nature rejoices, although he has no subject because he is not in love; he makes an effort nonetheless because he knows how to make a good poem—"e fatz esfortz, car sai faire / bo vers, pois no sui amaire," (29.7-8). In 26, although his lady or love has been cruel to him and he has not sung in two years, he wants to sing before winter sets in; when he does, the *vers*, at least, is excellent, without a defective word in it: "faihz es lo vers tot a randa / si que motz no'i deschapdolha" (26.36-37). But there is some humor in this claim, since there are three dissolute rhymes in each stanza. *Ab joi mou lo vers e'l comens* (1) would seem to be properly a *chans*, in as much as it is an expression of joy, but it is never called such, perhaps because it is also a poem in which plays with words, puns, and repeated stems, take precedence over both sound and meaning; in that sense, presumably, it is a *vers*.

By and large, if Bernart refers to his poem at all within the text, he calls it a "song;" often he speaks of "*My* song."[25] This indicates not so much possessiveness—Bernart does not often name himself in the poems—as strong attachment. The *chans* for Bernart, is an expression of joy, and *chantar* can be synonymous with *rire* (see 27.59 and 35.3). He sings when he is moved by love and joy and nature. In the spring when the plants bloom and the birds sing, Bernart, like Jaufré, is often moved to song himself, in such harmony with nature that he too "flowers," "leaves," and "turns green:"

> Lancan folhon bos i jarric
> . . . .
> autresi'm chant e m'esbaudei
> e reflorisc e reverdei
> e folh segon ma natura   (24.1-8);

(cf.10.1-4, 41.1-8, and 42.1-4). Even at night, when he is awakened by the sweet song of the nightingale, he sings with joy (33.1-7). But the joy from love is more powerful than the pleasure from nature and can move Bernart to song when nature does not: when there is no sun, the sun of love shines into his heart (7.1-8); the joy in his heart can make the cold seem like spring, ice like flowers, and snow like grass (44.1-12). Indeed, Bernart tells us that a song must come from the heart and from *fin'amors* within the heart if it is to be any good:

> Chantars no pot gaire valer
> s'ins dal cor no mou lo chans
> ni chans no pot dal cor mover
> si no i es fin'amors coraus.
> Per so es mos chantars cabaus
> qu'en joi d'amor ai et enten
> la boch' e'ls olhs e'l cor e'l sen   (15.1-7).

> (A song cannot be worthwhile if the song does not begin in the heart nor can a song come from the heart if there is not heartfelt fine love there. That is why my singing is excellent, because in the joy of love my mouth and eyes and heart and mind are immersed.)

It is his capacity for *fin'amor* that makes Bernart such a good poet: "It's no wonder if I sing better than any other poet (singer), because love draws my heart (body) more towards love, and I am more formed to her command" 31.1-4).

Often Bernart is not in the mood to sing, but he must because someone has asked him to. This is the dilemma of the professional poet who must sing at times whether he feels like it or not:

> Pois preyatz me, senhor
> qu'eu chan, eu chantarai;
> e can cuit chantar, plor
> . . . .
> Greu veiretz chantador,
> be chan, si mal li vai   (36.1-6).

> (Since you ask me, gentlemen, to sing, I shall sing; and when I think I am singing, I weep
> . . . .
> Only with difficulty will you see a singer sing well, if he is suffering.)

He can sing, in this case, since his problem is not unhappy love but separation. Again in 45, although he is in distress, he is not without hope; so, despite the somewhat ungracious response to the request—"let those who want to, sing" (45.4)—he does comply. He threatens to stop singing several times because his lady is mistreating him (30.22-25 and 43.59); occasionally, so he claims, he stops composing, but that does him no good—"the more I would remain mute, the more harm it will do me" (19.7-8). Fortunately, he never loses his ability to sing, despite the actions of his lady and her lover (19.50–51), for with all his suffering, he has a sense of responsibility to others, presumably because his singing can at least comfort them (19.5–6, cf. 13.7–9 and 26.6–7). It may be the same social motivation, if not the need to satisfy a patron, that leads him to pretend to a happiness he does not feel. At the end of three stanzas of complaint, in 25, he says: "I have so much pain that I am altogether without comfort; but I don't make a show of it, instead I sing and make light" (25.33–36). He does not, however, refer to this poem as a *chans*, and its structure reveals his real distress, both in the rhyme scheme, which is the only example of *coblas singolars* among his extant poems, and in the play on *olh* (eye)—her eyes cause him pain by looking in a mirror (25.45), his express the pain by weeping (25.70)—and *orgolh* (pride), which is enhanced by the rhyme sounds and inner rhymes of stanza one ("No crezatz qu'eu *volha* / flor ni *folha* vezer / car vas me s'or*golha* / so qu'eu plus *volh* aver" 25.5–8), and scattered through the poem, as though Bernart were trapped in the words.

But in disguising the pain he feels (see 35.1–4), Bernart deceives his friends as well as his enemies. This raises the whole question of the problems in language and communication. We know how much harm the *lauzenger* can do with a few ill-chosen words, and we sympathize with the poet when he manages to deceive them—"by my subterfuge and lies I have changed the dice on them" (35.39–40). But the poet can have difficulties with his own words, such as the inability to speak at the crucial moment; Bernart can be so tongue-tied in front of his lady that his only hope is that she will deign to look at a written message, since she knows how to read and understand (17.39–40, 49–56). Often Bernart's frustration is expressed through puns which suggest both the confusion in his mind and his desire to deceive. In 39, where he dare not even send a message, he wishes he could enchant (*enchantar*) his enemies so they would all become children (*efan*), unable to speak against the lovers; there are puns both in *enchantar*, as if he hoped to cast the spell with his poetry, and in *efan*, literally "unable to speak" (Latin *in* + *fans*). If he could find his lady alone ("Be la volgra sola trobar," 39.41— *trobar* is used only once by Bernart in the sense of composing a poem, presumably because he wants to play down the technical aspect in order to emphasize the natural outpouring of song, but it is tantalizing to imagine a double-entendre, "I would like to be the only one to celebrate her in song" or "I would like to celebrate only her in my song"), they would have to speak with a hidden sense, using cleverness where courage was lacking ("e pus no'ns val arditz, valgues nos *gens*" 39.48). He blames her for making him wait too long, for too much talk of love is annoying and seems like a trick ("que lonja paraula d'amar / es grans enois e par d'enjan" 39.51-52). Etymologically, *enjan* is related to *gens*, so his "cleverness" is really no different from her "trick." This is borne out by his suggestion that one can love and pretend otherwise, "lie nobly" (*gen mentir*) where there is no witness; the homonyms, "cleverness" and "nobly" add to the dubious nature of his position. Similarly, in line 56, he tells her if she will only love him he will never be troubled by lying ("ja per mentir eu no serai atens"); we can deceive others, but they will not deceive us. The envoi, however, subtly questions this assertion with a triple play on the stem *men*: "Messatger, vai, e no *m'en* prezes *mens* / s'eu del anar vas midons sui te*mens* (Messenger, go and let her not prize *me* the *less*, if I am *afraid* to go to my lady," 39.57-58, emphasis mine).

Bernart seems to be fascinated beyond any of the other Provençal poets with the inherent ambiguities in his language, making frequent and effective use of homonym rhymes and puns.[26] Because he limits himself to a fairly simple vocabulary of common and often monosyllabic words—in contrast, as we will see, to Raimbaut and Arnaut—which are capable of many different interpretations, he has rich possibilities for extension and confusion of meaning. But his purpose seems to be to create a harmony of sound, rather than confusion, to induce by the similarity of sound in the homonyms, inner rhymes, and frequent repetitions of related words, a sense of harmony which transcends the diversity of meaning. His rhyme schemes produce the same effect: thirty-two of the extant forty-four poems are *unissonans*, ten are *coblas doblas*, one is a variation of *unissonans*, and only one is *singolars*, with different sounds throughout. Nineteen have dissolute rhymes, usually only one per stanza (eleven of the nineteen); these give a temporary sense of unrest, but a final sense of harmony by tying the whole poem together. Raimbaut and Arnaut, by using many more dissolute rhymes per stanza, sometimes nothing else, create the opposite effect. Bernart's poems are thus "songs" not so much because the music is his primary concern, as it was with Jaufré,[27] but because the sound of the words, the verbal music, is as important as, and an essential complement to, the meaning.

Raimbaut d'Aurenga's interest is exclusively in the words, not in the harmony of sound, as Bernart's is, but in obscure meaning and unusual vocabulary. He seems to see poetry as a vehicle for displaying his cleverness with words and rhymes and strange sounds. He talks frequently about his vocabulary, distinguishing rich from simple, obscure from clear. Not surprisingly, he calls his poems *vers*, rather than *chans*, emphasizing the importance of the words. In one poem, 39, he puns on the word *vers* throughout the poem, revealing the pun only at the end: the first rhyme-word of each stanza is *enversa* or *enverse*, "invert," "reverse," which refers at times to the seasonal change in nature, to the confusion in the poet's mind, to evil in others, to the position he would like the lady to take; but in the last stanza, the opening line "Mos *vers* an—qu'aissi l'en*verse* (Let the poem go [or they have my poem]—for I invert [or enverse] it so 39.41), makes the pun explicit and encourages us to rethink lines 9 "Quar enaissi m'o en*verse*" ("for I so invert myself, i.e., by putting myself into verse) and 33 "Anat ai cum cauz, en*versa*" (I have gone like a thing in a poem).

When the poem is in the simple style, however, he does occasionally call it a *chanso*, but this is something of a put-down: "A mon vers dirai chanso / ab leus motz ez ab leu so / ez en rima vil'e plana" (I shall call my verse a song with easy words and easy music, in low and simple rhyme 30.1–3).[28] The music is apparently fitted to the words rather than the other way round (cf. "Apres mon vers vueilh sempr'ordre / una chanson leu per bordre" [After my poem, I want to arrange an easy song for fun 4.1–2]). In both these examples, *chanso* seems to mean just the music, though it can also mean singing or performing, e.g., "tals motz fai / c'anc mais non foron dig cantan" (who makes words never before said, singing 16.5–6); "e soy fols cantayre cortes / tan c'om m'en apela joglar" (and I am such a mad courtly singer, that people call me a *joglar*, i.e., a professional performer, 24.33–34); and a *vers* he writes when his lady has been hard on him, he will "sing" weeping ("en ploran serai chantaire" 11.19). In some cases, the verb *chantar* seems to mean "compose the poem," as when he says that he stops singing because his lady does not like it (7.8–12, 8.7 ff., 6.2–4), but sings again to greet a friend (6.1–7). It is unlikely that he means "perform" in these cases, but rather that he is moved to compose in their honor.

For the most part, a *chanso* (occasionally in the somewhat scornful diminutive, *chansoneta*, 3.1, 9.7) is something less than a *vers* for Raimbaut; it is either a poem in the simple style, or the relatively unimportant musical accompaniment. Singing is something lesser creatures, like birds and crickets, do (cf. 1.4–5, " 'lh grill pres del siure / chantan el mur" [the crickets sing on the wall near the cork-tree]), along with other less attractive sounds ("Braiz, chans, quils, critz / aug dels auzels" 8.1–2). It is the words, the *motz*, *digz*, or the whole *vers*, which fascinate Raimbaut, and the more obscure the better. Occasionally he pretends to write a simple poem, either to prove that he can, because that is what everyone seems to want (16.1–3), or because the audience is too foolish to appreciate anything else (18.1–6), but he clearly prefers to be obscure. Even when he sets out to do something simple, there is hidden meaning in it:

> Una chansoneta fera
> voluntiers laner'a dir;
> don tem que m'er a murir
> e far l'ai tal que sen sela   (3.1–4).
>
> (I would make a little song willingly, which is easy to say;
> from which I fear I will die and I have to make it so it hides
> the sense.)

The rhyme may be a problem—all but one are dissolute—but the words can be "uncovered" (*descubert*) by one who works it out with reason (3.5–8). In other words, if you are intelligent or experienced enough to follow the poem, it is simple. The poem seems to play on the need for a screen to hide the love ("no'y puesc nulh'escrima trobar" 3.14–15); *escrima*, "screen," may contain a pun on *rima*, "rhyme," and *trobar* can mean to compose a poem; the poet also begs God to "protect" him (*escrima*) form death long enough to enjoy his lady (3.57–59), and he ends with the comment "Qui trob'amor ses escrima . . . " (Who finds love without a screen—or composes a poem without hiding his meaning (?)—should not complain if he loses a fickle lady 60–62).[29]

There is a debate on *trobar clus* between Guiaut de Borneill, clearly named in the first line, and a "seign'en Lignaura," who is usually assumed to be Raimbaut; Raimbaut's recent editor, Pattison, prints it among his poems. Whether Raimbaut was directly involved[30] is less important than the attitudes expressed in his name which, if they do not tell us what he said, do tell us what other poets thought he believed. "Lignaura" attacks Guiaut for criticizing *trobar clus* and prizing what is common to all; he does not want his own poems to be praised by fools who cannot recognize real quality. He claims not to care if his poems are not popular, so long as they are well-made, an attitude that seems to be borne out in his poems.

Raimbaut is proud of his rich vocabulary and rhyme as well as his obscurity: "Cars, bruns e tenhz motz entrebesc" (I intertwine

rich, dark, and sombre words 1.19), he boasts, in a poem strongly
influenced by Marcabru. He is sure that another *vers, ab diz car*
(17.71) will win him the desired love, for love too is a complex
realm. Raimbaut has a book of the deeds of love in obscure words
("mos libres / de fag d'amor ab digz escurs" 10.12–13), which he
does not dare open; although he cannot therefore help himself, he
knows enough about the keys and secrets of love to tell others how
to get what they want. What he in fact tells them is not very
recondite—it is to punch obstinate ladies in the nose, use bad words
and ugly singing along with threats and force. Nonetheless, he
boasts openly about his knowledge of love—"if good lovers knew
how finely I loved, they would come to me as students to be taught,
and so would five hundred ladies" (17.37–44). But even more than
his knowledge of love, he boasts of his poetic abilities in comparison
to other poets: "let no other trobador try to compete . . . for his
poetry is not worth a radish compared to mine" (13.49–53); he is
confident that he will take the prize in a contest of twenty poets
(21.1–7—one wonders in this case if he means this as a serious boast
or if he is being tongue-in-cheek, knowing that the lord of Orange
must win if he chooses to). He takes particular pride in the unusual
aspects of his poetry, making words that have never been heard
before in song (16.5–6). But his pleasure is in expounding his "true
knowledge" with new meaning ("Ab sen novelh / dic e favelh / mon
saber ver," 17.23–25), so that even the best speakers seem children
beside him (cf. Marcabru 37 and 25). He often applies "new," *nou* or
novel, to his work in this way: "Aissi mou / un sonet nou"(18.1–2);
"Ab nou cor et ab nou talen / ab nou saber et ab nou sen . . . vuoill
un bon nou vers commensar" (35.1–4). This poem is indeed *nou*, in
that one word dominates each stanza, appearing in all but the last
line; the last line introduces the word which will dominate the next
stanza.

The most unusual of all Raimbaut's poems is his nonsense
poem, *Escotatz, mas no say que s'es* (Listen, but I don't know what
it is 24.1); it is not a *vers* or an *estribot* or *sirventes*, he tells us, or
any other known form, but something noone has seen, in this
century or the last. He emphasizes its uniqueness by "baptizing" it,
giving an identity to the new form, but the name he gives it is "no-
say-que-s'es." If someone asks who composed it, the one reciting is
to answer: he who knows how to do well whatever (or whenever) he
wants. What is unusual about this poem is that each stanza is part
verse (six lines) and part prose, so what Raimbaut is boasting of is
his ability to write a poem that is half prose and that, in a sense,

incorporates its own gloss.[31] Of course what it also reveals is the tremendous freedom Raimbaut feels in his writing. This may have something to do with the fact that he is his own master; as he reminds us in 22, he does not sing for money: "Ben sai c'a sels seria fer / que'm blasmon qar tan soven chan / si lor costavon mei chantar" (I know it would be hard on those who blame me for singing so much if they had to pay for it 22.1–3).

Since he does not have to please a patron, Raimbaut can experiment freely with forms. He has several run-on stanzas (see 2, 20, 26, and 39). He uses an extraordinary number of dissolute rhymes; they occur in twenty-seven of the thirty-nine poems, usually only one or two per poem, but in four poems there are four dissolute rhymes, in three, five, and in one, six, a device Arnaut Daniel will carry much further. In one poem (29), the dissolute rhyme is connected with rhymes in the previous stanza in a scheme which looks like a forerunner of Dante's terza rima: I abacdcd II bdbcaca III dadcbcb IV ab. . . . In other poems, the jarring sound effect of the dissonant rhymes is echoed in Raimbaut's use of unusual words or forms (e.g., *bederesc* and *entrebesc, grill* and *brezill, picvaira, aerc, siure,* and *caire,* all in 1), and plays on words through a poem, particularly words which have to do with poetry, like *rima* (both "rhyme" and "burn") and *vers.*[32] The use of many *rimas derivatius* (based on the stem rather than the ending) within one poem, as in 1 and 39, points up contrasts between masculine and feminine (*grezesc / grezesca,* 1.10 and 18), between indicative and subjunctive (*espresc / espresca,* 1.37 and 45), noun and verb (*caire / escaira,* 1.5 and 6), and infinitive and inflected forms (*pliure / pliura,* 1.13 and 16). These various effects, grammatical rhymes, punning and equivocal rhymes, run-on stanzas, dissolute rhymes, all tend to keep the audience in suspense, off-balance, surprised, just the opposite of the harmony Bernart strived to create with sound.

Like Raimbaut, Arnaut is primarily interested in the technical aspects of poetry and in displaying his virtuosity. He admits to laboring over his poetry, "filing" and "planing" it; he draws his images from the work of artisans because he sees his own work as a craft, a *bell'obra* (12.7):[33] "obre e lim / motz de valor / ab art d'Amor" (I work over and file words of worth with the art of love 2.12–14); "fauc motz e capuig e doli / que serant verai e cert / qan n'aurai passat la lima / q'Amors marves plan' e daura / mon chantar" (I make and construct and plane words which will be true and sure when I have passed the file over them, for Love smoothes and gilds my singing 10.2–6). Rhetoric is part of the poet's equipment; Arnaut mentions the technical terms of *color* and *flor* (2.4–5 and 13.5–6) as natural images but with overtones of the rhetorical figures, and draws on the "arts" of Love's school (16.3–5 and 2.14), a reference to Ovid and / or the earlier Provençal poets. He is concerned with all aspects of his craft, taking pains to make the words accord with the melody—"amors mi asauta / qui'ls motz ab lo son acorda," love assaults [with a possible pun on *azauta*, "exalts"] me so that I make the words harmonize with the melody 8.8–9); "en cest sonet coind' e leri / fauc motz e capuig e doli" (on this lovely and gay melody, I make the words and construct and plane them 10.1–2)—because the music is an integral part of the work (cf. 15.44).

Thus, although Arnaut is even more attracted by odd words, sounds, and rhymes than Raimbaut, he does not disparage the musical aspect, perhaps because he is more concerned with the effect on his audience and must consider the total product. *Chanso*, in his works, means what it has come to mean for later critics, a form of poetry. Arnaut does not call his poems *vers*; they are *chans* or *chanso*. "Chansson do'ill mot son plan e prim / farai" (2.1–2), he says, where earlier poets would have said "Vers farai" (cf. "esper a far bona chanson," 6.4, and "farai . . . breu chansson," 16.3–4). In his envois he often calls the poem a *chanson*, addressing it directly several times, as if it had a life of its own (3, 5, 13, and in the last full stanza of 9). Once he distinguishes it from the melody: "Era't para / chans e condutz / formir" (Now, song and melody, prepare to deliver . . . 9.86–88), so it is clear that *chans* is his word for the poem. But when he boasts of his technical abilities, it is the words Arnaut takes particular pride in, the "mot . . . plan e prim"(2.1), the "motz de valor / ab art d'Amor" (2.13–14); they are what make his "chans . . . tan pros / e de ric pretz manenta" (3.54–56, so worthy and filled with rich value), and *tot nou* (14.44, altogether new).

Although Arnaut attributes his poetic success to his inspirations, love and the lady (who possesses his workshop), he takes no chance of others stealing them; he names himself clearly in fifteen of the eighteen extant poems.[34] He also adds a special signature in three of the poems: "I am Arnaut who loves the breeze and hunts the hare with the ox and swims against the current" (10.43–45); in another he refers to "that trouble I had a year ago when I hunted the hare with the ox" (14.3–4); and in a third, he boasts "I know so much that I can make the course of the current stop and my ox outruns the hare" (16.6–7). Despite the burst of self-confidence in the third example, the figure indicates the tremendous effort Arnaut puts into his life, his poetry as well as his love.

Arnaut's labor and care can certainly be seen in the technical aspects of his poems, the various tours de force of the *sestina*, a form he apparently invented[35] and which Dante took up, and the extravagant use of dissolute rhymes, in fourteen of the eighteen poems. The highest number occurs in *L'aura amara*, ten per stanza; in the other poems there are three in 5 and 6, four in 4, five in 7, seven in poems 8, 10, 13, 15, and 16 (all seven are dissolute with the exception of one answered rhyme in 8), and eight, all dissolute, in poems 11, 12, 14, and 17. Arnaut also prefers strange rhyme sounds, which are sometimes onomatopoeic and always difficult. The opening of *L'aura amara*, which describes the silence of the birds in winter, actually suggests their chirpings with its short lines, self-enclosed syllables—an unusual concentration of consonants—and alliteration:

> L'aur'amara
> fa'ls bruoills brancutz
> clarzir
> qu'l dous'espeis'ab fuoills,
> el's letz
> becs
> dels auzels ramencs
> ten balps e mutz   (9.1–8).

Arnaut is not content simply with a series of non-rhyming sounds, instead he plays with sounds which are connected by assonance or consonance rather than rhyme, e.g., *omba, embla, oma*, are the *b, c, d*, rhymes in 4.[36] In the *sestina*, the repeated words are *oncle,ongla, verga, arma, cambra*, and *intra*, also connected by sound, in a pattern of consonant pairs (ncl / ngl, rg / rm, mbr / ntr) which is reinforced by the pairing of the rhyme-words in the *tornada*. Such connections suggest that Arnaut was looking for variations on the technique of rhyme, seeking modified harmonies in similar rather than identical sounds. It may be for this reason, and not simply to tease his audience, that Arnaut claims that there is no *mot fals ni rim'estrampa* (false word or unrhymed rhyme 12.8) in a poem in which all the rhymes are dissolute (cf. 10.39, the only other time Arnaut mentions rhyme, again all are dissolute). In this, Arnaut differs from Bernart who sought a harmony of sound in identical words with different meanings.

Arnaut does use homonym rhymes, but since he tends to much longer words than Bernart, and long words do not lend themselves to equivocal rhymes, they are not as characterisitc of Arnaut's poetry. They are apparent, however, in 15, where the first rhyme word of each stanza is a *rima equivoca* (*sortz* is both "rises" in 1, and "deaf" in 8; *cortz*, "courts" in 15, "short" in 22; *bortz*, "evil" in 29, "tourneys" in 36; there is another equivocal rhyme, though not in the first line, in *puois*, "after" in 5, "hills" in 12). Occasionally Arnaut indulges in a triple equivocal rhyme: in 8, *us* is "usage," line 6, "some," 23, and "gate," 32; and *agre* in 11 is "harsh," line 8, "nest," 24, and perhaps "accord" 50. Arnaut also plays with inner rhymes and alliteration to create similar sound effects of modified harmony:

Doutz brais e critz	*ais c*
lais e cantars e voutas	*ais c*
aug dels auzels q'en lur latin fant precs	*au au l l p ecs*
qecs ab sa par (12.1–4)	*p ecs*

Arnaut uses alliteration to particular effect in the opening of a number of poems:

Lanquan vei fueill'e flor e frug
parer dels albres el ramel
e aug lo chan que faun e'l brug
ranas el riu, el bosc auzel,
doncs mi fueill' e'm floris e'm fruch' Amors   (5.1–5).

The alliterating "f's" in the nouns of the first line and the verbs of the fifth underscore the affinity between the poet and nature, and the gentler alliteration in between suggests the harmonies of different species within nature; the whole is presented in a fairly symmetrical pattern: fff / al(au) r / au f b / r r b au / fff. In poem 11, the heavy concentration of "b's" emphasizes the harshness of the time to come: "En breu brisara'l temps braus / e'll bisa busin'els brancs" (11.1–2); in 15, the "s's" of the first two lines underline the poet's suffering: "Sols sui qui sai lo sobrafan qe'm sortz / al cor, d'amor sofren per sobramar." But in 13, "v's," "bl's," and "pl's" are used to suggest the soft harmony within diversity of nature which inspires Arnaut to sing: "Er vei vermeills, vertz, blaus, blancs, gruocs / vergiers, plans, plais, tertres e vaus / e'il votz dels auzels."

There are only four poems in which Arnaut does not use dissolute rhymes, but he does something else of interest in all of them. *Quan chai la fuelha*, 3, has a fairly conventional *coblas singolars* pattern, 4a6b4a6b4b6a4b6a, but the *a* rhymes are always feminine, so the rhythm keeps shifting both in the length of line and in the last syllables; the feminine rhymes, along with the soft consonant sounds and the many vowels throughout the poem, create a rather soft, sweet effect. In contrast, the first poem, *Pois Raimons e'n Trucs Malecs*, which is also *singolars*, has only one rhyme sound per stanza and that often harsh (*grecs*, *utz*, *ort*), in keeping with the rather crude content. *Chansson do 'ill mot son plan e prim*, poem 2, is *unissonans*, but the rhymes occur in different order every two stanzas, a variation of *coblas doblas* (aaabbcddc for two stanzas; bbbddcaac for two; dddaacbbc for two); and the last rhyme word in each stanza is repeated, minus the final vowel, in the first line of the next. The remaining poem is, of course, the *sestina* (18), which uses the same six words as rhyme words throughout the poem, in different order but in a rigidly maintained pattern. What is particularly impressive in this poem is that Arnaut does not choose words which might lend themselves easily to different but related contexts; his six include "nail," "uncle," and "rod," along with "soul," "chamber," and "enter," a suggestive group which has led critics to assume a *trobar clus* aspect to the poem.[37]

Arnaut is probably the most inventive of the Provençal poets I have considered here; with the *sestina*, variations on standard rhyme schemes, shorter lines and longer stanzas, and lavish use of dissolute rhymes, he stretches the available forms as far as they will go, and creates new ones. Raimbaut had experimented in similar ways, but he was too idiosyncratic to be imitated easily. It is, apparently, this aspect of Arnaut's poetry, the technical virtuosity and originality, which attracted Dante, who acknowledges a debt to him in *De vulgari eloquentia* and gives him pride of place as the last lyric poet to speak in Purgatory. In the *Comedy*, Arnaut stands for the beginnings of the lyric tradition which Dante and the Italian poets were still working in. But he can also be seen as the culmination of a tradition which began with Guillem and moved through all the poets who have been discussed here; and he seems to be the first to call the poetic form in which they all composed a *chanso*, the name by which it was thereafter known, so in a sense he is the poet who gives it its official form for literary history.

The tradition, as we have seen, began with noble poets, Guillem and Jaufré, who wrote primarily for themselves and their friends, who played at poetry, albeit quite successfully, who were capable of writing serious and effective poems but who never took themselves too seriously as poets. They could and did make fun of themselves and their poetry, and their nonsense poems are among their greatest achievements. The only professional poet of the earlier period who has been discussed here, Marcabru, saw himself primarily as a social critic; he used poetry in an attempt to reform his audience. The later trobadors, whether professional (like Bernart and Arnaut) or not (like Raimbaut), were sophisticated and self-confident poets, who investigated the possibilities of their art and their language, both sound and meaning, and experimented in poetic patterns, unusual rhyme schemes, and variations which seem to reject rhyme. All three delight in plays on sound and meaning, in analyzing situations and emotions, but they differ in the postures they adopt. Bernart seems to regard himself as the spokesman for his audience, at least insofar as they were or aspired to be "courtly" lovers; Raimbaut is content to speak for himself and professes little interest in popular acclaim. Only Arnaut admits to laboring over his poetry, as any craftsman does over his work; in that sense, he is the first to regard himself, and invite his audience to regard him, as a professional poet.

By Dante's time, the poetic setting, particularly in Northern Italy, had changed considerably. Poems were not sung at court before patrons, but circulated among friends, male and female, bourgeois and noble, many of them fellow poets. Most of the poems were set to music and sung, but some were circulated privately and simply read.[38] The content, therefore, becomes even more important; the thoughts can be more complex, sometimes, particularly in the *canzoni*, philosophical and scientific; the logical development is tighter. Although they are meant for public consumption, at least within a small circle, the poems were sometimes presented as private exchanges of ideas and advice (as between Dante and Cino, Dante and Guido Cavalcanti) or of insult (see the sonnets between Dante and Forese Donati). Dante also addresses a number of poems to sympathetic ladies who understand about love, singling out a group that must have been included in the Provençal audience—ladies certainly listened to the poems at court and some were patrons of the poets, while others wrote poetry—but poems were addressed either to the lady being courted or to a male audience (*senhor*). For Dante, the women's understanding of love makes them part of his elite circle.

Despite the differences in audience, and to some extent, the changes in form, many of the characteristics we have observed among the earliest Provençal poets can still be found in the *Dolce stil nuovo*. Dante who writes almost a century later, and in a different language, still has much in common with the tradition which begins with Guillem. I cannot, in a brief epilogue, do justice to Dante's changing styles in the early and late lyrics,[39] nor to his response to earlier Italian poets. I shall simply point to a few of the ways in which Dante's lyrics echo the earliest Provençal poets, to show how that tradition endures.

The most popular lyric form among the Italian poets seems to have been the short poem we call a sonnet, a single-stanza form invented in the Sicilian school and not known to early Provençal poets, but the long stanzaic form, the *chanso* or *canzone* in Italian, was also still used frequently, along with the *ballata*. Dante, in *De vulgari eloquentia* (II,iii,3–5), ranks the *canzone* as the most excellent of the three forms, putting the *ballata* second, and the sonnet last, because the *canzone* achieves its purpose in itself, whereas the *ballata* has to be performed. It is interesting, in view of the development of the *chanso* among the early Provençal poets, that Dante offers as another argument for the nobility of the *canzone* that although everything in rhyme is a song (*cantio*), only the *canzone* has that root in its name, and preserves it because of its beauty. Not, presumably, because it was sung.

Although the name *canzone* has long since denoted a genre of lyric, the tension between words and music is not altogether gone. Dante writes one poem to a certain Lippo, to ask him to set another to music: the poem speaks for itself as a "humble sonnet," bringing a "naked maiden" for Lippo to clothe (8.10, 13–16). In a *ballata*, Dante tells us his "little words have dressed themselves in another's dress," presumably a borrowed melody (Le parolette mie novelle, / che di fiori fatto han ballata, / per leggiadria ci hanno tolt'elle / una vesta ch'altrui fu data, 21.18–21). The music is thus an adornment, fitted to the words. Generally, Dante speaks of his *dolci rime*, "sweet rhymes," and of his poems "speaking" (*parlando*) rather than singing. Clearly he is primarily concerned with the words, but the music, although it seems to be secondary, still has some importance, at least in the love poetry. In the *Vita Nuova*, the God of Love tells Dante in a vision to write a poem in order to explain something to his lady and to adorn the words with sweet music in which he, the God of Love, will be present (chap. 12).

The God of Love is a personification which often appears in Dante's lyrics in a far more dramatic way than he did in Provençal. Marcabru, alone of the Provençal poets discussed here, used personifications to any extent, but he simply described their actions; he did not have them speak. Dante tells one of his *ballate* to find Love and go with him to the lady; the poem is to sing Dante's excuses, Love to persuade her to accept them. "Your bearing is so courteous," he tells the poem, "that you shouldn't need company, but she mightn't receive you without Love" (24.5–14). The part Love plays in Dante's lyrics and in the visions he describes in the early part of the *Vita Nuova*, is denied in *V.N.* chapter 25, where Dante explains that Love is merely an accident in substance, a figure of speech, a license permitted to poets more than to prose writers.

It is a license Dante often avails himself of, particularly when he speaks directly to his poems as if they were people. Apparently not everyone accepted this custom, as Dante notes in *V.N.* chapter 12, when he promises to answer those who object to his speaking in the second person to his own words; the answer is presumably the explanation in chapter 25, mentioned above. In this personifying of the poems, Dante carries Arnaut's occasional envoi to his *chansos* to the logical extreme. He sends one of his poems to shoot an arrow through the lady's heart; "Canzone, vattene dritto a quella donna / . . . e dalle per lo cor d'una saetta" (80.79, 82). He tells another *canzone* not to allow anyone to touch her garments in order to see what the lovely lady hides, but if she should ever find a friend to virtue, she may reveal herself to him (81.91–100). In other words, the poem is to remain obscure except to those virtuous enough to penetrate its meaning. In another poem, he warns it to be wary of friendly gentlemen and not to get in with bad people (68.81–96).

Dante treats his poems not simply as people, but as his children: "Canzone . . . / t'ammonisco, perch'io t'ho allevata / per figliuola d'Amor giovane e piana" (*Canzone* . . . I charge you, having brought you up to be a modest, young daughter of love, 33.57–60). Because they are his children, they are siblings, the *canzoni* "sisters," the *sonetti* "brothers," but they do not necessarily resemble each other; some are happy, others sad (see 47.71–74). Sometimes they contradict one another: "Canzone, e' par che tu parli contraro / al dir d'una sorella che tu hai" (*Canzone*, it seems that you speak the opposite of a sister of yours, 61.73–74). At other times, they speak for one another: "Sonetto, se Meuccio t'è mostrato . . . va' correndo e gittaliti a' piedi . . . fa' che prenda per lo primo dono / questi tuoi frati, e a lor sì comanda / che stean con lui e qua non tornin mai" (19.1, 3, 12–14, Sonnet, if Meuccio is pointed out to you . . . run to him and throw yourself at his feet, . . . make him accept these brothers of yours as a first gift and order them to stay with him and never come back).

Although Dante does not speak as directly about "making his poems" as the early Provençal poets do, his personification of them calls attention to his authorship every bit as dramatically, if somewhat more subtly. He often addresses the poem in the first line, as if it had an independent existence: "Parole mie che per lo mondo siete" (My words, that wander through the world, 62.1); "O dolci rime che parlando andate" (O sweet rhymes, that go about speaking 63.1); "Ballata, i' vòi che tu ritrovi Amore / e con lui vade a madonna davante" (Ballad, I want you to find Love and go with him to my lady 24.1). Sometimes he even lets the poem speak for itself in the first person: "Se Lippo amico sei tu che mi leggi" (If you, Lippo, who read me, are a friend 8.1).

But Dante also calls attention to his work in more conventional ways, talking about changes in style: "Le dolci rime d'amor . . . convien ch'io lasci . . . diporrò giù lo mio soave stile . . . e dirò . . . con rima aspr'e sottile" (I must give up the sweet rhymes of love . . . I shall lay down my soft style . . . and speak . . . with harsh and subtle rhyme 69.1–14); and the difficulties he may cause his audience: "Canzone, io credo che saranno radi / color che tua ragione intendan bene / tanto la parli faticosa e forte" (Canzone, I think they will be rare, those who really understand your meaning, you speak with such difficulty and effort 59.53–55). Occasionally he calls attention to the fact that he is doing something unusual, either because of the content (59.2–3) or the technique; in a variation on the *sestina*, he tells the poem at the end: "Canzone . . . io ardisco a far . . . la novità che per tua forma luce, / che non fu mai pensata in alcun tempo" (*Canzone*, I dare to create the novelty that shines through your form, which has never been thought of before, at any time" 79.64–66). What he does in the poem is take five words as the only rhyme words through the five twelve-line stanzas; he retains the rhyme pattern (abaacaaddaee), but changes the position of the words, using the last of stanza one, the *e* rhyme, as the first, *a*, of the next, so the words replace each other in the same order, backwards through the poem. Dante is outdoing Arnaut in this poem, having already composed a simpler *sestina*, like Arnaut's, with six words repeated in six-line stanzas, in different but carefully patterned order.

The new *sestina* proves that Dante can perform a tour de force if he chooses to, but such virtuosic display for its own sake does not satisfy him. He gets restless with lyric forms early on[40] and begins to move away from them, first by analyzing the poems and giving them a significance they did not originally have, as in the *Vita Nuova* and the *Convivio*, and finally by finding a new poetic mode in the *Comedy*. He never finished the *Convivio*, and he ended the *Vita Nuova* with the determination not to say any more about Beatrice until he could do so properly, and with the hope that he would be able to say of her what had never been said of anyone. In other words, he was aware that he needed an entirely new mode of expression.

The *Comedy* differs from the lyrics not only in its long narrative form, but in its rhyme scheme, the *terza rima*, which Dante invented for it: the interlaced trios of rhyme sounds, at once three and one, reflecting, like the three parts of the poem, the God who inspired it. And yet, Dante does not reject the lyric tradition in the *Comedy*; rather, he incorporates it, through the presentation of a series of lyric poets, Provençal and Italian, and quotations from his own lyrics, by which he traces his "poetic biography."[41] He puts the lyric tradition in its proper perspective, and suggests its limitations, by leaving the lyric poets literally fixed at certain points, and allowing only the epic poets to move with him, as well as by giving not very subtle hints that his fame will surpass that of other lyric poets. In Purgatory 11, he is told that a third poet has perhaps been born who will drive both Guido's out of the nest, in other words, replace them, though he may also be implying that their poetry will take on new importance in relation to his, as the new bird forces the older ones to fly. He acknowledges his debt to some of them, to Guinizelli, whom he calls "il padre / mio e de li altri miei miglior che mai / rime d'amor usar dolci e leggiadre" (my father and the father of my betters, those who ever used the sweet and lovely rhymes of love Pur. 26.97–99), and to Arnaut Daniel, whom Guido points to as a "miglior fabbro del parlar materno" (a better craftsman of the mother tongue Pur. 26.117), a phrase which unites Italian and Provençal, the languages of the poets, and which recognizes Arnaut as the craftsman he took pride in being. But finally, Dante transcends both traditions; the only poets he meets in Paradise are religious figures, Folquet, who began as a secular poet but became a monk and a bishop, David, the author of the psalms, and St. Bernard. Dante is the sole contemporary and secular poet among them.[42]

Guillem, who to all intents and purposes began the tradition, boasts that he will make a poem out of nothing (*Farai un vers de dreyt nien*) and writes one in which he denies or contradicts everything, so that all we are left with at the end is the poem as a technical structure (and a joke). Dante, at the peak of the same tradition, writes a poem "to which heaven and earth put their hands," a poem which contains the whole of his world and which, in its basic structure, reflects the creator of that world.

——— NOTES ———

[1]For a study of the possible influence of Latin grammar and rhetoric on the development of early Provençal poetic techniques. see my "Was Vernacular Poetic Practice a Response to Latin Language Theory?," *RPh* 35 (1982), 586–600.

[2]L. T. Topsfield, *Troubadours and Love* (Cambridge, 1975), divides the same poets into "early" (Guillem, Jaufré, and Marcabru), "the generation of 1170" (Bernart and Raimbaut), and "the generation of 1200" (Arnaut).

[3]His *vida* claims he was "*gentils hom*" who became a *joglar*, J. Boutière and A. H. Schutz, *Biographies des Troubadours* (Paris, 1964), p. 59.

[4]See Roger Dragonetti, *Aux frontières du langage poétique*, Romanica Gandenica 9 (Gent, 1961), for Dante's views on this issue in the *De vulgari eloquentia*.

[5]Of Jaufré's six extant poems, we have the music for four, of Bernart's forty-four poems, the music for eighteen, as compared to one in ten (or eleven) for Guillem, four in forty-four for Marcabru, one in forty-one for Raimbaut, and two in eighteen for Arnaut. I will not consider the melodies in this study, only references to the music within the poems. Much remains to be done on the relation of the extant melodies to the poems, but there have recently been solid efforts in this direction. See, for example, G. Scherner-von Ortmerssen, *Die Text-Melodiestruktur in den Liedern des Bernart de Ventadorn* (Münster, 1973).

[6]B5, as cited by Boutière and Schutz, *Biographies*, p. 12. For an extensive discussion of *vers*, particularly in relation to the *sirventes*, see Dietmar Rieger, *Gattungen und Gattungsbezeichnungen der Trobadorlyrik*, *ZRPh*, Beihefte 148 (1976), 185 ff.

[7]The *vida* of Peire d'Alverne says that Guiraut de Borneill was the first to write a *canson* (Boutière-Schutz, 5, p. 263), but in fact Guiraut continues to use the word *vers* as well; Arnaut is the first poet I know of who uses *chanso* exclusively. J. H. Marshall points out that *vers* is the term used for a lyric poem before 1150; *vers* and *chanso* are both used after 1150, but *vers* usually indicates a more serious style ("Le Vers au XIIe siècle: Genre poétique?," *Actes et Memoires du IIIe Congres International de langue et littérature d'Oc* [Bordeaux, 1961], pp. 55–63). L. M. Paterson notes that in the works of Bernart and Raimbaut, a *chanso* is in the light (*leu*) style, a *vers* is not (*Troubadours and Eloquence* [London, 1975], pp. 116, 173).

[8]Three poems, the *companho* poems, are written in three-line stanzas with the same rhyme sound through the poem, an extreme form of *unissonans*; F. Zufferey, "Notes sur la pièce III de Guillaume de Poitiers," *Romania*, 97 (1976), 117–22, argues for two rhyme sounds in a conscious pattern which follows the content in one of these poems, *Companho tant ai*

agutz. Another poem (*Mout jauzens*) is *unissonans*, abbaab, the same rhyme sounds in every stanza; one, *Ben vuelh*, is *coblas doblas*, the same sounds through two stanzas, in an aaaabab pattern; one, *Ab, la dolchor*, is a variation of *coblas doblas*, paired stanzas with the same sounds in different order, aabcbc, bbcaca. Four (or five) are *coblas singolars* (different sounds but the same rhyme scheme). Of these four two (or three) are aaabab with the same *b* sound throughout (*Farai un vers de dreyt nien, Pus vezem, Farai chansoneta nueva*), one is aaab with the same *b* sound (*Pos de chantar*), and one (*Farai un vers pos mi sonelh*) is aaabcb, with the dissolute *c* rhyme rarely answered in other stanzas. The "courtly" love poems are harmonious in sound as in content: one is *unissonans*, with only two rhyme sounds in the entire poem (*Mout jauzens*); two are *singolars* (*Pus vezem* and *Farai chansoneta*), with two sounds per stanza, one of which is repeated throughout the poem, drawing all the stanzas together. The poem about mutual love, not simply satisfied desire, *Ab la dolchor*, has the same rhyme-sounds throughout, but in varied order. I have used the edition of Nicolò Pasero, Guglielmo IX, *Poesie* (Modena, 1973). Questions have been raised about the authenticity of 8, *Farai chansoneta nueva*, which Pasero prints as an appendix to his edition. I have noted references to that poem in parentheses.

[9]In the three *companho* poems, Guillem speaks as a man who takes sex where and when he likes, who thinks of women as objects of lust. The structure of the poems is very simple, the language quite direct; what imagery there is is not subtle and there is little word-play (apart from the puns on *con*). But Guillem plays with his audience, pretending in 1 that he is making a fitting verse with a mixture of love, joy, and youth, words redolent of the courtly sphere.

[10]The rhyme scheme is basically aaabcb, but in the 8th and 9th, and 11th stanzas, it is aaabab, the dissolute rhyme disappearing, with no apparent relation to the sense. In the earlier stanzas, Guillem connects the stanzas with one rhyme sound, the *b* rhyme in the first, *als*, with the *a* rhyme of the second, *al*:

1	2	3	4	5	6	7	8	9	10	11	12	13	14	rhyme
elh	al	i	in	ut	en	el	os	os	os	at	en	en	etz	a
als	o	art	ent	an	utz	os	es	ent	ent	on	es	orn	es	b
ier	ar	entz	on	al	elh	iers	os	os	or	at	ers	ei	eg	c (a)

Breaks occur in the connecting patterns between stanzas 4 and 5, and at stanza 11; the *c* rhyme of the 6th is the *a* of the 1st; the *b* of the 7th becomes both the *a* and the *c* rhyme of the 8th and 9th, and the *a* of the 10th.

[11]See Frederick Goldin, *Lyrics of the Troubadours and Trouvères* (Garden City, NY, 1973), pp. 7–8, for an interesting analysis of the poem.

[12]A number of poets imitate Guillem's nonsense poem, Jaufré in *No sap chantar*, Raimbaut in *Escotatz, mas no say que s'es* (both of which will be discussed below), and Guiraut in *Un sonetz fatz malvatz e bon*). For a study

of the negative concepts of the poem, see Lynn Lawner, "Notes Towards an Interpretation of the *Vers de dreyt nien*," *CN*, 28 (1968), 147–64.

[13] The text follows the edition of J. M. L. Dejeanne, *Poésies complètes du Troubadour Marcabru* (Toulouse, 1909).

[14] Paterson, pp. 20 ff., notes that in this poem, *D'aisso lau Dieu*, Marcabru claims to be an astute exponent of verbal dispute, but normally his view of eloquence is negative. See her book for a detailed analysis of Marcabru's style and his connection with *trobar clus*. Aurelio Roncaglia, in his edition of the poem ("Il 'Gap' di Marcabruno," *SMed*, N.S. 17 [1951], 46–70), surveys the opposing critical views of the poem as a straight boast and as parody, and defends the latter view.

[15] P. 54; Paterson calls Marcabru the model for the style later known as *trobar braus* ("harsh style").

[16] *Semblansa* seems to mean "image" rather than "false appearance," as in line 6 of the same poem "qui ves Proeza balansa / semblansa fai de malvatz."

[17] For a discussion of Marcabru's odd word formations and metric schemes, see Stephen G. Nichols, Jr., "Toward an Aesthetic of the Provençal *Canso*" (I), in *The Disciplines of Criticism*, ed. P. Demetz, T. Greene, and L. Nelson, Jr. (New Haven, 1968), pp. 249–73), and (II) in *Italian Literature, Roots and Branches: Essays in Honor of Thomas G. Bergin*, ed. Giose Rimanelli and Kenneth J. Atchity (New Haven, 1976), pp. 15–37.

[18] Boutière and Schutz, p. 17, 3.

[19] The text follows the edition of Rupert Pickens, *The Songs of Jaufré Rudel* (Toronto, 1978). Pickens gives different versions of several poems and I have noted the particular version I am referring to in parentheses.

[20] The fourth stanza appears as the second in versions 1 and 2, as the third in 2a; the third only appears in 3 and 3a.

[21] In version one, the praise is hesitant: "Bos es lo vers s'ieu no'y falhi, / ni tot so que'y es, ben esta" (the verse is good if. . . .") But the warning to the performer is equally strong: "e selh que de mi l'apenra, / guart si que res no mi cambi" (. . . let him not change anything of mine in it).

[22] For an analysis of the audience in Bernart's poems, see Frederick Goldin, "The Array of Perspectives in the Early Courtly Love Lyric," *In Pursuit of Perfection*, ed. J. M. Ferrante and G. D. Economou (Port Washington, 1975), pp. 59 ff.

[23] Numbers and text follow the edition of Stephen G. Nichols, Jr., John A. Galm, et al., *The Songs of Bernart de Ventadorn*, Univ. of North Carolina Studies in the Romance Languages and Literatures, 39 (Chapel Hill, 1962). The edition is based on Appel's.

[24] See Paterson, p. 116, but *vers* does seem to mean the words as opposed to the whole work for Bernart, as I try to show. It is therefore inaccurate to translate *vers* "chanson" as Lazar does. Bernart's *vidas* make it clear that he

was known for both the words and the melodies: "e saup ben chantar e trobar" (A.3, Boutière and Schutz, p. 20); "et aveia sotilessa et art de trobar bos motz e gais sons" (B.2, p. 26).

[25] "Mos chans," "ma chanson," or "mos chantars," see 4, 6, 10, 15, 22, 26, 30, 33, 37, 42, 44; Bernart also calls the poem a "song" in 7, 8, 18, 24, 25, 29, 31, 35, 36, and 41.

[26] See M. L. Hansen, "A Linguistic Analysis of Selected *Cansos* by Bernart de Ventadorn," unpub. M.A. thesis, Univ. of California, Berkeley, 1975, for a study of the ambiguities in Bernart's language; see also Nathaniel B. Smith, *Figures of Repetition in the Old Provençal Lyric*, Univ. of North Carolina Studies in the Romance Languages and Literatures, 176 (Chapel Hill, 1976), for a study of the repeated words and sounds. I have also done a detailed analysis of Bernart's language, particularly in one poem in "Ab joi mou lo vers e'l comens," *The Interpretation of the Medieval Lyric*, ed. W. T. H. Jackson (New York, 1980), pp. 113-41. Typical examples of equivocal rhymes include *sens* meaning "girded," "directions," "sign" in 20, "feels," "sense," and "one-hundred" (spelled *cen*) in 1.

[27] In one poem, Bernart seems to imply that the music came first and the words were fitted to it ("com pogues bos motz assire / en est so c'ai [apedit]" 19.5-6). There is a discrepancy in MS readings for the last word; *apedit* is the most likely candidate.

[28] The text follows Walter T. Pattison, *The Life and Works of the Troubadour Raimbaut d'Orange* (Minneapolis, 1952). The first line of this poem may mean "I shall sing a *chanso* with my verse," as Paterson translates it, p. 171. Marshall, p. 57, says Raimbaut is the first poet to distinguish *vers* from *chanso* by the style. Raimbaut's *vida* emphasizes his interest in difficult words: "e fo bons trobaires de vers e de chansons; mas mout s'entendeit en far caras rimas e clusas" (Boutière-Schutz, p. 441,4).

[29] Paterson thinks Raimbaut is making fun of both the light and the closed styles in this poem, by calling it *laner*', "base," rather than light, and by hiding the sense, so pedants must dig it out. She takes the poem as a sexual *gap* in the Guillem style, pp. 163-64.

[30] Pattison, p. 36, notes that some manuscripts cite Raimbaut as co-author and concludes that the theory that Lignaura is Raimbaut is not pure speculation. Paterson seems to accept it as a real debate (pp. 110, n.2, 145 ff.), noting that Guiraut is deferential to Lignaura. That might, however, be so, even if Guiraut were writing both sides, since Raimbaut was a patron of his. I am more inclined to take Guiraut as the sole author, since he names himself so clearly, and since most of the debates we have from the early poets seem to be the work of one poet who often uses the form to make fun of his own postures, putting his clichés into the mouth of another and thereby arguing with himself. See Bernart, nos. 28 and 32.

[31] There is a tradition of mixing poetry and prose (the *prosimetrum*) in larger Latin works from Boethius' *De consolatione Philosophiae* and Martianus Capella's *De nuptiis Philologiae et Mercurii* to Bernard Sil-

vester's *Cosmographia* in the twelfth century, but nothing like it in lyric poetry, Latin or Provençal.

[32] *Bon vers*, "good poem," rhymes with *envers*, "contrary" (7.3 and 10), with *travers*, "reversed" (7.24), and as an inner rhyme with *Domna es vers*, "Lady, it is true that . . ." (7.26), although what is true is that others are slandering the poet / lover. See 39, *enversa* and *enverse* alternate as the first rhyme word in each stanza; the last stanza begins "Mos vers an . . . qu'aissi l'enverse" (let my verse go, for thus I invert it).

[33] The texts are from the edition by Gianluigi Toja, Arnaut Daniel, *Canzoni* (Florence, 1960). I have consulted the new edition by Maurizio Perugi, *Le Canzoni di Arnaut Daniel* (Milan, 1978), and found only minor differences in spelling for the passages I cited here. Unfortunately, the new edition and translation by James J. Wilhelm, *The Poetry of Arnaut Daniel* (New York, 1981), arrived too late to be used here.

[34] See nos. 2, 3, 5, 6, 7, 8, 9, 10, 11, 13, 14, 15, 16, 17, 18. This is an even higher percentage than in Marcabru's poems. The signature within the poem seems to be more characteristic of professional poets—even Bernart does it although sparingly, naming himself directly or indirectly only seven times, three of them in debates; Bernart de Ventadorn occurs three times, Bernart alone twice, Ventadorn alone twice. The nonprofessionals, Guillem and Jaufré, do not do it; Raimbaut names himself only twice in the thirty-nine poems, although he does mention Aurenga twice as well.

[35] See János Riesz, *Die Sestine* (Munich, 1971) for a recent study of the development of the genre, which includes a discussion of previous theories. Arnaut may have been inspired in part by Raimbaut's use of the same rhyme words through a poem, varying only the endings, as in 39. Arnaut's tendency to use recherché rhymes is noted in a *vida*: "e pres una maniera de trobar en caras rimas, per que soas cansons no son leus ad entendre ni ad aprendre" (Boutière and Schutz, p. 59, A.3.

[36] See *ors* and *orna*, the *c* and *e* rhymes in 5, the *b* and *d* rhymes in 7; *ama* and *anda* are *e* and *f* in 7; *etz, ecs, encs*, are *e, f, g*, in 9; *ara, ars, ortz, ers*, are *a, h, i, j*, also in 9; *eri* and *ert* are *a* and *c* in 10; *aura* and *erna, e* and *g* in 10; *am, em, endi* are *d, e, f*, in 12; *int, an, andres, c, e, g*, in 13; *erc, ers, ecs, b, g*, and *h*, in 14; *ortz* and *ors*, a and *d* in 15; *anchas* and *anda* are *a* and *c* in 16; *uoilla, oigna, ola* are *b, d, e*, also in 16; *arga, arc* are *a* and *c* in 17; *omba, om, d* and *e*, in 17.

[37] There is much literature on this subject; for opposite extremes, see Charles Jernigan, "The Song of Nail and Uncle: Arnaut Daniel's *Sestina*," *SP*, 71 (1974), 127–51, for a sexual interpretation and Paterson (193–201) for a spiritual one. The structure of the poem has also elicited different treatments, tracing the rhyme-word patterns either in a kind of graph— Carleton W. Carroll, "A Comparative Structural Analysis of Arnaut Daniel's 'Lo ferm voler' and Peire Vidal's 'Mout m'es bon e bel," *Neophilologus*, 54 (1970), 340; and Hamlin, Ricketts, and Hathaway, *Introduction à l'Etude de l'Ancien Provençal* (Geneva, 1967), p. 198—or as

a spiral—Roger Dragonetti, "The Double Play of Arnaut Daniel's *Sestina* and Dante's *Divine Comedy*," *YFS*, (1977), 232.

[38]See Kenelm Foster and Patrick Boyde, *Dante's Lyric Poetry* (Oxford, 1967), 8.1 ("Se Lippo amico se' tu che mi leggi") and 76.1–4 (". . . questa pulzelletta . . . vuol esser letta"). I have used their edition for my texts.

[39]For a comprehensive study of Dante's style in his lyrics, see Patrick Boyde, *Dante's Style in His Lyric Poetry* (Cambridge, 1971).

[40]He has problems with lyric forms in the *Vita Nuova*, e.g., the abbreviated *canzoni* in chapters 27 and 33 and the false start in 34, although he continues to write lyrics long after.

[41]The phrase is taken from a study of Dante's attitudes towards poetry as revealed by his treatment of poets in the *Comedy* see Teodolinda Barolini, *Dante and the Poets of the Divine Comedy* (Princeton, forthcoming).

[42]For a study of Dante's poetic techniques in the *Paradiso*, where he stretches the limits of his language apparently as far as they can go, see my "Words and Images in the *Paradiso*: Reflections of the Divine," *Dante, Petrarch, Boccaccio: Studies in the Italian Trecento in Honor of Charles Singleton*, eds. Aldo Bernardo and Anthony Pellegrini (Binghamton, 1982).

THE DIFFERING SEED:
DANTE'S BRUNETTO LATINI
EUGENE VANCE

IN THIS ESSAY I shall consider Canto XV of Dante's *Inferno* as a brilliant poetic clustering of three notions commonly associated in the Middle Ages, from St. Augustine onward: those of erotic desire, rhetoric, and text. Canto XV deals with the example of Brunetto Latini, the distinguished Florentine rhetorician, politician, and poet whose juxtaposition with the sodomists in the *Inferno* has never been justified on historical grounds but has been accepted by modern scholars with a certain intellectual complacency.[1] The notable exception to this statement is of course André Pezard, whose remarkable book, *Dante sous la pluie de feu* (Paris, 1950), has heavily influenced my reading of this Canto.

In the case of Brunetto Latini, Dante does not seem to be concerned specifically with sodomy as a perversion of those organic sexual duties that humans share with all other animals who must be fruitful and multiply in order to replenish their species—it is a matter of historical record that Brunetto did, in fact, acquit himself of that very duty.[2] Dante seems concerned, rather, with what for him were yet graver perversions of higher, and more specifically human, properties of that rational animal called man, which are to be *social* and to be a *maker of signs*, especially verbal signs (whether oral or written), by which individuals in society may engender truth in each other. I am assuming, in other words, that in this Canto, Dante is situating Brunetto, as poet and rhetorician, in a perspective that is above all political, and he is asking us to ponder, through Brunetto, what ethical parameters must prevail in that delicate bond between the individual and society, insofar as that bond may be seen as a linguistic one.

However, in exploring the capacity of medieval intellectuals to identify perversion as a social and linguistic problem, and not merely as a sexual one, my purpose is hardly to vindicate Brunetto; and on this point I differ somewhat from Pezard, even though I agree to the pertinence of many of his arguments to the problems posed by this Canto. But I differ more radically from Pezard on questions of method. I shall rely less than he on *a priori* cultural and ideological models that may have "influenced" Dante's text from without: to the contrary, I shall concern myself no less with Dante's manipulation of these models in complex rhetorical strategies within the poem. Dante is a poet whose art is constantly both asserting and calling into question its own legitimacy as a discursive performance. To recognize the validity of such a claim is little else than to recognize that poets, whose art belonged to rhetoric, could express within their discipline priorities consonant with those in the other two medieval disciplines of language—dialectics and grammar—especially, perhaps, the latter: Dante's century was also that of the *Modistae*, that is, of those speculative grammarians who were concerned with the different *modes* of signification of verbal signs.[3] Though his method relies more on performance than on rational demonstration, Dante is nonetheless actively concerned with exploring modes of signification of poetic signs.

It was generally held in Dante's time, and by Dante as well, that the political order was situated midway in a hierarchy of being between the natural order and the divine. In his *Commentary on the Politics of Aristotle*, St. Thomas had affirmed that the city (*civitas*) is the most important (*principalissimum*) work of human reason,[4] and in this context in Aristotle we read, further, that those who by nature remain outside of the political order are either superhuman or violent men given to war:

> Hence it is evident that the state is a creation of nature, and that man is by nature a political animal. And he who by nature and not by mere accident is without a state, is either a bad man or above humanity; he is like the "tribeless, lawless, heartless one," whom Homer denounces—the outcast is forthwith a lover of war. . . .[5]

If exile, for Aristotle, is closely linked with a penchant for military violence, in this canto Dante will explore the violence of an exile as it is manifested within the realm of language, of language understood as the living expression of the political order.

Throughout the Middle Ages, it was held that the orders of language and of society are co-natural, St. Thomas states very succinctly both the social origin of verbal signs and their social function:

> Now if man were by nature a solitary animal the passions of the soul by which he was conformed to things so as to have knowledge of them would be sufficient for him; but since he is by nature a political and social animal it was necessary that his conceptions be made known to others. This he does through vocal sound. Therefore there had to be significant vocal sounds in order that men might live together. Whence those who speak different languages find it difficult to live together in social unity.[6]

St. Thomas says that the social order reigns by virtue of laws whose purpose, as the etymology of the word "law" suggests, is to *bind together* (*ligare*) individuals in the body politic,[7] and these same ideas are extended by Dante to a yet broader notion of *authority* which, for etymological reasons as well, remains centered upon the action of the proper *binding of words together* (*legare parole*), and which may be understood, therefore, to include the notion of *author* as someone whose words are of the "highest authority" (*altissima autoritade*), as is the case, says Dante, with Aristotle himself (*Convivio* IV.vi.).

In the Middle Ages, the concept of sodomy included not only homosexuality and copulation with animals, but any other sexual practice (for instance incest or anal intercourse) which was deemed "unnatural"; and though it is a matter of historical record that sodomists were occasionally burned alive by both Catholics and Protestants alike, in accordance with God's exemplary punishment of the Biblical city which gave the vice (if it *is* a vice) a name, it is also true that (with some exceptions) acts of sodomy tended to be treated in canonic law rather as occasions for excommunication— that is, for exile from the Christian community—or, in the case of clergy, for removal from their clerical functions.[8] Moreover, Canto XV may be considered as a profound meditation on human exile in all of its various modes. Such a flexibility of association (the sexual, the political, the metaphysical) was possible in the Middle Ages only because the concept of "nature" over and against which sodomy was believed to constitute a class of corruptive behavior had become such a broad ideological construct by Dante's time that sodomy could not easily be seen as but one member of a whole family of more subtle—and for poets, perhaps, more interesting—perversions.

In the aftermath of the twelfth-century Platonists Bernard Sylvester and Alain de Lille, the concept of nature as a *mater generationis* or as a *mater procreatrix* had not only come to integrate the erotic element of man's desiring nature into a comprehensive cosmology of procreation, but had been expanded to express an imposing ideology of human culture and of social order: the principle of culture belonged to nature, and "culture as nature" was conceived in dialectical opposition to the "corruptive" principle of Chaos. God as *maggior fattore*, to use a term of Dante's, is to nature what man is to civilization. As Brian Stock says, "More emphasis is placed on man's role as creator rather than as the object of creation."[9] The importance of doctrines of analogy to later medieval thought has been explored by many scholars, and recently Robert M. Durling has demonstrated how Dante himself drew on theories relating man's bodily functions to the order of the macrocosm as a whole.[10] One may also recall with profit that these analogies extend no less to man's capacities to act upon the physical world *around* him. The Latin *Asclepius*, which was an important source for Bernard of Sylvester's *Cosmographia*, had already ventured such notions. As Brian Stock writes of the *Asclepius* (p. 201):

> Hermes says that mortal things not only include the two elements, earth and water, which Nature has placed under man's government, but everything which man makes in or out of these, including agriculture, navigation and social relations: "This earthly part of the world is preserved by the knowledge and use of arts and disciplines, without which God would not have wished the world to be completed."

Similarly, in Bernard, the disciplines of music and poetry are seen as crucial implements to aid the cause of nature against the "corruptive" principle of Chaos, which he elaborately personifies as *Silva*, or "forest." *Silva*, in Bernard's *Cosmographia*, is the locus of violence and conflict, but not that of a Darwinian violence of becoming: rather, it is a violence of pure anarchy and dispersion. In her opposition to *Silva*, Nature speaks of artistic order as a privileged antidote to the corruptive lawlessness of Chaos—especially musical art, which includes poetry. Bernard Silvester expresses the opposition thus:

> Silva rigens, informe chaos, concretio pugnax,
> discolor usie vultus, sibi dissona massa!
> Turbida temperiem, formam rudis, hispida cultum
> optat et a veteri cupiens exire tumultu
> artifices numeros et musica vincla requerit. . . .[11]
>
> (Silva—a stiff, formless chaos, a bellicose compound. The discoloured face of Being, a mass dissonant unto itself! Being turbid, she desires tempering, being ugly, beauty, being uncultivated, refinement. Desiring to escape from her ancient tumult, she asks for skilful proportions and the harmonious bonds of music.)

Dante's readiness to exploit such analogies as a poet may be explained in part by a conceptual opposition in his mind between the urban and the rustic as it applied to the past history of his own city, which he came to see as a tragic admixture of the two, as is implied in the complex political message of Cacciaguida's chronicle of Florence's origins and decline in *Paradiso* XVI. There is a close doctrinal affinity, in any case, between Bernard's concept of *Silva* and Dante's notion that there is a class of words called the *sylvestria* because of their roughness of sound: it is the duty of the poet to banish the *sylvestria* from the lyric art of the *canzone*, whose proper discourse is *urbana*.[12] Nor is it difficult to see an affinity between Bernard's *Silva* and Dante's *selva oscura* as a locus of disruptive passion whose proper remedy is a return to the *dritta via*, the "straight path" by means of a straight moral epic: *grammatica*, as the art *de recte scribendi*, was an art of the "line" (*gramma*), rather, of *rectilinearity*.[13] In the context of Canto XV, which is merely one of three cantos (XIV–XVI) dealing with violence in its different forms, one will remember that the suicidals have not been allowed the annihilation of their being that they sought by their violence, but rather have been punished for their deed by being transformed into the timeless trees of an infernal *Silva*: only God, it seems, prevails over the principle of Being.

Against such an ideological backdrop, one will readily understand how the order of the *polis* could be seen in the later Middle Ages and by Dante as a manifestation, within the sphere of *homo microcosmus*, of generative forces operative in the macrocosm of God's creation. And it will follow, I hope, that we may also see how, in juxtaposing Brunetto with the sodomists, Dante chose to deal with the problem of sodomy in its most extended sense: that is, as a problem involving not just an individual's physical relationship to his species, but rather, his relationship to his *polis* and his culture: Sodom, after all, was a city before it was a vice. In this case, however, the relationship is embodied above all in the order and the processes of language.

That the order of language, understood as a system of conventional signs, may be conceived as the living expression of the social order was an idea especially prevalent in a Ciceronian tradition that Brunetto himself espoused in his *Trésor* and his *Rettorica*, the latter being a liberal translation of Cicero's *De inventione*; moreover, Dante himself had explored many of these same assumptions elaborately and with great originality in *De vulgari eloquentia* and the *Convivio*. Though I shall not attempt to summarize here Dante's abundant thoughts about the equation between the order of language and that of culture, let us recall for our immediate purposes that Dante considered verbal signs to be the "seeds of action" (*seme d'operazione*), seeds which must be very discretely sustained and dispensed (*lasciare*) by individuals in the social order if they are to be properly received (*ricevute*) and come to fruition (*fruttifere vegnano*); otherwise, the "seeds" of words will be undone in sterility (*difetto di sterilitade*).[14] The word as seed can also be sown with malice, however, as in the case of Ugolino (*Inf.* XXXIII. 8–9), who speaks out his horrible sins of the past solely in the hope that his words will become "seeds" (*seme*) whose fruit will be infamy for Archbishop Ruggieri, whose corpse he still devours.

Dante is exploiting here a long exegetical tradition centered upon the powerful parable in Matt. 13, where Christ compares the revelation of the word of God to the sowing of seeds, a parable which gave rise, in the Middle Ages, to many daring analogies between speaking and the ejaculation of semen.[15] (Such ideas will perhaps seem less extravagant to us if we recall that it was thought during the Middle Ages that semen flows from the brain through the spinal column into the loins during intercourse: what is not used up goes back to the brain.[16]) Among Dante's more recent predecessors, Alain de Lille had gone especially far in underscoring the common ideological basis for laws of copulation that must govern the proper regeneration of natural species and laws of grammar, dialectics, and rhetoric as those disciplines of language (*artes sermocinales*) by which we combine verbal signs with each other to engender true and proper utterances. In his *De planctu naturae*, Alain elaborates upon the equivalence of errors in speech with the vice of sodomy, and in the following passage, where Nature bewails the generalized prevalence of sexual perversion among men, Alain conflates sexual with grammatical perversion:

> Man alone rejects the music of my harp, and raves under the lyre of frenzied Orpheus. For the human race, derogate from its high birth, commits barbarous acts (*barbarizans*) in its union of genders, perverts the rules of love by a practice of extreme and abnormal irregularity (*metaplasmo*). Thus too, man, drawn from love into irregularity (*a Venere tiresiatus anomala*), turns the predicate into direct contraposition, against all the rules. Drawing away from the power to spell, he is proved to be an unlettered sophist (*sophista falsigraphus invenitur*). Avoiding proper analogies of the Dionean art, he falls into vicious constructions. . . . Of such of these men as profess the grammar of love, some embrace only the masculine gender, some the feminine, others the common or indiscriminate. Some as of a heteroclite gender, are declined irregularly, through the winter in the feminine, through the summer in the masculine. . . .[17]

Alains extends his analogy, moreover, to cover all three branches of the trivium. Alain is no less forceful in depicting the relationship between the misdirected seminal flows of phallus and of pen, an analogy that would later be made more famous by Jean de Meun. Less immediately familiar to us, perhaps, is the following corollary of such ideas: if language could be considered as the living expression of the present social order, so too the written text was imagined by thinkers such as John of Salisbury and St. Thomas to be the ultimate expression of social order in its most abstract temporal and spatial sense. St. Thomas expressed the utopian function of the textual order very succinctly:

> If man had only sensitive cognition, which is of the here and now, such significant vocal sounds as the other animals use to manifest their conceptions to each other would be sufficient for him to live with others. But man also has the advantage of intellectual cognition, which abstracts from the here and now, and as a consequence is concerned with things distant in place and future in time as well as things present according to time and place. Hence the use of writing was necessary so that he might manifest his conceptions to those who are distant according to place and to those who will come in future time.[18]

Not only does Dante conflate the notion of "author" with the "authority" of imperial power ("Be it known, then, that 'authority' is nought else than the act of an author" *Convivio* IV.vi), but, inversely, he sees writing as a device of reason which allows men to govern their wills and, further, he sees the office of the emperor as one where the specific power of writing is primordial to social order:

> Wherefore Augustine says: "If it (equity) were known of men, and when known were observed, there would be no need of written reason (*Raggione scritta*)." And therefore it is written in the beginning of the Old Digest: "Written reason is the art of good and of equity." It is to write, to demonstrate, and to enforce this equity that the official is appointed of whom we are discoursing, to wit the emperor. . . .[19]

By the same reasoning it follows that the written text could also be seen as a locus of social or cultural perversion as well, and I shall suggest at the end of this essay that it is in the perspective of such an ideological vision that we must be ready, finally, to understand Dante's judgment of Brunetto Latini and the deviant *litterati* in his company in Canto XV of the *Inferno*.

It is not difficult to understand why Dante considered Brunetto Latini an opportunist who turned against his "natural" language and against all *carità del natio loco*, to borrow Dante's expression in another context, for Brunetto himself declares his preferences for the French language, in which his major work was written, over all other languages:

> And if anyone asked why this book is written in French (*roumanc*), according to the custom of the French, since we are Italian, I would say that it is for two reasons: one, that we are in France, the other, because that language (*parleure*) is the most delectable and the most common of all languages (*langages*).[20]

While it is true that in his *De vulgari eloquentia* (I.x) Dante recognizes the established claims for each of the languages of *oc*, *oïl*, and *sì* based on the different uses to which these languages had been put (French is reputedly most suitable for translations and compositions in prose), I would suggest that in the present context languages are taken by Dante above all as emblems of distinct political groups: hence, Brunetto's choice of the French language is seen by Dante as a political choice that is also moral. In other words, though Brunetto was accidentally exiled in France by political circumstances, he *voluntarily* exiled himself from his culture through language. Similarly, if sodomists were punished with spiritual exile,

136

it is because their lust was, in itself, already seen as a manifestation of exile. Alain de Lille says: "Reason allows man to talk (*disputare*) with angels; lust forces him to wanton (*debacchari*) with animals. Reason teaches man to find in exile a home; lust forces him in his home to be an exile."[21] André Pezard summarizes the ideological equation between sexual and discursive perversion in the Middle Ages thus:

> just as the sodomite turns carnal love away from its proper end, so too those who renounce their language turn from its proper end the first gift that God gave to man by his love—a gift made for the purpose of love, since the community of language is the primary spiritual bond of the family and of the nation. Thus, Brunetto Latini, a writer and a deserter, by refusing to give life to his language, denies its purpose and takes away its means of giving life to new beings: literary works as daughters of the intellect which must grow on the soil of one's native land. At the very least, he deprives his language of the hope to make viable, through the intellect, the sons of Italy, both born and unborn, since he refuses to communicate his knowledge to all of the "famished poor" who do not know French. He has frustrated his idiom with regard to its natural end, which is to disseminate and multiply the spirit.[22]

If Dante shared such notions, inversely, on a more cheery note, just as Aristotle saw the state as being prior to the family (*Pol.* I.2), so Dante saw language, which is the living expression of social order, as the mediator of his own very being. It was thanks to the Italian language that his mother and father first knew each other, were united in marriage, and begot him:

> Now this my vernacular it was that brought together them who begat me, for by it they spoke; even as the fire disposes the iron for the smith who is making the knife; wherefore it is manifest that it took part in my begetting and so was a certain cause of my being (*Convivio* I.xiii).

Though Pezard has distilled from the historical and intellectual background what I believe to be the proper ideological matrix for an understanding of the Brunetto Latini episode of the *Inferno*, much remains to be said about Dante's strategies in the dramatization of this model in his own text. Thus, that Dante chose to emphasize the political backdrop against which we are to witness Brunetto's life as an example of violence against social order is

137

already strongly indicated by the sequence of metaphors at the beginning of Canto XV. There Dante compares the firm dikes of the divine but not-yet-nameable "masterbuilder" ("whoever he is," as Dante says), which hold back the river of blood from the burning sand, with the constructive efforts of organized social groups to preserve, through their common labor, the physical existence of their cities from the chaos of the unbridled natural elements. Dante mentions, in particular, the Flemish of Bruges and of Wissant, who must erect dikes against the sea, and the Padovans who must build fortifications *Per difender lor ville e lor castelli* against the Brenta River and against the meltoff of the snows from the mountains in the spring—especially in April, no doubt, the month of Aphrodite, goddess of moisture and of love. The opposition between the constructive labors of technology (or what St. Thomas calls *artes mechanicae*[23]) and the subversive forces of unbridled desire had already been strikingly celebrated by Virgil in the example of Dido, Queen of Carthage and a city-builder who gave up her city-building and went out to fornicate in the forest. But in a more specifically medieval context, if we may properly assume that Dante was conscious, as was Chaucer, of those astrological myths which allegorize the life-giving period of spring as the result of the cosmic orgasm which must occur, yet whose excess must be controlled (as must all passion) in order for such a flood to be properly life-giving. That Dante posits elsewhere the analogy of the flood with orgasm seems clear: Robert M. Durling shows in great detail how in the first of his *rime petrose* Dante draws on the same mythical tradition as Bernard Sylvester, who calls the flow of semen during intercourse a flooding, a "little death," during which nature "survives the world" as she "flows into herself and yet remains unchanged: to that extent she is nourished by her own flux."[24] In the macrocosm, this same process of regeneration occurs, though without the need for those genital members which are necessary to humans as animals. I am suggesting, in other words, that there is a latent analogy between the "heat" (*caldo*) which gives rise to floods in the spring and human erotic passion—the fire of Mars in man—which excites man's animal being to overflow its bodily limits. Each flood of passion must occur, but it must be contained, just as the *duri margini* of the "masterbuilder" now contain the river of passionate blood that flows through Hell. Dante's metaphors are involved in a triple process of analogy (a process called *proportionalitas* in the later Middle Ages), and he is telling us that *reason* is to *passion*, as *construction* is to *flooding*, as *God's creative power* is to the elements of *Chaos*. *Proportionalitas*, one will recall, is a comparison, not of *things* to each other, but of *relationships*.

If Dante's metaphors at the outset of Canto XV stress the fragility of man's social order before the physical violence unleashed upon it by the natural elements from without, Dante is no less concerned to show us that man's culture is no less fragile with regard to the forces of alienation and subversion—subtle, yet no less violent—which may overwhelm it from within. Dante's conception of the inner life of the city reflects, moreover, a distinction between two opposed, yet necessary, tendencies: first, that of the *division of labor* into specialized groups, each of which provides some necessary service to the whole; second, that of the *integration* of separate groups by language and by law put to the service of proper authority. Indeed, Dante's interpretation of the Babel episode in *Genesis* proposes, basically, that linguistic confusion affected first and foremost the integrity of the body politic, whose division into different labor groups became an obstacle to understanding between those groups: the division of labor became, in other words, a division of speech against itself.[25] Political science has as its object not the material or technological aspects of the body politic, but rather those relationships which must prevail between individuals and groups, relationships which depend first and foremost on language. St. Thomas distinguishes political art from the practical arts in the following way:

> Furthermore, reason can operate about things either as making something (*per modum factionis*), in which case its action passes on to some external material, as we see in the mechanical arts of the smith and the shipwright; or by doing something (*per modum actionis*), in which case the action remains intrinsic to the agent, as we see in deliberation, making choice, willing, and all that pertains to moral science. It is clear that political science, which is concerned with the ordered relationship between men, belongs, not to the realm of making or factitive science or mechanical art, but rather to the realm of doing or the moral sciences.[26]

In this strongly politically oriented Canto of the *Comedy*, Dante's own poetic discourse is clearly no neutral agent, and we should be aware that in those same metaphorical gestures, those *signa translata*, in which Dante posits the fragility of organized culture before the tumult of the elements, he is enlisting his own poetic discourse as a potentially regenerative force in the contest for survival of the body politic. A metaphor (*translatio*) is a "trope," that is, a "turning" (*tropare*) of verbal signs from their proper to an improper signification: technically speaking, the later scholastics saw metaphor (whether the motives behind it are "good" or "bad") as an act of what they called *improper supposition*.[27] Good metaphors (for instance, the *signa translata* of the Scriptures, or the metaphors to which theologians must occasionally take recourse) have a potential to edify us and make us fecund with the truth; bad metaphors, on the other hand, are tropes that subvert truth by turning the polysemous word from its appropriate end in such a way it leaves us barren of the truth. This is a moment in Dante's text where the crucial question arises: what are the political consequences of Dante's own poetics of desire? The ideological prejudice against poets in the Middle Ages is well known, and because we are dealing with a region of Hell populated by *litterati grandi e di granda fama*, Dante was no doubt unusually sensitive to the possibility that his own poetic metaphors, if not his fiction of human love as a whole, might, themselves, somehow be considered as subversive. Joseph Mazzeo describes thus the problematical status of the poetic word with regard to theology:

> Poetry . . . is merely the lowest of the kinds of knowledge (*est infima inter omnes doctrinas*). Its function is to make pleasing pictures of representation, since man, by nature, is pleased by such pictures. St. Thomas thus maintains that the use of metaphor is common to both poetry and theology, but in the former it obscures a lower truth whereas in the latter it discloses a truth which would not otherwise be known. This particular emphasis is made clear in a passage on metaphor from his commentary on Peter Lombard's "Sentences," where he argues that the methods of branches of knowledge which are entirely different cannot be the same. Although poetry, which contains the least portion of truth, uses metaphor in common with theology, the science of poetry concerns things which cannot be comprehended by reason because of their lack of truth, and the reason must therefore be deluded by similarities; but in theology the symbolical method is used to lead the mind to the suprarational.
>
> Thus St. Thomas accepts metaphor in theology as the only way to a suprarational truth, but not, as we have seen, in philosophy where discourse must be proportionate to reason. Metaphor in poetry lures the mind into some kind of pseudo-understanding by "seducing" it with mere similitudes.[28]

Though Dante both questions and vindicates the methods of the poets in many ways in the *Comedy* and in his other treatises, in this instance, I would suggest that Dante had already begun to dramatize this problem in a deliberate and interesting way in Canto XIV, of which XV is merely a prolongation.

One will recall that the *vendetta di Dio* reserved for the sodomists, as well as for their contiguous co-sinners of the seventh circle—the blasphemers and usurers, each of whom in his distinct way violates some creative faculty bestowed by God upon man—is a rain of fire which falls down upon the sterile sand and burns the naked sinners. To postulate the oxymoron of *rain* that is also *fire*—heat that is moisture—is to postulate, of course, a supremely "unnatural" occurrence, all the more since it is a property of fire not to fall but rather to rise to its "natural place," as both neo-Platonic and Aristotelian teachings agreed. So long as transgressions of natural law could be understood as supernatural events produced by God, they were not especially problematical to the medieval mind. In the case of rain-that-is-fire we are dealing with a "literal" event recorded in the Scriptures: hence, the legitimacy of Dante's example of God's *orribil arte di giustizia*, as Dante calls it, in Canto XIV. However, we may suspect that Dante's motives for punishing the sodomists with a rain of fire included more than an appeal to Scriptural authority, since, as Joseph Mazzeo has written, in the later Middle Ages

> the notion of natural place was extended to the spiritual realm so that appetition or love became simply the desire of all things, corporeal and spiritual, to attain the "place" in the universe, material or immaterial, that was proper or "natural" to them. Thus as air and fire go up and earth and water naturally go down, so all things seek their place and man seeks his "true place" in heaven. It is in this form, not in the more properly Aristotelian form, that St. Thomas expounds, that we find the doctrine of love as a cosmic principle in Dante; his "spiritual gravity" is the correspondence between states of soul and their proper or natural place in the universe.[29]

What could be more supernaturally "natural" than to punish with fire that falls those who turn love from its proper end?

Such conjectures about Dante's intentions cannot, of course, finally be proven. However, what follows Dante's Scripturally motivated example of God's justice (however "poetic" such justice may *also* be) allows us to grasp the complexities of Dante's rhetorical strategies with somewhat more certainty. Dante deigns to supplement God's "horrible art" specifically with the art of the poets when he compares the falling fire to "snow falling in the alps without wind," now an oxymoron of fire and ice that is both stunning and—seemingly, at least—gratuitous, all the more because the comparison hearkens not to the Scripture but rather to an erotic *canzo* in the illustrious vernacular by Guido Cavalcanti.[30] In this poem (a remarkable piece in itself) Cavalcanti accumulates a whole sequence of images of worldly beauty which are surpassed, he declares, by the beauty of his lady. If one is willing to assume that Dante's use of "sources" is always deliberate and strategically motivated, Dante's perfectly "unnatural" comparison of fire to falling snow is an erotic oxymoron that functions as an icon, so to speak, of the poetic and, more specifically, of the *dolce stil novo* as the very principle of poetic metaphor that is at once impassioned and rational.[31] Quite clearly, a poetic discourse expressing a movement of charitable love that is both human and divine is being brought by Dante into a spiritual counter-position with the vindictive and unredeemed letter of the Old Testament, indeed with the text dealing with the perversion of Sodom.

If there is any warrant for my claim that Dante's performance here is one that both asserts and vindicates the fiction-making capacity of poets—that faculty of making what Augustine had earlier called "reasonable lies"—by contrast, Dante continues by demonstrating, in the encounter with Brunetto Latini, how easy it is for *litterati* to stray in their writings—*in scriptis errare*, as Alain de Lille put it—or to *deviate* from the art of the straight path, *la dritta via*. Though there is a strong tendency for critics of Dante to be moved by the terribly "human" sentiments exchanged between Dante and Brunetto Latini, it seems to me that these exchanges are mined with traps which are intended to snare us (as men of letters) in affections that we are subsequently led to reprove in ourselves as we progress through the Canto: Dante frequently demands that we read "backwards."

One will recall that Brunetto's band of *litterati grandi et di granda fama* (his insistence on their grandure reveals a certain ambition for his own) wander eternally and without direction about the desert of burning sand, dramatically in contrast with Dante and Virgil, who must walk prudently along the narrow dike separating the river of blood (in which the violent are being boiled) from the burning desert where the sodomites wander. Brunetto turns back (*ritorno in dietro*) in order to converse with Dante. This is but one of several *motifs* of turning, wandering, delaying and dispersion in this Canto which may possibly be linked with tropes as a dangerous art of "turning" (*tropare*) and not inconceivably even with the figure *tourn* mentioned by Brunetto in the *Livres dou tresor* as a strategy of rhetorical amplification achieved through substitution: "tu changeras les propres mos et remueras les nons des choses et des persones en plusors paroles tot belement environ le fait. . . ."[32] The potential for perversion in such "turns" of tongue is of course high, and Alain de Lille had already compared such "turning" with the act of "turning" one's desires towards members of the same sex. One may perhaps see Brunetto's own ingenious *tourn* in which he calls the death of the sodomite Francesco D'Accorso a "quitting of his sinfully distended muscles" (*lascio li mal protesi nervi, Inf.* XV. 114), as a speech act dangerously close in its effects to the act that it both names and conceals. In any case, the pederast, Alain says, cannot be called an artist: "art does not please him, only the trope (*tropus*); however, this trope cannot be called a metaphor (*translatio*): into far greater vice it falls."[33]

The horribly sooty appearance of Brunetto contrasts violently with Dante's memory of the man. However, aside from its stunning dramatic effect, this scene may very well harbor deeper meanings. Like the Sodomites, Brunetto has been burned. However, for St. Augustine, Sodom was a real city, one which subsisted even after its punishment by divine fire, and, though the place is infertile, it continues to produce apples which are deceptive because they are filled not with fruit, but with ashes. As St. Augustine writes in his *City of God*:

> The land of Sodom was not always as it now is; but once it had the appearance of other lands, and enjoyed equal if not richer fertility; for, in the divine narrative, it was compared to the Paradise of God. But after it was touched by fire from heaven, as even pagan history testifies, and as is now witnessed by those who visit the spot, it became unnaturally and horribly sooty in appearance; and its apples, under a deceitful appearance of ripeness, contain ashes within.[34]

Sodomites, then, are people whose perversion extends, now, even to the techniques of agriculture, but in this canto Dante is less concerned with the false fruit of the bad farmers of Sodom than with the false fruit of the Sodomite as rhetorician.

Dante's reply to Brunetto's greeting reveals, to be sure, a high degree of reverence for Brunetto's achievement, a reverence that we ourselves can scarcely refrain from sharing. However, at the very same time that Dante acknowledges Brunetto as a *buona imagine paterna*, a father-figure to whom Dante was once a spiritual *figluol*, Dante also reveals that for selfish reasons he too has been vulnerable to passions that would turn him away from his culture, passions therefore improper to the *grammaticus* as a man of letters. Brunetto not only blasphemes the people of his native Florence, calling them beasts that devour each other, but he opposes the crudeness of their rustic origins to the "holy seed" (*sementa santa*) of Roman culture, a culture that Brunetto no doubt understood as consisting primarily in the literary achievements of rhetoric and a culture that Brunetto now yearns to endow with his own fame.[35] The model of the poetic word as a sowing and fructification is invoked a second time by Brunetto (again, perversely) when he bids Dante to believe that the sweet "fig-tree" of his poetic talent is incompatible with the bitter fruits of the "sorb-apple tree" that is the culture of Florence. Ambition, then, has caused Brunetto to flatter Dante by belittling the society that begot them both. I believe that there is a political lesson imbedded in this exchange that may be clarified by St. Thomas, who says in his *De regimine principium* that

> the desire of human glory (*cupido gloriae*) destroys magnanimity of soul. For whoever seeks favour of men must consider their desires in all that he says and does; thus, because of his desire to please men he becomes the servant of individuals. For this reason the same Cicero in his *De Officiis*, warns us to beware the desire of glory. It is this in fact which destroys liberty of spirit (*animi libertatem*) which should be the greatest aspiration of the magnanimous man.[36]

Although Dante does not overtly reprove either Brunetto for uttering such words or himself for hearing them—we must remember that Virgil is present—we know very well from Dante's other writings that his real attitudes toward his culture are quite the opposite: though Dante himself will later excoriate the vaingloriousness of certain Florentines, especially those who take excessive pride in the blood ancestry of their great families (*Par.* XVI), and though he too has been a political exile from Florence, Dante obviously continues to see the bond between individuals and their society as a sacred one. Implicit in the contrasting cultural attitudes of Brunetto and Dante is also a contrast of doctrines of history: as had Horace and Ovid, Brunetto subscribes to an ideal of the permanent cultural supremacy of the Romans, and he ignores the contrary possibility, that the temporal succession of cultures is also the unfolding, in time, of a revelation whose truth could not be known until the vehicle of language had matured to a point where such truth could be accommodated. Dante, however, saw in the undeniable reality of linguistic change the ontological necessity for the individual to acknowledge and respect the primacy of his native language in the acquisition of all other languages, including Latin; and he also was aware of the potential of a new language (especially the language of *si*) both to rival the old and, what is more, to express certain moral values (for instance, the virtue of humility and that of a charitable love) whose expression had remained yet unfulfilled in the language of the ancients.[37] Even Cicero himself, as Dante reminds us in the *Convivio* (I.i.), had once had to remonstrate with those who "found fault with the Latin of the Romans and commended the Grammar of the Greeks, for the like reasons for which these others now make the Italian speech cheap and that of Provence precious."

In this encounter, Dante reveals that, at least momentarily, he has now put aside Brunetto's incurable pride in worldly fame— *come l'uom s'eterna*—a pride compulsively reiterated in Brunetto's plea at the end of Canto XV that Dante remember him on earth for his *Trésor*. Brunetto, by contrast, is still laying up treasures for himself on earth, "where rust and moth consume," instead of "treasures in heaven" (Matt. 6.19). Dante considers earthly fame to be a false creativity, a vain fiction: *fama* is a rumor which flourishes, he tells us in *Convivio* I.iii, because it is "dilated" by men's minds as it passes from person to person, just as Brunetto himself dilates the *vecchia fama* ("old rumour") of Florence's avarice and pride as he speaks to Dante and Virgil (*Inf.* XV. 68). Opposed to this false goal of earthly fame is Dante's more humble desire to invent a text worthy to be glossed (*chiosar*) by a higher intelligence moved by charitable and transcendant love, that is, Beatrice, *la donna che sapra*, who is already among the saved. As Dante uses it here, the model of text and gloss now implicates the word as "seed" (as opposed to the word as "husk" or "chaff") in a less social and more theological sense, though with this interesting variant: normally the hermeneutic gesture is to be undertaken by those living in time who must recover a hidden truth of the Word-as-seed that has been obscured by time; but in this instance, a being in time is planting the seed of his individual historicity in a text whose beloved hermeneutician is in heaven, and whose charitable *operazione* will redeem his seed so that it may fructify, not in the world, but beyond.

The encounter between Dante and Brunetto now situates the problem of perverted love in a context of hermeneutical action. A hermeneutics motivated by charity induces us to read beyond the letter and beyond the individual who produced that letter as well: hence, Augustine's insistence that we read his autobiographical text exactly as we read the Scriptures, with charity.[38] To believe in Augustine is to believe in God. A concupiscent hermeneutics leads us to a carnal knowledge of both the letter and its maker. It causes us to hope, in vain, that texts can be the vehicle of an intersubjectivity which is true in the sense that truth is constituted by the mind of our interlocutor and that his mind is a proper goal of our understanding. As we shall see shortly, Brunetto's love for Dante and for his companions in Hell is uncharitable in the extreme (again, in St. Augustine's sense of the word) in that he loves people or things (words too are things) for their own sakes, or for his own sake, but never for and in God's sake.[39] Indeed, it is with this question in mind that I shall venture some concluding remarks on the notion of *litteratus* that Brunetto evokes with regard to the company of sinners in which he appears, and I shall also comment upon the presence of Priscian in this group.

The term *litteratura* was the Latin equivalent of the Greek *grammatica*: as St. Augustine had said of the art of *grammatica*, "by its very name it proclaims that it knows letters—indeed, on this account it is called *litteratura* in Latin."[40] As an instrument of culture, then, "literature" is not first and foremost a corpus of texts or a norm of correct writing, but rather, a signifying operation that begins with the function of that special type of sign that is called the *littera*, or letter. The letter is nothing but a line, a *gramma*, which signifies merely by virtue of a completely arbitrary association with a spoken sound whose words (*voces*), in turn, are no less arbitrarily related to their meanings than a sound is to its letter. Written signs never signify necessarily, as do "natural" signs (e.g., smoke that signifies fire), but, on the contrary, only where there is a will to signify (*voluntas significandi*) and to understand on the part of those who exchange them. Moreover, understanding is an experience that occurs strictly within our being, and not corporeally. Obviously, the written, corporeal letter is only the most extrinsic dimension of meaning: it is meaning in exile. Although such problems had been articulated primarily with regard to the search for a true understanding of the Scripture, as I have indicated,

146

already St. Augustine had begun to deal with them as problems of communication involving mortal readers and writers of other texts, including autobiography. Hence, we may safely imagine that no writer could have been more aware than Dante that, as love's vernacular scribe, he too was begetting dangerous hermeneutical problems by seeming to invest the previously empty zero-sign "I" of the medieval erotic poem with the plenitude of his own, singular, historical intelligence. A similar problem was obviously apparent to Chaucer, who created a fictive "I" who understands far less than his readers do, and whose "presence" only makes Chaucer "himself" all the more inscrutible. Although Dante's strategies in dealing with the alluring but dangerous fiction of the "I" in the body of the text are not always easily grasped, the example of Brunetto does illustrate, pragmatically, at least some of Dante's ambivalence about *littera-tura* in its relationship to the individual, writing self. Indeed, we may suggest that Brunetto himself had gone quite far, however unwittingly, to make himself a focal point for such a problem: if he could speak of his *magnum opus* as a "treasure" that serves princes like *deniers contans pour despendre tousjours es coses besoignables*, and if he could further compare the parts of his book devoted to rhetoric to "fine gold," now Brunetto wants to keep this treasure for himself. Dante understood very well that inordinate love of such verbal gold and its fruits was not better than adoration of a golden calf: it was idolatrous. The moral consequences of such idolatry are displayed in Brunetto's own conduct at the end of the canto, where he vaingloriously pleads, not that Dante intercede for him in heaven, but that he recall to those on *earth* his *Book of the Treasure*. Then Brunetto compulsively wheels away from Dante (*si revolse*) to greet some unknown new arrival in Hell—as if, Dante says, he were a footracer competing for a prize. As the willing emblem of the classical rhetorician, Brunetto is enacting all of the vices for which rhetoricians since Plato had been typically censured—love of money, opportunism, devotion to external things, and so on—vices which persist in Brunetto even though he is now suffering for them in Hell. Brunetto's self-adulation and his ambition lead us retrospectively to suspect his motives for praising Dante so warmly when they first met in Hell. Was it flattery whose purpose was to evince reciprocal praise from the younger poet? Was it a desire to corrupt Dante once again with a perverted love of letters? With hindsight, the very moving meeting of Dante and Brunetto becomes disturbingly ambiguous, all the more because it invites us, as readers, to re-evaluate the motives behind our own responses to Dante's text.

147

The presence of the grammarian Priscian among the *litterati grandi* of the *Inferno* has puzzled many generations of Dante scholars, and with good reason: not only was Priscian, with Donatus (who is in Paradise), one of the most important pillars of the *trivium*, but strictly nothing seems to have been known about the person of Priscian during the Middle Ages—much less about what may have been his sexual proclivities. However, there was a legend that circulated about Priscian during the Middle Ages, an entirely apocryphal one, but one that explains, I believe, his presence in the *Inferno*. Priscian had dedicated his *Institutiones grammaticae* to a certain "Julius, Consul and Patricus," and this Julian later came to be confused with the Emperor Julian the Apostate, who had decreed that Christians did not have the right to sign their names to any published text. On this basis it was surmised during the Middle Ages that Priscian had renounced his religion in order to sign his grammar. In his *Anticlaudianus*, Alain de Lille berates the memory of Priscian in the following terms:

> Our Apostate strings out tracts on grammar, and, somewhat tiresome in style, is the victim of sluggish dreams. As he strays (*errans*) far and wide in his writings, he is thought to be drunk or quite insane or to be drowsy. He falters in his faith to prevent the reputation (*fama*) of his book from faltering and he sells his faith not to lose the sales from his book; his faith goes astray to prevent popular fame from straying away from him.[41]

Shortly afterward, we are further told that Priscian is one of those "base grammarians who rejoice in mere husks, whom the richness of the marrow within does not set apart: if they seek chippings (*fragmenta*) from the outside (*foris*), content with mere shells, they cannot taste the flavour of the nut (*nuclei*)." Though Pezard is aware of this legend, he attributes the presence of Priscian in Hell above all to prejudice in certain medieval circles against those who hold to the necessity of *grammatica* as a science that is a precondition for all rational knowledge.[42] However, such a prejudice is not prevalent in Alain, since he also bestows lavish praise on Donatus in the very same context; nor is such prejudice in any way proper to Dante. Not only does Dante situate *grammatica* in the first sphere in the "cosmos" of human understanding in the *Convivio*, but he puts Donatus in Paradise. Yet, if we conceive of grammar as the law of the *gramma*, of the letter as a corporeal, material object that is the exteriority of language in its most extreme form, then we may

understand that Dante is alleging of Priscian an idolatry of the text
that is fatal to meaning as the inner life of the soul. Such attitudes, if
they may be said to exist in Dante, reflect, of course, a longstanding
doctrinal fear among Christians of an idolatry of the written sign.
Such a fear is already clearly expressed by St. Paul (2 Cor. 3:3–9),
but it is elaborated upon with great eloquence by St. Augustine in
his famous treatise, *On Spirit and the Letter* (chs. xxiii–xxiv). In this
text, Augustine insists heavily upon the analogous relationships
between the killing letter and the killing law of the decalogue and
the inert tables of stone, as opposed to the tables of the heart in
which the merciful spirit of the living God writes his truth. Moreover, Augustine gives sharp dramatic relief to such ideas in his
Confessions in his account of being taught as a schoolboy to write to
the tune of the whip. Such pain and labor are necessary for the "sons
of Adam," which is to say that learning to write letters is the scourge
of a vindictive God—the letter kills.[42]

There is an interesting case of possible wordplay in the line in
which Priscian is mentioned in this canto: *Priscien sen va con quella
turba* (Priscian goes off with the miserable crowd.). If we may
presume, with Pezard (p. 162), that Dante was alert to the similarity
of the adjective *grama* (a Germanic word cognate with the English
"grim") to the word *gramma*, or "letter," which could also be spelled
by medieval writers such as John of Salisbury as *grama*,[44] then there
is an interesting semantic continuity here of the notion of the letter
of the text with the notion of a dismal, milling crowd in which one
may become eternally lost. Whether or not this semantic trick is
being played by Dante the *figluol* on an unsuspecting "father,"
Brunetto—that is, on a *litteratus* who was himself patricidal with
regard to his native culture and who, himself, suddenly deserts his
former spiritual son in order to greet some newcomer to the crowd
of wandering rhetoricians and sodomites from which he had earlier
turned away—we are witnessing an ironic dramatization of the
potential for rhetoric to become, finally, a self-defeating art and a
process of deception whose first victim is always none other than the
deceiver himself.

NOTES

[1]A recent summary of the debate about Dante's portrayal of Brunetto
Latini and its historical validity may be found in the essay by Francesco
Mazzoni, "Brunetto in Dante," which is the introduction to his edition of
Brunetto's *Il tresoretto, Il favolello* (Alpignano, 1967).

[2]See J. Carmody's introduction to his edition of Brunetto's *Li livres dou tresor* (Berkeley and Los Angeles, 1948), p. xx.

[3]G. L. Bursill-Hall, *Speculative Grammars of the Middle Ages* (The Hague, 1971).

[4]St. Thomas, *Commentum in Libros Politicorum Seu De Rebus Civilibus* I.i.

[5]Aristotle, *Politics* I.ii, tr. B. Jowett, in *Introduction to Aristotle*, ed. R. McKeon (New York, 1947), p. 556; compare, *Convivio* IV.iv.

[6]Aristotle, *On Interpretation: Commentary by St. Thomas and Cajetan*, tr. J. Oesterle (Milwaukee, 1962), lesson II.2, p. 24. I have cited St. Thomas not with the supposition that Dante was influenced directly by this passage in Thomas, but rather because this passage summarizes succinctly attitudes that were broadly held throughout the Middle Ages, from St. Augustine onward. See St. Augustine, *De ordine* II.xii.35 on the question of the co-originality of signs with the social order. How "Thomist" is Thomas?

[7]St. Thomas, *Summa theologica, Qestio* XC: "*De essentia legis,*" art. 1., as published in *Aquinas: Selected Political Writings*, tr. J. G. Dawson, ed. A. P. D'Entreves (Oxford, 1959), p. 109.

[8]Albert Gauthier, "La sodomie dans le droit canonique médiéval," in *L'erotisme au moyen-age*, ed. B. Roy and G. -H. Allard, (Montréal, 1977), pp. 111-21.

[9]Brian Stock, *Myth and Science in the Twelfth Century* (Princeton, 1972), p. 201. See also Winthrop Wetherbee, *Platonism and Poetry in the Twelfth Century: The Literary Influence of the School of Chartres* (Princeton, 1972).

[10]Robert M. Durling, "'Io son venuto': Seneca, Plato, and the Microcosm," *DSARDS*, 93 (1975), 95–129.

[11]Bernard Sylvester, *Cosmographia* I.i.18–46, as cited and translated by Stock, *Myth and Science*, p. 69.

[12]Dante, *De vulgari eloquentia* II.viii.

[13]John of Salisbury says that grammar is the "scientia recte loquendi scribendique et origo omnium liberalium disciplinarum." Grammar is therefore a "linear" art: "*Grama* enim littera uel linea est, et inde litteralis, eo quod litteras doceat; quo nomine tam simplicium uocum figure quam elementa, id est uoces figurarum, intelliguntur; aut etiam linearis est . . . 2 *Metalogicon* I. 13, ed. Webb, (Oxford, 1929), pp. 31–32. "*Grama* means a letter or line, and grammar is "literal," since it teaches letters, that is, both the symbols which stand for simple sounds, and the elementary sounds represented by the symbols. It is also in a way linear . . ." *Metalogicon,* trans. McGarry (Berkeley, 1955), pp. 37–38.

[14]*Convivio* IV.xx.8, ed. Cordati (Turino, 1968), pp. 165–66.

[15]Pezard, pp. 303 ff.

16See Stock, p. 218. Alain de Lille compares the flow of semen to the flow of the mind; verboseness is the seed (*semen*) which does not fructify, but leaves its audience sterile. See Pezard, p. 303, n. 5.

17Alain de Lille, *De planctu naturae*, prosa IV, ed. Wright, in *Satirical Poets of the Twelfth Century*, vol. 2 (London, 1872), and as translated by D. M. Moffat in *The Complaint of Nature by Alain de Lille* (New York, 1908), p. 36.

18St. Thomas, *Commentary*, *loc. cit*, in note 6 above; compare, St. Augustine, *De doctrina christiana* I. vi. 5, and John of Salisbury, *Policraticus* I, introduction, trans. J. B. Pike (Minneapolis, 1938), pp. 6–7.

19*Convivio* IV. ix, as translated by Wicksteed (London, 1903), p. 271.

20Brunetto Latini, *Trésor*, I. 7, p. 18.

21Alain de Lille, *De planctu naturae*, prosa III, trans. Moffat, p. 26.

22Pezard, p. 302, translation mine.

23St. Thomas, *Commentary on the Politics* I. lectio 1.

24Durling, pp. 108–10; see Stock, pp. 216–19.

25*De vulgari eloquentia* I. vi.

26St. Thomas, *Commentary on the Politics*, I. lectio 1.

27Gordon Leff, *William of Ockham: The Metamorphosis of Scholastic Discourse* (Manchester, 1975), p. 137.

28Joseph Anthony Mazzeo, *Medieval Cultural Traditions in Dante's Comedy* (Ithaca, 1960), pp. 67–68; see also the Chapter entitled "Dante's Conception of Expression," in *Structure and Thought in the* Paradiso (Ithaca, 1958), p. 49.

29Mazzeo, *Structure and Thought*, p. 51.

30Guido Cavalcanti, "Biltà di donna e di saccente core," in *Poeti del duecento*, ed. Gianfranco Contini (Milan-Naples, 1960), vol. 2, p. 494.

31Mazzeo, *Structure and Thought*, p. 41.

32Brunetto Latini, *Trésor* XXX.xiii. 2–3, p. 330. If rhetoricians and sodomists are held by diverse compulsions to "turn," Paradise, Dante tells us, is a place where man's appetitive self is *not* twisted or turned, *là dove appetito non si torce* (*Paradiso* XVI.5).

33Alain de Lille, *De planctu naturae*, metrum I, trans. Moffatt, pp. 3–4.

34St. Augustine, *The City of God*, trans. Marcus Dods (New York, 1950), Bk. XX, 1.8, p. 777.

35In his *Rettorica*, ed. Francesco Maggini (Florence, n.d.), p. 19, Brunetto says that before the invention of rhetoric, men lived like beasts, eating raw flesh and plants and other things that beasts eat. Rhetoric, in other words, is the *technè* primal to all others in organized society, and it is on these grounds that Dante is calling into question Brunetto's actions in life.

[36]St. Thomas, *De regimine principium* I. vii, trans. Dawson, in *Aquinas: Selected Political Writings*, p. 37.

[37]*De vulgari eloquentia* II. ii–iii.

[38]St. Augustine, *Confessions* X. iii. 3.

[39]St. Augustine, *De doctrina christiana* I. xxii. 20–21.

[40]St. Augustine, *De ordine* II. xii.37, trans. Russell, under the title, *Divine Providence and the Problem of Evil* (New York, 1942), p. 143.

[41]Alain de Lille, *Anticlaudianus* ii. 500–13, trans. J. J. Sheridan (Toronto, 1973), p. 90.

[42]Pezard, pp. 160 ff.

[43]St. Augustine, *Confessions* I. ix. 14.

[44]See note 13 above.

"PER TE POETA FUI,
PER TE CRISTIANO:"
DANTE, STATIUS,
AND THE NARRATOR
OF CHAUCER'S *TROILUS*
WINTHROP WETHERBEE

ATHOUGH MUCH excellent work has been done on the literary relations of Chaucer's *Troilus*, the results have been curiously indecisive, even where his most obvious sources are concerned. Despite the best efforts of Lewis and Muscatine, we still are not sure what Chaucer intended in doing what he did to *Il Filostrato*, though we can see the details of his reworking of Boccaccio's poem clearly enough; and we cannot agree on whether his use of Boethius is itself "Boethian" or anti-Boethian. The intricacy of the poem's interplay with these two major sources is of course fundamental to its meaning, for the sources are essential foils to Chaucer's dramatization of the complex appeal of love and beauty, and the uncertain relation of human life to the larger forces of fate and an all too dimly apprehended providence. But criticism based on these relationships has tended to dwell on the inner complexities of the *Troilus* to the neglect of the larger question of the poem's scope and purpose. Though we recognize that the poet and his narrator finally reject the worldly attachments with which their poem is concerned, or at least withdraw from them, we have found it easier to characterize the poem's world and its inhabitants than to define the process or assess the implications of their rejection.

In this essay I propose to approach the poem in a somewhat

different way, to attempt to indicate its true dimensions and define its relation to poetic tradition by considering some less obvious allusive presences. Specifically, I want to indicate certain thematic correspondences between Chaucer's poem, the *Thebaid* of the Roman poet Statius, and Dante's treatment of the figure of Statius in his *Purgatorio*. Statius' attitude as narrator of his *Thebaid* offers what seems to me virtually a unique precedent for the experience of Chaucer's narrator—finally the most important character in the *Troilus*. Bound to follow his "auctor" and tell the tragic story he has inherited, the narrator is subject at the same time to intuitions which draw him away from a tragic perspective and charge his narrative with hints of transcendence. Dante's *Commedia*, and particularly the Statius Cantos, provide an allegorical framework for viewing the narrator and his hero, thus enabling us to gauge the spiritual significance of the love depicted in the *Troilus* and assess the spiritual experience of the narrator as he responds to it. The essence of the narrator's experience, as I will try to show, is his discovery of the real nature of his vocation—of what it means to be, first, a *poet*, and, second, a *Christian* poet. It is this discovery that makes it possible for him to distance himself, finally and decisively, from the world of his poem, while at the same time it enables him to preserve a modicum of sympathy with Troilus and the wholly human love he embodies.

The relation of the narrator to his hero closely parallels the relationship which he comes gradually to recognize between his own activity as poet and the poetic tradition to which his poem is finally and inevitably "subject." Just as he finds at the heart of Troilus' experience of love an intuition of beauty and harmony which he and his medieval audience can appreciate at its full value from their truer religious perspective, and which thus becomes a means of moving beyond desire and entering the realm of charity, so the narrator comes at last to realize that the vehicle of his insight into love has been "the forme of olde clerkes speche / In poetrie," that his own final vision is largely dependent on the sympathetic, even reverent, assimilation of the tentative vision of the great poetic *auctores*. Only when he has realized the vast extent of his obligation to the poets of the past can he appreciate the meaning and value of his own autonomy, his privileged Christian perspective on the pagan world, and his own final responsibility for the effect of his appropriation to the English vernacular of the resources of "alle poesie."

The *Troilus* is, thus, both a great exposition of the relations between human and divine love and a major statement on the re-

lationship between Christian vernacular poetry and the pagan
classical tradition. The process of transcendence which it dramatizes
and the exploration of the status of the Christian poet which leads
to this transcendence show Chaucer everywhere responsive to the
great example of Dante's *Commedia*, and, though the differences
between the attitudes of the two poets are in the end almost as
striking as their affinities, Chaucer is plainly concerned to set his
work in clear relation to that of his greatest predecessor in the
vernacular. Their most significant contact, I would suggest, occurs
within that area of poetic experience defined in the central Cantos of
the *Purgatorio*, where Dante presents a Christianized Statius,
created by his own art of invention on the basis of hints in the
Thebaid, as the prototype for that experience of the assimilation
and transcendence of classical poetry which he in the *Commedia*
and Chaucer in the *Troilus* are to undergo in turn. Without attempting to argue that Chaucer deliberately patterned his narrator's
experience of poetry on the career of Dante's Statius (though I think
it highly likely that he did so), I will try to show that comparison
between the two, as well as between the themes of the *Troilus* and
Statius' own *Thebaid*, can illuminate Chaucer's poetic purpose and
provide us with a new sense of what he saw the true dimensions of
his poem to be.

We are invited to consider Chaucer's relations with Dante and
Statius from the outset. The theme of the *Troilus*, as stated in the
opening line, is Troilus' "double sorrow." There is an obvious
similarity between this formulation and the line of Dante's
Purgatorio in which the shade of Vergil refers to Statius as having
sung in his *Thebaid* of the warfare of "la doppia trestizia," the
"double sorrow" of Jocasta.[1] This similarity may be only coinci-
dental, but certainly the *Thebaid* offers a unique precedent for
Chaucer's invocation of Tisiphone as his Muse: the narrator, in his
darkness appealing to the "cruel furie sorwynge evere in peyne,"[2]
bears an odd and striking resemblance to the blinded Oedipus who
calls out from the "eternal night" of his self-damnation to summon
this same "cruel goddess," and in doing so sets in motion the plot of
Statius' poem.[3] Equally striking is what this comparison suggests
about the situation of Chaucer's narrator. Statius begins his poem
by claiming for himself the inspiration of the Muses, *Pierius calor*,
and reviews Theban history from the initial banishment of Cadmus
by Agenor, before settling on the house of Oedipus and the war of
the Seven against Thebes as his subject. It is only after he has given
us a summary of the war and dwelt briefly on the fates of the Argive

heroes, revealing in the process a moral perspective on the violence to come and compassion for the human suffering it causes, that Oedipus appears to pronounce his curse and give utterance to all that is impious and savage in the world of the *Thebaid*. Chaucer's narrator, too, begins with an overview of his subject, but within the very opening stanza of the *Troilus* he is drawn abruptly to a position like that of Oedipus, a virtual collaboration with the forces which are to determine the fate of his protagonists. Throughout the somber and moving proem to the opening book of *Troilus*, hints of detachment and pity coexist with an explicit acquiescence in the dominion of the finally destructive passion of love. In one aspect the narrator presents himself as a quasi-priest, seeking by means of his story to minister to the emotional needs of lovers and offer them the hope of a future "solas." In another, he is obsessively involved with fate, and "Thesiphone" becomes, not simply the necessary catalyst of the tragic action, but the power to whom the poet himself looks for inspiration.

The narrator's ambivalence is entirely unconscious. He seems to recognize that sorrow is the essential link between himself and those whom he seeks to "serve" by soliciting for them the prayers of those more favored by love, but he seems utterly unaware of the irony implicit in his position and dwells on certain paradoxical aspects of his office with no sense of contradiction. Though devoted to love, he is himself chronically alienated from the power he invokes, resigned to a vicarious identification with the joys and sorrows of others. Even in his "priestly" role he can point to no better solution for the despairing lover than a quick and easy end to sorrow through death. From the beginning, he must pit his will to affirm the reality and value of the "gladness" attained by happy lovers against his knowledge that "peyne and wo" are the lot of most lovers most of the time.

In many ways the narrator's engagement with his subject is one of what Dante would call *pietà*; his feeling for the lovers tends toward an enlightened, charitable sympathy, though these qualities are in constant danger of subversion by a strong and potentially debilitating need to identify himself vicariously with the lovers and their fate.[4] Toward the end of his Proem he attains a momentary detachment and hints at a possible religious perspective on his theme:

> For so hope I my soule best avaunce,
> To preye for hem that loves servauntes be,
> And write hire wo, and lyve in charite.

156

And for to have of hem compassioun,
As though I were hire owne brother dere.   (1.47-51)

Here, at the very beginning of the *Troilus*, these lines foreshadow
the shift to a larger world of experience, a new and redemptive
distancing of the poet from his subject matter; but this climatic
event will take place only in the final stanzas of the poem, and only
after the seductive dangers of the story have been exorcised once
and for all, leaving behind a *scintilla* of essential human significance
with which the poet can identify himself in full confidence.

We will gradually come to recognize that the narrator's problem is caused by his compelling need to reduce to the limits of a
conventional love-romance a story which in fact has far larger
implications. He has chosen to adopt the conventional posture of a
courtly "maker" in a situation which demands a "poet" in the larger
sense. For the moment, however, all that is clear is that he cannot
distinguish among his various motivations. We can hardly suppose
Chaucer's narrator capable of any such malign intention toward his
lovers as that which leads Oedipus to incite Tisiphone against his
progeny, but we must recognize that he, like Oedipus, is motivated
in large part by deprivation: the sympathy and optimism which he
brings to his vicarious identification with the fortunes of Troilus and
Criseyde are largely a willed alternative to frustration, envy, and
bitterness, and his willful blindness to the transitoriness of the bliss
of happy lovers is an essential antidote to despair. Like Pandarus,
who is in this respect his surrogate within the poem and whose
emotional involvement with the story we can never wholly trust, the
narrator has invested all his hope of happiness in the lovers, to the
point at which, during the consummation scene in book three, he
can imagine trading his very soul for a moment of such bliss as he
imagines them to know (3.1317-20). Thus the intensity of his
involvement, the sense in which he both possesses and is possessed
by them, imposes on the story a foreshortening of spiritual perspective which complements Pandarus' emphasis on the finite end of
sexual consummation. Together, Pandarus and the narrator
maneuver the lovers into an unwitting collaboration with the laws of
change and the inevitabilities of history, fulfilling the dire prophecy
of the Proem, which thus comes to loom over the action with
something of the effect of Oedipus' curse on the city of Thebes.

The notion of a "double sorrow," in fact, bears as much on the
narrator's relation with his material and the assumptions about love
it embodies, as on the fortunes of his hero. The narrator's involvement with the story of Troilus precedes his own telling of it: though

he professes not to share completely the attitude of his "auctor" toward love, auctor and story together provide a reflection of his own desire, enshrining as they do the pseudo-religion of love and its elusive promise of happiness. And of course they reflect as well the narrator's inner darkness: one effect of his engagement with his "auctor," with literary tradition, and with history, is seemingly to exclude the spiritual as a valid category of response to the story he is telling. The tradition has no place for a *pietas* capable of transcending the world view implied by the poem's machinery. The only outlets for response to the story's unhappy outcome are wrath and grief, and the only appropriate conclusion, beyond moralism ("Swich is this world . . ."), is the death of the hero. The message of the story of Troilus is finally despairing, and the narrator's attachment to it is desperate. That the enterprise is doomed from the outset reveals Chaucer's sense of what it can mean to be heir to the tragic vision of ancient poetry—a poetry cut off from hope, informed by no saving awareness of a spiritual goal.

All of this the poet knows before he begins the poem, and the result, as I have suggested, is to create a tension between the pressure of this knowledge and the moral it implies on the one hand, and on the other a desire to keep this knowledge at bay, to enjoy and as nearly as possible vindicate the love depicted in the poem as an end in itself. But even at its most affirmative, the narrator's attitude shows signs of strain: like the occasionally disturbing ambiguity which surrounds the attachment of Pandarus to the lovers, an uneasiness in the narrator's own mind contaminates his enthusiasm. He senses in spite of himself a certain "disease" in what Pandarus' campaign seems to make of love, and at the very moment of the lovers' fulfillment he is haunted by the voices of imaginary detractors, materialistic debasers of love who would challenge his desperately affirmative attitude (3.1373–93).[5] The narrator is sufficiently aware of his misgivings to seek to explain them away by claiming to be at the mercy of his source, and hence of the sexual *mores* of a remote place and time, in rendering the action of the poem (2.12–49); and at times he excuses possible discords in his language on the grounds of his ignorance of love (2.19–21; 3.1401–14). But he is never quite able to bring himself to question the meaning and value of the tradition in which he is working until the moralizing outbursts of the poem's concluding stanzas. In the meantime the story and the conventions which program his narrative override his better judgment, providing him with Ovidian rationalizations and the pseudo-religious assumptions of *courtoisie* as seductive alternatives to a recognition of the true nature of his involvement with his material. The result is that when he is inevitably betrayed by these conventions and compelled to recognize their inadequacy to control the larger forces which determine the course of human life, he is easily led into a capitulation to the powers of darkness. So at the beginning of book four he summons up the Furies again, and asks their aid in bringing both the doomed love and the unhappy life of Troilus to the quickest possible conclusion:

> O ye Herynes, Nyghtes doughtren thre,
> That endeles compleynen evere in pyne,
> Megera, Alete, and ek Thesiphone,
> Thow cruel Mars ek, father to Quyryne,
> This ilke ferthe book me helpeth fyne,
> So that the losse of lyf and love yfeere
> Of Troilus be fully shewed here.   (4.22–28)

It is this controlling influence exercised on the narrator by the conventions and values of his authorities, the sense in which literary tradition itself becomes an incubus on his sensibilty, subverting knowledge and leaving him in spiritual jeopardy, that the Dante-Statius allusions of the proem serve to announce. It is dramatized again in a brief vignette which appears at the beginning of book two, when Pandarus, in his initial mission as Troilus' ambassador, comes upon Criseyde and her ladies listening to the story of the siege of Thebes. He interrupts the reader just as she is about to begin the chapter which would have described the earth's swallowing up of the still-living Amphiaraus, the priest of Apollo who had joined the campaign against Thebes in spite of his clear foreknowledge that he and his companions were doomed.[6] The scene has certain possible implications for Criseyde, whose own father is a seer more opportunistic than Amphiaraus; and it is appropriate to Pandarus' role that he should distract the women from a story likely to give rise to disturbing reflections with a brisk "do wey youre book" (2.111). But the vignette of Amphiaraus' fall seems to me most of all to suggest the plight of the poet, the privileged figure whose vision is capable of encompassing both "drede and sikernesse," tragedy and spiritual redemption, yet whose vision and *pietas* are all too liable to be rendered inoperative by his involvement with the tide of events.

Amid the plight of Chaucer's narrator, burdened and constrained by his engagement with tradition, the figure of Statius might almost be said to point the way to liberation. To a great

159

extent this is a matter of the posture adopted by Statius in his own poetry, the balance of deep reverence and independence in his attitude toward his great predecessor Vergil and his special perspective on the subject matter of the *Thebaid.* As C. S. Lewis has shown, there are many anticipations of medieval Christian values in Statius' treatment of man and the gods,[7] and indeed it seems to have been this that led Dante to invent the history of Statius' conversion. But once appropriated by Dante, Statius' meaning is inseparable from the biography Dante creates for him; it is easy enough to demonstrate that the *Troilus* owes a clear and significant debt to the *Thebaid* itself, but the most important "Statian" element in the poem, as I have suggested, is the correspondence between Dante's fiction of the crypto-Christian epic poet and the experience of Chaucer's narrator. Both figures are presented as having been moved, Statius in the shadows of paganism and Chaucer's narrator in the dark depths of his preoccupation with the pains of love, to sing of "double sorrow," and the "meaning" of both poems depends largely on how we understand the two poets to have come to terms with their material. The Statius who dates his baptism by a reference to the writing of the *Thebaid* (*Pur.* 22.88–89) and describes the stages of his spiritual development in terms of a progressively clearer understanding of Vergil (*Pur.* 22.27–73), corresponds closely to the narrator of the *Troilus,* whose experience of his own story finally issues in a spiritual perspective upon it, together with a heightened appreciation of his relation to the great poets of the past.

The primary significance of Statius, then, for Chaucer as for Dante, would have been largely symbolic: he stands for a kind of spiritual enlightenment accessible only through a profound experience of great poetry and impossible to describe in objective terms. It may, however, be worth pointing out certain affinities between Statius' poem and Chaucer's, connections which, as I will try to show, must be viewed in the light of the Dantean-Christian view of Statius' career. So viewed, they serve to reinforce his symbolic role and bear signficantly on the conclusion of the *Troilus.* To give an adequate account of this relationship it will be necessary first to spend a little time on the *Thebaid* itself, and then suggest how the relevant aspects of that poem would have been colored for Chaucer by the mediating influence of Dante.

It is a striking feature of the *Thebaid* that it makes a powerful affirmation of human *pietas* and *virtus* with scarcely any regard to the fortunes of these qualities on the level of history. Statius' view of human nature is very dark: nothing in the course of events in his poem runs counter to the emphasis established at the outset by the curse of Oedipus. The pervasive effect of evil dominates the lives of most of the characters, who come to embody wrath, envy, despair, and madness as the fate of Thebes works itself out. Even the great peacemaker, Theseus, gains his end and vindicates natural law and divine order only by adding to the chain of violence its final link, the death of Creon.[8] The most powerful embodiments of *pietas*, Amphiaraus and Menoeceus, perform heroically under the burden of certain knowledge that they are doomed. The purity and fidelity with which Statius endows Argia, Antigone, and the other women of the poem only serve to heighten the painfulness of their bereavement. At Menoeceus' death the *virtus* which has inspired his expiatory suicide bears his soul to the seat of Jove, and Amphiaraus' integrity gains him something like immortality at the court of Dis. But these deliberately equivocal hints that there is an ultimate reward for virtue are set against an overwhelming body of evidence that fate and the gods are fundamentally opposed to the activity of good men. The very "goddess" *Clementia*, whom Statius celebrates in lines which have seemed to express a virtual Christian humanism, whose altar is at Athens but who has her true home in human hearts and minds, is emphatically a last resort, the one hope in a world where man is inevitably a victim. Laments and ceremonies for the dead occupy a large portion of the poem, and the sense of loss dominates the final lines.

A focal point for this sense of loss, though he can only be viewed as a potential embodiment of meaningful *virtus*,[9] is the young Arcadian warrior Parthenopaeus. Of the seven Argive heroes he contributes least to the action of the poem, but his origins, physical appearance, and final *aristeia* are given special prominence. He is a uniquely privileged figure: from his primitive Arcadian background he derives an innocence which serves as a sort of insulation against the realities of the war. For him alone battle is a sport; Diana protects him and guides his arrows; his youthful beauty, reminding the Theban warriors of their own sons, makes them reluctant to attack him; and when he finally falls both armies lament his death.

It would be hard to say with any precision what we are to see as embodied in Parthenopaeus, or why his presence and fate should be so strongly emphasized. Very tentatively I would suggest that his embryonic heroism, and the elaborate means by which Statius dramatizes his beauty and innocence, are an adumbration of the fulfillment of something intrinsically noble, the ritual assumption of a kind of ideal natural manhood uncontaminated by any debasing passion and untroubled by a mature, worldly awareness of fate and responsibility. This ideal can hardly be elaborated, for it exists only as a promise, and the promise is inevitably aborted by circumstance. The summons to war, though it finds Parthenopaeus already restless in Arcadia and eager for battle, is untimely; and in his final speech he acknowledges that recklessness has brought about his premature death. The role of Parthenopaeus inevitably recalls the figures of Pallas and Camilla in the *Aeneid*, and we are probably to see in his brief intrusion into the world, as in Vergil's depiction of the destruction of Saturnian Italy at the hands of the Trojans, a suggestion of the inevitably alienating effect of history on man's relations with what is simple and natural.

Whatever Statius' reasons for celebrating Parthenopaeus as he does, his motives may well seem to reduce themselves to mere nostalgia when this pastoral figure is set against the austere heroism of Menoeceus, the son of Creon, whose ritual suicide, undertaken in response to the prophecy of Tiresias that this alone can avert a Theban defeat, marks the spiritual high point of the poem. It is essential to Parthanopaeus' role that he exist as nearly as possible outside of history, while Menoeceus, as the last of the Thebans, is deeply involved in the world of events. He is at least believed to have affected the course of history through his expiatory death, and, through the *virtus* which inspires his action, he seems finally to transcend it.

Statius is at pains to stress the inner, spiritual aspect of the experience which Menoeceus undergoes in preparation for death. Before the hero himself is introduced we are shown the goddess *Virtus* joyfully descending from the seat of Jove to make one of her rare incursions into human life. Whereas the other heroes in the poem are impelled in their final *aristeia* by a *furor* which intensifies their valor as death approaches,[10] Virtus finds Menoeceus already fighting at the height of his powers, and her function is not to goad him to a heroic madness but to imbue him with a sense of his patriotic and spiritual mission. Assuming the form of the priestess Manto, she compels him to forsake *humiles pugnas* and raise his mind to the consideration of a higher destiny:

> ... non haec tibi debita virtus:
> Astra vocant, caeloque animam, plus concipe, mittes.
> (10.664–65)

(This sort of virtue is not meant for you: The stars summon
you; only set your mind on higher things and you will send
your soul to heaven.)

His death, which prepares the way for a new order on earth, gives
release to a soul which has long been disdainful of bodily existence
and which has already entered into the presence of Jove even as
pietas is bearing his body to the ground.

Statius offers no final assessment of Menoeceus' heroism: his
importance for the meaning of the *Thebaid* as a whole remains
uncertain, one of a number of dark questions which the action
leaves unresolved. As the poem draws to its close the poet seems to
move toward a milder and more simply compassionate attitude
toward his human subjects, and the final lines of the narrative,
which allude briefly to the funerals of the several Argive heroes,
conclude by lingering over the Arcadian boy, Parthenopaeus:

> Arcada, quo planctu genetrix Erymanthia clamet,
> Arcada, consumpto servantem sanguine vultus,
> Arcada, quem geminae pariter flevere cohortes.   (12.805–07)

> (The Arcadian, and how his mother cried out in her
> mourning; the Arcadian, his face still beautiful despite his
> loss of blood; the Arcadian, for whom the two armies felt
> equal grief.)

The *Thebaid* is pervaded by pessimism about the benevolence
of the divine order: the goddess *Pietas* defines her role as opposition
to the cruel desire of gods and men alike (II.465–66), and there is no
equivalent in the poem to the remorseless *pietas* of the *Aeneid*,
which vindicates the great achievement of the founding of Rome as
worth the price of so much loss and slaughter.[11] Thus Statius seems
unwilling to express full approval of the rigorous *virtus* of
Menoeceus, which is exercised in response to Fate, and we may
perhaps see his curious attachment to Parthenopaeus as symbolic of
a purely personal attitude, a dissent from the harsh world of epic
values for which no explicit justification can be given. It is perhaps
worth noting the similarity between the well-known lines of the
epilogue to the *Thebaid* in which Statius defines his relation to
Vergil and the earlier passage in which Amphiaraus, seeking
auguries of the outcome of the war, describes the flight of a bird
which foretells the doom of Parthenopaeus. The epilogue establishes an attitude of reverent subordination:

> nec tu divinam Aeneida tempta,
> sed longe sequere et *vestigia* semper *adora*.   (12.816-17)
> (Do not seek to rival the divine *Aeneid*, but follow at a
> distance, and ever venerate its footsteps.)

In Amphiaraus' words the pathos of Parthenopaeus' immature
venture is gently evoked:

> illum *vestigia adortum*
> maiorum volucrum tenerae deponitis alae.   (3.540-41)
> (As that one seeks to pursue the path of the greater birds,
> you bear him, O tender wings, to earth.)

If the correspondence of language and idea here is more than mere
coincidence, I think it suggests that Statius is conscious of something unheroic in his stance as epic poet; he seems to hint at moral
and spiritual doubts which make it impossible for him to identify
himself fully with Menoeceus, Theseus, and the *pietas* they embody,
and for which Parthenopaeus may perhaps be seen as a sort of
private symbol.

I would like to suggest that it was just the indecisiveness of
Statius' final vision that would have commended him to Dante and
Chaucer. His "conversion," I think, may be viewed retrospectively
in terms of the resolution of problems apparently left open in the
Thebaid—most strikingly in relation to the opposition of Parthenopaeus and Menoeceus. Dante represents Statius' conversion as
having come to pass through a revisionist reading of Vergil's famous
Messianic eclogue, with its prophecy of a return to the Golden Age
(*Pur.* 22.67-73). His purpose is to dramatize Statius' spiritual
growth as a reorientation of that yearning for a lost innocence which
seems so strong a note in the treatment of Parthenopaeus and to
show him coming to terms with history and its underlying spiritual
economy. In effect, Statius' "conversion" is a shift from his pre-
Christian nostalgia for the world of Parthenopaeus to the more
demanding spiritual challenge represented by the fate of Menoeceus.

The confirmation of this shift appears in Statius' major contribution to the spiritual theme of the *Commedia*, his discourse on the
informing of the embryonic human soul by divine *virtù* (*Pur.*
25.34-108), for this discourse is modelled on Menoeceus' experience
of the infusion of *virtus* in *Thebaid* 10. In both cases the infusion is a
glad bestowal of the divine upon a creature which has attained a
state of natural perfection sufficient to make it a worthy receptacle,
and the effect in both cases is the absorption and reordering of the

natural powers by the divine. This total transformation is conveyed in the *Purgatorio* by the wonderful analogy of the sun's heat, which becomes wine in union with the grape (*Pur.* 25.76–78), and in the *Thebaid* by the more violent image of a tree struck by lightning, which "drinks" the fire and becomes itself consumed by its power.[12] As Menoeceus' soul, immediately smitten with the love of death, moves unfalteringly toward the destiny which will translate it to heaven, so in *Purgatorio* the soul, once perfected, lives only to die,[13] and then, *sanza restarsi*, goes forward to learn its destination in the afterlife.

In delegating Statius to trace the development of human life from the origin of the natural embryo to its consummation in the *alma*, Dante is actually pointing to the presence of a kind of "embryonic" spirituality in the *Thebaid* itself; Statius' intuition of the inner experience of Menoeceus becomes the germ of his own experience of liberation from the psychological chaos of Thebes. The conversion which forms a bridge between the *Thebaid* and the *Purgatorio* is of course impossible to locate or define, and by inventing it Dante is positing the existence of a mode of uniquely *poetic* experience, grounded in intuitive sympathy and culminating in enlightenment, an interaction of literary sensibility and spirituality as impervious to analysis as Dante-Statius' image of the transformation of sunlight into wine.

If we cannot analyze this experience, however, we can at least gauge its importance by noting that, in effect, what the apotheosis of Menoeceus comes to represent in the spiritual career of Statius as "invented" by Dante is what *this same act of invention* represents for Dante himself. Statius' conversion is finally most important as a symbolic prefiguration of Dante's own growth to spiritual maturity through poetry, a growth which will be illustrated in his encounters with Bonagiunta da Lucca and other poets in later Cantos of *Purgatorio*. By a series of engagements in which poetic and spiritual experience are indistinguishable, Menoeceus' encounter with *virtus* leads directly to that moment in which Dante will respond to Bonagiunta by describing his poetry as a response to the inbreathing of divine *Amor* (*Pur.* 24.52–54). It is appropriate to the nature of this mode of experience, in which poetry and spirituality influence one another reciprocally, that the series should lead back to Statius: Dante's famous words to Bonagiunta correspond closely to Statius' description, in the following Canto, of the infusion of a *spirito novo* into the soul (*Pur.* 25.70–75).[14]

At this point we may return at last to Chaucer. In a sense the key to the affinity between the *Troilus* and the *Thebaid*, and to the role of Dante as a mediating link between them, is the recognition that Troilus is at once the Parthenopaeus and the Menoeceus of Chaucer's poem. Like Parthenopaeus he is a privileged figure whose innocence must be preserved at all costs, and who exists on his own plane of reality, unaffected by the long war and the worldly stratagems of Pandarus. His imaginative world, his equivalent to the idyllic Arcadian atmosphere in which Parthenopaeus is inseparably involved, is the lyric world of the religion of love, and he can have no real life outside it. But he is also, like Menoeceus, the vessel of an incipient spirituality, a *virtù* which withstands and finally transcends the prevailing emphasis of the poem's action. The intensity of his feeling is the essential catalyst which carries the action forward after the love story has run its course. Love is dominated, though not displaced, by wrath, in the brief *aristeia* which leads to his death, and then reappears transmuted in the posthumous Boethian vision which, both in its suddenness and in its equivocal relation to the larger meaning of the poem, is his equivalent to the apotheosis of Menoeceus.

It is moreover the very *virtù* which has inspired Troilus' love and elevated him to the Dantean transports of book three that drives him forward to his final destruction. By the terms of his love-religion the only release from the insupportable pain of the loss of love is death. Thus we see him in book four, faced with the initial threat of the loss of Criseyde, and praying to the gods

> To doon hym sone out of this world to pace;
> For wel he thoughte ther was non other grace.   (4.951–52)

The death of Hector and the discovery of Criseyde's infidelity turn this desire into a firm resolve: for the first time in the poem Troilus prepares to act on sure knowledge and toward a definite end, a determination which finds expression in his final speech:

> And certeynly, withoute moore speche,
> From hennesforth, as ferforth as I may,
> Myn owen deth in armes wol I seche;
> I recche nat how soone be the day.   (5.1716–19)

At this point Troilus and his story are about to shift to a new plane of action. The narrator, in the first of a series of attempts to bring his poem to a decorous conclusion, steps in to call attention to the new departure which Troilus' resolution represents:

And if I hadde ytaken for to write
The armes of this ilke worthi man,
Than wolde ich of his batailles endite.
But for that I to writen first began
Of his love, I have sayd as I can,———
His worthy dedes, whoso list hem heere,
Rede Dares, he can telle hem alle ifeere.———

(5.1765-71)

The fifth line of this stanza, surely as weak and halting as any line Chaucer ever wrote, seems intended to represent the final exhaustion of the narrator's inspiration as a love-poet. The love story is over, and to pursue Troilus' career any further will require his entering the larger and more serious world of epic. Then follows the narrator's vain attempt to cap his story of unhappy love with a moral capable of satisfying both the male and female portions of his courtly audience, and then a stanza which, ostensibly an *envoi*, serves in fact to bring the poem to a crucial turning point:

Go litel book, go litel myn tragedye
Ther god thi makere yit, or that he dye,
So sende myght to make in som comedye!
But, litel book, no makyng thow nenvie,
But subgit be to alle poesie;
And kis the steppes, where as thow seest space
Virgile, Ovide, Omer, Lucan, and Stace.   (5.1786-92)

The opposition of tragedy to comedy here has lately been explained as a balancing of the *Troilus*, now almost complete, against the *Canterbury Tales*, the work which will constitute Chaucer's most serious claim to poetic eminence.[15] In fact, however, the lines assume a far richer meaning if they are read, not as pointing forward to a work still to come, but as referring to the precarious generic status of the *Troilus* itself at this crucial stage in its narrative unfolding. The apotheosis of Menoeceus had confronted Statius with a spiritual experience which could not be assimilated to the religious world of the *Thebaid* and remained an unresolved element in Statius' vision until both the poet and his hero were transformed by Dante. In a similar manner the persistence of Troilus' *virtus* in seeking final expression compels Chaucer's narrator to acknowledge the limitations of his own imaginative world and forces him to come at last to a radically new perspective on his material. From this new perspective the story of Troilus, in itself a story of tragic and final loss, will be seen to contain intimations of what Chaucer's narrator and his audience may read as the hope of redemption.

In the course of rising to a new awareness of the meaning of his poem, the narrator undergoes an experience which corresponds in many ways to Dante's discovery of his own role and voice as poet in the *Purgatorio*. He becomes aware of the relation of his work to that of earlier poets and, at the same time, of its separate status as a product of his own place, time, and language. With a newfound sense of purpose he resolves the story of Troilus, considers its moral significance *sub specie aeternitatis*, and in a final half-dozen stanzas gives expression to those spiritual implications of his theme which his earlier overinvolvement with the love-story had concealed from him. From a poet of love he becomes, for a brief interval, a poet of heroic virtue, and finally a religious poet.

The first stage of this process is the subordination of the narrator's sense of himself as a "maker" to the recognition of his more significant role as a participant in the continuum of poetic experience and poetic tradition. Whether we take "maker" as meaning simply "craftsman," the practicioner of an art, or understand it in a more specific sense as denoting one who writes love-verses to the specifications of a courtly audience, Chaucer clearly intends to set this function in contrast to the larger responsibilities of poetry.[16] After the insistent repetition of "makere," "make" and "makyng" in 1787–89, the word "poesie" is introduced into the poem for the first time in 1790. Now, also for the first time, references to the tyrannizing book of "myn auctor" and the chimerical Lollius are replaced by the naming of real poets and an implicit acknowledgment of their true authority. The poets named are those ancient poets to whom Dante, too, had given special prominence, and in bidding his own poem "kiss the steps" where they have passed Chaucer recalls both Statius' own injunction to his *Thebaid* to venerate the footsteps of the *Aeneid* and his gesture of reverence on meeting Vergil in Dante's Purgatory. It is a gesture which implies something very different from the hapless subservience with which the narrator, overwhelmed by his obsession with the sorrows of love, had acquiesced in the pagan, tragic view of his material at the opening of the poem. Now the poet is "subject" to his chosen *auctores*, but in a way which implies an emerging sense of his own identity, and the change in attitude becomes clearer in the next stanza, as Chaucer's narrator, for the first time, accepts responsibility for the language of his poem, pleading that care be shown in the rendering of the letters, syllables, and rhythms of his native English.

There is no moment in the poem at which Chaucer is closer to Dante, and as for the Dante of *Purgatorio* so for the narrator of the *Troilus* the discovery that he is at once "subject" to his great poetic models and independent of them at the primary level of linguistic inspiration has important spiritual implications.[17] But unlike Dante, Chaucer's narrator seems hardly to appreciate what is happening to him. When he bids farewell to his "litel book" he is clearly unaware that he is soon to gain a new perspective on his story and break free once and for all from his acquiescence in its tragic message. When he "subjects" his poem to poetic tradition it is with none of Dante's confidence in his own power to rival the great poets of antiquity and go beyond them into new areas of experience. His emphasis is on his own subject status, and his injunction to his book to "kis the steppes" of the epic poets, even as it evokes the Statius of the *Thebaid* and the *Purgatorio*, serves by its literalism to suggest the lingering sense of his own rather comic ineptitude in contrast to the great masters. Even the lines which urge respect for the poem's language are primarily an exprssion of anxiety: though they stand in significant contrast to the narrator's earlier disclaimers, their main concern is with the dangers of misconstruction to which the linguistic enterprise of the *Troilus* had rendered him liable. Certainly there is no hint of anything like Dante's pride in his refinement of the mother tongue. If the process through which Dante achieves poetic self-awareness in Purgatory is left somewhat obscure, its equivalent in the case of Chaucer's narrator seems to be an impulse which never becomes fully conscious. That intuitive sympathy which had made possible Statius' appropriation of Vergil and Dante's Christianizing of Statius is here reduced to a sort of providential instinct, which carries the poet forward almost in spite of himself.

In reducing the narrator to a virtually unconscious collaboration in the discovery of his true poetic vocation Chaucer is not simply exhibiting his characteristic humility. His purpose is to show by this comic means just how far it is possible to proceed in the direction of spiritual enlightenment under the influence of the "olde clerkes." In the absence of any conscious application of craft or knowledge on the part of the narrator, it is "poesie" itself, the normative influence of poetic tradition, that guides his hand, enabling him to complete his artistic task and give full expression to the implications of Troilus' experience. And it is only by thus following out the dictates of "poesie" that he comes to the most crucial turning point of all.

As the narrator returns abruptly "to purpos of my rather speche" after his remarks on language, both he and his hero are, as it were, poised for flight. Troilus, like Statius' Menoeceus, is on the threshold of death and a posthumous transcendence of the tragic world in which he has been drawn by his special *virtù* toward his inevitable end. But as for Statius, viewed in terms of Dante's version of his spiritual career, the hero's moment of transcendence is not of primary significance in itself. Its real meaning is in its foreshadowing of the poet's transcendence of the world of his poem. Troilus ascends through the spheres and comes to see at last the terms on which life is lived in a pagan universe, and books have been devoted to the meaning of his final vision; but he is actually suspended in a spiritual void, and there is no category of religious experience to which we can confidently refer his celestial journey. He ascends to the eighth sphere only to go forth again and vanish with Mercury, we know not where.

But this final flight, which both fully articulates and finally circumscribes the aspirations of Troilus' *virtù*, also dramatizes the first exercise of the narrator in his newfound role of *poet*. True to his resolve to be "subject" to the greatest poets, the narrator's attitude is hardly distinguishable from Troilus' own as they ascend the spheres, and he speaks for both of them in his sensitive rendering of the moral and cosmological vision of neo-Platonism. Only then, after relegating Troilus once and for all to the unknown, does he emerge, suddenly and powerfully, as a *Christian* poet.

The final six stanzas of the *Troilus* may be read as two triads; each begins with an almost frenetic rejection of earthly vanity and pagan folly and ends in prayer. In the first, the finally abortive love of Troilus is balanced against the *virtù* of the young lovers in Chaucer's audience, which is not confined by the tragic world view and which can be matured and refined in the light of inner vision, to the point at which it becomes an all-consuming love of God. The three stanzas and the three types or stages of love with which they deal bear the relation of Inferno, Purgatory and Paradise, and confirm the poet's emancipation from the world of his poem: he has sent forth his book and commended his poetic fortunes to God, only to have the "litel tragedye" return to him transformed into a divine comedy.

170

But the transformation of the poet and his distancing from the world of the poem are not so absolute as may appear. Though the powerful anaphora of lines 1828–32 ("Swich fyn . . .! Swich Fyn . . .!") seems intended to exorcise any lingering attachment to Troilus and his experience, there is in fact a significant similarity between the moral content of this passage and that of Troilus' posthumous vision in the preceding stanzas. Looking down on the world, Troilus had recognized and dismissed

> al oure werke that folweth so
> The blynde lust, the which that may nat laste;
> And sholden al oure herte on heven caste. . . .   (5.1823–25)

So the narrator condemns the futility of Troilus' love, the squandering of his nobility in the pursuit of "false worldes brotelness," before appealing to the young to "cast up" their inner vision to God. The correspondence between Troilus' final insight and that which the narrator urges upon his audience is a way of asserting that the love which "up groweth" in Chaucer's young Christian readers had grown as well in Troilus. The difference between his "blynde lust" and their power to arrive at the vision of God and Christ is a body of knowledge which the poet then recalls with paternal simplicity: we see most truly with the eyes of the spirit; we are made in the image of God; the beauty we behold outwardly will pass away. The absence of this knowledge, so fundamental as to be taken for granted and all but forgotten by the "yonge fresshe" medieval reader, is what kept Troilus from realizing the divine element which he had sensed so strongly at the heart of his experience of love.

This complex relationship between human and divine love is, of course, what the *Troilus* is most nearly "about," and as its exposition has required the narrating of the full inner and outer history of Troilus' love, so the final awareness which the narrator now seeks to communicate dawns on him only after he has pursued the implications of Troilus' experience to the very limits of the speculative and visionary universe of paganism. His relation to his pagan story and its sources is as complex as the theme of love with which the story deals, and the final three stanzas of the poem reveal both his new independence and his continuing involvement. This final triad again follows an ascendant, Dantean pattern, moving from an exorcism of the themes and cosmology of classical poetry through the presentation of Chaucer's own text for the scrutiny of learned friends to the final prayer.

171

Perhaps the most striking thing about the final triad is its intermingling of powerful, decisive rhythms, and a moral tone which carries us an impossible distance from the world of ancient poetry, with incongruous hints of nostalgia and reluctance, as though Chaucer, like the Statius of the *Thebaid*, could not finally break away from the world of purely human love and loss.[18] The vigorous rejection of the pagans and their gods ends with a couplet which states plainly the narrator's debt to the world he is rejecting:

> Lo here, the forme of olde clerkes speche
> In poetrie. . . .   (5.1854–55)

Though Chaucer has finally transformed his pagan vehicle by infusing its form with a *virtus* derived from his own surer knowledge, he has learned all but a few essential truths (*the* essential truths) from his subjection to the poets. The extent of his dependency is further suggested by his address to Gower and Strode. Unlike Dante, who presents himself frankly as having realized the truth-telling capacities of his idiom more fully than other poets, Chaucer appeals to his friends as one conscious of the danger that he may not have realized his intention, that in seeking to do justice to human love he may have failed to satisfy the demands of truth.

Even his concluding prayer seems to look back to the world, for it is based on the invocation used by those souls in the *Paradiso* who await the perfecting sacrament of reunion with their earthly bodies:

> Quell'uno e due e tre che sempre vive
> e regna sempre in tre e 'n due e 'n uno,
> non circunscritto, e tutto circunscrive. . . .   (*Par.* 14.28–30)
> (That One and Two and Three which ever lives, and ever reigns in Three and Two and One, uncircumscribed, and circumscribing all things. . . .)

Chaucer's allusion may have been prompted in part by Boccaccio, who refers to God the creator in the same terms in the second section of the *Filostrato*, where Pandaro declares to Criseida that no soul so perfect as Troiolo's has informed another being "since He who circumscribed the universe made the first man."[19] The intention of this allusion in Boccaccio is hard to gauge: it is one of many instances in the *Filostrato* in which the appropriation of Dantean rhetoric to the celebration of earthly love seems almost an end in itself. But it is easy to imagine its ironic appeal for Chaucer, who has rendered in so much more depth the sorrow of Troilus' abortive vision. If we can imagine him as thinking simultaneously of the fatally compromised spirituality of Troilus and of the glory of the bodily regeneration promised to the souls in Paradise, then his use of Dante's lines may be seen as a plea for the reintegration of human life, for the redemption of the imagination and a resolution of that psychological schism which has allowed Troilus to invoke love in the language of Dante's St. Bernard, praying to Mary at the summit of the *Paradiso*, yet has allowed him also to believe that Paradise is the love of Criseyde.

It is in many ways appropriate that Chaucer should conclude his poem with lines borrowed from Dante. From no poet could he have learned better the true value of classical tradition and the necessity of living through ancient poetry in full imaginative sympathy before seeking to impose meaning on it from a Christian perspective. But this final allusion also serves to illustrate the difference of emphasis which separates the two poets. Dante allows his disembodied souls a lingering concern with the spiritual well-being of others who had been dear to them in the world, but his emphasis is on the supernatural radiance which the resurrected body will exhibit. Poetry, too, is for Dante only a means and must in the end be rejected along with the world. Chaucer never turns so decisively away, and to the end he makes us aware of the importance for him of poetry as a mode of vision. His concern is with aspiration as much as with transcendence, and in the violent, secular world of the *Canterbury Tales* he will continue to seek out the spiritual element in the imaginative lives of even his most worldly and tormented characters. He sees deeply into Dante's achievement, and makes it in many ways the measure of his own achievement in the *Troilus*, but he finally chooses to follow a different path.

———— NOTES ————

[1] *Pur.* 22.56. Quotations from the *Commedia* are from the edition of Charles S. Singleton, 6 vols. (Princeton, 1970–75).

[2] *TC* 1.9. Quotations from *Troilus* are from the edition of R. K. Root, *The Book of Troilus and Criseyde* (Princeton, 1926)

[3] *Thebaid* 1.56–87. Quotations from the *Thebaid* are from the Loeb Library Statius, ed. J. H. Mozley, 2 vols. (Cambridge, MA. and London, 1928). Translations from Statius are my own.

[4] Dante distinguished true *pietà* or *pietade*, a noble disposition of mind apt to receive "caritative passioni," from the mere passion of pity, which consists in sorrow for the ills of others (*Convivio* 2.10.6). The implications of their opposition for the poet of love are shown in a remarkable article by

173

Roger Dragonetti, "L'épisode de Francesca dans le cadre de la convention courtoise," in his *Aux frontières du langage poétique*, *Rom G*, 9 (Ghent, 1961), pp. 93–116. On *pietà* itself see pp. 95–96.

[5]Even Antigone's idealizing *cantus* in book two contains a certain amount of such wrangling (see ll. 855–68), and there is a certain defensiveness in her subsequent remarks to Criseyde (890–96).

[5]On the thematic implications of this interruption, which occurs at a point which corresponds to the end of the sixth book, and hence the exact mid-point, of Statius' *Thebaid*, see John Norton-Smith, *Geoffrey Chaucer* (London, 1974), pp. 90–91.

[7]"Dante's Statius," *MÆ*, 25 (1956), 133–39.

[8]Few readers will agree with David Vessey, *Statius and the Thebaid* (Cambridge, 1973), who sees Theseus' intervention as transforming the poem into "an epic not of sin but of redemption, a chronicle not of evil but of triumphant good" (p. 316). For a strongly opposed view of the poem see Giuseppe Aricò, "Adrasto e la Guerra Tebana," in his *Ricerche Staziane* (Palermo, 1972), pp. 109–31. Lewis (see above, n. 7) provides abundant illustration of that "dark" aspect of the poem which would have been most likely to impress medieval readers such as Dante and Chaucer. See also John F. Burgess, "Statius' Altar of Mercy," *Class Q*, 22 (1972), 344.

[9]"Nec desunt animi, veniat modo fortior aetas" ("nor is courage lacking, if only he attain the strength of maturity") is the narrator's comment as Parthenopaeus appears amid the host (4.253).

[10]See Paola Venini, *"Furor* e psicologia nella Tebaide di Stazio," *Athenaeum*, n.s. 42 (1964), 208.

[11]See Burgess, "Pietas in Virgil and Statius," *PVS*, 11 (1971–72), 48–61.

[12]Fulminis haud citius radiis adflata cupressus
  combibit infestas et stirpe et vertice flammas
  quam iuvenis multo possessus numine pectus
  erexit sensus letique invasit amorem.   (10.674–77)
(Not more quickly does the cypress blasted by lightning drink in the flames attacking trunk and crown than the youth, his breast filled by the divine spirit, drew together his powers of mind and embraced his death.) The suggestive phrase "erexit sensus" (677) may be seen as corresponding to the moment when the *spirito novo* reconstitutes the *attivo* of the embryonic human nature which it informs (*Pur.* 25.71–75).

[13]The abrupt transition from the moment of the consummation of human nature by *virtù* to the moment of death (*Pur.* 25.79–81) corresponds to the radical separation of spiritual from earthly existence in Menoeceus, emphasized at the moment of his death when, even as Piety and Virtue are lowering his body to the ground, his spirit has ascended to appeal before Jove for its place among the stars (*Thebaid* 10.780–82).

[14]For a richly suggestive discussion of the relationship between Cantos

24 and 25 see Giuseppe Mazzotta, "Dante's Literary Typology," *MLN*, 87 (1972), 10–13.

[15]Donald R. Howard, *The Idea of the Canterbury Tales* (Berkeley, 1976), pp. 30–36, 75.

[16]On the implications of courtly "making" as opposed to poetry in the higher sense see Glending Olson, "Deschamps' *Art de dictier* and Chaucer's Literary Environment," *Speculum* 48 (1973), 719–23. For a reading of Chaucer's lines which emphasizes "making" as art or technique see Ida L. Gordon, *The Double Sorrow of Troilus* (Oxford, 1970), pp. 88–90; Robert O. Payne, *The Key of Remembrance* (New Haven, 1963), p. 84.

[17]It is worth noting that the problem of language is discussed earlier in the poem in terms which strongly recall Dante. Though the most obvious foil to the present passage is 3.1401–14, where the narrator diffidently submits his language to the "correccioun / Of yow that felyng han in loves art," it also contradicts the observations on language in the proem to book two. There Chaucer's gloomy comparison of himself to a blind man who "kan nat juggen wel in hewis" (2.21) resembles Dante's rebuke to those "idiots" who, insensitive to the linguistic values of the *volgare*, burst into song with no understanding of poetic construction, and whom "non aliter deridemus quam caecum de coloribus distinguentem" (*De vulgari eloquentia* 2.6.3.). In addition ll. 22–25, on the mutability of language, seem to recall *Convivio* 1.5, where the nobility and permanence of Latin are contrasted with the unstable and corruptible vernacular. (See J. L. Lowes, "Chaucer and Dante," *MP*, 14 [1917] 710–11.)

The attitude of the *Convivio* passage is of course one which Dante later strongly rejected, explicitly in the *De vulgari eloquentia* and implicitly in his encounters with earlier Italian poets in Purgatory: it is tempting to see Chaucer as having consciously defined his narrator's earlier benightedness in Dantean terms as an insensitivity to the importance of his own *volgare*, in order to indicate the starting-point of the process of evolution which culminates in the linguistic self-discovery of 5.1793–98. (A prior question, of course, is whether Chaucer could have known the *De Vulgari eloquentia*.)

[18]On this element see E. Talbot Donaldson, "The Ending of Chaucer's *Troilus*," in *Early English and Norse Studies presented to Hugh Smith*, eds., Arthur Brown and Peter Foote (London, 1963), pp. 26–45; rpt. in Donaldson, *Speaking of Chaucer* (London, 1970), pp. 84–101.

[19]*Filostrato* 2.31 (ed. Vincenzo Pernicone, *Scrittori d'Italia*, no. 165 [Bari, 1937]):

poi che colui che 'l mondo circoscrisse
fece il primo uom, non credo più perfetta
anima mai 'n alcun altro venisse,
che quella di colui che t'ama tanto,
che dir non si potrebbe giammai quanto.
(Since He who circumscribed the world made the first man, I do not believe

that a more perfect soul has ever entered any other than that of him whose love for you is so great that its greatness cannot be expressed.) Chaucer may also be recalling the explanation by Dante's Statius of how the soul is reconstituted posthumously by its formative *virtù* once it has been "circumscribed" by the space of the after-world (*Pur.* 25.88–90). This transitional condition will cease with the reunion of body and soul to which the souls of *Paradiso* 14 look forward.

SELF-CONSCIOUSNESS
OF POETIC ACTIVITY
IN DANTE AND LANGLAND
GEORGE D. ECONOMOU

TWO OF THE GREATEST poets of fourteenth-century western Europe
have written verse (and, in one case, some prose as well) in which
they reveal their unique self-awareness as poets. Dante and
Langland both have something to say—to themselves, perhaps as
well as—to their medieval and future audiences about what it means
to them to be poets. To pursue the implications of what I take to be
their respective revelations along these lines is surely a speculative
activity. Since this speculation will take the form of a critical
meditation on some passages of poetry that disclose the poets' views
and images of themselves, ideally it ought to represent both its
medieval sense as a mirroring and its modern one as a conjecture. A
mixture of these medieval and modern senses is indeed inevitable,
though I hope my observations will provide reflections of these
poets that are objectively convincing. At the same time, I will not
disavow the possibility that what we often see as a carefully worked-
out and argued piece of criticism owes its existence to a good
(presumably because it is educated) guess.

Without reducing two individuals of their creative power and
complexity to a single notion, we can begin by isolating one of the
central images of the self as poet that Dante and Langland have
established, basically insofar as received critical opinion is con-

cerned. As in other aspects of their work, these poets stand out from most of their contemporaries in their capacities for self-observation and -definition, not necessarily of the sort practiced by writers of later periods. Briefly, both poets try to distinguish themselves from the company of poets with whom they perceive themselves as sharing a primary and dynamic identification. On the one hand, Dante places himself within and measures himself against what was for him the tradition of poetry itself, not only naming the poets most important to his self-evaluation but also introducing a considerable number of them as participants, in varying degrees, in his poem's action. Yet, he seems to want to probe more deeply and personally by exploring the meaning and design of his own career. Langland, on the other hand, appears to begin by judging himself within the context of contemporary minstrelsy. He continues by justifying himself through a separation from that body and by an association with a special class of minstrels. Finally, I would add, he is able to assert that in his life's work as a poet lies his salvation.

It is not only from the early nineteenth century to the present that poets have been intensely self-conscious of their being poets. While "the poet's ego" as "the primary reality," as Octavio Paz puts it,[1] was hardly the central and exclusive subject of our poets' writing, they each develop a sense or image of the self-as-poet that is singularly compelling. And, I would venture, each of these poet's sense of himself was based on a strong, though profoundly different, recognition of his special worth as a poet.

It is a commonplace of Dante criticism that the poet candidly (and, in some viewpoints, rather immodestly) places himself in the company of the great. Arriving in Limbo with Virgil, Dante is eventually greeted and taken into the company of poets by Homer, Horace, Ovid, and Lucan. He becomes "the sixth amid so much wisdom,"[2] walking and talking, presumably of matters to do with poetry; for Dante says that it is fitting he be silent concerning the subjects of their conversation, "even as it was well to speak of them there" (*Inf.* 4.105). In the *Purgatorio*, however, we are treated to direct accounts of Dante's conversations with the poets he finds there, most notably in cantos 24 and 26, where the always courteous and modest mixture of shop-talk and mutual praise yields a picture of the evolution of the poetry Dante and his original audience would have thought of as "modern." Of particular interest in this context is Bonagiunta's acknowledgment of Dante as initiator of the "dolce stil novo" (*Pur.* 24.57). A few lines before Bonagiunta introduces the world to one of its most renowned literary terms (49–51), he asks if the individual in front of him is he "who brought forth the new rhymes, beginning: 'Ladies that have understanding of love'" (che fore / trasse le nove rime, cominciando / "Donne ch'avete intelletto d'amore"). Dante's response, which prompts Bonagiunta's praise, takes the form of a definition of himself as poet:

> I mi son un che, quando
> Amor mi spira, noto, e a quel modo
> ch'e' ditta dentro vo significando.   (52–54)[3]
>
> (I am one who, when Love inspires me, takes note, and goes setting it forth after the fashion which he dictates within me.)

Episodes such as these, along with the characterizations and interactions of other poets like Virgil, Sordello, and Statius, Bertran de Born, and Folquet de Marseille in the *Commedia*,[4] as well as passages in other works such as *Vita Nuova* 25 and the second book of *De Vulgari Eloquentia*, all show Dante keenly interested both in accounting for and understanding the poetic past and in assessing his place in the literary continuity we call tradition.

Nowhere in the *Commedia* does Dante more subtly explore his status as poet than in the great liberation canto (2) of the *Purgatorio*. Standing at the foot of the mountain at dawn, Dante and Virgil have witnessed the arrival of the angel of God with a crowd of souls—more than a hundred, he specifies—that had gathered at the mouth of the Tiber to begin the long journey of purification. After an exchange with Virgil about the way up the mountain, the fortunate souls perceive that Dante lives. They pause to look at him, as if they have forgotten their purpose in being there, literally, "to go make themselves fair" (75). Then the first individual among these saved souls, "la nova gente" (58) as opposed to "la perduta gente" (*Inf.* 3.3) whom pilgrim and guide have recently been among, emerges from the group and moves towards Dante:

> Io vidi una di lor trarresi avante
> per abbracciarmi, con sì grande affetto,
> che mosse me a far lo somigliante.
>
> Ohi ombre vane, fuor che ne l'aspetto!
> tre volte dietro a lei le mani avvinsi,
> e tante me tornai con esse al petto.   (76–81)
>
> (I saw one of them with such great affection drawing forward to embrace me that he moved me to do the same. O empty shades except in aspect! Three times I clasped my

hands behind him and as often brought them back to my
breast.)

In this touching description of mutual recognition between Dante
and Casella, his musician-singer friend who had reputedly set some
of Dante's *canzoni* and *ballate* to music,[5] the poet not only
introduces the first encounter of the poem with a saved soul (the
circumstances of Cato's salvation and his custodial position put him
in a class of his own) but also evokes the epic tradition through an
ingenious adaptation of a well-known motif from that genre.

Unlike *Inferno* 25 where he explicitly invites comparison with
Lucan and Ovid in a metamorphosis competition (94 f.), in this
passage Dante merely alludes to a memorable episode in the *Aeneid*
(and indirectly, of course, to Homer's *Odyssey*). He makes the
allusion in such a way that he identifies himself with the classical
tradition on two levels, as poet and as protagonist.

The motif of the impossible embrace between the living Dante
and the dead Casella is modelled on two episodes of the *Aeneid*,
primarily—as critical tradition would have it—on the attempted
embrace between Aeneas and Anchises in the underworld but also
on the earlier attempt by Aeneas to embrace the shade of his
recently killed wife, Creusa, as he flees burning Troy. In both
episodes, partly because they are thematically related, Virgil uses the
same words to describe the unsuccessful embrace.

> Ter conatus ibi collo dare bracchia circum,
> ter frustra comprensa manus effugit imago,
> par levibus ventis volucrique simillima somno.
> (ii. 792–94; vi. 700–02)
> (Thrice there he tried to throw his arms around his neck,
> thrice the form fled his hands, clasped in vain, like light
> winds and most like a winged dream.)

It is possible, though not essential to this discussion, that Dante was
aware of Odysseus' meeting with the shade of his mother, Anticlea,
in the eleventh *Odyssey* as the prototypical episode; for in
Macrobius' account in the *Saturnalia* of Virgil's indebtedness to
Homer, the Homeric passage is twice-cited as the source of the
Virgilian ones:

> Thus she spake, but I pondered in my mind and was fain to
> embrace the spirit of my mother, dead. Thrice I sprang
> toward her and my heart bade me embrace her, but thrice
> from my hands, like a shadow or even as a dream, she flitted
> away, and my keen grief grew yet keener in my breast.[6]

180

In the classical epics, the failed embrace with a loved one occurs within a context of a significant turning point in the educational journey of the hero: just before Aeneas tries to embrace Creusa, she briefly states that his destiny awaits him in the west (ii. 780–84), a direction that is fully explored and supported in the great destinal vision of future personal and Roman glory that Anchises gives Aeneas immediately following their attempted embrace. (And Odysseus learns important things about wife, son, father, and kingdom from his departed mother.) Dante repeats the motif in a context no less important for his poem. That this opening scene of the *Purgatorio* is a major turning point of the poem, controlled as it is by the Exodus figure of conversion, is virtually axiomatic.[7] Dante has chosen a meaningful moment in his journey through the otherworld for this appropriation from the epic tradition, a pivotal moment that steadies the pilgrim in his movement towards the kingdom of heaven even as the vision of that other, earthly empire steadied Virgil's hero by filling him with the evidence and assurances he needed to continue his quest.[8]

If it does not come as a surprise—and it should not—that Dante's treatment of the motif includes a contextual and thematic parallel, there is something surprising about his choice of partner. Odysseus had attempted to embrace his mother, Aeneas his wife and father. It could be observed, with small satisfaction, that Dante's choice of Casella was one that allowed him to stake a claim of originality, Homer and Virgil having used up, as it were, three of the fundamental relationships available to a man. Dante's choice, however, reflects not only a characteristic avoidance of imitation but also, and more importantly, a characteristic ingeniousness in the construction of episodes, whatever their literary provenance, that are arrestingly singular in their literal actions and intriguingly complex in their implications. Repetition and continuity, thus, involve the making of something altogether new. The choice of Casella and the consequent exchange between the dead and living pilgrims reminds us that the pilgrim-hero of the poem is also a poet. While this identity has been worrisome to some critics, raising problems for them at other points in the narrative, here it is irresistibly drawn to our attention that the poet Dante, who uses the classical tradition in his poem, also appears in that poem, discusses that tradition with its chief practitioners in a conversation we are expected *to imagine*, and participates in the enactment of a motif borrowed from that tradition in an episode that dramatizes the meaning of his poetic career in a way that is finally—and sur- prisingly—affirmative.

If Dante and Casella could not embrace in the next world, they could be, and are, reunited for a brief time through the performance by Casella of Dante's *Amor che ne la mente mi ragiona*. Aware of the transitional status of these souls, himself weary in body and soul and thus nostalgic for a familiar comfort, Dante requests a song— provided it is possible for Casella to deliver it in his new condition:

> E io: "Se nuova legge non ti toglie
> memoria o uso a l'amoroso canto
> che me solea quetar tutte mie voglie,
>
> di ció to piaccia consolare alquanto
> l'anima mia, che, con la sua persona
> venendo qui, è affanata tanto!"   (ii. 106–11)
>
> (And I, "If a new law does not take from you memory or
> practice of the songs of love which used to quiet in me all my
> longings, may it please you therewith to comfort my soul
> somewhat, which coming hither with its body is so
> wearied.")

There is, of course, nothing to prevent Casella from attempting to accommodate the request.

It is as noteworthy that the choice of the *canzone*—possibly in response to a hint in Dante's speech—is made by Casella within the narrative frame of reference, as that the choice of Dante the maker of the poem is made within the intentional frame of reference. To better appreciate the implications of these choices, it is important to consider the performance of the song in terms of some of Dante's observations on the *canzone* in *De Vulgari Eloquentia*. Most obvious in this connection is Dante's inclusion of this poem in the sixth chapter of the second book as the tenth and last example of illustrious *canzoni* that represent the highest grade of poetic construction.[9] There is nothing unusual about Dante's high regard for this particular poem, to which he devoted an entire tractate, the third, of the *Convivio*. Perhaps more pertinent is the passage in the eighth chapter of *De Vulgari Eloquentia*, following the list of *canzoni*, in which Dante seeks to explain the term. Aiming for the conclusion that attribution must always go to the writer of the poem rather than to a performer, Dante states that *canzone* can be understood in an active or a passive sense. In the active sense it is to be understood as the composition of its author, as something created, acted upon. In the passive sense it is to be understood as being performed, by the author or by another, with or without music, as something that acts upon someone:

182

> And because it must be acted upon before it can act upon another, it is therefore more the action of someone, and should certainly seem to get its name from the one who acts upon it than from the one which it acts upon. The evidence for this is that we never say, "This is Peter's *canzone*," referring to the person who performs it, but rather to the person who composed it.[10]

Thus, though poet and performer are united in the latter's sweet singing and have finally consummated the mutual affection that had originally impelled them towards each other, a sense of separateness nonetheless prevails.[11] The reunion of poet and composer in the singing, i.e., in the *canzone*, effects a retrospective perception of their unique collaboration in this world. But, though Dante stands among those who are rapt by Casella's singing, and thus acted upon by the *canzone* through its performance, *by his own theory* it is he, Dante the poet, whom we should regard first and foremost at this moment.

Awareness of Dante's insistence that we concentrate on his authorship of the song carries with it an obligation to honor the poem's original significance. Just as there is no reason to assume that Dante did not write the *Amor che ne la mente mi ragiona* as a poem in praise ("lo stilo de la loda") of philosophy in the first place,[12] there is no reason to assume—as some editors and commentators do—that in this episode he intended or expected from his audience an abnegation of the poem's essential subject.[13] And in responding to Dante's request with this particular choice, does not Casella show unusual sensitivity to the language of that request, especially, "consolare alquanto / l'anima mia" (109-10), the first word of which refers to that famous work of Boethius which, with the Old Testament sapiential books Proverbs and Wisdom, constituted the major sources of the *donna* of this *canzone*?

Once a philosopher—that is, having once taken this *donna* as mistress—always a philosopher, Dante suggests in *Convivio* III. xiii, not as a way of doubting philosophy's subservience to theology but as an affirmation of its ability to confer temporal happiness on men. In the view of Gilson, one of our most distinguished commentators on the *Convivio*,

> Dante speaks there as a man who has already been won back by the heavenly Beatrice, a man who therefore cannot doubt the preeminence of religion over philosophy, but who, convinced that philosophy remains none the less legitimate in its own sphere and for its special purpose, undertakes to

183

become its interpreter. In other words, we should be dealing with a Dante who has already emerged from a crisis of pure philosophism—which moreover, he unequivocally admits that he experienced—but who is convinced that a legitimate place remains for philosophy, and is bent on defining it.[14]

Thus, at this moment that signals a major transition in Dante's journey in the otherworld, as we read of Casella's performance we must heed Dante's theory and never say it is Casella's *canzone*. We must rather attend to the report of its singing by acknowledging our prior experience of it and our understanding that it is indeed Dante's *canzone*. The fact that we are not told at what point Cato interrupts Casella's singing preserves the poem's integrity in our minds without undercutting the dramatic point of the interruption.

This unusual assertion of poetic individuality ought not to be confused with the major dramatic effect of the scene; in other words, the singing of Dante's *canzone* should not be regarded categorically and exclusively as representing an inappropriate yearning for our little, imperfect world, a malingering mix, both intellectual and sensual, of an earthly pleasure. The reaction of the pilgrim souls to Cato's stern rebuke, which is likened to the sudden flight, because of a greater care, of a flock of feeding doves (124–33), is certainly appropriate to them, as their rapt attention to the performance of the *canzone* is, strictly speaking, inappropriate; for they are passing into that spiritual discipline that will lead them up the mountain towards God. In the dynamic of salvation, their look back is only a momentary dilation, a fleeting, harmless farewell to a world lost forever before they eagerly recommence their journey to heaven— just as Aeneas sensed, almost as simultaneously, the sudden loss of an old way of life and the beginning of a new in his meeting with Creusa.[15] As pilgrim, Dante has ties with this group, though his actions are independent of them; as poet, he has ties with his audience, through their mutual awareness of his poetic activity, past and present. Curiously, we the audience can delay as long as we need to appreciate the *canzone* in the midst of the greater poem's urgent action. As we do, we realize that the two poems complement rather than contradict each other, that in their concentric-positioning—if I may coin a term for this occasion—they express a unique integration of the earthly and the divine. It is fitting that this nexus occurs in Purgatory, itself the place that bridges the two worlds until Judgment Day.

Casella's appearance as a representative of *la nova gente*—with whom he sings *ad una voce* and in its entirety, we are told, the great Exodus psalm 113 [114] *"In exitu Israel de Aegypto"* (46–48)— before emerging as an individual to enact the scene we have been discussing, suggests yet another union between singer and poet. As it has been their destiny to share a past in their earthly collaboration (commemorated by Casella's solo), Dante and Casella share the mutual status of being among the saved (signalled by the singer's participation in the psalmody). Because they are saved and he is not, Virgil responds to Cato's reprimand with shame and remorse at the beginning of the next canto. Casella's singing stayed, the pilgrim souls scatter to continue their individual journeys, and Dante returns to his guide, the one who will bring him up the mountain, only to see him "smitten with self-reproach." The pilgrim exclaims, "O pure and noble conscience, how bitter a sting is a little fault to you" (*Pur.* 3.7–9). It has been argued that "Virgil appears to be stung by his own conscience rather than by Cato's rebuke (which does not apply to him directly, since he is not a soul undergoing purgation)."[16] It is equally possible, especially since the only explicit reproach for the lingering does come from Cato, that Virgil is in fact responding to it, but in his own way. Unlike Dante and the pilgrim souls, he is particularly smitten because he is *not*, like them, a soul undergoing purgation; that is, Virgil's individuated response to the interruption of the *canzone* emphasizes his isolation and reminds him, without diminishing his nobility, that the philosophy whose limits he, as Dante's guide, knows so well (and will soon begin to expound) has imposed its limits on him eternally.

Conversely, Dante, in whose experience philosophy and theology are bonded rather than divided, responds to Cato's rebuke with no sign of remorse or self-reproach. It is true that if we concentrate on the allegorical relationship between them, we can rest assured that Virgil's reaction signifies a reaction by Dante as well. But, if we concentrate on the more immediate and complex literal level and keep Dante and Virgil on an equal footing there, all we can read is that their departure was no less quick than that of the other souls at the end of the dove simile and the canto itself, and that Virgil reacted as we have already seen at the beginning of the next canto. In the only explicit reaction to the singing of his *canzone*, a self-conscious Dante shifts the focus from his role as pilgrim to that of poet. His own protagonist, the Christian pilgrim-poet who has seen the ultimate truth, justice, and beauty and returned to write it, writes, on this side of eternity, of one incident in his grand vision and speaks simply and boldly of its effect on him:

"*Amor che ne la mente mi ragiona*"
cominció elli allor sì dolcemente,
che la dolcezza ancor dentro me suona.   (112–14)

("*Love that discourses in my mind*," he then began so
sweetly that the sweetness still within me sounds.)

At this remarkable moment, the voice of the poet separates from the
pilgrim in purgatory to report how it feels, not to journey through
the otherworld, but to remember and to write about it—to remind
his audience that his poem, however spiritual its destination, was
written and is read and heard in this world. The reverberations of
the departed Casella's singing of his *canzone* in Dante's being even
as he writes these lines suggest a connection between the earthly and
divine that can only be described as anagogical.

In one of the crucial and pivotal moments within the epic of
mankind's destiny and fulfillment in the next world, we are
dramatically reminded of a crucial and pivotal moment in the poet's
past education and preparation in this world for the creation of that
very poem. *Non simplex natura* [*poetae*], to borrow a phrase from
Prudentius. Paradoxically, the *canzone* can be heard in these two
worlds simultaneously, and without interruption in this one because
as long as it exists it will provide human consciousness with
intimations of the next one. Recognizing that it is the proper motion
of the pilgrim souls to continue their journey after willingly listening
to the song is not so different from recognizing the proper continuity suggested in the description of the philosophical *donna*:

Cose appariscon ne lo suo aspetto
che mostran de'piacer di Paradiso.   (55–56)
(In her aspect things appear that show the joys of Paradise.)

Thus, as the poet of the *Commedia*—which is to say, its author-
narrator-protagonist—translates the meaning of his earthly experience and career to a context under the aspect of eternity, he remains
steady in his conviction of the rightness of that career, founded as it
is on a commitment stated in the closing lines of the *canzone* in
which the poem, like the Dante of this episode, speaks for itself *in
propria persona*:

"Madonna, s'ello v'è a grato,
io parlerò di voi in ciascunlato."   (89–90)
("Lady, if it be your wish,
I will speak of you everywhere.")

As Dante's activity as a poet inevitably contributes to his characterization of the narrator-pilgrim of the *Commedia*, so does Langland's contribute to the narrator-dreamer of *Piers Plowman*. Despite the differences between them, the poems share, among other elements, a basic conception of the narrator. Writing primarily of Langland and Chaucer, George Kane has made some observations about the concept in a way that also applies to Dante:

> The situation arising out of the conventions of the dream-vision, and extending to other fourteenth-century poetry narrated in the first person, is then that there exists an inferentially necessary distinction of a designedly indeterminable character between the life and circumstances of the poet, whose imagination and language have brought narrator and narrative into existence, and that narrator, apparently speaking with the poet's voice, even named after him, to whom necessarily fictitious things happen in a structure of fiction. One part of the poet's technique is to suggest that these personalities are identical, another part to imply the caution that we fix on particulars of identity at our peril.[17]

The purpose of this concise analysis, of course, is to warn us against making unwarranted inferences about the poet's life from his works. Accordingly, the identification of Dante the poet with the narrator-pilgrim in the Casella episode should and does have the support of external evidence for its particular claim on our attention. The audience *knows* from sources other than the *Commedia* not only the fact that Dante wrote a poem *Amor che ne la mente mi ragiona* but also the poem itself. And although it is not essential, we have some reason—the original audience perhaps had better reason—to believe that Casella did in fact musically set and perform some of Dante's *canzoni*. This information has served more to implement than to imperil our recognition of Dante-the-poet in Dante-the-pilgrim in such distinct and definite terms. This may well be so because the "autobiographical" particulars pertain to poetic activity rather than to other circumstances and facets of the poet's life and personality, an activity which elicits its primary credibility from the very poem— itself a product of that activity—that has required we respond to this situation in the first place.

The immediately preceding argument applies as well to the famous autobiographical passage in *Piers Plowman* C, vi. 1–104, which I read as being fundamentally concerned with Langland's activity as a poet. Putting aside the question of this interpretation for the moment, we can note that it has already been especially well-argued that the passage can be considered a piece of truthful rather than ficitonal autobiography: R. W. Chambers has pointed out that those who contend that the passage is fictional have never been able "to produce a precedent" for its being so, and E. Talbot Donaldson has most cogently observed "that the rejection of the poet's account of himself entails one great responsibility that no one has ever attempted to meet: that is, to explain what purpose the auto-biographical passage was meant to serve if it is fictional."[18] Finally, the fact that the passage is set outside of the dream-vision frame as a waking allegory argues for its being read on different terms from those that prevail in the dreams. This is true even though Will's interaction with Reason and Conscience in the passage superficially reminds us of the dreamer's life-like contact with characters in other parts of the poem.

Bridging the first two dreams of the poem in the C-text, the passage introduces the dreamer in a wakened state in which he examines the motives and manner of his life and work.

> Thus ich a-waked, god wot · whanne ich wonede on Cornehulle,
> Kytte and ich in a cote · clothed as a lollere,
> And lytel y-lete by · leyue me for sothe,
> Among lollares of London · and lewede heremytes;
> For ich made of tho men · as reson me tauhte.
> For as ich cam by Conscience · with Reson ich mette
> In an hote heruest · whenne ich hadde myn hele,
> And lymes to labore with · and louede wel fare,
> And no dede to do · bote drynke and to slepe.
> In hele and in vnite · on me aposede;
> Romynge in remembraunce · thus Reson me aratede.
> (C, vi. 1–11)[19]

Before Reason, joined by Conscience towards the end, is done with him, the narrator has spoken of his reluctance to do physical labor, of his schooling as a youth in Holy Writ, of his supporting himself by praying for his benefactors, arguing that this is more fitting work for a cleric than various kinds of other labor, and of his awareness that he has misspent his time, though he hopes finally to turn it to his spiritual profit. As this brief summation might suggest, critical opinion about this passage has hardly turned out to be unanimous; in fact, it ranges from a view in which the passage is characterized as "powerfully condemnatory" to one that is exactly opposite in which the narrator is said to find "verification by Reason and Conscience that he is doing the right thing."[20]

Despite their apparent serious difference, these two views share a basic assumption about the passage and the poem as a whole. This agreement is founded upon a common recognition of Langland's view of his work as a poetic activity "which *as a mode of life* must be justified before God and man."[21] Central to this view is Langland's preoccupation with the meaning of minstrelsy and the classification of minstrels. It is a concern that is altered and refined as it runs through the three versions of the poem, and the question of its relevance to Langland's life as a poet or maker, in my opinion, is finally resolved in the famous C-text autobiographical passage.

As Donaldson has pointed out, minstrelsy is the only occupation that does not receive consistent treatment in the Prologues of the three versions: AB, Pro. 33–39 distinguish between those minstrels who guiltlessly "geten gold with hire glee" and those "Iapers and Iangelers, Iudas children," who could work if they wanted to; in contrast, C, i. 35–40 eliminates the distinction and describes one bad class of minstrels, those "That wollen neyther swynke ne swete."[22] While the A and B-texts appear to proceed with some confusion from their original distinction between good and wicked minstels, the C-text moves from its one-class definition to a view that distinguishes between the original class of minstrels and "godes mynstrales" (C, viii. 100), a phrase deriving ultimately from Franciscan tradition. The B-text, between passūs x and xiii, begins to show a severe judgment against all but the most pious kind of minstrelsy, while at the same time tending to disassociate the dreamer from the vocation. Still, in its identification of Hawkin as a minstrel, the B-text appears to persist in its preoccupation with minstrelsy, possibly even contributing to the connection between Hawkin and the poet so many readers see. But it is in the C-text, with its explicit separation of God's minstrels from the body of everyday minstrelsy and entertainment, that we find the clearest expression of the poet's "conscious assimilation of himself to a minstrel" along the basic line of development found in all three texts: "first, an honest, plausible, idealistic entertainer and ultimately an apostolic-Franciscan *ioculator Dei*."[23]

Among the many differences between the B and C-texts, there is one that not only points significantly towards the poet's final view of himself as one of God's minstrels, but also gives strong indications that he came to believe in the validity of his poem as his life's

189

work. This is the beginning of the Imaginative episode in which, in B, xii, the recently appeared character's rebuke of the dreamer for writing poetry elicits a defensive response from him. In C, xv, these lines have been completely deleted because they would have contradicted the sense of the autobiographical passage, which preceded it by nine passūs.[24]

In the B treatment of the episode, Imaginative, defined by the *MED* at 4 (c) as "the ability to form images of things not experienced, e.g., of past or future events" and by a recent critic as "reason using the resources of the imagination in an imaginatively reasonable way" and as "the proper perspective on experience,"[25] challenges the narrator's poetic activity:

> And þow medlest þee wiþ makynges and myȝtest go seye
> þi sauter,
> And bidde for hem þat ȝyueþ þee breed, for þer are
> bokes y[n]owe
> To telle men what dowel is, dobet and dobest boþe,
> And prechours to preuen what it is of many a peire freres.
> (B, xii. 16–19)

The dreamer-narrator's defense begins rather weakly with a reference to the recreational value of writing poetry:

> I seiȝ wel he seide me sooþ, and somwhat me to excuse
> Seide, Caton conforted his sone þat, clerk þouȝ he were,
> To solacen hym som tyme; [so] I do whan I make: .
> *Interpone tuis interdum gaudia curis.*
> And of holy men I her [e], quod I, how þei
> ouþerwhile
> [In manye places pleyden þe parfiter to ben].   (20–24)

But it closes on a definitely stronger note:

> Ac if þer were any wight þat wolde me telle
> What were dowel and dobet and dobest at þe laste,
> Wolde i neuere do werk, but wende to holi chirche
> And þere bidde my bedes but whan ich ete or slepe.
> (25–28)

It is especially noteworthy that he seems to identify his making with his search for salvation, a quest which is finally profoundly affected and directed by this entire crucial encounter with Imaginative, a vivid example, incidentally, of self-consciousness fourteenth-century style. If he could get his answers elsewhere—the reader is aware of an earlier failure of a pair of friars to provide any—the narrator would give up his "werke" and go to church to do his more conventional duty. The assertion that poetry is his proper work and the suggestion that for him it is something more serious than play are indeed remarkable, all the more so when we consider that after Langland arrived at his view of himself as one of God's minstrels, they became superfluous.

While it is the autobiographical section unique to C, vi that this revision by deletion seems to relate back to most directly and meaningfully, there is an intermediate speech common to all three versions that provides further insight into the poet's changing position on the significance of his work. In A, vii. 231 f., Hunger explains to Piers that natural intelligence, *Kynde wyt*, calls for every man to work, whether it be teaching or tilling or travailing in prayers, and that Christ requires it as well.[26] In B, vi. 249 f., Hunger says essentially the same things, and, as in A and C, invokes the authority of Psalm 127, "*Labores manuum tuarum quia manducabis; beatus es, et bene tibi erit: et cetera.*" But in C, ix. 260 f., the verses immediately preceding the scriptural quotation have been drastically reduced: the lines referring to natural intelligence and Christ have been omitted as well as the references to different kinds of labor and living. While retaining the general sense that work is both necessary and blessed, the speech in C introduces the words from the psalm with two lines (261–62) that occur only in this last version of the poem.

> "Yblessed be alle tho · that here by-lyue byswynken
> Thorw eny leel labour · as thorgh lymes and handes."

The accommodation of "any faithful labor" to the notion that one will be nourished by the labors of one's hands, and the equation of that general sense of honest work with the work of limbs and hands, emphasize what appears to be an important point in the C-text: the concept of acceptable forms of work must be expanded to contain the calling of poetry when it is specifically committed to serving God.

If it is possible that a revision in an earlier part of the C version of the poem helps in part to explain the deletion from C. xv of the defense of making that occurs in B. xii, it is possible that the way the B-text was completed also helps explain the revision of a passage such as the one with which this same passus, C. xv, opens. The writing, which mostly means the rewriting, of *Piers Plowman* incorporates poetic activity into the subject matter of the poem. What was written in B, especially from this very point in the text on, becomes part of the personal experience the narrator-dreamer brings to bear on his subsequent treatment of his continuing quest, the ongoing nature of which will be confirmed by the identical conclusions of B and C when Conscience announces his intention to seek out Piers the Plowman. Thus, the accomplishment of B in its explorations of Dowel, Dobet, and Dobest influences the removal of a passage that predicates its justification of making on the condition of acquiring knowledge about those three lives; it also influences the rewriting of the lines that introduce the figure that has already initiated the acquisition of that knowledge in the previous version.

After beginning with similar first lines, the openings of B, xii and C, xv proceed in remarkably different ways. In B, Imaginative tells the narrator-dreamer (who now follows him) that he, Imaginative, has followed him these five and forty winters, "And manye tymes haue meued þee to [mynne] on þyn ende, / And how fele fernyeres are faren and so fewe to come" (3–4). Imaginative's emphasis on the brevity and limitations of the human condition and the necessity for amending one's ways leads directly into the attack on poetry-writing: you have been warned of the precariousness of your position and have been shown the way to escape damnation. "And þow medlest þee wiþ makynges." But C moves along very different lines.

> "Ich am Ymaginatif," quath he · "ydel was ich neuere,
> Thauh ich sitte by my-self · suche is my grace;
> Ich haue yfolwed the in faith · more than fourty wynter,
> And wissede the ful ofte · what Dowel was to mene,
> And counsailede the for Cristes sake · no creature to by-gyle,
> Nother to lye nother to lacke · ne lere that is defendid,
> Ne to spille speche · as to speke an ydell,
> And no tyme to tyne · ne trewe thyng to teenen;
> Lowe the to lyue forth · in the lawe of holy churche;
> Thenne dost thow wel, with-oute drede · he can do bet,
>   no forse!"   (1–10)

Rather than leading up to a condemnation of making, these lines grow out of an increasing recognition of its validity. The contrast is sharply initiated and epitomized by the fourth lines of each version—B representing Imaginative as saying that he has moved the narrator many times to think on his end, and C that he has often instructed him in the meaning of Dowel. This clearly indicates one instance of the way the completed B-text has been assimilated to and subsumed in the C-text narrator's life experience, a change in perspective that is also supported by the substitution of the more general "more than fourty wynter" for the specific "fyue and fourty" in the third lines of C and B, respectively. Instead of stressing life's limitations and the need for reform, C's Imaginative recounts the various ways in which he has counselled the narrator. That most of this counsel has concentrated on virtuous uses of language suggests at least an awareness of the resolution concerning the role and significance of making that I believe is achieved in the earlier autobiographical passage. And the echo of C, vi's line in which the narrator admits, "That ich haue tynt tyme · and tyme mysspended" (93), by the present passage's "And no tyme to tyne," argues for the close relationship between the two passages in Langland's mind during the composition of the C-text and especially for the crucial status he seems to have accorded the new autobiographical addition to his poem.

Just as Will's admission that he has wasted time (and his resolution a few lines later not to waste it further) in his closing speech of the autobiographical passage foreshadows Imaginative's claim that he has taught the narrator-dreamer not to waste time some nine passūs later, the unique connection between these two parts of the poem is also probably partially based on a rather subtle but unmistakable connection between their personified inter-locutors at the conclusion of the passage's opening paragraph. We have already read there that Reason, "Romynge in remembraunce," reproached the conscious narrator for his past and current attitude towards work. Considering that part of Imaginative's function, represented by the scholastic *ars commemorativa*, operates through memory, we can see that Reason and Imaginative resemble each other in their vivid representations of experience to the narrator in both dream and non-dream states. Indeed, their similarity is symptomatic of a much deeper connection—Imaginative's attack on the narrator's making in B, xii was deleted because it had been preempted by Reason's more broadly based attack on his manner of working, an attack which results in the narrator's proposal of a commitment and hope in his making,[27] just as Imaginative's attack had resulted in a definite, though weaker, defense of it.

Reacting to Reason's rebuke by saying he knows in his conscience "what Crist wolde that ich wrouhte" (83), prayers of a perfect man and discreet penance, he arouses a further attack by the character Conscience, who tells him it is no perfection to go begging in cities. Now he responds by admitting his error and continuing in a new vein about his work in the sense we have been attempting to grasp throughout this discussion:

> "That ys soth," ich seide · "and so ich by-knowe,
> That ich haue tynt tyme · and tyme mysspended;
> And ȝut, ich hope, as he · that ofte haueth chaffared,
> That ay hath lost and lost · and atte laste hym happed
> He bouhte suche a bargayn · he was the bet euere,
> And sette hus lost at a lef · at the laste ende,
> Suche a wynnynge hym warth · thorw wordes of hus grace;
>> *Simile est regnum celorum thesauro abscondito in agro,*
>> *& cetera:*
>> *Mulier que inuenit dragmam vnam, et cetera;*
> So hope ich to haue · of hym that is al-myghty
> A gobet of hus grace · and bygynne a tyme,
> That alle tymes of my tyme · to profit shal turne."
>   (C, vi. 92–101)

Beginning by comparing himself to a merchant—maintaining even in a simile the aversion for manual labor—who has finally made the deal that pays off so well that all previous losses become negligible, Langland gradually shifts the focus to the speaking Will, the third-person merchant playing, as it were, the tenor to the first-person vehicle of Langland himself. But the possibility that he is talking about himself as a maker is only suggested: the line that introduces the scriptural references, "Suche a wynnynge hym warth · thorw wordes of hus grace," hints at a double meaning as it makes the transition from the merchant of similitude to the poet of reality. Those words of his grace refer certainly to the salvation parables from Matthew 13:44 and Luke 15:9. But the line can also be read as saying such a winning of the Lord's grace, still represented by the parables, came to him through his, that is the poet's words. If such a reading is possible, then we must also be receptive to the possibility that when he states his hope to "bygynne a tyme, / That alle tymes of my tyme · to profit shal turne," he is referring to his work as poet. The charm of the third try, supported by the merchant's successful bargain after two losses, tempts a comparison with the three versions of his poem, the third and last of which he has already begun—not merely for the sake of the revision but for the sake of the completion that will justify for eternity the lifetime of labor it has taken.[28] And the relevance of the sense of *time* as it pertains to prosody, which it has had since the mid-eleventh century (*OED* at 10), as well as the primary relevance of the more common sense of

194

"the period contemporary with the life, occupancy, or activity of some one" (*OED* at 4), contributes to the conviction that an understanding of these lines that includes the notion of poetic activity is based on more than suspicion. And what could be more appropriate as a measure of the Almighty's grace with which a maker with words hopes to begin his redemptive work than a *gobet*, literally a mouthful?

If Langland is writing about his making here, as so much evidence in the passage and other parts of the poem indicates, then why does he appear to be reluctant to write of it explicitly, as he has in other places? To put it differently, if he has resolved the question of the worth of his poetic activity, why does he express that resolution in an oblique, almost secretive, way? The answer, I believe, comes in two stages. First, Langland, wishing to raise this very question, deliberately writes in this indirect way about his making—as if in the narrative moment of this speech he felt compelled to hide what he has found, though he is also moved to publicize it. Thus, the passage signals a paradoxical message of simultaneous, though differently realized, assertion and suppression of the poet's discovery. The explanation of his communicating both the need to keep it hidden as well as to reveal that he is hiding it comes from a brilliant instance of Langland's use of scriptural quotation. The two parables of salvation, as mentioned above, speak for Langland as if they were his own words, leading us to a full recognition of what has happened and why. We are required merely to complete each quotation in order to establish the context in which we may understand the two-fold significance of the form Langland's own discourse has taken. "The kingdom of heaven is like unto a treasure hidden in a field," goes the Vulgate translation of the line quoted from Matthew in the poem, and the apostle continues,

> Which a man having found, hid it, and for joy thereof
> goeth, and selleth all that he hath, and buyeth that field.
> (... quem qui invenit homo, abscondit, et prae gaudio illius
> vadit, et vendit universa quae habet, et emit agrum illum.)

Langland's making is that field, to which he as the poet-merchant, united finally in the parable, has invested all he has. That he, as one man, has found the treasure of his salvation in it is cause enough for him to joyously purchase it and keep it hid. But as a poet, his voice joins with that of the woman in Luke, who finding the silver coin she had lost, calls her friends and neighbors to rejoice with her, *Congratulamini mihi*, for his poem-making has led him to the

195

exalted service of his God and Maker as His minstrel. And greater cause, still, for his joy in his minstrelsy must lie in the realization that his service is treasured as well in the court of Heaven, which the traditional interpretation of the woman in the parable as *Dei Sapientia* both inspires and affirms.

—— NOTES ——

[1] *Children of the Mire, Modern Poetry from Romanticism to the Avant-Garde*, The Charles Eliot Norton Lectures, 1971–72, trans. Rachel Phillips (Cambridge, MA., 1974), p. 61.

[2] *Inferno* IV. 102. All quotations from and references to Dante's *Commedia* are from the edition of Charles S. Singleton, *The Divine Comedy*, 3 vols., Bollingen Series 80 (Princeton, 1970–75).

[3] I am aware of the lack of unanimity among Dante students on the precise significance of this episode; however, even a radically individualistic interpretation like Mark Musa's in *Advent at the Gates: Dante's Comedy* (Bloomington, IN., 1974), pp. 111–28, does not appreciably affect the basic point I am making here.

[4] See, for example, Thomas Goddard Bergin, "Dante's Provençal Gallery," *A Diversity of Dante* (New Brunswick, NJ, 1969), pp. 87–111; orig. pub. *Speculum*, 40 (1965). See also, Teodolinda Barolini, "Bertran de Born and Sordello: The Poetry of Politics in Dante's *Comedy*," *PMLA*, 94 (1979), 395–405.

[5] See Singleton's note, *Purgatorio*, Vol. 2, Commentary, II. 76 ff., pp. 35–36.

[6] *Odyssey* XI. 204 f. See Macrobius, *The Saturnalia*, trans. Percival Vaughan Davies (New York, 1969), Book 5, Chapters 5.14 and 7.8, pp. 302, 308–09.

[7] For the definitive discussion of the Exodus conversion figure, see Charles S. Singleton, "In Exitu Israel de Aegypto," *Dante: A Collection of Critical Essays*, ed. John Freccero (Englewood Cliffs, NJ., 1965), pp. 102–21; orig. pub. *78th Annual Report of the Dante Society of America* (1960).

[8] It is worth noting here that in the commentaries on the *Aeneid* by Fulgentius and Bernardus Silvestris, Anchises is interpreted as the supreme deity and father of all. See "The Exposition of the Content of Virgil," 22, *Fulgentius the Mythographer*, trans. Leslie George Whitbread (Columbus, OH., 1971), p. 132; *Commentum Bernardi Silvestris super sex libros Eneidos Virgilii*, ed. William Riedel (Greifswald, 1924), p. 9.

[9] *The Literary Criticism of Dante Alighieri*, trans. and ed. Robert S. Haller (Lincoln, NE., 1973); *The Latin Works of Dante* (New York, 1969, orig. pub. J. M. Dent, 1904).

[10] *De Vulgari Eloquentia* II.8.4, Haller, p. 49.

[11] It is noteworthy that this non-visual union of poet and musician is supported by the absence of attempts to depict the episode in manuscript miniatures. See Peter Brieger, Millard Meiss, and Charles S. Singleton, *Illuminated Manuscripts of the Divine Comedy*, 2 vols., Bollingen Series 81 (Princeton, 1969), I, 159–60; II, 332–35.

[12] K. Foster and P. Boyde, *Dante's Lyric Poetry*, 2 vols. (Oxford, 1967), II, Commentary, pp. 166–67, 173; for text, see I, The Poems, Text and Translation, no. 61, pp. 107–11.

[13] In addition to the testimony of Dante's own *Convivio*, ed. G. Busnelli and G. Vandelli (Florence, 1934); English trans. *Dante's Convivio*, William Walrond Jackson (Oxford, 1909), there is a long line of scholarly support for this view: see, for example, John Smyth Carroll, *Prisoners of Hope* (London, 1906), p. 33; and Pietro Calí, *Allegory and Vision in Dante and Langland* (Cork, 1971), p. 78 and notes 10–11.

[14] Etienne Gilson, *Dante and Philosophy*, trans. David Moore (New York, 1963), p. 93.

[15] See W. F. Jackson Knight, *Vergil, Epic and Anthropology* (New York, 1967), p. 71.

[16] Singleton, *Purgatorio*, Vol. 2, Commentary, p. 42.

[17] George Kane, *The Autobiographical Fallacy in Chaucer and Langland Studies*, The Chambers Memorial Lecture Delivered at University College London 2 March 1965 (London, 1965), p. 16.

[18] R. W. Chambers, *Man's Unconquerable Mind* (1939; rpt. Philadelphia, 1953), p. 109; E. Talbot Donaldson, *Piers Plowman, The C-Text and Its Poet*, Yale Studies in English, 113 (1949; rpt. London, 1966), p. 220.

[19] This and all subsequent quotations and references to the C-Text are from the three-text edition of Walter W. Skeat, *The Vision of William Concerning Piers the Plowman*, Vol. 1, Text (London, 1886, rpt. 1924 and 1954).

[20] Respectively, George Kane, *Piers Plowman: The Evidence for Authorship* (London, 1965), p. 64; and S. T. Knight, "Satire in *Piers Plowman*," in *Piers Plowman: Critical Approaches*, ed. S. S. Hussey (London, 1969), p. 291.

[21] Anne Middleton, "The Idea of Public Poetry in the Reign of Richard II," *Speculum*, 53 (1978), 103.

[22] See *The C-Text and Its Poet*, p. 136. The following discussion of minstrelsy in the poem is based on Donaldson's keen analysis of the subject, pp. 136–55. All quotations and references to the B-text are from the edition of George Kane and E. Talbot Donaldson, *Piers Plowman: The B Version* (London, 1975).

[23] Donaldson, *The C-Text and Its Poet*, p. 155.

[24] The connection between the openings of B, xii and C, vi was pointed out by Mabel Day, "The Revisions of 'Piers Plowman,'" *MLR*, 23 (1928),

2, in terms of the earlier passage, along with others, contributing personal details to the later passage. Day believes the autobiographical passage is an interpolation and speculates that it was at this point in C's revisions of B that "he decided to insert an autobiographical passage earlier in the poem." Day favors multiple authorship and generally views the C-poet as inferior, while I understand the revisions to be the result of a single highly self-conscious poet who is deeply engrossed—*not tinkering*—with his poem. See Donaldson, *The C-Text and Its Poet*, Chap. I, "The C-Text and Its Critics," pp. 1–19 *passim*.

[25] Judith H. Anderson, *The Growth of a Personal Voice*, Piers Plowman *and* The Faerie Queene (New Haven, 1976), p. 84. My discussion of this episode is also indebted to the erudition and insights of Morton W. Bloomfield, *Piers Plowman as a Fourteenth-Century Apocalypse* (New Brunswick, N.J., 1961), pp. 170–74; Elizabeth D. Kirk, *The Dream Thought of Piers Plowman* (New Haven, 1972), pp. 139–45; A. C. Spearing, *Medieval Dream-Poetry* (Cambridge, 1976), pp. 155–62; and Joseph S. Wittig, "'Piers Plowman' B, Passus IX-XII: Elements in the Design of the Inward Journey," *Traditio*, 28 (1972), 264–79.

[26] *Piers Plowman: The A Version, Will's Visions of Piers Plowman and Do-Well*, ed. George Kane (London, 1960). For a cogent argument for reading the lines as representing the triad of Mixed Life—teaching, Active Life—husbandry, and Contemplative Life—travailing in prayers, see Kane's note on line 232, p. 449.

[27] In light of this interpretation, it is likely that Skeat was right to read the *made of* in line 5 of this section as "made verses about," and that Kenneth Sisam, ed., *Fourteenth-Century Verse and Prose* (Oxford, 1923), p. 233, and Donaldson, *The C-Text and Its Poet*, p. 201 note 8 are wrong to insist that Skeat's is a forced translation.

[28] Perhaps this view of the poem in some way qualifies the sense of "partialness and inadequacy" that Mary Carruthers concludes is its "anguished premise" in her *The Search for St. Truth: A Study of Meaning in* Piers Plowman (Evanston, 1973), p. 173.

GRAMMAR, POETIC FORM, AND THE LYRIC EGO: A MEDIEVAL *A PRIORI*
JUDSON BOYCE ALLEN

THE BUSINESS of this essay is to define a mode of the lyric, which was supremely enacted in the medieval experience, and was then normal. It is a mode which has also been enacted in other eras; in our own it tends to occur primarily as popular song. I presume, in discussing it, that poetry exists not as instances of synchronic textuality, but as instances of human behavior—hence the word "enact." Within this presumption, I must begin with a distinction: some lyrics are clear and immediately intelligible. Others seem obscure and hermetic but are not properly read until their obscurities are so clarified that the achieved experience of reading is of something clear and intelligible. Still others are difficult in a way which is intrinsic to their existence. The second category, as I shall show, is a disguised version of the first. My fundamental distinction then is between the clear or immediately intelligible lyric, and the difficult lyric.

The second is the normally esteemed modern form. Our lyrics are printed things, which we deal with by radically attentive reading, laboriously repeated. When properly accomplished, this reading amounts to a de-coding of an encoded text. The code, of course, is intended. The difficulties are deliberately imposed by the poet-maker of the text. Coping with them is somehow the necessary action by which the ego of the poem—its silent speaker—is discovered. In this discovery, the possibility of relation between the self and the Other becomes a difference[1] which, though never overcome, is strongly and even clearly realized. This realization is the point of the text, and of its reading. What the lyric enacts is the simultaneous presence to each other, realization of each other, of two ego centers.

The medieval version of this difference, as might be expected, is the distance between man and God, and the discourse which relates man and God works in precisely the same way as does the difficult lyric. Overcoming the unintelligibilities of God's word requires exertions whose violence, may I say, enacts that cognition which is relation to God. Saint Gregory defines this process for us in neatly conventional Christian terms, in the prologue of his commentary on *Canticles*.

> Postquam a paradisi gaudiis expulsum est genus humanum, in istam peregrinationem uitae praesentis ueniens caecum cor ab spiritali intellectu habet. Cui caeco cordi si diceretur uoce diuina: "Sequere deum" vel "Dilige deum," sicut ei in lege dictum est, semel foris missum et per torporem infidelitatis frigidum non caperet, quod audiret. Idcirco per quaedam enigmata sermo diuinus animae torpenti et frigidae loquitur et de rebus, quas nouit, latenter insinuat ei amore, quem non nouit.
>
> Allegoria enim animae longe a deo positae quasi quandam machinam facit, ut per illam leuetur ad deum. Interpositis quippe enigmatibus, dum quiddam in uerbis cognoscit, quod suum est, in sensu uerborum intellegit, quod non est suum, et per terrena uerba separatur a terra. Per hoc enim, quod non abhorret cognitum, intellegit quiddam incognitum. Rebus enim nobis notis, per quas allegoriae conficiuntur, sententiae diuinae uestiuntur et, dum recognoscimus exteriora uerba, peruenimus ad interiorem intellegentiam.[2]
>
> (After the human race was expelled from the joys of paradise, coming into the wandering of this present life mankind had a heart blind to spiritual understanding. So if the divine voice were to say to persons blind of heart, "Follow God" or "Love God," as the law does say to them, they cannot get what they hear, both because they have been cast out, and because of the cold listlessness of their infidelity. On account of this condition the divine word speaks to the cold, listless soul in puzzles, and from things which the soul knows, God secretly insinuates in it a love which it does not know.

> Allegory operates like a kind of machine on the soul which is far from God, that through it the soul may be raised to God. The puzzles in fact are put in the way, and while one recognizes something in the words which is familiar, he understands in the meaning of the words something which is not familiar, and is separated from the earth by earthly words. By explicitly not rejecting the known, one understands something unknown. For things known to us, out of which allegories are constructed, are dressed with divine significance, and, while we recognize the words which are obvious, we come through to the deep truth.)[3]

I do not claim, of course, that the allegorical hermeneutic which Gregory follows in decoding Canticles is the same one which we use to decode the more hermetic lyrics of Wallace Stevens. I do claim that the two decoding processes are semiotically identical, in that in both cases their object, their ideal result, is the achievement of a meaningful communication between reader and Other. In both cases, difficulties are imposed upon the act of reading which "quasi quadam machina" effect for the coping reader an accomplishment of understanding which could not, presumably, have been communicated by direct and simple statement. The allegorical enigmata work because the reader is fallen—a sinner—and therefore incapable of direct and unmediated experience of God. The difficulties of the encoded lyric work because the modern reader, like the modern poet, is a solipsist—that is, he lives in a social and linguistic culture which permits him no easy and literal access to meanings other than his own. The Other which allegory helps the reader attain is God. The Other which the encoded lyric permits one to sense is an alien ego and its statement.

This is the difficult lyric—a language event to which difficulties are intrinsic, which would fail if it were clear, because there can be no perception of Otherness in clarity. Distinguished from this type of lyric is its opposite, the clear lyric—the kind typically made in the Middle Ages. It is this lyric which is my subject. I have defined its opposite with such care at the outset in order to make explicit this opposite's concern with the Other, because there is no evocation of the Other in the clear lyric. Rather, the clear lyric is a genre in which the question of the Other, in all its dark and violent imponderability, does not come up. Instead, we have the lyric ego, which this paper defines.

The clarity of many medieval lyrics is obvious even to modern readers. Other medieval lyrics, however, are allusive or conventional in ways which present great difficulties to modern scholarship and require for their understanding a great deal of reconstruction of historical context, as well as of the form and meaning of the rhetorical or symbolic conventions which they enact. But there is an important difference, easily obscured by the passage of time, between a text whose difficult code its ideally expected reader experiences by decoding, and a text whose complex use of convention intends for its ideally expected reader a refined and even mannerist but immediately intelligible experience. To the modern scholar, the two kinds of text may seem the same, since he experiences equal and similar difficulties in decoding the cryptic utterances of the first and the no longer active conventions of the second.

We face the further difficulty that a text in the difficult category may, with the passage of time and in the presence of readers with different presumptions, become a text which is taken as, and which has become, clear. Canticles is such a text. Even in Gregory's time, the allegorical meanings upon whose discovery his "machine" depended were, in point of fact, both conventional and clear, even though they were to be further elaborated by devout exegesis. Nevertheless, since his theme is the achievement of communication between God and fallen man, it is the obscurity—the difficulty— which he emphasizes in his hermeneutic theory. By the time of Nicholas of Lyra, what gets emphasis is clarity. In his comment, Nicholas takes Canticles as the third part of Solomon's collected works; its point is "inducens ad amorem superne felicitatis" (persuasion to the love of heavenly happiness). The obvious literal meaning of the words, which describe a carnal love relationship, must not be taken seriously, "propter quod descriptio talis amoris non videtur ad libros sacre scripture canonicos pertinere" (because the description of such a love does not seem to be suitable to the canonical books of holy scripture). The book must be taken "parabolice" (parabolically); this done, "tunc facile esset hunc librum exponere" (it should be easy to expound this book).[4] The convention is established; the clear, literal meaning of Canticles is the love between Christ and the Church. Nicholas does not neglect the devotional component of this understanding, of course. In that it persuades to a particular kind of love, the book is obviously taken as primarily affective. But the strategy by which this love is induced is not that exegetical exercise which overcomes difficulties in a text deliberately made obscure; rather, it happens by following a text, which, under the power of a well-exercised convention, repeats and celebrates a meaning already well known. Here, as in Pope, "true wit is nature to advantage dressed, / what oft was thought, but ne'er so well expressed."

My claim in this paper is that the medieval lyric, even in those courtly modes whose conventions and allusions often baffle us, is, in terms of my basic distinction, clear rather than difficult. Medieval lyric does not enact the kind of code whose reading effects, by means of "quadam machina" (a sort of machine), a link of communication between reader and Other. Rather, it uses the strategy of clarity to achieve quite different effects. In order to argue this claim, and to describe these effects, I must make one assumption and answer two related questions. The assumption I make is that Canticles, at least from the twelfth century and onwards, may be taken as an example of the clear lyric, and that therefore the medieval experience of Canticles can be presumed to be like the experience of other medieval lyrics.[5] The first question, to which I have already alluded, is the question of the lyric ego—in the clear lyric as I define it, who is speaking? Who can be speaking, if there is no Other, and so in a sense, no communication? The second question is the question of process—if the difficult lyric requires for its reading an achievement of decoding (which probably in most cases is holistic rather than linear) leading to the intuition of a communicating Other, then by contrast what process defines the experience of the lyric of clarity?

I have argued elsewhere that the medieval courtly lyric, exemplified in the *grand chant courtois* and particularly in the definitive poems of Bernard de Ventadour, does not exist in linguistic circularity, as a merely narcissistic code enclosed only in self-referential language, but that it does have reference and a referent. I tried to discuss this reference in terms of audience, and showed that, at least in the case of the *grand chant courtois*, lyrics refer to audience with a tropological effect, tending to displace audience into its ideal or anagogical mode of existence.[6] This conclusion depended on the presumption, which medieval literary critics make necessary,[7] that the rhetorical effect of a text, and the glosses which accumulate around it, are intrinsic parts of its whole integrity. Medieval poems, that is, are larger than textuality, and in that article I based my conclusion on extra-textual considerations. Here, I concentrate on the text as such—its content and its form. For the medieval lyric, the question of content is above all else a question of speaker, because of the ubiquitous literal presence of first and second person pronouns—regardless of specific subject matter, whether love, worship, or whatever, it is the lyric ego which the lyric most significantly contains and presents. Forms vary—there are, for instance, a number of lyric stanzas—but there is, as we shall see, a consistent formal process. Both the ego and the process have distinctively medieval definitions.

Except for the autobiographical criticism of lyrics in the tradition of the *grand chant courtois* preserved for us in the thirteenth and fourteenth century *razos* of poems and "biographies" of troubadours, the great bulk of what medieval critics wrote about what we would call poetry (including, under my presumptions, Canticles) is rhetorical and ethical criticism, or formalist criticism in the narrow sense of discussions of meters and ornaments. What they wrote in addition about specific texts was mostly paraphrase or precis, including, of course, allegorization. With regard to the questions that this essay attempts to answer, medieval critics have very little to say. But since one thing they make unmistakably clear is that the existence of poems constitutes no special category, we are justified in casting a larger net for evidence. Discussions of grammar, by defining language, necessarily define the language of poetry. Further, what is not said directly may be said indirectly; from statements which in some way exist as betrayal[8] as well as discourse, it is possible to discover what was presumed about poems.

One such betrayal, which is the ground of my medieval definition of the lyric ego, was discussed long ago by Leo Spitzer. When Pierre de Roissy, Chancellor of Chartres, composed his *Manuale de mysteriis ecclesiae* by plagiarizing from the *Poenitentiale* of Robert of Flamborough,

> he even borrowed from him, *tel quel*, certain autobiographical facts which, in the light of historical evidence, could not possibly apply to himself. For example, when we read in Roissy: "Ego tamen ... a duobus parisiensibus episcopis, Odone et Petry, habui ut ubique eorum auctoritate dispensarem ..." (I nevertheless had the right from two Paris bishops, Odo and Peter, to dispense everywhere by their authority), we must realize that the privilege of dispensation of which he speaks was granted only to Flamborough, just as it was Flamborough alone who transferred to papal authority the case referred to in the words: "superstitem, ut ordinaretur, ad papam transmisi" (I sent the witness to the pope according to regulations). Thus, Roissy is substituting his own ego to [sic] that of his source.[9]

Spitzer goes on to show that Marie de France did the same thing, raises the central question of Dante, and then discusses such figures

as Francois Villon and the Archpriest of Hita. What the article seeks
to define in all this is the "poetic 'I' of the medieval tradition, which
speaks in the name of man in general" (p. 419), and which exists in
contrast to the "empirical 'I'" which Proust wittily defined as "un
monsieur qui raconte et qui dit 'je' . . . qui est Je et qui n'est pas
toujours moi" [a somebody who tells a story and says 'I' . . . who is I
and who is not always me] (p. 418).

This easy medieval plagiarism of first person pronouns does
indeed loosen medieval from autobiographical reference, as Spitzer
claims, and does therefore tend toward the achievement of a
discourse which is that of generic rather than particular man. But to
what end? Spitzer has, I think, failed to make certain necessary
distinctions, which I can most efficiently make by example. I may
listen to a person tell me about Paris for at least three reasons:
because he can help me feel what it is like to be there, because I am
going there next week and wish recent data on restaurants, libraries,
and the possible presence of friends, or, finally, because the person
talking is imposing on the Eiffel Tower a phallic significance which
may help me diagnose his psychosis. All three of these interactions
may exist in poetic as well as empirical modes, but in either case the
first asks that I displace myself to become the ego of the description,
the second, that I receive information which comes from a presumably trustworthy witness, and the third, that I achieve insight
into the mode and significance of a point of view of someone other
than myself. My examples, which refer to Paris, are empirical; in the
poetic mode, the first example corresponds most precisely to
Spitzer's ego which speaks for Everyman, the second is supremely
represented by Dante, and the third corresponds to Proust's "monsieur qui raconte," and to the encoded modern lyric, as well as,
mutatis mutandis, to Canticles under Gregory's definition. Spitzer
has unnecessarily confused his point by including Dante and Villon,
but the fundamental betrayal stands—authors who can without
embarrassment plagiarize first person statements presume a certain
interchangeability of speakers, that is, they presume that certain
kinds of statements which include the first person pronoun may be
validly made by anyone, not because they are true statements about
any possible world or situation, but because they are the kind of true
statements because of which any given speaker, by attaching himself
to them, becomes himself true.

Paul Zumthor, speaking about the *grand chant courtois*, in the
context of a discussion of the possibility of medieval autobiography,[10] says that the *chant* "est un mode de dire entierement référé
à un *je* qui, tout en fixant le plan et les modalités du discours, n'a

d'autre existence pour nous que grammaticale" (is a mode of speech totally in reference to an "I" which, while it fixes the plane and modality of discourse, has for us no other existence than grammatical).[11] The grammar which Zumthor has in mind is modern, and his consequent analysis is dominated by linguistic concerns, but he raises nevertheless an extremely important question for which there is a medieval as well as a modern answer: what is the nature of grammatical existence? The imagery of solecism and sodomy in the *Complaint of Nature* of Alanus de Insulis would lead us to expect an answer both serious and ontological; medieval grammatical discussion satisfies this expectation, and with a distinction which sheds upon the lyric ego—the grammatical "je" of lyric poetry—a great deal of helpful light.

The course of grammatical studies in the eleventh and twelfth centuries has been defined in two seminal articles by R. W. Hunt.[12] He begins with two collections of glosses prior to Peter Helias' *Summa* on Priscian, in which the then fashionable willingness to involve logic in grammatical discussion was clearly established. In the light of these glosses, he makes clear that Peter Helias, far from being the innovator who related logic and grammar, was rather one "whose part was ordering and integration" (39), and who, though he did indeed use logic in his analysis of grammar, did not mix the two disciplines needlessly or carelessly. After Peter Helias, Hunt places emphasis on Ralph of Beauvais and glosses related to him; his work is innovative in considering "the development of syntax and the reapplication of the study of authors to grammar" (ibid.). But Ralph has been since forgotten, because "the development of grammar did not proceed along the lines he marked out. The assimilation of the new Aristotle and the works of Arabic logicians led to a new speculative grammar; and the discussions on syntax were conducted on rigorously logical lines" (ibid.).

The literary study of grammar never absolutely died out; the classics continued to be taught as well as read, as surviving school commentaries prove. But the ability of medieval Latin poets to write in classical meters diminishes markedly after the twelfth century; the logical and philosophical significance of grammar dominates. There is not room here to document, or even illustrate this situation in general; my point is that this logical, philosophic, speculative handling of grammar deposited with regard to pronouns, and especially with regard to the first person and second person pronouns which dominate lyric utterance, definitions which both define the lyric ego and confirm, in that definition, what other

206

internal and external evidence connected with lyrics would seem to imply.

Priscian defines pronouns as words which "substantiam solum sine qualitate significant" (signify substance only without quality),[13] and further distinguishes between first and second person pronouns, which are "semper demonstrativa—utraque enim, ut dictum est, praesens ostenditur persona" (XII. 3, p. 578, always demonstrative, for in each, as was said, a present person is shown), and the others, which may be demonstrative, but are often relative, in that they do not guarantee the presence of anything without some specifying noun. The speculative grammarians made much of both these points,[14] and the distinction which accorded special substantiality to first and second person pronouns persisted into at least the Renaissance.[15] "Substance without quality" narrowly and carefully understood, of course, does not guarantee the real presence of any primordial material, as Peter Helias was careful to point out,[16] but such care was probably unusual. The word "demonstrative" as applied in these analyses to first and second person pronouns in a manner contradicted his distinction; what the medieval grammarians meant by it was a kind of guarantee of presence, and not the mere pointing which the word now means in grammatical contexts. Of this presence the most explicit statement I have found, and the one which will permit the greatest clarity of approach to the lyric ego, occurs in an early gloss on the *Doctrinale* of Alexander Villedieu:

> Ad aliud dicendum est quod talis modus loquendi inventus est ad exhibendum reverentiam persona excellenti. Sed maior reverentia exhibetur ei presenti, quam absenti, causa favoris acquirendi. Propter hoc potius pronomine prime vel secunde peronse utimur, quod rem presentem vel quasi presentem significat, quam pronomine tertie rem absentem designante.[17]

> (Otherwise it should be said that this manner of speaking was invented to show reverence to an important person. But greater reverence is shown to a present person than to an absent one, for the sake of gaining favor. Therefore we rather use the first or second person pronoun, which signifies a thing present or as if present, than the third person pronoun which designates something absent.)

In the light of all this grammatical doctrine, the ego, which in medieval terms is only grammatical, is nevertheless quite powerful, and in a way which defines precisely what we should expect from medieval lyric, which in most cases utters the position of a definite but unspecified ego whose position the audience is invited to occupy. Like my hypothetical tourist friend, the lyric tells me what it feels like—to be in Paris, to be in love, to despair of love, to pity the pains of Christ or the sorrows of the virgin, or whatever. That the pronoun signifies substance without quality both makes demands on reality, in involving substance, and invites qualification. That first and second person pronouns are demonstrative, that is, presume or guarantee presence, again makes demands upon reality—uttered in the lyric poem, they exist as ideal or universal to each member of the audience's own particularity and invite him to perfect or universalize himself by occupying that language as his own. Acting in this way, the lyric does not communicate—the physical ego of the performer is not relevant but enacts itself only to invite plagiarization—rather, it is, a definite and informing ego position within which any given human hearer is invited to become true.

Lyric of this kind is, of course, still being made and performed. Popular love songs still exist to permit lovers to say to one another, "They're singing our song," and to find in the performed words of a phonograph the postures of emotion which are to them truer and more affective than any they could invent for themselves. From time to time, especially with adolescents, the pronoun position occupied is that of the second person, and the love emotion is directed toward the performer. But even here the ego is more plagiarized than merely real; public adulation of Elvis Presley was essentially directed toward a persona—which Elvis the person was of course careful to occupy—just as religious devotion is directed toward saints which customarily hagiography has made out of persons who as human beings have been taken unaware by martyrdom or some other behavior whose appearance can be seen as especially holy. But the essence is not the "you" but the "I"—regardless of the object toward which the attention of the poem is directed, and regardless of whether that attention is directed by a statement by the "I" or to the "you," the poem remains an invitation to each hearer to displace himself, as particular ego, into the ideal monologue (or dialogue) of the poem.[18]

When the hearer displaces himself thus, what he experiences is the form of the poem. If my initial schema holds, what this means is not a meditation on an array of difficulties, read through and then analysed wholistically in an effort to reach an Other and hidden ego, but rather a serial experience of significant words, taken as one's own utterance, in the course of which one is identified, or identifies one's self in growing insight, as an ego of a certain type of essence. Once again, as in the case of medieval grammar, I have a comment which states, in medieval terms, a useful definition of this experience.

The doctrinal context of this comment is the convention under which late medieval literary critics discussed the form of the texts in which they were interested. Normally, they held that the formal cause of any given text was double, and involved a *forma tractandi* and a *forma tractatus*.[19] The *forma tractatus* is simple enough; it is that form of a text which is defined by its table of contents, or by the fact that there is a part or paragraph one, which is followed by part or paragraph two, and so on. By virtue of this form, parts relate "adinvicem" in serial order. In addition there is the *forma tractandi*. It derives from and adapts an earlier topic, that of the *modus agendi*, under which commentators of the twelfth century and before usually specified that a given text proceeded "metrice" or "poetice." The *forma tractandi*, as a techical term related to the concept of formal cause, cannot of course antedate the adoption of Aristotelian terminology of the causes, but the discursive and logical concerns which it reports of course existed earlier. Medieval discussion of the *forma tractandi* self-consciously presumes a norm—that the *forma tractandi* is a fivefold scheme, and that its modes are definition, division, proof, refutation, and the giving of examples (*definitiva, divisiva, probativa, reprobativa, et exemplorum positiva*). In general ideological harmony with this norm, there is a good deal of variation; the specific modes which most significantly occur as variation are praise and blame, which elicit a punning second meaning, of which medieval critics were aware, from the mode *reprobativa*. Under these presumptions, medieval texts have two simultaneous forms—one that of the literal text, as an arrangement of words, and the other that of the text's discursive or thematic strategy. This second form may, and often does, exist independent of the text in question; this possibility generates complex relations between texts, and between any given text and its real world.

In these terms, *Canticles* seems to have been normally taken as the third part of a three-part work—that is, the writings of Solomon, which include also *Proverbs* and *Ecclesiastes*. This grouping and the different modality of each part, are already established in the *glosa ordinaria*.[20] Hugh of St. Cher refers to the three as a "triplex opus" (triple work).[21] Thus it is only natural that discussions of *forma tractandi* and *forma tractatus* should be made in terms of the entire *opus triplex* and that commentators should consequently permit themselves to ignore the question of the form of Canticles taken by itself. At least this is what Nicholas of Lyra does.[22] But there does exist one commentary on Canticles which raises, for it alone, the question of form, and comes to conclusions which, as might be expected from the lyric character of Canticles, neatly define the process of the lyric experience. This commentary is the one written by Aegidius Romanus, a prolific and intellectually conventional writer of the later thirteenth century, from whom one may be justified in expecting opinions which are intelligent, but not notably creative or eccentric. His comment is as follows:

> Consueuit enim distingui duplex forma scilicet forma tractandi, que est modus agendi, et forma tractatus, quae est ordinatio capitulorum adinuicem. Modus autem agendi in aliis scientiis est approbatiuus, et improbatiuus. In doctrina vero sacra potissime in canone esse videtur inspiratiuus, idest reuelatiuus, quia magis talis textus innititur reuelationi quam probationi. Modus autem in isto libro specialiter videtur esse affectiuus, desideratiuus, et contemplatiuus. Vnde et glossa tenet quod modus huius libri est ostensiuus quali desiderio membra capiti adhaereant, et ei placere contendant, et quali affectione sponsus ecclesiam diligat. Vnde modus agendi huius libri conuenienter notatur per huiusmodi dulcedinem, cum dicit (Vox tua dulcis.) quia complacentia, affectio, et desiderium, quandam dulcedinem amoris important. Ex hoc etiam potest haberi forma tractatus, quae talis debet esse, quale requirit modus agendi, immo quia ipse ordo capitulorum adinuicem bene intellectus animam demulcet et delectat, non inconuenienter forma tractatus per dulcendine[m] intelligitur.[23]

> (The form [of a text] is normally understood as double; there is a form of the treatment, which is the mode of procedure, and the form of the treatise, which is the ordering of the chapters in relation to one another. The mode of procedure in other sciences is proof and refutation.[24] In religious works and above all in the Bible the mode would seem to be inspirational, that is, revelational, because a text of this kind depends more on revelation than proof. But the mode in this book seems especially to be emotional, desiring, and contemplative; therefore the glosa states that the mode of this book is to show with what desire the members adhere to the head, and seek to please him, and with what affection the spouse loves the church. Therefore the mode of

procedure of this book is conveniently defined by a sweetness of this sort, when it says, "Your voice is sweet," because
pleasure, affection, and desire stimulate a certain sweetness
of love. The same situation determines the form of the
treatise, which ought to be what the mode of procedure
requires, and so because the order of the chapters in regard
to one another, as such well understood, soothes and
delights the soul, it is not inconvenient to understand the
form of the treatise through [the experience of] sweetness.)

This is an enormously dense and suggestive piece of criticism.
Though it presumes the traditional meaning for Canticles, and
though it reports as the effect of Canticles upon the reader the kind
of reaction which any sympathetic reading of the text itself would
elicit, it is unusual in medieval criticism[25] in describing this meaning
and effect in experiential rather than in merely cognitive terms. His
"ordinatio capitulorum adinuicem" makes of medieval additive
organization something highly coherent, if not organic; though the
modi through which scripture works effect cognition, they do so in
affective ways. Specifically in Canticles, the subject is love; the mode
of Canticles is to show that love, not as something objective, to be
known, but as something caused or "imported" by pleasure, affection, and desire. The sweetness of love, therefore, is that which the
book enacts for and in one who follows "ipse ordo capitulorum
adinuicem bene intellectus"—that is, who reads with the expectation
that this ordered experience which the text enacts for him will make
him sensible of what the text intends that he know and be. In the
case of Canticles and the *grand chant courtois*, what is enacted is
love and the condition of the lover and the beloved.[26] In the case of
much English lyric, what is enacted is the appropriate emotional
attitude toward the fact that some relatively simple Christian event
or doctrine is true. In all these cases, the human experience of the
text, or in the text, is as Aegidius describes it. Displaced, the ego of
the audience occupies the ego of the text and experiences its words
as a *forma tractatus*—a serially ordered event—whose experience is
its meaning and its mode of communication.

This, then, is my *a priori*—that the typical medieval lyric is a
"clear" poem, whose ego invites the occupation of audience, and
whose meaning is the serial experience of the text. That this *a priori*
should be true of some lyrics should be intuitively axiomatic—
rhetorically there are only three ways to hear my hypothetical
reporter on Paris. That it should be true of most medieval lyrics
should also be intuitively axiomatic, both because achieved medi-

eval self-hood normally involved subsuming one's particularity under some norm or type of status, condition, or estate, and "private" tended to mean "deprived," and because medieval activities, whether of rule, love, or service, tended to follow pre-written scripts, of which the Rule of St. Benedict and the rules of chivalry are obvious examples. Thus, though I shall begin the practical criticism which this *a priori* makes possible with a few obvious examples, whose exemplarity I shall try to cast into sharp relief by relating them to poems from other periods, I shall be dealing primarily with hard cases, presuming that if they can be seen to fit, then the easier cases will be obvious.

The justly famous Middle English lyric, "Sunset on Calvary,"[27] begins with the third person report of a sunset. But this is a common experience, which first person takes over in the second line, announcing pity and sympathy for Mary. The pun in the third line, which relates sunset to the passion in Christ, evokes a medieval association; the fourth line renews the pity on a more comprehensive scale. The poem, in expressing it, asks the reader to feel it; the sunset in the beginning, which of course everyone has seen, by its very banality displaces the poem into common experience, where it becomes anyone's words. To the extent that the pun is merely a convention, this common quality is enhanced; to the extent that it does generate a sense of insight, the insight is prepared for by the pity offered to Mary in the second line. There are no surprises.

A longer version of the rhetorical strategy of "Nou goth sonne vnder wod" is the Occitan lyric by Bernard de Ventadour, "Can vei la lauzeta mover."[28] Like the lyric "Nou goth sonne vnder wod," Bernard's poem begins with a common human experience—a sight of a bird. His strategy reminds us of Keats, and Hopkin's "The Windhover." Unlike Hopkins, and in a way like Keats, he evokes this experience only to alienate himself from it, and the poem continues inside a self-preoccupied love-accidia whose end is death. Neither the language nor the human condition being described is alien or impossible for any hearer; the progress of this emotion is conventional and predictable. Bernard announces that he has lost his heart and has left only desire. The natural comparison is to Narcissus; it is made. Then there are generalizations leading to particulars: "De las domnas me dezesper" (of ladies I despair); "Merces es perduda per ver" (Mercy is lost, in truth). The particulars of his situation are typical—at one point, proverbial. The alienated self is speaking really to himself; the absorption is one the audience is invited to share. Probably for most hearers, the ego of the audience does, in performance, become the ego of the poem; if so, then the final envoy, addressed to Tristan, is from a poetic ego to a character of romance—that is, an address entirely enclosed in poetry. If at this point the audience still has detachment left, the poem effects the same enclosure at the level of second person. The serial experience of the poem is its meaning. By combining enactions of alienation with acts of self-inclusion under generalizations, the words achieve an ever more radical enclosure of the speaker, and by extension the audience which, in overhearing, speaks. The envoy, then, by presuming this enclosure, is its final proof.[29] *Forma tractandi* is *forma tractatus*, they exist together at that point where psychological and logical processes intersect, as self is subsumed under a universal—in this case, despairing death.

In these cases the lyric ego achieves our displacement by beginning with a universal empirical experience, in relation to which (or alienation from which) audience and poem occupy together a common emotional ground, which is itself explicitly, and even at length, reported. The same effect may be achieved by empirical or narrative means alone. For instance, the Latin pastourelle, "Exiit diluculo,"[30] which Peter Dronke defends as both complete and of high quality,[31] describes a shepherdess going out with an odd little flock of three pairs of animals. In the meadow she notices a lone student, to whom she says, "veni mecum ludere" (come play with me). In so speaking she evokes the universal male fantasy of the willing maiden; she and the student will make a fourth pair, and every student or otherwise appropriate person in the poet's audience will project himself as half the pair. This narrative strategy leading to ego displacement is probably the one which dominates love song in all periods.[32] The "storybook romance" is possible only because human sentiment seems by nature accommodated to love according to one of a few often repeated formulaic scripts, and the fact that the *grand chant courtois* tends to achieve its effects more often by direct reporting of the lover's psychic condition than by examination of his love story is therefore consistent with *fin amors'* tendency to be more often aspiring and frustrated than active. But in both cases the appeal is to the ego of the audience, for whom the ego of the poem exists as a possible act or condition.

This same appeal is even more obvious in the case of the exclamatory lyric, such as "Sumer is icumen in" (*EL* XIII, no. 6). Words of celebration cannot be said without enacting, in some manner, the celebration which they are, and to enact by speaking is to be the speaker, the ego, of the utterance. The same is also true of proverbial or sententious utterance, which, whether in verse or not, is the kind of language most often involved when someone quotes language not his own if it were his own, in application to some particular of his own experience.[33] The medieval lyric is of course full of proverbs, both stated and implicit, as well as of analogous religious truisms, whose statement cannot avoid affirmation, and so commitment. According to Raymond Oliver, the English lyric exists to celebrate, persuade, and define; it is public, practical, and anonymous, spoken by types;[34] rhetorically, such poetry could not fail to implicate the ego of any audience not protected by the solipsism.

All these are, however, easy cases. I turn now to more difficult ones, which are, I suggest, of three kinds. First and most obviously, there are the lyrics with apparently unavoidable autobiographical significance. Related to these are lyrics which consist of, or are enclosed within, some kind of third person statement, to which they are necessarily then relative. Third, there are the lyrics which are "difficult" in ways which cannot be rationalized in terms of some originally clear but now inexplicable allusion or convention. Under this heading would seem to go all poems with ironic effects, unless the irony were so stable as to be banal.

By autobiographical significance, I mean only those rhetorical effects which a given lyric, in performance, might have upon the relation between audience and performer-author, and upon the interpretation which the lyric in performance would elicit of itself and of its maker. I do not mean the "biographical" details and stories later attached, by way of commentary, to the lyrics of the *chansonniers*. These stories, it seems to me, impose nothing autobiographical, but rather the reverse—they are evidence that medieval scribes and compilers felt, in the lyric texts, the need for some supplied concrete ego—some qualification of the first person "substantia sine qualitate" which could be supplied by making up a particular narrative for displacement into the ego of the poem. As concrete narrative, they are analogous to the schematic stories imposed as tropological interpretation on Ovid's *Metamorphoses*, whose contradictory number and variety did not embarrass the commentators who, inventing them, introduced them with the formula "Ovidius vult." What their existence betrays is no positivist interest in factual context of texts, but rather a philosophical conviction that universal or ideal statements expect particular illustration, just as particulars expect to be subsumed under some type or definition.

Any discussion of poems with autobiographical reference must begin with a distinction between poems performed by their author, for an audience who know that this is true, and poems which are performed by someone other than their author, in which autobiographical reference, including naming one's self in the third person, as in the famous, "Ieu sui Arnautz, q'amas l'aura" (Press, p. 184),[35] is plagiarized by a performer who is not the author. This distinction is imposed by the fact that the *grand chant courtois* in particular and medieval lyric in general, is more sung than read and can, therefore, never be properly considered without major emphasis on its existence as public behavior. Of poems performed by their author, a good test case is the work of the first troubadour, William, Count of Poitou. A genuine noble could most plausibly perform with autobiographical reference songs in the aristocratizing register; a mere troubadour of no distinguished background sings either in an ego of substance without quality, or confirms scandalous gossip. The second, of course, is uncourtly, and so rhetorically impossible, even if from time to time true. For William's poetry we must further distinguish, by asking whether his songs were sung in his own court, or at the court of his lord or a peer. In the second case he may rhetorically be or impersonate a troubadour, though his lyric ego is of course inevitably qualified by his presence in it; the first case raises the question of autobiography in its rhetorically purest form.

Some of William's poems, such as "Farai chansoneta nueva" (Press, pp. 20–23), express praising love of a lady which is quite general—it is, as it were, textually unqualified. In performance, it would be public, and common—the presence of William's voice would not so much appropriate it into autobiography, but underline its generality by the exemplary presence of his own nobility. As he sings, the general song displaces him into itself, and is reinforced. On the other hand, his "Companho, faray un vers [. . .] convinen" (Press, pp. 12–13) is very specific and allusive—riddling in a self-referential way—and at the same time quite self-conscious of the craft of poetry. One may presume that William does have the castles of Gimel and Nieul, and that the audience knows this. One may not, I think, presume that the ladies Agnes and Arsen are notorious as his mistresses, since "kiss and tell" has never been a convention of *fin amors*. But one may suppose that they are in William's audience, ladies of unimpeachable virtue, whether because of extreme youth, withered age, or invincible protection we may not guess; or on the other hand we may suppose they are absent and unknown. In either case William's relation to them is hypothetical—a tease—made all the more outrageous and hypothetical by its sudden juxtaposition with William's real castles, and the suddenly more intrusive three-vowel rhymes ending with "sagramen"—sacrament. Leading up to this is a discussion of horses which only a "vilan" would not understand, and which contains "mais de foudaz noy a de sen." Tone is difficult to gauge after more then eight centuries, but to my ear the poem clowns its way to Lady Arsen, so much so that it is, as performance, distanced even from its performer. At the same time it does let the audience know "what it feels like"—comic distance is here the same for comic and his audience. William is not communicating, but posing; the castles at the end add substance to the pose, without, I think, ejecting the absorbed audience.

I find the same tone in the famous "Farai un vers de dreyt nien" (Press, pp. 14–17); what the audience is invited to occupy here is not a loving ego, but an act of virtuosity. No one knows what might be its meaning,[36] in the presence of its brilliance, just as no one now knows what might be the meaning of "Twas brillig, and the slithy toves . . .," a poem universally admired, and even translated into both French and German, without compromising in any way the clear emptiness of its formal linguistic virtuosity. On the other hand, the lyric of death and parting, "Pos de chantar m'es pres talentz" (Press, pp. 22–25), is unavoidably autobiographical, in the sense that William like all men, will die, and like many, will leave behind a son. But this poem is in the future tense, and so distanced. We share it because, in the matter of death, all futures are the same. William's reference to himself qualified this future, without delivering us in any way from it; "any man's death diminishes me, because I am involved in mankind."

What William's presence gives to his poems is a certain exemplary reinforcement. They may, in fact, be literally autobiographical. But in performance, rhetorically taken as the courtly behavior of a noble host, they are the acts of a public man, who becomes, by being public and noble, universal. We may occupy his words, by hearing, or repeating them, and so qualify his lyric ego with our presence. We may hear his words as his, and order ourselves by analogy to his exemplum. In either case, we, the audience, are particulars in the presence of our definition, and the definition is clear.

Exemplum, of course, is third person narrative. Autobiographical significance, heard as such in a poem by an audience, is displaced third person qualification, which exists in parallel to the audience as its ego also occupies the poem. Explicit third person

216

qualification is, except for authors who name themselves, rare in lyric. But this complex relation between autobiography, lyric ego, audience, and third person exemplary qualification can be explicitly illustrated, in a context in which autobiographical facts are clearly established, and in which all these relationships are therefore matters of fact rather than speculation. My illustration is Abelard's set of *planctus* on Old Testament characters, and specifically his *planctus* on Sampson. For Dronke, these poems are evidence of "poetic originality"[37] ultimately because in them, and especially in the *Sampson*, Abelard achieves an irony which Dronke compares to the Archpoet and to Brecht. In this comparison he suggests that these *planctus* belong to my category of difficult lyric, and that their ultimate achievement is to bring us into contact with the full complexity of Abelard's own suffering, part-religious, part-sexual, part-poetic self consciousness. At the same time, Dronke also says that these planctus can "subsume them [Abelard's sufferings] in a creation that gives them objective dignity—no longer the private, helpless laceration of one or two human beings, but the meaningful sorrow of the artist's persona, the dramatic creation that can enfold the private thoughts and yet as artefact [sic] can take its place in the outer world in its own right" (pp. 118–19).

All of this is on the way to right, I think. The suggestion that Abelard's sufferings are subsumed "in a creation that gives them objective dignity" refers from the other side to precisely that displacement which the lyric ego, as I have described it, invites. But Dronke neglects to notice that the thoughts and sufferings of Dinah, Jephthah's daughter, Sampson, and the rest, though they are poetically created by Abelard in the sense that we cannot account for all the elements of his poem elsewhere, are not, once made, his creation. They are characters from the Bible. As such, they are authoritative. The "corroborative detail" supplied by Abelard is diachronically new, but it is devotionally correct, and is, as such, eternal. Abelard's relation to these characters is not that of the modern poet, who wishes readers to contact him in his uniqueness by penetrating his ironies and his codes; rather, Abelard's relation is the same as Augustine's to the objective creation story with which he climaxes his *Confessions*. In that relation, Augustine, the *vendor verborum*, accepts the condition of silence in becoming one of the created Words of God; in Abelard's relation to the Biblical characters whom his poetry discovers to be analogous to himself Abelard finds the truth for which his sufferings have enabled him to search. Sublimation (and I take the etymological pun seriously) and not self-expression, is the achievement of these poems—the displacement of particular self-hood into truth.

There is, admittedly, irony in the *Sampson*. There is, in fact, one more layer than Dronke mentions, since Abelard's line, "sinum aspide" (bosom with an asp), evokes the death of Cleopatra, which Abelard would have known from Suetonius.[38] By this allusion, Sampson is equated with the exemplary case of the woman who dies for love, and the compliment to Eloise is reinforced. Abelard's *planctus* is literally only the story of a suffering suicide, just as Abelard's own literal biography, and Eloise's, is a chronicle of human suffering. But human destiny is not to escape suffering, but to achieve the typology of it—Adam, David, Solomon, and Sampson are good figures, and their figural existence is the end of their *exitium*, toward which the "femineis illecebris" (feminine wiles) invite. Thus, "ad exitium / properare certissimum / cum predictis" (to hasten with the others to certain disaster) leads not to catastrophe, but merely through catastrophe to truth.

Abelard's own relation to his poem is not ironic, but allusive. He need not decode it, because of course he knows the facts of his own life, and the facts of Bible narrative, as well as their accumulated figural meanings. His own relation is thus to something clear, into which he displaces himself. The relativity of third person narrative is compensated for by Biblical authority; in these examples, he can become true. For the larger audience, as Abelard well knew, because he knew his own fame, an analogous displacement was possible. If we see now the suffering poet more largely and clearly than the types of the Suffering Servant, this is our own bent, and not the achievement of Abelard.

My final hard case, I have suggested, is the ironic one—that is, the case of lyrics whose language yields no certainty except the author's fundamental mistrust of language. Here, difficulty is imposed by a literary version of the Heisenberg principle—to raise the question at all is to answer it in favor of irony. Our modern linguistic predicament betrays us, and we read Dante's *De vulgari eloquentia* and the "trapassar del segno" (trespass of the sign) of *Paradise* XXVI as admissions that language is absolutely, and not merely relatively and redeemably, fallen. I think we go too far. There is certainly medieval awareness of the duplicity of signs, but not, I think, of signing altogether. Chaucer's ironies are stable, and so are Abelard's. Before Petrarch[39] and Villon, and the whole Renaissance notion of mimesis which in claiming imitation admits the gap that act must bridge, I would propose *a priori* that if such irony were to be found anywhere, it would be found in Latin lyric, where a book-learned bi-lingualism would have permitted one most easily to intuit the essential artificiality of language. I am almost persuaded of its presence in a few lyrics, such as "Dum Diana vitrea," "Si linguis angelicis," and "Dum rutilans Pegasei." But it is not common—there are too many easy cases, too much naive linguistic realism, for such a co-existence.

What, then, is the medieval lyric ego? It is a "substantia sine qualitate"—a substance, may one say, seeking qualification. One qualifies it by entering it—by submitting to the *tractatus* of the poem, its linear process, as an enactment of *tractandi*, and so true. In so doing, one becomes one's self a true self—whether lover, Christian, warrior, or suffering type. Such a displacement is the central medieval paradigm of personality and personhood. The *exemplum*, which works by analogy, is the more familiar case, but it merely suggests this displacement, without enacting it. The lyric, by saying "I," does enact it, for all who will repeat it, and so invites the plagiarism apart from which there is no truth.

——— NOTES ———

[1]The extreme version of this position, of course, is defined by Jacques Derrida, *Writing and Difference*, tr. Alan Bass (Chicago, 1978), especially the essay "Violence and Metaphysics, An Essay on the Thought of Emmanuel Levinas," pp. 79-153.

[2]*Sancti Gregorii Magni Expositiones in Canticum Canticorum*, ed. Patrick Verbraken, O. S. B. (Turnholt, 1963), pp. 3-4. (Corpus Christianorum, Series Latina CXLIV)

[3]The normal Latin preposition which modifies allegorical signification is "per," which occurs here; it is significant, however, that the word "dum" is really more prominent—that is, the experience of the puzzle as puzzle, as enigma, is in a sense already the cognition of God.

[4]*Biblia sacra, cum glosa ordinaria et postilla Nicolai Lyrani* (Lyons, 1520), fol. 355r.

[5]My presumption that Canticles, as understood by Gregory, is a text in the mode of modern difficult lyric, I base on the fact that his description of reading it fits the normal modern experience of reading lyrics. But later commentary, though in content like Gregory's, presumes and describes in some detail a different kind of reading, which seems perfectly to describe the kind of reading medieval lyrics normally ask. I therefore call Canticles lyric; being able, as it were, to have Canticles both ways makes it, in Roland Barthes' terms, a "writerly" text; see *S/Z*, tr. Richard Miller (New York, 1974), pp. 4-6. But this protean relation to readings is normal to sacred texts, since God is both mysterious and (dogmatically) clear.

[6]"The Grand Chant Courtois and the Wholeness of the Poem: The

Medieval Assimilation of Text, Audience, and Commentary," *E Cr*, 18 (Fall, 1978), 5–17.

[7]Late medieval literary theory can be established in great detail, both from theoretical manuals such as Geoffrey of Vinsauf's *Poetry nova* and Hermann the German's Averroistic version of Aristotle's *Poetics*, and even more from the commentaries made at the time on texts we now call poems. For a full discussion of the evidence and its meaning, see my *The Ethical Poetic of the Later Middle Ages: A Decorum of Convenient Distinction* (Toronto, 1982). The briefest medieval illustration that I know of this four-aspect existence of poetry is the conventional commentary definition of the hymn as "laus dei in canticum" (praise of God in song), in which praise is content, God is audience, and song is form. Commentary, of course, specifies these things.

[8]All medieval legislation exists as betrayal, in that it proves the existence of the prohibited behavior. Alcuin's condemnation of the public reading of heroic poems in Lindisfarne is, in this sense, valuable evidence for the popularity of works like the *Beowulf* in monastic contexts. When we wish to find out what past ages thought about questions that interest *us* (such as the question of literary genre—or even the question of literature as such, in the sense of *belles lettres*) we usually have to find out from betrayals, rather than direct statements.

[9]"Note on the Poetic and the Empirical 'I' in Medieval Authors," *Traditio*, 4 (1946), 414.

[10]On which see also the collection of essays in *Genre*, 6 (1973), and especially the essay by Eugene Vance, "Augustine's Confession and the Grammar of Selfhood," pp. 1–28.

[11]*Langue, texte, énigme* (Paris, 1975), p. 171.

[12]R. W. Hunt, "Studies in Priscian in the Eleventh and Twelfth Centuries," *Medieval and Renaissance Studies* 1 (1941–43), 194–231; 2 (1950), 1–56.

[13]Priscian, *Institutionum grammaticarum Libri XVIII*, ed. H. Keil, in *Grammatici Latini*, Vols. I–II (Leipzig, 1864), XVII. 37, p. 131.

[14]G. L. Bursill-Hall, *Speculative Grammars of the Middle Ages: The Doctrine of* Partes Orationis *of the Modistae* (The Hague, 1971), pp. 180 ff.

[15]In a Renaissance edition of the *Doctrinale*, at line 356: "monstrant et referunt et quasi fixa manebunt" (they point out and refer and remain as if fixed), Ludovicus de Guascis glosses as follows: "Hic auctor ostendit proprietatem predictorum pronominum dicens quod hec pronomina pre-dicta monstrant idest demonstrativa sunt et referunt idest relativa sunt et manebunt quasi fixa idest substantiva, quasi dicere quod predictorum pronominum aliqua sunt demonstrativa ut hic et iste ego tu aliqua relativa ut is et sui et manebunt quasi fixa idest substantiva quasi dicere ad demonstrandum ipsa non penitus substantiva. Nam licet substantiva ponantur, ut ego curro, tamen recipere possunt substantivum tanquam si

essent adiectiva ut ego pater. Alii dicunt quod Alexander dixit quasi ad notandum quasi ipse esse substantiva significatione et non notent [cod. nocent] is et ipse aliqua voce et significatione ut ego et tu. Alii tamen dicunt quasi idest certe vel vere substantiva, quia secundum Priscianum pronomen loco proprii nominis et certam significat personam. Postea dicit quod hoc nomen ille refert idest relativum est monstrat idest demonstrativum est: et nullum aliud pronomen hoc significabit, idest poterit esse relativum et demonstrativum" (Here the author shows the property of the above pronouns, saying that these specified pronouns point out, that is, are demonstrative, and refer, that is, are relative, and remain as if fixed, that is, are substantive—as if to say that of the specified pronouns, some are demonstrative, such as 'this' and 'that,' 'I,' 'thou,' some are relative, such as 'he' and 'his' and remain as if fixed that is substantive, as if to say to show themselves not entirely substantive. For though pronouns may be put as substantives, as in the phrase 'I run,' nevertheless they can receive substance as if they were adjectives, as in the phrase 'I father.' Others say that Alexander said 'as if' in order to note that being itself was substantive by signification. And 'he' and 'himself' do not signify by a particular voice and signification as do 'I' and 'thou.' Others still say that 'as if' means certain or true substance, because according to Priscian the pronoun is put in the place of a proper name and signifies a specific person. Afterwards he says that this word 'he' refers, that is, is relative, [and] shows, that is, is demonstrative, and no other pronoun will signify in this manner, that is, can be relative and demonstrative). *Alexandri Grammatici opus, una cum facili Interprete plurimis erroribus expurgatum* (Brixiae, 1539) fol. Bii[r]. I am happy to thank John Alford for notice of this book, and for the use of his personal copy.

[16]"Pronomen uero significat substantiam sine qualitate . . . Antiqui dicebant pronomen meram substantiam significare, non quod informem et ab omni qualitate exutam significat, (hoc enim esset primordialem materiam significare), sed quia rem ut substat et sine respectu forme significat" (A pronoun indeed signifies substance without quality . . . The ancients said that the pronoun signified mere substance, not that it signified something without form and stripped of quality [for that would be to signify prime matter] but because it signified a thing as present and without respect to its form). Paris, Bibliothèque nationale, MS. BN lat. 16220, fol. 35va, as quoted in R. W. Hunt, "Studies in Priscian," p. 201.

[17]Orléans, Bibliothèque municipale, MS. M 252, fol. 18?[r], as quoted in Charles Thurot, *Extraits de divers manuscrits latins pour servir à l'histoire des doctrines grammaticales au moyen âge* (1869; rpt. Frankfurt, 1964), p. 265. The manuscript is described on p. 33; the gloss is the one identified by its incipit as the gloss "Admirantes."

[18]The fact that modern lyrics of this kind tend to be without aesthetic or high cultural value should not invalidate their value as examples rhetorically and generically identical to the *grand chant courtois*, as well as

to religious lyrics in the ego-displacing mode. The difference in quality may relate to a difference in register, a concept to which I was introduced by Pierre Bec in a seminar in 1976, and which is a theme of much of his work. "Register" is a quality of text, but it is a quality which suggests and presumes the appropriate audience. The issue may be complicated by ironic use of registers. However, the medieval *chant* was clearly "aristocratizing" in register, while the modern love song is "popularizing." Love postures which we dismiss as adolescent and immature had, in the Middle Ages, the power to enhance the nobility of powerful aristocrats functioning in a world even more dangerous and demanding than our own. In our own day, the rich and powerful are expected to be "cooler" and even ironic in their postures of public love. A structural shift has taken place. The relation between distributional structures of emotional behavior and social arrangements for the exercise of power, which love lyric permits us to see in diachronic variation, should elicit a most interesting anthropological analysis, which is beyond the scope of this paper.

[19]For a preliminary discussion of these terms, see my "Commentary as Criticism: Formal Cause, Discursive Form, and the Late Medieval Accessus," in *Acta Conventus Neo-Latini Lovaniensis*, ed. J. Ijsewijn and E. Kessler (Munich, 1973), pp. 29–48.

[20]*Biblia sacra*, ed. cit., fols. 354^v–355^v.

[21]*Opera Omnia* (Venice, 1732), Vol. III, fol. 105^v.

[22]At the beginning of his commentary on Canticles, Nicholas passes quickly over general matters, about which "dictum fuit plenius in principio primi libri, ubi posui quandam prefationem pro istis tribus libris" (there is full treatment at the beginning of the first book, where I have put a certain preface for these three books). *Biblia Sacra*, loc. cit. In the preface to which he refers, he deals with the question of form as follows: "Est autem duplex forma, scilicet forma tractandi, et forma tractatus. Forma tractandi est modus agendi, qui triplex est in libris sapientialibus, quia procedunt monitive, comminative, et promissive. De quo potest accipi quod dicitur Ecclesiastes iiii. c. Funiculus triplex difficile rumpitur, quia si aliquis non acquiescit monitiis, compellitur tamen comminationibus, vel attrahitur promissis. Et in hoc etiam huius doctrine soliditas designatur. Forma vero tractatus est divisio huius doctrine, que ut iam dictum est, in tres libros dividitur, scilicet Proverbia, Ecclesiasten, et Cantica canticorum" (The form is double, that is the form of the treatment and the form of the treatise. The form of the treatment is the mode of procedure, which is triple in the sapiential books, because they proceed by exhortation, condemnation, and promise. For this procedure there is a text in Ecclesiastes 4:12—"A triple cord is difficult to break," because if one does not agree to exhortation, one may nevertheless be compelled by condemnation or attracted by promises. In this also the solidity of doctrine is designated. The form of the treatise is the division of this doctrine, which, as was already said, is divided into three books, that is, Proverbs, Ecclesiastes, and Canticles [fol. 308^v].)

[23] Aegidius Romanus, *In Librum Solomonis qui cantica canticorum inscribitur Commentaria* (1555; rpt. Frankfurt, 1968), fol. 2ᵛ.

[24] In normal medieval usage, proof and refutation are meant in this context. But praise and blame are meanings of whose possibility the medieval critics were not unaware.

[25] This is very preliminry judgement. I have not yet investigated the manuscript tradition. Bernard's descriptions of the devotional processes which are the allegorical meaning of the text are, of course, most affective, but Bernard is describing the Christian's relation to God, while Aegidius is describing the experience of a text. Medieval criticism is full of descriptions of texts and explications of their meanings or contents, but this explicit attention to the point in between is unusual. Aegidius' comment deserves an analysis which brings to bear upon it as full as possible a restoration of its context and intellectual tradition.

[26] The mode of love which dominates the *grand chant courtois* is an absolutely dedicated but unconsummated desire, which, though it professes to expect realization in the flesh, usually gets no more than to serve and wait. According to a paper by Theresa Moritz, "William of St. Thierry and Romantic Love," presented at the Thirteenth Conference on Medieval Studies, 4–7 May 1978 (Kalamazoo, MI.), this same mode of love as longing is central to William's notion of the fit love of God. William exploits imagery of human love in his description of religion, but never in such a way as to honor the flesh, human marriage, or physical consummation. Mrs. Moritz suggests that he may have been influenced in his conception by the imagery of the courtly lyric. My own reading of commentary on Canticles suggests that the influence may have been quite general—what commentary achieved was the transformation of radically carnal love poetry into allegories of precisely this unconsummated love longing. Sometimes, as in the *glosa*, the relation between Christ and the Church of the allegory does indeed exist, however spiritually. But in Aegidius Romanus, it is further comprised by being made potential. The test case is the orgasmic "Dilectus meus misit manum suam per foramen, et venter meus intremuit ad tactum eius" (5:4 My beloved put his hand through the hole, and my womb trembled at his touch), which is even more explicit in the Hebrew. For Aegidius, in this verse "ponitur Christi attractio . . . Quasi diceret, tanta fuit virtus Christi, quod non solum fortiores partes animae fuerunt parate ad obediendum Christo, sed etiam debiliores" (fol. 11ᵛ the attraction of Christ is described . . . as if it said, such was the virtue of Christ, that not only the stronger parts of the soul were prepared to obey Him, but also the weaker). But the energy of this spirituality is desire. This focus of attention puts the burden of loving on the speaker, whose love longing fails: "idest, propter amorem deficio: volo in amorem eius rapi, et dulcedinem contemplationis eius sentire, et non valeo, sed deficio." (fol. 12ʳ that is, I fail because of love: I wish to be carried away in his love, and feel the sweetness of his contemplation, and I cannot, but I fail). The interpreta-

tion might serve as a precis of any of a large number of courtly lyrics. One may explain the coincidence in various ways; a possibility that needs to be taken most seriously is that of direct influence—in this case, of vernacular texts on the learned ones. Our habit has been to suspect influence, when we do at all, only in the other direction—but this is to allow a value judgement about learnedness and authority to prejudge an historically possible fact.

[27]Nou goth sone vnder wod,—
  me reweth, marie, þi faire Rode.
  Nou goþ sonne vnder tre,—
  me reweþ, marie, þi sone and þe.
Carleton Brown, *English Lyrics of the XIIIth Century* (Oxford, 1953), 1, p. 1. Unless otherwise noted, I shall refer to Middle English lyrics as printed in the Brown and Robbins Oxford editions, by citing short title and poem number.

[28]I have used for Bernard's poems the edition of Moshé Lazar, *Chansons d'amour, édition critique avec traduction, introduction, notes et glossaire* (Paris, 1966). Unless otherwise noted, I have for convenience cited all these Occitan poems from Alan R. Press, *Anthology of Troubadour Lyric Poetry*, Edinburgh Bilingual Library 3 (Austin, 1971); "Can vei la lauzeta mover" is pp. 76 ff. The largest and best recent anthology is Martin de Riquer, *Los trovadores: Historia literaria y textos*, 3 vols. (Barcelona, 1975).

[29]The love-accidia which this enclosure enacts can be a real problem, as well as a poetic achievement; the medieval lyric ego has moral and ontological as well as aesthetic power. For Chaucer's coping with this love-accidia, as a part of the process of finding for himself a way of writing poetry that was not morally and spiritually self-destructive, see R. A. Shoaf, "'Mutatio amoris': Revision and Penitence in Chaucer's *The Book of the Duchess*," Diss. Cornell 1977.

[30]Alfons Hilka and Otto Schumann, *Carmina Burana*, Band 1.2, *Die Liebeslieder* (Heidelberg, 1941), no. 90. p. 86.

[31]Peter Dronke, "Poetic Meaning in the Carmina Burana," *Mit J*, 10 (1974–75), 116–37.

[32]The poetry of modern pop music provides instructive comparison. A particularly complex example of ego displacement occurs in a song in which a passing woman, seeing a little girl eyeing a toyshop doll and remembering that she had herself once been in the same situation, bought the doll for the child. On both dolls there hung the sign, "Shake me I rattle, squeeze me I cry / Please take me home and love me" (*Song Hits Magazine*, 42 [May, 1978], 46). This couplet, used repeatedly as a refrain, makes it clear by the end of the song that the passing woman narrator considers herself also a purchasable doll, whose sign is addressed to the audience—her displacement effects that of the audience, by evoking the same male fantasy as did "Exiit diluculo."

[33]According to a commentary on Geoffrey of Vinsauf's *Poetria Nova*: "Secundum Tullium et autorem istum proverbium est idem quod sententia, prout sententia est color rethorici. Quem sic diffinit Tullius in 5o nove rethorice: sententia est oratio sumpta de vita que aut quid sit aut esse oporteat in vita breviter ostenditur, cui consonat Aristoteles, sic diffiniens sententiam in 2o rethoricorum: Sententia est enunciatio non de singularibus sed de universalibus. Nec de omnibus universalibus, puta: rectum curvo est contrarium, sed de quibuscumque. Actiones sunt et eligenda sunt aut fugienda sunt adoperari. Ysidorus vero libro ethymologiarum 2o in tractatu de rethorica dicit quod sententia est dictum impersonale idest sine persona" (Assisi, Biblioteca communale, MS. 309, fol 9[v], According to Cicero and this author a proverb is the same as a proposition, insofar as a proposition is a color of rhetoric. Cicero defines it thus in the fifth of the *New Rhetoric*: a proposition is a saying taken from life in which either what might be or what ought to be is shown briefly; Aristotle agrees, defining a proposition thus in the second of the *Rhetoric*: a proposition is a statement about universals, not particulars. Not about all universals, such as "a curved straight line is a contradiction," but about certain ones. They are actions, and the actor must choose or reject them. Isidore indeed in the second book of the *Etymologies* in the tractate on rhetoric says that a proposition is an impersonal saying, that is, one without a person). Impersonal, of course, means not relative to any person—and therefore useful as truth for any and all. None of this makes sense, obviously, except to a culture willing to take universals seriously.

[34]*Poems Without Names: The English Lyric, 1200-1500* (Berkeley, 1970).

[35]In the manuscripts, the envoys of Arnaut's poems are not always present, but when they are, the name they mention is clearly his. If any medieval singers ever substituted their own names, I find recorded no manuscript evidence for it. See U. A. Canello, ed., *La vita e le opere del trovatore Arnaldo Daniello* (Halle, 1883), pp. 139-85.

[36]Except, of course, some modern critics, whose seriousness lacks proper appreciation of rhetoric. For a list of interpretations and the author's own interesting proposal, see L. T. Topsfield, *Troubadours and Love* (Cambridge, 1975), pp. 28-35.

[37]"Peter Abelard: *Planctus* and Satire," in Dronke's *Poetic Individuality in the Middle Ages: New Departures in Poetry 1000-1150* (Oxford, 1970), pp. 114-45. The *planctus* on Jephthah's daughter he treats in "Medieval Poetry—I: Abelard," *The Listener*, 74 (25 November, 1965), 841-45.

[38]Whom Abelard cites twice: in his letter to Eloise on the origins of nuns, and in his *Christian Theology*, giving the impression that *Suetonius* is a text he knows quite well. See *Petri Abaelardi Opera*, ed. Victor Cousin

(Paris, 1849–59), I, p. 148; II, pp. 437–38. Cleopatra is described in Suetonius, *Julius Caesar*. 35.

[39]For an argument that Petrarch is the first modern poet in terms which complement the distinction I have argued here, see John Freccero, "The Fig Tee and the Laurel: Petrarch's Poetics," *Diacritics*, 5 (Spring, 1975), 34–40.

TOWARD A POETICS
OF THE
LATE MEDIEVAL COURT LYRIC
GLENDING OLSON

MY SUBJECT is the court lyric of the later Middle Ages—all those balades, virelays, rondels, usually about love, and not only by recognized authors like Machaut, Froissart, and Chaucer, but also by lesser-known makers like Philipoctus de Caserta and Jacomi Senleches, by undistingushed amateurs like Jean de Garencières and Humfrey Newton, and by the anonymous writers who fill the courtly love lyric portion of R. H. Robbins' *Secular Lyrics of the XIVth and XVth Centuries.* This body of work does not enjoy a very high reputation among literary scholars, whether French or English. It is normal to read that these lyrics, imaginatively constrained by the domination of courtly love conventions and the rigors of the fixed-forms, are at best graceful and charming and at worst (the condition that usually obtains) repetitive and vapid. Arthur K. Moore refers to the English tradition as "moribund," "irreparably damaged by formalism and abstractness," "fundamentally inefficacious," and "turgid and discursive." Edmund Reiss has argued that the Middle English lyric is more "interesting" and "complex" than generally acknowledged, yet of the twenty-five poems he analyzes closely not one is a fixed-form lyric in the Machaut-Chaucer tradition. Nigel Wilkins' edition of late medieval French lyrics is offered as a refutation of the received opinion that all such verse is "empty and artificial."[1] Most modern readers probably have sympathies similar to the conventional wisdom; we are delighted with *To Rosemounde* because it seems to be a balade in which Chaucer slyly pokes fun at the conventions, and we are just as happy to forget about *Womanly Noblesse*, because it is a balade in which he does not.

Surely the principal reason for this disparaging attitude is that we expect these lyrics, implicitly, to meet our standards of what a *poem* is, standards inherited in one way or another from a later body of lyric poetry, often perceived under the aegis of Brooks and Warren. I do not want to argue that late medieval court lyrics really do meet these standards, that if we look closely enough we will find richness of imagery, irony, ambiguity, or—Moore's central value—"concrete representation,"[2] though in some cases we do. Rather I would argue that the fixed-form lyrics should not be held against these standards at all, that in a very real sense we are not dealing with poetry but with some other kind of discourse. My aim is to discuss certain aspects of late medieval lyric theory which will suggest how these works seem to have been thought of, what kind of cultural and aesthetic context surrounded them, as a first step toward a more sympathetic understanding of the poetics of the tradition. The term "theory" in this case has to be taken very broadly, to include any kind of evidence that suggests the ways in which these compositions were perceived.

I limit the discussion to those lyrics written in the fixed forms in the fourteenth and early fifteenth centuries, principally in France but also in England and Italy. Some of what will be said is applicable to other medieval lyrics as well, say, to troubadour performance or to the work of the thirteenth-century trouvères; and some of it will echo points made often about the Renaissance lyric, where the fusion of music and poetry and the social function of lyric performance have received more appreciative attention. Still, the delimitation is reasonable. The lyric production of the court makers has a coherence of its own that is due, as we will see, not just to the use of certain set forms and to observable literary connections among the countries involved,[3] but also, and more significantly, to a particular attitude toward lyric poetry that was part of the ethical, educational, and recreational ideas of the late medieval courts and other similarly cultivated segments of society.

We may come to understand something about these lyrics if we get to know the company they keep. In the *Ménagier de Paris*, a late fourteenth-century, well-to-do Parisian citizen instructs his young wife on the value of fidelity in marriage by citing, among others, the ancient story of Lucretia's violation by Sextus Tarquinius and her subsequent suicide. Among Lucretia's virtues is her deportment. When her husband is not with her, she does not seek out revelry but spends her time profitably at home, in contrast to other wives, who are discovered at various games,

> les unes devisans, les autres jouans au *bric*, les autres à *qui féry?* les autres à *pince-merille*, les autres jouans aux *cartes* et aux autres jeux d'esbatemens avecques leurs voisines; les autres qui avoient souppé ensemble, disoient des chançons, des fables, des contes, des jeux-partis; les autres estoient en la rue avecques leurs voisines jouans au *tiers* et au *bric*, et ainsi semblablement de plusieurs jeux. . . .
>
> (. . . and some ladies they found talking, others playing at *bric*, others at hot cockles, others at "pinch me," others playing at cards and other games of play with their neighbors; others, who had supped together, were singing songs and telling fables and tales and asking riddles; others were in the road with their neighbors playing at blind-man's-buff and at *bric* and so likewise at other games. . . .)[4]

Since Lucretia, a few lines later, is recorded as saying her hours, we may assume that this list of wifely recreations is a reflection of late fourteenth-century society, not the author's attempt to recapture Roman customs. Principally concerned with propriety and devotion, the story is not critical of entertainment *per se*; Lucretia participates in communal disports whenever she gets a letter from her husband, and elsewhere the author of *Le Ménagier* indicates that his wife should know about games and recreations in order to function well in social situations (I, 7). The passage is most interesting because it groups games with what we think of as literature. The songs and stories are seen as "jeux," as entertainment, and are listed as part of a series of recreations. The reference to "chançons" is vague enough perhaps that we cannot be sure exactly what kind of compositions it refers to, but the mention of "jeux-partis" clearly puts us in the realm of established lyric forms. These verbal and musical entertainments, in addition to being categorized as games, are also put in the context of a particular time and circumstance: they are after-dinner entertainments.

There is no need to cite at length comparable testimony to the occurrence of lyrics and fictions in a similar context, for the evidence is abundant and familiar. One example from Chaucer suggests the tenor of many such passages, though it too is ostensibly

229

about an ancient event. In Book III of *Troilus and Criseyde*, the widow and her entourage come to the house of her uncle, Pandarus; they dine lavishly,

> And after soper gonnen they to rise,
> At ese wel, with hertes fresshe and glade,
> And wel was hym that koude best devyse
> To lyken hire, or that hire laughen made.
> He song; she pleyde; he tolde tale of Wade.[5]

Froissart describes a similar scene, but this time a real one: his visit in 1388 to the court of Gaston Fébus, where, as part of the count's grand feasts, "il prenoit grant esbatement en menestraudie, car bien s'i cognoissoit; il faisoit devant lui ses clercs volentiers chanter chançons, rondiaux et virelaiz" (he took great pleasure in minstrelsy, for he understood the art well; he would have his clerks before him gladly singing chansons, rondels, and virelays).[6] In passages like these such terms as "song" and "menestraudie" indicate primarily a musical performance, and indeed the most extensive documentation of references of this sort has usually come from historians of music.[7] But the songs *are* the lyrics under consideration. Although it is commonplace to talk about the second half of the fourteenth century as a transition period during which lyric and music became separate, and to speak of Machaut as the last important trouvère, in fact even late in the century a number of composer-lyricists worked in that tradition, and many fifteenth-century English courtly love lyrics were meant to be sung. It is easy to forget the musical dimension of such lyrics when they appear in anthologies designed for classes in medieval literature, and it is a helpful reminder of their original status to consult them in such editions as Willi Apel's *French Secular Compositions of the Four-teenth Century* (3 vols., American Institute of Musicology, 1970–72), Nino Pirotta's *The Music of Fourteenth-Century Italy* (4 vols., American Institute of Musicology, 1954–63), and Sir John Stainer's *Early Bodleian Music* (2 vols., London, 1901). Even among those makers who did not write music, such as Deschamps and Chaucer, the conceptual sense of lyric as music remained.[8]

   The people who are trying to please Criseyde with their songs, with what their craft enables them to "devyse," are performing the kind of after-dinner entertainment that we know to have occurred in English and continental circles during the fourteenth and fifteenth centuries.Though one can find criticisms of such activity for its triviality, and concern for its excesses, it was an established part of court life. There is even Biblical justification, if one needs it. In *De proprietatibus rerum*, Bartholomaeus Anglicus includes a chapter on supper in which he lists various things that improve and embellish it, such as diverse wines and dishes, courteous servants, the proper time and place. The eighth item, in Trevisa's translation, is "mirþe of song and of instrumentis of musik," and the supporting authority is a line from the parable of the prodigal son, where the father celebrates his return with feasting, music, and dancing.[9]

The environment in which these "songs" occur, their connection with music, and their function as established social recreation are well-known but easily neglected aspects of the poetics of the court lyric. If we take these contexts seriously, though, then it will affect the kind of expectations we have in regard to the lyrics and even the way in which we conceptualize them. For we are dealing less with a literary situation than with a social one; the lyrics supply entertainment, and insofar as a maker makes lyrics he is functioning—whether amateur or professional—as an entertainer. His work is circumscribed by the conditions that prompt it: people together, looking for recreation, usually at the appropriate postprandial time. This social situation suggests a moral context for the writing of verses. In the *Nicomachean Ethics* Aristotle categorizes three virtues that deal with social interaction; though different, "they are all concerned with human relations in speech and action." The first is truthfulness, the mean, as opposed to the extremes of boastfulness and self-depreciation. The remaining two are concerned with pleasantness rather than truth. Pleasantness in daily life is affability, the mean between the two defects of obsequiousness and quarrelsomeness. Pleasantness in amusement is the third virtue; the mean is *eutrapelia*, wittiness, the extremes buffoonery and boorishness. The logic of defining a virtue in regard to amusement is as follows, in Aquinas' explanation:

> As man sometimes needs to give his body rest from labors, so also he sometimes needs to rest his soul from mental strain that ensues from his application to serious affairs. This is done by amusement (*ludus*). . . . It follows that in amusement there can be a certain agreeable association of men with one another, so they may say and hear such things as are proper in the proper way.[10]

Aristotle and Aquinas go on to distinguish suitable amusements and the degree one should attend to them. People should avoid scandalous stories just to get a laugh; most have a tendency to take more pleasure in amusement than they should, and hence they often mistake the buffoon, who regales them with jokes, for the truly witty person.

These Aristotelian attitudes concerning the way people speak and act in relationship to one another influenced late medieval thinking through the various adaptations, commentaries, and translations that accrued to the *Nicomachean Ethics* in the thirteenth and fourteenth centuries. Book II of Brunetto Latini's *Trésor* relies not only on the *Ethics* but also on the *Compendium Alexandrinum*, an abridgment of Aristotle's work that entered western Europe through a translation credited to Hermannus Alemannus. Latini's briefer treatment of Aristotle's discussion of affability (IV, 6) is introduced in a way that offers a general recommendation for proper social behavior:

> Aprés ce deviserons des choses ki afierent a compaignie des gens et en la conversation des homes et en lor parleure, pour ce que tenir le mi en ces choses fet a loer, et tenir les estremités fet a blasmer. Et en tenir le mi doit on estre plaisant en parler, et en demorer avec les gens et en converser entre les homes, et k'il soit de bele compaignie et soit communaus as choses qui se covient et en maniere et en leu et en tans k'il covient.[11]

> (Now let us discuss those things which pertain to people in social situations, their association and conversation, because holding to the mean in these matters is praiseworthy, whereas going to extremes is blameworthy. In observing the mean one should be affable in speech, both in familiar relationships and in conversation with anyone else; and one should be agreeable and receptive to suitable things in the appropriate manner, time, and place.)

Being "de bele compaignie" is observing the mean in social behavior, and in a later chapter Latini returns to "compaignie" as a topic, where he briefly defines the mean and the extremes in regard to the two virtues of pleasantness. Concerning pleasantness in amusement he says:

> Gengleour est celui ki gengle entre les gens a ris et a gieu, et moke soi et sa feme et ses fiz et tous autres. Et son contraire est cil ki tousjors se moustre cruel et sa face torblee, et ne s'esleece avoec les autres, et ne parle et ne demeure avoec ceaus ki s'esleecent; mais cil ki tient le mi entr'aus use la moieneté amesureement.[12]

(A jangler is one who talks frivolously in social situations, for the sake of laughter and amusement, and derides himself, his wife, his sons, and everyone else. His opposite is the person who always appears stern, with a pained expression, and does not enjoy himself with others, nor speak or associate with people having a good time. A person observing the mean between these extremes practices moderation appropriately.)

Throughout these discussions, the context seems to be polite social conversation. The amusements referred to are apparently jokes, witticisms, anecdotes, and they may seem far removed from the formally contrived lyrics under discussion. But Latini's general statement that the proper mean in social relationships involves pleasant conversation permits a substantial range of verbal behavior; and his reference to the "gengleour," even though it defines a personality type rather than a profession here, nevertheless carries connotations not just of casual conversation but of more planned performance. Earlier Latini had defined the person excessive "en choses de jeu et de solas" as "jougleour et menestrier" (II, 16; Carmody, p. 185). This lack of a clear dividing line between personal inclinations and professional accomplishments is true to such fourteenth-century phenomena as Boccaccio's "uomini di corte" (see *Decameron* I, 7 and 8), men whose ready wit becomes their source of income, and noblemen-makers like Oton de Graunson and Sir John Montagu, whose creative talents were thought of at least in part as an aspect of their status as "gentil" men. At least theoretically, the moderate pursuit of social pleasure through making or hearing lyrics would appear to lie comfortably within the moral virtue of *eutrapelia*.

The relevance of the Aristotelian categories is apparent too when one considers the semantic range of the word for play or amusement, *ludus*: it includes not only physical recreations but mental ones as well, not only jokes but more elaborate verbal constructions that we now call poems and drama. It creates some juxtapositions that might strike a modern reader as incongruous. William Fitzstephen's famous description of London in the twelfth century has a section on the city's entertainments which puts religious plays at the head of a list that includes cock-fighting, jousting, archery, and ice-skating.[13] At the beginning of the *Book of the Duchess* the narrator finds Ovid "beter play" than chess or backgammon (50–51). The conceptual extension of *ludus* to include formal literary productions as well as games and spontaneous verbal play is apparent in the passages cited earlier: the "jeux" in the *Ménagier de Paris* include "chançons" as well as card games; and in Chaucer we have the English equivalent of *ludus*—"He song; she pleyde." Played a musical instrument? Told an entertaining story? Acted out a small dramatic monologue? Did acrobatics? The first choice seems the most reasonable, but any of these activities is possible as a kind of "playing."

The influence of this Aristotelian perspective on medieval views of social behavior is evident in various treatises on conduct and in descriptions of courtly attainments. The statement in a fifteenth-century courtesy book that one should "in companies be neuere to tale-wiis, / Ne ouer myrie, ne ouer sadde" is a specific reflection of the Aristotelian mean regarding pleasantness in amusement. That accomplishments in lyric composition or performance were seen in the context of social pleasantness is apparent, of course, in Chaucer's Squire, whose making of songs is grouped with such other abilities as knowing how to ride, joust, dance, and write. Earlier, in Italy, Francesco da Barberino, in a treatise on the social education of women, carefully delineated the proper limits for ladies to observe in their attention to lyrics and dance. And later we find Charles d'Orléans speaking of the ability to compose lyrics as one of the six attributes a good lover should have:

> Le sixiesme point et le derrenier
> Est qu'il sera diligent escollier,
> En aprenant tous les gracieux tours,
> A son povoir, qui servent en amours.
> C'est assavoir à chanter et dansser,
> Faire chançons et balades rimer,
> Et tous autres joyeux esbatemens.[14]
>
> (The sixth and last rule is that he be a diligent student in learning as well as he can all the gracious manners that belong to love: singing, dancing, making chansons and rhyming balades, and all the other joyous recreations.)

The most explicit connection between the lyrics and Aristotelian ideas of social amusement is the recreational justification that Eustache Deschamps gives in the *Art de dictier*. Here, in a treatise by a court maker written to explain the various lyric types that any would-be writer needs to know, Deschamps categorizes all the fixed forms as a kind of music, and defines music as the one liberal art that refreshes people who have labored hard at the others.

The language and logic are both out of the Aristotelian explanation of the recreative value of *ludus*.[15] Deschamps' insistence that music serves a practical function, that it renders people "plus habiles apres a estudier et labourer aux autres .VI. ars" (VII, 269), may be profitably compared to Nicole Oresme's more comprehensive view of music. In his translation of and commentary on Aristotle's *Politics*, completed in the early 1370s after his translation of the *Ethics*, Oresme offers the following summary of the varying purposes Aristotle assigns to music in Book VIII:

> Or avons donques que musique est bonne pour gieu et pour deduction et sunt .ii. choses differentes. . . . Et me semble que elles different ainsi; car gieu est seulement pour remede et pour delectation contre tristece, et est un repos et recreation. Mes deduction ne est pas principalment pour oster tristesce, mes est delectation qui esmuet et excite le corage a pensees nobles et honestes et a speculation, et principalment a contemplation des choses divines. Et a toutes ces choses vault musique.[16]

> (Music has value both as play and as intellectual pleasure, and these are two different things. . . . I think they differ in this way: play functions solely as a remedy, as delight that combats sadness; it is a kind of rest and recreation. But intellectual pleasure does not serve principally to alleviate sadness; it is a kind of delight that moves and excites the mind to noble and virtuous thoughts, to speculation, and especially to the contemplation of divine subjects. Music promotes all these activities.)

Music offers both recreative and contemplative pleasures. Insofar as it is appreciated "pour gieu" it offers a respite from the "tristece" that accompanies work; insofar as it is appreciated "pour deduction" it leads one not to "repos" but to the highest forms of mental activity. And as Oresme's translation of the *Ethics* reminds us, "repos n'est pas la fin humaine. Car repos est fait et ordené pour operacion" (rest is not the goal of human life; it is created and ordained for the sake of activity). Recreational "repos," justifiable only in that it leads to further work, differs from heavenly rest, Oresme explains in his commentary, because in heaven not all activity ceases—there is only "cessacion d'operacion triste, penible et laborieuse."[17] It is precisely that "laborieuse" activity of earthly life which Deschamps claims his *musique naturele*, the music of recited lyric poetry, will refresh. He offers it as "medicine," as

235

recreation, and his classification should be seen in the context of an Aristotelian ethical tradition which recognizes both the value and the limitations of such pleasure. His silence on the more speculative functions of music, which would have been well known not only through Aristotle but through Boethius and other theorists of *musica mundana*, must be due to the fact that he views the composition of lyric poetry as activity "pour gieu" rather than "pour deduction," activity that belongs in the arena delimited by Aristotelian notions of recreation and its proper place in secular society.

What Deschamps implies theoretically about the social position of lyric poetry appears in more particularized form in the anonymous biography of Marshal Boucicaut written about a generation later. In a chapter on Boucicaut's way of life, the author notes his continual concern to do good works and avoid idleness, but points out that such "ardeur" leads Boucicaut to avoid taking any "repos" or "esbatement." The biographer then proceeds to describe how various wise authorities explain the psychological dangers of such "grande sollicitude" and counsel "joyeuseté et esbatement" in order to "reconforter nature." He devotes a sentence to some specific examples of such recreations: "Si est moult à propos au reconfort de telle lasseté oüir chanter doucement, ou joüer d'aucuns doulx instrumens, oüir paroles joyeuses sans peché, ne vice, ou quelque chose qui face rire, et qui reconforte aulcunement nature, laquelle est en creature humaine si tendre, que elle est de peu de chose grevée et affoiblie" (Especially useful in the recovery from such weariness is hearing songs sweetly sung, or playing some soft instrument, or hearing merry talk [as long as it is not indecent] or something which promotes laughter and restores somewhat one's natural condition, for it is so vulnerable that it is easily weakened and debilitated). He ends the chapter with the familiar story of a saintly recluse justifying recreation by explaining that a bow cannot always be bent without losing its strength, an exemplum which concludes with the same reasoning Deschamps presents for the value of music: "si convient donner quelque plaisir à l'esprit, et qu'il se joüe quelques fois, affin qu'il soit apres plus prompt et plus prest à ouvrer de son entendement" (thus it is appropriate to give some pleasure to one's spirit, and to enjoy oneself at times, so that subsequently one will be more ready and willing to set his mind to serious work).[18] Telling jokes or pleasant stories, singing, and playing instruments are proper kinds of recreation; lyric poetry is among the natural and fitting diversions of Boucicaut's society, and the *Livre des faicts* thinks of them essentially in a psychological and ethical rather than an aesthetic context.

In fact, when he was younger, Boucicaut did allow himself some recreation, for as his biographer notes elsewhere, he was one of the joint authors of the *Cent Ballades*, composed during a sojourn in the East that included a pilgrimage to the Holy Land. The combination of religious devotion and secular love lyric composition is not incongruous when one thinks of the latter as a kind of pastime which implicitly acknowledges the prior values of the former, and it is worth noting that interest in lyric making during the age of Chaucer was not restricted merely to effete aristocrats and frivolous young squires. Both Boucicaut and Oton de Graunson wrote amorous balades *and* joined Philippe de Mézières' crusading order. In England, Sir John Montagu, like other Lollard knights, combined cultivated social tastes with firm religious convictions. Jean Creton, who was with Montagu and Richard II in Ireland in 1399, was requested by the Earl of Salisbury to accompany him back to England "pour rire & pour chanter," and in his catalogue of Montagu's virtues lyric composition takes a major place along with humility, courtesy, generosity, and valor: "Hardi estoit, et fier comme lions; / Et si faisoit balades & chancons, / Rondeaulx & laiz, / Tresbien & bel" (Bold he was, and courageous as a lion. Right well and beautifully did he also make ballads, songs, roundels, and lays). The easy juxtaposition of songwriting with courage and Christian worthiness may possibly say more about Creton's own sensibility than Montagu's, but it points once again to the perspective from which such activity was seen and to its practice by noblemen of some substance and seriousness.[19]

At this point it is appropriate to acknowledge a more serious side to the lyrics themselves. I have been concerned principally with those lyrics meant to function as social entertainment, within which category most love songs seem to fit, at least on the testimony of Christine de Pisan, who says that if one undertakes to write "biaulz et plaisans" compositions, "Le sentement qui est le plus legier, / Et qui mieulx plaist a tous de commun cours, / C'est d'amours" (the sentiment that is the easiest and generally the most pleasing to everyone is that of love).[20] But Aristotle's social virtues include truthfulness as well as pleasantness, and although he is talking about the way in which a person represents himself, a more extended application of the polarity of truth and pleasantness is useful. Not every maker was content solely to follow the amorous formulas, and in some cases we find lyrics reflecting other concerns. Deschamps, the clearest example of the maker as journalist-moralist-social commentator, says at the beginning of one balade that he is not disposed toward love lyrics because of the condition of his society:

> En mon cuer n'a, ce jour de May, verdure,
> Joye, deduit n'amoureus sentement.
> Pour quoy? Pour ce que mainte creature
> Voy au jour d'ui en paine et en tourment,
> Ne je ne voy nul bon gouvernement
> Au bien commun ne en fait de justice.   (VI, 258)
>
> (On this day in May there is no freshness, joy, delight, nor feeling of love in my heart. Why? Because today I see many people in pain and anguish, and I see no proper governance in the interest of common profit or justice.)

Chaucer's few surviving lyrics reveal him in a variety of roles that reflect almost as wide a range of purpose as his longer fictions. The lyric form of the *Envoy to Bukton* memorializes, apparently, a bachelor party joke, the *Complaint to his Purse* a matter of personal finances. And in *Truth* and *Lak of Stedfastnesse* Chaucer speaks directly as moral counselor, the versification serving to heighten the impact of essentially ethical and religious precepts and arguments. The social circumstances and purposes of such speech are always apparent, as with the love lyrics, only in these cases the goals are truth and common profit. In contrast to Moore's observation that "the serious Boethian ballades read rather well, even if the tone is usually homiletical" (p. 130), I would suggest that they read well because of their homiletical tone, conversational but assured, and that that tone is achieved in part because lyric poetry was thought of as a species of social communication, a proper vehicle for the expression of wisdom as well as pleasantness.

In a very real sense, then, late medieval lyrics are more a manifestation of manners, broadly taken, than of literary inspiration; and perhaps they should be thought of as versified conversation rather than poetry. They aim at truth and pleasantness, though more often at the latter. Generally speaking, they are essentially affable works, their platitudes keyed to reinforcing social and ethical norms, their language suitably decorous. Their goal more often than not is enjoyment at the level of recreation, refreshment— the kind of unchallenging satisfactions associated today with the popular arts. I will return to this comparison later, but there is another aspect of lyric theory to be dealt with first.

In addition to the social dimension of lyric composition, there is a personal one as well, comparable on a private level to the lyric's ability to provide public entertainment. It is often a feature of medieval depictions of the act of lyric creation, and a passage from the *Troilus*, where the hero laments the loss of Criseyde, may be taken as representative:

> ... hym likede in his songes shewe
> Th'enchesoun of his wo, as he best myghte,
> And made a song of wordes but a fewe,
> Somwhat his woful herte for to lighte.   (V, 631–34)

The making of songs is in some way therapeutic: it alleviates, lightens, one's woe. And what appears here in narrative form, or is asserted in the lyrics themselves as a motive, is confirmed in non-fictional sources. Francesco da Barberino acknowledges the usefulness of lyric composition in dealing with sadness (Vecchi, 17–18). Jean Creton tells us that upon his return to France after Richard II's capture by the future Henry IV, he wrote a balade about the treacheries done to the king; he includes the poem in his history, and it reviles Henry. Creton says that after writing it "Je ne fui maiz si tresmalade / Que Javoie este pardevant / De courroux" (I was no longer as sickened with anger as I had been before) [Webb, 380]. As an expression of one's state of mind, particularly if that state is of sorrow or anger, writing lyrics brings some kind of relief. The articulation of feelings is itself useful, as Aquinas acknowledges in discussing remedies for sorrow:

> ... a hurtful thing hurts yet more if we keep it shut up,
> because the soul is more intent on it: whereas if it be allowed
> to escape, the soul's intention is dispersed as it were on
> outward things, so that the inward sorrow is lessened. This is
> why when men, burdened with sorrow, make outward show
> of their sorrow, by tears or groans or even by words, their
> sorrow is assuaged.[21]

Many love lyrics are just such words. Even those composed out of joy or hope rather than sorrow or fear work to enhance one's well-being, and not only for the pragmatic reasons of pleasing or persuading one's lady. A passage from Bartholomaeus Anglicus focuses on the effects of a good voice, in relation to the speaker as well as to the listener:

239

> Also a swete voys and ordynat gladeþ and sturieþ to loue,
> and schewiþ out þe passiouns of þe soule, and witnes þe
> strengþe and vertue of spiritualle membres, and schewiþ
> purenesse and goodnesse of good disposicioun þerof, and
> releueþ trauaile, and puttiþ of noye and sorwe. . . .
>   Also by swete voys and songes and armonye, acoord,
> and musik, sike men and mad and frenetik comeþ ofte to
> hire witt aʒee and hele of body.   (V, 23; Seymour, I, 213)

I would argue that the formal attributes of lyric composition—
meter and rhyme and structural patterns—are among those things
which render a voice "swete" and "ordynat." This is certainly
implied by Deschamps when he argues that both sung and spoken
lyrics deserve the name of music "pour la douceur tant du chant
comme des paroles qui toutes sont prononcées et pointoyées par
douçour de voix et ouverture de bouche" (because of the sweetness
both of the melody and of the words, which are all uttered and given
shape by the sweet sound of the voice and the articulation of the
mouth) [VII, 271]. Lyric composition in this sense is a heightened
use of the voice, and the ease with which Bartholomaeus moves
from "swete voys" to "songes and armonye" suggests that music,
singing, and recited poetry all share a common power which
"schewiþ out þe passiouns of þe soule" and in so doing "puttiþ of
noye and sorwe."

Another personal virtue claimed for lyric composition is a
corollary to the idea that there is therapy in speaking one's feelings.
The first version of the *Leys d'amors*, written about 1330 to codify
the rules of the literary society in Toulouse, notes that one of the
"cauzas" of the science of *trobar* is the avoidance of sloth. Late in
the fifteenth century the editor of an anthology of love questions
and riddles adduces the same motive to explain partially why he
worked on the collection.[22] The clearest statement of the idea comes
from the grieving knight in Chaucer's *Book of the Duchess*, as he
describes how he acted in his youthful love:

> But, for to kepe me fro ydelnesse,
> Trewly I dide my besynesse
> To make songes, as I best koude,
> And ofte tyme I song hem loude;
> And made songes thus a gret del.   (1155–59)

He notes that he had no experience or skill in the art, but nevertheless he composed songs "Of my felynge, myn herte to glade," and
he even recites his first effort (1160–80). The making of lyrics,

according to this view, is worthwhile because as an activity it opposes idleness. The logic seems to be a highly secularized version of the familiar medieval idea that good works combat *acedia*, which appears in more traditional form in the *Canterbury Tales* at the beginning of the Second Nun's translation of the life of St. Cecilia. It seems unlikely that the Second Nun would consider the writing of love lyrics an act of genuinely "feithful bisynesse"; in fact, such secular composition is identified precisely as a product of idleness in Deguileville's *Pilgrimage of the Life of Man*.[23] But within the social context of young love, I think we are meant to take the logic seriously. Excessive brooding or sadness as a result of love can be dangerous: this is the problem encountered by Boccaccio's *donne oziose*, for whom the *Decameron* will act as distraction, as well as a number of Chaucerian lovers. One kind of sadness, torpor (*acedia*), may even result in losing one's voice, says Aquinas, adding that of all man's outward motions "the voice is the best expression of the inward thought and desire" (*ST*, I–II, q. 35, a. 8, resp.). Given such a secular situation, lyric composition can thus be justified as productive: the very exercise of the voice is a kind of work that combats the tendency to progressively greater sorrow and torpor.

For the audience, then, the lyrics provide pleasure and sometimes profit. For the lover-maker they provide a constructive outlet for the expression of feeling, and for the professional maker, too, even though he or she may be representing someone else's feelings. Christine de Pisan, who often distinguishes her own emotions from those in her lyrics, indicates in one virelay that even though her "sentement" is sorrowful, writing happier lyrics at the request of others will "un pou alegier / La doulour" (I, 116–17). The fusion of private and public functions is attained principally through music, taking that term in its largest sense to include not only Machaut's polyphony but Deschamps' natural music of the spoken voice. Testimony to the therapeutic value of music is widespread in the period (as indeed throughout the Middle Ages), and it appears in Nicole Oresme's speculative work as well as in Deschamps' practical *Art de dictier*. When Oresme notes the power of music to cure "many sicknesses, such as the one that the doctors call *amor-hereos* as well as many others, and most of all those diseases which arise from the accidents of the soul," he alludes to a firmly established medical analysis of love and other passions which often indicates that such conditions can be alleviated by music.[24] Thus through the lyric poem, which manifests the regularizing and harmonizing effects of music, both maker and audience can find solace.

241

The social and psychological aspects of the court lyric may be seen as extrinsic to the works themselves, yet they are to my mind the most interesting components of the poetics of the genre, and they are the ones most often attended to in medieval evidence. For the most part the treatises on vernacular lyrics from this period are rather thin; none approaches the richness of *De vulgari eloquentia*. Nor do many of the songs themselves yield great dividends when analyzed closely in the established ways of modern criticism. This literary situation parallels that involving other types of discourse; as John G. Cawelti has pointed out, in most criticism "high art is commonly treated as aesthetic structure or individual vision; the popular arts are studied as social and psychological data."[25] Cawelti goes on to propose a principle of analysis, based on *auteur* criticism of film, that might do more justice to the aesthetic values of popular art, and it is one that could be readily adapted to analysis of the lyrics under discussion. But my reason for citing him is to establish, however briefly and incompletely, the affinities between late medieval court lyrics, particularly the love lyric, and what today is known as popular song. The lyric conventions operate much like the formulas of current popular genres, and the experience offered by the performance of a lyric would seem to involve the same kind of escapism that Cawelti posits for stereotyped narrative forms: "a simple and emotionally charged style that encourages immediate involvement in a character's actions without much sense of complex irony or subtlety." Substitute "feelings" for "actions" and we are not far from a statement about the methods and effects of popular songs, whether written in the 1380s or the 1980s.[26]

I am aware of the problems in trying to distinguish between popular and elite art, and the added difficulties of a diachronic comparison; also, it is somewhat awkward thinking of the court lyric as popular art because of the longstanding habit of distinguishing "courtly" from "popular" verse in the Middle Ages.[27] But the approach complements, and perhaps will vivify, the historical material cited above which testifies to the lyrics being perceived as songs and entertainment. There are songwriters, and then there are poets, and we do not expect to find in Oscar Hammerstein or Neil Diamond what we find in Richard Wilbur, even though a poet may (as Wilbur has) choose to become a songwriter on occasion. The authors of the court lyrics were songwriters in the main, though a very few were poets who did some songwriting as well. Chaucer is an example of the latter, and it is possible to see much of his work, particularly parts of the *Book of the Duchess* and the *Troilus*, as the

242

efforts of a poet to come to terms with the songs written around him, to recognize the limitations of a discourse that tends to present pure *sentement* without irony or subtlety.[28]

But my concern has been to see the lyrics as sympathetically as possible. To conceive of them genuinely as songs goes a long way in helping to understand some of their most obvious and most denigrated features: the restrictions of fixed verse forms, the lack of complex imagery, the repetition of stock themes, situations, and abstract diction. Such works are the words of friends, peers, rather than authorities; they console by appealing to familiar and generalized responses, by giving to private feelings an implicit community sanction. If we are tempted to scoff at such formulaic expression and easy consolation, it is useful to recall that even Thomas Aquinas in the *Summa Theologica* (I–II, q. 38) notes that *any* kind of pleasure is a remedy for sadness and devotes attention not only to the contemplation of truth but to the less exalted correctives of crying, sympathy from friends, sleeping, and bathing. The delights of lyric are limited, but we can at least acknowledge what they do offer. The late medieval court composition gives us what we have heard in popular songs for decades: relatively simple statements of basic emotions and truths, projections of intense feelings, repeated depictions of particularly critical situations in love relationships, all of which are heightened by melody and rhythm and offered to an audience for its sympathy and pleasure. In more ways than one, it's still the same old story.

Seeing the lyrics as formulaic popular art helps in one way to locate their social role. It remains only to indicate briefly how the principles of the court lyric delineated here fit in with other developments in vernacular poetics in the later Middle Ages. If we recognize that lyric production belongs more to the ongoing social life of a group than to the evolving aesthetic of any individual artist, we will see that its poetics are complementary to rather than a part of the efforts of major writers to come to terms with the values and potential of literature in the vernacular. The measure of the distance between poets and lyric makers is most acutely seen in the difference between Dante's treatment of lyric poetry in *De vulgari eloquentia* and subsequent vernacular treatises.[29] In that work Dante distinguishes between the "sententia" of a text and the "verbis" with which its meaning is communicated (II, 1); and in the *Convivio* he notes a comparable distinction between the "bontade" and the "bellezza" of a discourse: goodness lies in "sentenza," beauty in "l'ornamento de le parole," and of the two goodness gives the greater delight (II, ll).

Whereas that concern with goodness led Dante ultimately to the *Commedia*, to a poetics in which the beauty of words serves a content dictated by supreme Love, and whereas the very problem of the relationship between goodness and poetry seems to have animated so much of Chaucer's work, the court lyrics appear to reflect the casual acceptance of the possibility of vernacular eloquence without any corresponding concern for the depth or nature of their *sententia*. They are somewhat unwitting testimony to a widespread, easy confidence in the capabilities of the vernacular.

But the court lyric is not unrelated to important developments in late medieval poetics. Its intensive and often reverential exploration of feeling, of *sentement*, almost invariably in the most decorous language, is doubtless part of the shift in secular sensibility that D. W. Robertson, Jr., has noted in regard to late medieval views of the *Roman de la Rose* and that John V. Fleming has rather acidly characterized as "the moist chivalry of the Middle Ages in decline."[30] Also, the lyric's concern with beautiful, "musical" speech, in a way that makes the pleasing use of language theoretically accessible to anyone willing to learn the rules, accounts in part for an increased emphasis in the fifteenth century on the poet as a craftsman of language.[31] But these matters are part of complex cultural developments. Neither the practitioners nor the early observers of the fixed form lyrics seem to have had much interest in their historical or theoretical significance. As the evidence assembled here indicates, late medieval society talked about the lyrics in a variety of ways: as recreation, as conversation, as personal expression, as music. That variety, with its greater interest in social than in literary values, is indicative of the real place of the fixed form lyric in its time. It gives us vernacular poetics at leisure; and leisure, as we know, presupposes greater exertions elsewhere.

——— NOTES ———

[1]Moore, *The Secular Lyric in Middle English* (Lexington, 1951), pp. 124–27. Reiss, *The Art of the Middle English Lyric* (Athens, Ga., 1972), pp. ix–xv. Wilkins, *One Hundred Ballades, Rondeaulx and Virelais From the Late Middle Ages* (Cambridge, 1969), p. vii. For more appreciative criticism, see Daniel Poirion's comprehensive study, *Le Poète et le prince: L'évolution du lyrisme courtois de Guillaume de Machaut à Charles d'Orléans* (Paris, 1965) and John Stevens, *Music and Poetry in the Early Tudor Court* (Lincoln, 1961). "Music and Poetry," the appendix to Douglas Kelly's *Medieval Imagination* (Madison, 1978), is a valuable contribution which appeared after the writing of this essay.

[2]Moore, p. 127.

[3]The dominant influence is certainly French. Chaucer's importation of some of the fixed forms into England is well known, and French influence on Catalonian and Italian lyric production has been demonstrated, though Italian traditions are by no means identical to those of France. On these matters see, in addition to the standard treatments of *ars nova* in the major histories of music, Nigel Wilkins, "The Post-Machaut Generation of Poet-Musicians," *NMS*, 12 (1968), 40–84; Adelmo Damerini's brief *Guglielmo de Machaut e l' "Ars nova" italiana* (Florence, 1960); Alberto Ghislanzoni, "Les Formes littéraires et musicales italiennes au commencement du XIVe siècle," *Les Colloques de Wégimont II—1955, L'Ars Nova* (Paris, 1959), pp. 149–63; Amédée Pagès, *La Poésie française en Catalogne du XIIIe siècle à la fin du XVe* (Paris, 1936). As an illustration of the unified nature of late medieval lyric "making," one may note the remarks of a Spanish friar who visited both France and Italy; he says that in the former country people are always singing and dancing and that Neapolitan woman also sing and talk of love "axi com fan les dones generoses de França" (Pagès, pp. 46–47).

[4]Ed. Jérôme Pichon (Paris, 1846), I, 71–72. Trans. Eileen Power, *The Goodman of Paris* (New York, 1928), p. 102. For notes on the games, see Pichon, I, lxxvii and 71, and Power, p. 317.

[5]Lines 610–14, in *The Works of Geoffrey Chaucer*, ed. F. N. Robinson, 2nd ed. (Boston, 1957). Subsequent references to Chaucer in the text will be to line numbers of this edition.

[6]Quoted in Wilkins, "The Post-Machaut Generation," 43.

[7]See e.g., André Pirro, *Histoire de la musique de la fin du XIVe siècle à la fin du XVIe* (Paris, 1940); Nanie Bridgman, "La Musique dans la société française au temps de l'ars nova," in *L'ars nova italiana del Trecento*, ed. Bianca Becherini (Certaldo, 1962), pp. 83–96.

[8]See my article, "Deschamps' *Art de dictier* and Chaucer's Literary Environment," *Speculum*, 48 (1973), 714–23.

[9]VI, 23. *On the Properties of Things*, ed. M. C. Seymour et al. (Oxford, 1975), I, 330–31. Nicole Oresme, in the text cited below in n. 16, p. 342, quotes *Ecclus.* 32:8 in support of music at dinner. Since the writing of this essay, two contributions have further established the need to see the court lyric in its immediate social context: Richard Firth Green, *Poets and Princepleasers: Literature and the English Court in the Late Middle Ages* (Toronto, 1980), esp. pp. 101–34; and Rossell Hope Robbins, "The Middle English Court Love Lyric," in *The Interpretation of Medieval Lyric Poetry*, ed. W. T. H. Jackson (New York, 1980), pp. 205–32. These and other studies approach principally from the standpoint of social history concerns that I address here principally from the standpoint of literary thought.

[10]*Commentary on the Nicomachean Ethics*, trans. C. I. Litzinger, O.P. (Chicago, 1964), I, 368. For Aristotle I have used the translation of Martin Ostwald (Indianapolis, 1962); the virtues are first mentioned in II, 7 and then at greater length in IV, 6–8.

[11]II, 25. *Li Livres dou Trésor de Brunetto Latini*, ed. Francis J. Carmody, University of California Publications in Modern Philology, 22 (Berkeley, 1948), p. 196.

[12]II, 37. Carmody, p. 204. Latini's use of "gengleour" is based not on the *Ethics* but the *Compendium*: "medius in solatio et ludo est apte iocans, et superfluens in hoc potest dici ioculator, deficiens uero homo uel incultus aggrestis (*sic*) dicitur." Concetto Marchesi, *L'Etica Nicomachea nella tradizione latina medievale* (Messina, 1904), appendix, p. xlix. Cf. R. T. Lenaghan, "The Clerk of Venus: Chaucer and Medieval Romance," in *The Learned and the Lewed*, ed. Larry D. Benson, Harvard English Studies 5 (Cambridge, Mass., 1974), p. 43.

[13]*Materials for the History of Thomas Becket*, ed. J. C. Robertson, Rolls Series 67, pt. 3 (London, 1878), pp. 8–12. H. E. Butler's translation of this text has been reprinted in *The World of* Piers Plowman, ed. Jeanne Krochalis and Edward Peters (Univ. of Pennsylvania Press, 1975), pp. 24–34.

[14]Quoted in William Allen Neilson, *The Origins and Sources of the Court of Love* (1899; rpt. New York, 1967), p. 201. For Francesco da Barberino, see Giuseppe Vecchi, "Educazione musicale, scuola e società nell'opera didascalica di Francesco da Barberino," *Quadrivium*, 7 (1966), 5–29, esp. 7–15. For Chaucer see *CT* A 94–96, and the comparable list in the ME *Romaunt of the Rose*, 2311–28. For the courtesy book, see *The Babees Book*, ed. F. J. Furnivall, EETS o.s. 32 (London, 1868), p. 34.

[15]*Oeuvres complètes*, ed. M. de Queux de Saint-Hilaire and Gaston Raynaud, 11 vols., SATF (Paris, 1878–1903), VII, 266–92. For further discussion of this logic see my article in *SP*, 71 (1974), 291–313, and for more on the *Art de dictier*, the article cited above in n. 8.

[16]*Maistre Nicole Oresme: Le Livre de Politiques d'Aristote*, ed. A. D. Menut, *Transactions of the American Philosophical Society*, 60, pt. 6 (1970), p. 348.

[17]*Le Livre de Ethiques d'Aristote*, ed. A. D. Menut (New York, 1940), p. 517.

[18]*Le Livre des faicts du bon messire Jean le Maingre, dit Boucicaut*, ed. Petitot in *Collection complète des mémoires relatifs à l'histoire de France*, 6–7 (Paris, 1819), VII, 214–18.

[19]For the composition of the *Cent Ballades*, see Gaston Raynaud's introduction to his SATF edition (Paris, 1905), pp. xl–lvi. For Montagu and his associates, K. B. McFarlane, *Lancastrian Kings and Lollard Knights* (Oxford, 1972) and V. J. Scattergood, "The Authorship of 'The Boke of Cupide,'" *Anglia*, 82 (1964), 143–49. For Creton's text and translation, John Webb, "Translation of a French Metrical History of the Deposition of King Richard the Second," *Archaeologia*, 20 (1824), 314, 320, 72. Christine de Pisan also testifies to Montagu's reputation as a "gracieux dicteur" (Webb, 72 n.).

[20] *Oeuvres poétiques*, ed. M. Roy, SATF, I (Paris, 1886), 51.

[21] *Summa Theologica*, I–II, q. 38, a. 2, trans. Fathers of the English Dominican Province, I (New York, 1947), p. 754.

[22] *Monumens de la littérature romane*, ed. A. F. Gatien-Arnoult, I (Toulouse, 1841), 10. *Amorous Games: A Critical Edition of* Les Adevineaux amoureux, ed. James Woodrow Hassell, Jr. (Austin, 1974), p. 200.

[23] Trans. John Lydgate, ed. F. J. Furnivall, EETS o.s. 77, 83, 92 (1899–1904; rpt. Millwood, N. Y., 1973), p. 317.

[24] *Nicole Oresme and the Medieval Geometry of Qualities and Motions*, ed. and trans. Marshall Clagett (Madison, 1968), p. 330; for the medical precedents see pp. 478–79. Bartholomaeus' assertion of the therapeutic value of voice and music, quoted above, is followed by a citation to and an anecdote from Constantinus Africanus. For further, abundant evidence of medieval views of music as therapy, see Madeleine Pelner Cosman, "Machaut's Medical Musical World," in *Machaut's World: Science and Art in the Fourteenth Century*, ed. Madeleine Cosman and Bruce Chandler, *Annals of the New York Academy of Sciences*, 314 (1978), 1–36.

[25] "Notes toward an Aesthetic of Popular Culture," *JPC*, 5 (1971), 258. I owe this and the following reference to Paul Solon and Gary Engle.

[26] *Adventure, Mystery, and Romance: Formula Stories as Art and Popular Culture* (Chicago, 1976), p. 19. The entire discussion of the artistic characteristics of formula literature, pp. 8–20, is relevant. For parallels in verbal and situational stylization between some medieval and modern love songs, see Ruth Harvey, "Minnesang and the 'Sweet Lyric,'" *GL & L*, n. s. 17 (1963), 14–26. Though concerned only with music of the 1950s, Donald Horton's "The Dialogue of Courtship in Popular Songs," *Am Jnl Soc*, 62 (1957), 569–78, makes some similar points about the conventionality of popular lyrics and their social and psychological usefulness.

[27] In "A Short Essay on the Middle English Secular Lyric," *NM*, 73 (1972), 117–18, George Kane offers a variety of objections to the traditional terminology.

[28] Various studies of Chaucer have made this point in varying ways. Nancy Dean, "Chaucer's *Complaint*, A Genre Descended from the *Heroides*," *CL*, 19 (1967), 1–27, shows that Chaucer's complaints are less abstract, more subject to irony, than is usual in the genre. John Burrow comments on Chaucer's less "lyric" reworkings of Boccaccio in *Ricardian Poetry* (New Haven, 1971), pp. 52–57. In "The Terms of Love: A Study of Troilus's Style," *Speculum*, 51 (1975), 69–90, Davis Taylor associates Troilus' speech patterns with "lyric conventions" and then indicates ways in which those attitudes are qualified by other perspectives in the poem. The *Book of the Duchess* is also in one sense a critique of the limitations of conventional lyric diction; for a recent view along these lines, see Phillip C. Boardman, "Courtly Language and the Strategy of Consolation in the *Book of the Duchess*," *ELH*, 44 (1977), 567–79.

[29]For documentation of these texts, and for evidence of the distinction at this time between poets and writers of lyrics, see my article "Making and Poetry in the Age of Chaucer," *CL*, 31 (1979), 272–90.

[30]*A Preface to Chaucer* (Princeton, 1963), pp. 361–65. "Hoccleve's 'Letter of Cupid' and the 'Quarrel' over the *Roman de la Rose*," *MÆ*, 40 (1971), 38.

[31]See e.g., Lois Ebin's comparison of Lydgate and Chaucer in this regard, in "Lydgate's Views on Poetry," *AnM*, 18 (1977), 89–90.

LATE MEDIEVAL IMAGES
AND SELF-IMAGES OF THE POET:
CHAUCER, GOWER, LYDGATE,
HENRYSON, DUNBAR
ROBERT O. PAYNE

IN THE INTRODUCTORY chapter of his excellent study of John
Lydgate,[1] Derek Pearsall remarks that for Lydgate,

> ... poetry is a public art, its existence conditioned and
> determined by outer needs and pressures, not by inner ones.
> In this sense, all his poetry is occasional poetry. Writing of a
> Romantic poet, one would be tempted to create, even if
> there were not extant chronological evidence, a chronologi-
> cal structure in which each poem was so placed as to
> illustrate the growth of the poet's mind, or some mythical
> prototype of it. . . . It is not profitable to study a medieval
> poet like Lydgate in this way. . . . Every mask he puts on is a
> well-worn medieval one, and it is well to recognize these
> masks for what they are, otherwise we may find ourselves
> interpreting poems like the *Testament* as personal
> documents.

Now, in the sense in which it is offered, that statement seems to me
unexceptionable. But at the same time, it is a little troublesome. To
distinguish between a monitory art and an expressionistic one is
surely critically useful—and Pearsall's paragraph might well bring
to mind Yeats' dictum (which Lydgate would never have understood) that "out of the quarrel with others we make rhetoric; out of

the quarrel with ourselves we make poetry." The trouble is that, especially in the context of late Middle English and Scots poetry, the Pearsall-Yeats distinction does not allow for some very interesting alternatives. Indeed, it seems to rule them out *a priori*.

The one I particularly want to suggest here is that there is an important difference between poems that present themselves to us in the speaking voice of an author for whom a framing *persona* is provided, and poems which do not, or which do so only minimally. In this matter, it is of little consequence whether or how the voice and *persona* might correlate with the historical personage and personality of the poet. The question is rather one of alternative models for the poetic process, and although it is a larger issue that I do not wish to pursue here, some quite significantly different models can be seen in the late medieval poets.

Several recent historical critics have assumed, for some very good reasons, that the most appropriate conceptual model for most medieval poems is the binary, idea / language one.[2] The rhetorical decorum that should then follow ought to drive the poet toward anonymity, toward the suppression of an identifiable voice. And it would seem to follow also that readers of poems see through language to ideas, rather than listen to other fallible men speaking. Yet all the poets named in my title go to considerable pains to present images of themselves both as poets and as readers, although for none of them is the idea / language model fully appropriate, and only Lydgate closely approaches it.

I think it was to explore such issues that Chaucer made his marvelous trip to the house of Fame. The encyclopedic aquiline pedagogue who conducts Geffrey to "fames hous" puts it with a nice precision at mid-flight:[3]

> Loo, this sentence ys knowen kouth
> Of every philosophres mouth,
> As Aristotle and daun Platon,
> And other clerkys many oon;
> And to confirme my resoun,
> Thou wost wel this, that spech is soun,
> Or elles no man myghte hyt here;
> Now herke what y wol the lere.
>   "Soun ys noght but eyr ybroken,
> And every speche that ys spoken,
> Lowd or pryvee, foul or fair,
> In his substaunce ys but air;
> For as flaumbe ys but lyghted smoke,

250

Ryght soo soun ys air ybroke.
But this may be in many wyse,
Of which I wil the two devyse,
As soun that cometh of pipe or harpe.
For whan that a pipe is blowen sharpe,
The air ys twyst with violence
And rent; loo, thys ys my sentence;
Eke, whan men harpe-strynges smyte,
Whether hyt be moche or lyte,
Loo, with the strok the ayr tobreketh;
And ryght so breketh it when men speketh.   (*HF*, 757–80)

That is, Geffrey, as a mortal consumer of the literary tradition, has
all along actually been hearing speeches; but since mortal Geffrey
hears them only after they have echoed down through time, he now
needs to visit the record library where they are preserved as first
spoken—and at the same time to identify (as he will in the allegory
of Book III) the particular individual speakers who made the
speeches. *Elocutio* and *ethos*, after the Eagle's introductory lecture
in Book II, will merge in the figures of the ancient writers Geffrey
sees (and partly hears) in Book III.

An understanding of what Chaucer is about in the *Hous of
Fame* depends to a considerable degree upon our perception of the
Eagle's reopening of an ancient quarrel dear to Sophistic rhetoricians. If, for instance, Geffrey perceives Vergil (as he does in Book I)
in terms of the idea / language conceptual model, then the *Aeneid*
crystalizes into the permanent, eternal "table of bras" on the walls of
the Temple of Venus. If, on the other hand, Geffrey is to perceive
the *Aeneid* in terms of the Eagle's explication of the speaker /
speech / hearer model, then he hears a very mortal Vergil breaking
wind down the centuries.

My main point is that Chaucer manipulates his self-image as
narrator not (insofar as we can tell) for any overt psychological
revelation, but to help try to define the poetic process. Before going
on to some of his contemporaries and successors, I should make a
couple of minor and interestingly related points. First, Chaucer's
images of himself as author and as reader are indeed obverse and
reverse of the same theoretical coin. He fully expects us to experience the same difficulties and frustrations with his poetry as he had
with Vergil's. A little earlier in the *Hous of Fame*, at the beginning
of Book II, his proem worries typically about future readers and his
ability to speak to them:

Now herkeneth, every maner man
That Englissh understonde kan,
And listeneth of my drem to lere.
For now at erste shul ye here
So sely an avisyoun
That Isaye, ne Scipion,
Ne kyng Nabugodonosor,
Pharoo, Turnus, ne Elcanor,
ne mette such a drem as this!
Now faire blisfull, O Cipris,
So be my favour at this tyme!
And ye, me to endite and ryme
Helpeth, that on Parnaso duelle,
Be Elicon, the clere welle.
O Thought, that wrot al that I mette,
And in the tresorye hyt shette
Of my brayn, now shal men se
Yf any vertu in the be,
To tellen al my drem aryght.
Now kythe thyn engyn and thy myght.   (509–28)

Second, and in a more literally historical perspective, nearly all of the poems Chaucer depicts himself as concerned with in his self-images are spoken by voices enormously remote in time, language, and culture. Again, we must look at the image, rather than at what we know or suspect to be its referent. We may know, for example, that the voice Chaucer hears, echoes, and alters in *Troilus and Criseyde* is really Boccaccio's, but in the imagery of his poem Chaucer assigns it to the old Roman Lollius. That is, in the tropes Chaucer develops for the relationship of his poetry to his predecessors in the craft, there is nothing at all like the figure he is himself to become in the self-imagery of Lydgate, Henryson and Dunbar.

Many of us may immediately think of John Gower as an exception, if not a negation, to this last assertion. Yet whatever may have been the course of the friendship between the two poets, or their influence on each other, neither figures in the other's imagery of his relationship to past tradition. For neither do the echoing voices they must learn to hear include any recent English ones, or each other's.

However, Gower is, like Chaucer, painstakingly concerned (especially in the *Confessio*) to invent a *persona* to control the voice we hear in his work. And not even in the *Vox clamantis* does the etymological definition of *persona* very accurately indicate how we perceive its author. Gower is never just the medium through which

252

some ultimate truth speaks (*per-sonare*); the voice we listen to decrying the wilderness of *fin de siècle* Ricardian politics has to be authenticated by a *persona* we can believe and trust because he is an experienced, scarred survivor of his own humanity:[4]

> No matter how much a dullness of perception may hinder me, I shall nevertheless render without any embarrassment the things for which my ingenuousness is adequate. Knowing very little used to be a great disgrace for an old man, because of the magnitude of the time he had lost. But nowadays if old age is wise in any way or teaches what it has learned earlier, its voice hardly receives the welcome of a youth's. Even if they are fervent in their zeal, the words which old men write are, as a rule, acceptable to young men only quite rarely. Yet no matter how much the voices of the dogs may bark in objection, I shall not run away, but instead I shall sing out my words.

For certain kinds of historians of ideas, it seems satisfactorily accurate to label both the *persona* of Geffrey in *Hous of Fame* and the passage I have just quoted from Gower's *Vox clamantis* as manifestations of the "humility topos" and let it go at that. But in fact, that superficial categorization obscures, a good deal more than it clarifies, the two poets' deployments of their *personae*. One short-cut to an explanation of the point (admittedly more metaphorical than analytical) might go this way: none of us really believes that the Geffrey of the second book of the *Hous of Fame* correlates in any but the most oblique and figurative way with the "real Chaucer"; nearly all of us feel that the "real Gower" must have sounded nearly exactly like the speaker of the *Vox clamantis*. There is in fact no kind of available evidence to support either view. We are dealing with two deliberately constructed self-images—and the historians of medieval rhetoric incidentally notify us that their forms have several features in common. Because Gower's is a stylistically consistent *persona* throughout his work, and though often ironic and self-deprecatory, never comic, we find it easy to say "that is the *real* moral Gower." Because Chaucer's *persona* is comic and not identical with several of his alternative *personae*, we find it hard to correlate with the putative unified personality of a serious "real Chaucer."

But to switch back to theoretical and historical terms more appropriate to my own argument, Chaucer's deployment of his self-image—his argument from *ethos*—is essentially Aristotelian; Gower's is much closer to Quintilian.

Early in the first book of his *Rhetoric*, Aristotle exhorts the persuasive speaker to construct a *persona* for himself as one of his prime agencies of persuasion:[5]

> Of the modes of persuasion furnished by the spoken word there are three kinds. The first kind depends on the personal character of the speaker; . . . This kind of persuasion, like the others should be achieved by what the speaker says, not by what people think of his character before he begins to speak.

And although Chaucer almost certainly could never have read that passage, it is an apt prescription for his usual procedure—to recreate himself in each new poem as part of the machinery for achieving the ends that poem seeks.

Gower, on the other hand, carefully builds through all his work a consistent *persona* which will authenticate the voice we hear in those poems, a procedure succinctly prescribed by Quintilian at the beginning of the *Institutio*:[6] "I hold that no one can be a true orator unless he is also a good man and even if he could be, I would not have it so." In fact—and again with a perspective quite different from Chaucer's—Gower's image of his precedent *auctores* is pretty much as a succession of good old boys who have (like him) lived, suffered, learned, won and lost, and so earned the right to their utterance and our attention:[7]

> For hier in erthe amonges ous,
> If no man write hou that it stode,
> The pris of hem that weren goode
> Scholde, as who seith, a gret partie
> Be lost; so for to magnifie
> The worthi princes that tho were,
> The bokes schewen hiere and there,
> Wherof the world ensampled is;
> And tho that deden thanne amis
> Thurgh tirannie and crualte,
> Right as thei stoden in degre,
> So was the wrytinge of hire werk.
> Thus I, which am a burel clerk,
> Purpose forto wryte a bok
> After the world that whilom tok
> Long tyme in olde daies passed:
> But for men sein it is now lassed,
> In worse plit than it was tho,
> I thenke forto touche also

The world which neweth every dai,
So as I can, so as I mai.
Thogh I seknesse have upon honde
And longe have had, yit woll I fonde
To wryte and do my bisinesse,
That in some part, so as I gesse,
The wyse man mai ben avised.

Within a generation, John Lydgate had conceived a very different image of those poets of the past against whom he had to define himself—different not only because the image is so dominated by Chaucer, but also because Chaucer has come to mean for Lydgate a particular skill in the ordering of language. That is, the authentication Lydgate seeks for his own voice is that it echoes a doubly valid model: Chaucer the immediate father of English poetry,[8]

Noble Galfride, poete of Breteyne,
Among oure englische that made first to reyne
The gold dewe-dropis of rhetorik so fyne,
Oure rude langage only t'enlumyne;

and Chaucer the nonpareil wordsmith:[9]

Flour of Poetes thorghout all breteyne,
Which sothly hadde most of excellence
In rethorike and in eloquence
(Rede his making who list the trouthe fynde)
Which neuer shal appallen in my mynde,
But alwey fressh ben in my memorye:
To whom be yiue pris honure and glorye
Of wel seyinge first in oure language
Chief Registrer of this pilgrimage,
Al that was tolde foryeting noght at al,
Feyned tailis nor thing Historial,
With many prouerbe diuers and unkouth,
Be rehersaile of his Sugrid mouth,
Of eche thynge keping in substance
The sentence hool with-oute variance,
Voyding the chaf sothly for to seyn,
Enlumynyng the trewe piked greyn
Be crafty writing of his sawes swete.

It was probably a little snide of Derek Pearsall to remark that when Lydgate invokes the "humility topos" we really believe him, but I think Pearsall's observation penetrates to the heart of the matter we

255

are concerned with here. Lydgate quite literally means to measure himself against Chaucer—a Chaucer who is far more intimidating to Lydgate than Ovid had been to Chaucer, both because of Lydgate's chauvinistic awe of the "well of purest English undefiled" and because of his conviction that to write well was to write like Chaucer. For Lydgate, his voice will be authenticated largely to the extent that it sounds like Chaucer's, and so for him the idea / language model for the poetic process has very nearly merged with the speaker / hearer one.

Why Lydgate never seems to have recognized Chaucer's dramatic and rhetorical exploitations of his poetic voice and *persona* remains a puzzle, as does the suddenness of Chaucer's apotheosis in the metaphors Hoccleve and Lydgate offer for their sense of themselves as poets in the great tradition. Their personal and patriotic identification with Chaucer seems almost spontaneously to have generated what is to be itself a conventional *topos* for the next two centuries of English poets. Gower, whatever his personal relationship with Chaucer may have been, gives us in the 1390 version of the *Confessio amantis* a very different image of his sense of their relationships with each other and to the great tradition:

> And gret wel Chaucer whan ye mete,
> As mi disciple and mi poete:
> For in the floures of his youthe
> In sondri wise, as he wel couthe,
> Of Ditees and of songes glade,
> The which he for mi sake made,
> The lond fulfild is overal. . . .   (VIII, 2941–47)

Undoubtedly, some part of the slightly avuncular, faintly condescending tone of this passage has to be charged to Venus, who speaks it, rather than to Gower. But equally surely, it was Gower rather than Venus who cancelled it in a subsequent revision. The main point, in any case, is that neither the original passage nor its cancellation would have been possible for Lydgate.

It would probably have come as a considerable surprise to all three of these poets that within a few years after Lydgate's death in 1449, their names had become solidly linked to form for late fifteenth- and early sixteenth-century poets what might almost be labeled an "auctoritee topos." Dunbar coins the image in typical form in his moving *Lament for the Makaris*:[10]

> The noble Chaucer, of makaris flour,
> The Monk of Bery, and Gower, all thre.   (50–51)

Even the form in which Dunbar casts the image calls to mind at once Chaucer's injunction to his book, at the end of *Troilus and Criseyde*, to

> ... kis the steppes, where as thow seest pace
> Virgile, Ovid, Omer, Lucan and Stace.　(V, 1791–92)

Yet the differences between the two images, in their contexts, are nearly as great as their similarities. Chaucer's image is unmistakably of the enthroned immortals of a distant time and another language. Dunbar's is one in his litany of *ubi sunt* images supporting his *timor mortis* theme, whose poignancy depends largely on his awareness of Chaucer and Lydgate and Gower as very near to him and very like him.

But like Chaucer, Dunbar exploits both his images of other poets and his self-images quite variously—I am tempted to say playfully. In the *Flyting of Dunbar and Kennedie*, for instance, we get a bravura comic *reductio ad absurdum* of the image of poets as mortal men speaking to each other, one which takes us far beyond where the eagle and Geffrey left us in the second book of the *Hous of Fame*:

> Commirwald crawdoun, na man comptis the ane kers,
> 　Sueir swappit swanky, swynekeper ay for swaittis;
> Thy commissar Quintyne biddis the cum kis his ers,
> 　He luvis nocht sic ane forlane loun of laittis;
> 　He sayis, thow skaffis and beggis mair beir and aitis
> Nor ony cripill in Karrik land abowt;
> 　Uther pure beggaris and thow ar at debaittis,
> Decretpit karlingis on Kennedy cryis owt.　(129–36)

On the other hand, in *Dunbar at Oxinfurde*, we see a Dunbar who could have come straight out of Quintilian via Gower:

> The curious probatioun logicall
> 　The eloquence of ornat rhetorie,
> The naturall science philosophicall
> 　The dirk apperance of astronomie,
> 　The theologis sermoun, the fablis of poetrie,
> Without gud lyfe all in the selfe dois de,
> 　As Maii flouris dois in September dry:
> A paralous lyfe is vane prosperite.　(9–16)

And in the familiar passage in the *Goldyn Targe*, he out-Lydgates Lydgate in his apotheosis of Chaucer:

257

O reverend Chaucere, rose of rethoris all
As in oure tong ane flour imperiall,
   That raise in Britaine evir, quho redis rycht,
Thou beris of makaris the tryumph riall;
Thy fresch anamalit termes celicall
   This mater could illumynit have full brycht.
   Was thou noucht of our Inglisch all the lycht
Surmounting eviry tong terrestriall,
   Alls fer as Mayis morow dois mydnycht?   (253–61)

What I particularly want to emphasize is the exuberant variety of Dunbar's exploitation of the images of himself and his fellow poets. Like Chaucer, he seems to feel free to construct and develop whatever self-image best suits the mood and needs of a particular poem. Like Chaucer, he sees his fellow makers sometimes as nearly unapproachable models of verbal craft, sometimes as equals or less, and at least as mortally flawed as himself.

But for one final and, I think, still different deployment of the poet's voice and *persona*, let us look at another of the makers whose death Dunbar lamented, his fellow Scot, Robert Henryson.

At the beginning of the *Testament of Cresseid*, Henryson carefully details for us the icy, blustery March night on which he began to write:[11]

Richt sa it wes quhen I began to wryte
This tragedie; the wedder richt feruent,
Quhen Aries, in middis of the Lent,
Schouris of haill [gart] fra the north discend,
That scantlie fra the cauld I micht defend.

Yit neuertheles within myne oratur
I stude, quhen Titan had his bemis bricht
Withdrawin doun and sylit under cure,
And fair Venus, the bewtie of the nicht,
Uprais and set unto the west full richt
Hir Goldin face, in oppositioun
Of God Phebus, direct discending doun.

Throw out the glas hir bemis brast sa fair
That I micht se on euerie syde me by;
The northin wind had purifyit the air
And sched the mistie cloudis fra the sky;
The froist freisit, the blastis bitterly
Fra Pole Artick come quhisling loud and schill,
And causit me remufe aganis my will.   (3–21)

Except for the conventional astronomical personifications, this is clear, circumstantially detailed, highly visualized realism. And so the first-person narrator who gradually materializes in that very specific setting emerges also as solidly human, a visibly present speaker whom we have just joined in his study to while away a raw night. Then our friendly, sophisticated, urbane host pokes up the fire, pours himself a double scotch, pulls a favorite book off the shelf, and prepares to tell us a marvellous story:

> I mend the fyre and beikit me about,
> Than tuik ane drink, my spreitis to comfort,
> And armit me weill fra the cauld thairout.
> To cut the winter nicht and mak it schort
> I tuik ane quair—and left all vther sport—
> Writtin be worthie Chaucer glorious
> Of fair Creisseid and worthie Troylus.   (36–42)

It is not that we should try to see in Henryson what many Victorian critics wanted to find in Chaucer, a "modern" something-or-other, two or three centuries ahead of his time. Rather, I suggest that Henryson had just discovered yet another way to develop and exploit that self-image that had become so important a device to his fellow English poets since Chaucer. And what Henryson wants for his *persona* here is neither moral credibility nor the ambivalent perspectives of irony, but simply (in anticipation of a Lamb or a Poe) the embodiment of the compelling tale-teller. In a sense, the wind howling around the shutters, the blazing fire, the drink, the good old book, our friendly host, all certify in advance the quality of the story we are to hear. These are exactly the circumstances under which fine tales are told—even down to the unimportant but titillating touch of mystery thrown in a couple of stanzas later:

> To breik my sleip ane vther quair I tuik,
> In quhilk I fand the fatal destenie
> Of fair Cresseid, that endit wretchitlie.
>
> Quha wait gif all that Chauceir wrait was trew?
> Nor I wait nocht gif this narratioun
> Be authoreist, or fenyeit of the new
> Be sum poeit. . . .   (61–67)

Not to sell Maister Henryson short, we must acknowledge that much is hidden under that oblique implication that even "glorious Chaucer" might not always be trusted; and it would be most interesting to know exactly how Henryson distinguished between a narrative that was "authoreist" and one that was "newly imagined by some poet." But the more important point is that in the *Testament* Henryson does not manage his self-image in such a way as to explore or develop those issues, as Chaucer so repeatedly does in his poems.

To conclude with a bit of generalization: what I have most wished to point out here is that late Middle English poets regularly image forth themselves and their predecessors in the craft as part of the process of making poems. But for us critics, there are two mistakes perhaps too easily made about their procedures. Because we are dealing with self-images, we may (as too many historical critics have warned us) press them too hard for direct personal revelations, and when those are not forthcoming, dismiss the images as "merely conventional." On the other hand, seeing such imagery as conventional, we may fail to pursue adequately its integration into the strategies and purposes of various poems and so miss much of what the poems do after all reveal about their author's attitudes toward their craft and themselves as practitioners of it.

For a couple of centuries now, we have been offered a variety of historical definitions of medieval poetry as language decorously embodying ideas—as constantly seeking that total impersonality T. S. Eliot recommended for all poetry. I think all the poets discussed here thought of themselves as men trying to speak to us through their poems.

—— NOTES ——

[1] Derek Pearsall, *John Lydgate* (Charlottesville, 1970), p. 5.

[2] Of several quite recent examples, an especially good one is Ernest Gallo, "The *Poetria Nova* of Geoffrey of Vinsauf," in *Medieval Eloquence*, ed. James J. Murphy (Berkeley, 1978), pp. 68–84. Gallo quotes the well-known passage from the *Poetria* which Chaucer paraphrased in *Troilus and Criseyde*, I. 1065–69 ("If anyone is to lay the foundation of a house his impetuous hand does not leap into action . . ."), and comments: "Of interest here is the notion of the mental model, the *archetypus*, to which we will return later. I will suggest that it is precisely the *archetypus* which is to be expressed in the opening lines of the poem."

[3] All quotations from Chaucer are from F. N. Robinson, *The Works of Geoffrey Chaucer*, 2nd ed. (Boston, 1957).

[4] *Vox clamantis*, Bk. II, Prologue, trans. Eric W. Stockton in *The Major Latin Works of John Gower* (Seattle, 1962), p. 97.

[5]*Rhetorica*, Bk. I.2,1356^a, trans. W. Rhys Roberts in *The Works of Aristotle*, ed. W. D. Ross (Oxford, 1946), vol. XI.

[6]*Institutio oratoria*, I.ii.3, ed. and trans. H. E. Butler (London and New York, 1921).

[7]*Confessio amantis*, Prologue, 11. 40–65, ed. Russell A. Peck (New York, 1968).

[8]*Troy Book*, 4697–4700, ed. Henry Bergen, *EETS*, nos. 97, 103, 106, 126 (1906–1935).

[9]*Siege of Thebes*, 40–57, ed. Axel Erdman, *Publications of the Chaucer Society*, Ser. 2, no. 46 (1911).

[10]All quotations from Dunbar's poetry are from *The Poems of William Dunbar*, ed. W. Mackay Mackenzie (Edinburgh, 1932).

[11]Quotations from the *Testament of Cresseid* are from *Robert Henryson: The Testament of Cresseid*, ed. Denton Fox (London, 1968).

POETICS AND STYLE
IN LATE MEDIEVAL LITERATURE
LOIS EBIN

ONE OF THE MOST distinctive and, to moderns, troubling features of late medieval poetry is its preoccupation with high style. In Italy, this tendency finds form in post-Petrarchan elegance, in France in the theory and practices of the Grands Rhétoriquers. In England and Scotland, it is evident in the pronounced shift toward an increasing use of elevated style in both secular and religious verse which occurs at the outset of the fifteenth century, a change which is perhaps even more striking than its continental counterpart since the high stylistic mode is virtually absent from Middle English literature before this time. When high style begins to appear with some frequency in the works of the late fourteenth-century poets, it is, in contrast to fifteenth-century practices, generally undercut or treated ironically. For the most part, critics have viewed the shift in attitude toward high style as an embarrassing symptom of decline.[1] But this feature of late medieval poetry, because of its very pervasiveness, deserves a more inquisitive response. We have not recognized that the use of high style in the late Middle Ages is an important indication of a changed conception of poetry and the role of the poet, and, rather than being a perversion or misrepresentation of earlier practices, the fifteenth-century poets' style is linked directly to ideals and assumptions about poetry which are different from those of their so-called "maisters." While, as Burrow de-monstrates, the uneasiness about the unequivocal use of high style in the English poetry of the late fourteenth century is a mark of ambivalence about the truthfulness of poetry and the limits of mortal man as artist,[2] these dilemmas are no longer apparent in the fifteenth century. Poetry is viewed as ennobling; the poet's effort leads man to truth, and his heightened style is seen as the medium which is most appropriate to his noble purpose.

The attitudes of uneasiness and enthusiasm about high style and the contrasting views of poetry of the late fourteenth- and fifteenth-century English and Scots poets are aspects of a much larger debate, inherited from classical antiquity, which pervades the discussions of poetry throughout the Middle Ages. In its earliest and most familiar form, the dualism between positive and negative visions of poetry is introduced in the writings of Plato and Aristotle, particularly in their considerations of the truthfulness of poetry and its relation to philosophy and the effects of the poet's and the rhetor's language . While Plato argues that poetry as an imitative art provides only an inferior or partial version of truth and debases man's vision by arousing the lower element of his mind at the expense of the higher, Aristotle defends the process of poetic imitation as one which enables man to see reality more clearly by allowing him to consider truths represented in art which are either too incoherent or too painful to view directly in life.[3] Likewise, although Plato acknowledges the appeal of poetic language, he emphasizes that it belongs to a lower sphere of action and is useful only when subordinated to dialectic.[4] Aristotle, in contrast, distin-guishes between two types of rhetorical and poetic language, the honest and the dishonest, defending the proper use of heightened language on the side of truth and justice as a counterpart or equal art to dialectic.[5] As Lanham demonstrates, the dual attitude toward poetry is reflected again in the Roman period, not only in the rhetorical and philosophical treatises, but also in the writings of the poets themselves, for example in the Virgilian and Ovidian strate-gies of representing reality as mythic ideal in the one case, and as rhetorical creation, dependent upon the poet's language in the other.[6]

At the outset of the Middle Ages, the controversy about poetry was cast in somewhat different terms and continued with renewed intensity. In the attempt to accommodate pagan writing to the demands of the new Christian belief, the early Church Fathers debated the value of poetry and poetic style. On the one hand, classical literature, especially Virgil's *Aeneid* and the rhetorical writings of Cicero and Quintilian were much admired, both for their enormous aesthetic appeal and for their didactic use as the basis for medieval instruction in grammar and rhetoric. Morally and ethically, classical poetry embodied the best of pagan tradition and, thus, as Bolgar points out, it could not be rejected out of hand by anyone who was not, at the same time, prepared to cut himself off from the whole of existing civilization.[7] Yet, the form and content of this literature clashed in many ways with the new Christian ideals, and, therefore, was vehemently condemned by some writers. The conflict is illustrated effectively by the famous dream of St. Jerome, who, imagining himself before God's judgment seat, suddenly heard a thundering voice accuse him, "Thou art no Christian—thou art a Ciceronian!"[8] While Jerome ultimately addressed this dilemma by enlarging the concept of poetry to include certain books of the Bible and by beginning a process of separating form and content in dealing with pagan authors, it is St. Augustine in the late fourth and early fifth centuries who provides an even more significant defense of poetry and poetic style and establishes a new basis for Christian poetry. Redefining the aesthetic appeal of poetry, Augustine distinguishes between use and enjoyment and suggests that poetic eloquence is pleasurable in so far as it helps us move toward the blessed. Arguing that words are signs which point to a meaning higher than the apparent one, he demonstrates that the enjoyment one derives from poetry is in the labor of penetrating the hard outer shell of its language to discover the sweet kernel of meaning inside. While eloquence is desirable when directed to the end of wisdom, the model of style for Augustine finally becomes the Bible rather than classical sources. In examining the range of styles which this sacred book contains, Augustine discovers the underlying paradox that the most humble style, like the most humble of men, Christ, is ultimately the most sublime and, for him, the humble style or *sermo humilis* replaces the classical ideal of high style.[9]

While Augustine bases his consideration of poetry upon the enduring text of the Bible, many later writers with their eyes not on sacred but on secular texts are increasingly aware of the limitations of mortal man as poet and the uncertainty of his fallen, ambiguous, and changing language to direct man to wisdom. In the centuries which follow Augustine, both the negative view of poetry as a source of delusion and the positive vision of poetry as a means of leading man to truth survive, the former tradition represented in the works of Boethius, Bernard de Silvestris, Alain de Lille, Jean de

Meun and the latter in the writings of John of Salisbury, Bonaventura, Dante, and Boccaccio among others.[10] The tension between these two attitudes is a characteristic of medieval poetics and becomes, in many cases, a central concern in the poems themselves.

With the rise of vernacular literature on the continent in the twelfth and thirteenth centuries, one finds a number of interesting attempts on the part of poets to resolve this conflict. Two striking examples are provided by the *Tristan* of Gottfried von Strasbourg and the poetry of Dante. Characteristic of both of these efforts is a new sense of poetry as ennobling and a corresponding return to an ideal of high style. In the *Tristan*, as W. T. H. Jackson points out, Gottfried justifies his activities as a writer by defining a new relation between author, text, and audience.[11] Turning from the critics who would misunderstand the work and deny the poet fame, the quality which makes the poem blossom, Gottfried suggests that the poet is an originator whose style makes the familiar story suitable for a new type of audience, the *edele herzen* or "noble hearts" who are capable of understanding his subject, the bitter sweet quality of love, in its sorrow and joy. This love, the highest of human experience, finds form in the poet's special use of language, the paradoxes of his words, and the intricate design of sound and meaning which he introduces, and which, when received by the appropriate reader, will transform and ennoble him: "It will make love lovable, ennoble the mind, fortify constancy, and enrich their lives."[12] Finally, Gottfried links the experience of the writer's story with the holy eucharist, suggesting that what the poet offers to his select audience is the "bread" which will inspire them and give them life. Dante, carrying to its fullest implications the conceptions of Augustine and Bonaventura, introduces in the *Vita Nuova* an ideal of the poet as an imitator of God, whose book, like the divine book of the universe, when "opened up" (*aprire*) reveals significant truths. Moving beyond the *stilnovisti* vision of the love poet, he expands the significance of their traditional subject matter and style to suggest the way in which the poet's love leads to the contemplation of higher truths and his heightened language directs the chosen reader ("those who have intelligence of love") to its underlying meaning.[13]

In the late Middle Ages, with the development of English and later Scots as important literary languages, a similar reassessment of the value of poetry and the role of the poet occurs. As Kean demonstrates, after the mid-fourteenth century, one discovers in English poetry a new self-consciouness about the importance of poetry, the limitations of the poet's craft, and the need for developing an effective poetic medium in the vernacular.[14] These concerns, as well as the traditional dilemma about the truthfulness of poetry, are central themes in the poems of the period. While the responses of the fifteenth-century poets to these issues and the shift in attitude from the Ricardian uneasiness about the truthfulness of poetry and high style owe a great deal to the increasing number of defenses of poetry which appear on the continent, particularly to Boccaccio's *De genealogia deorum*, Books XIV and XV, these poets' solutions are not simply a reiteration of earlier views. Although they share certain assumptions about poetry with their continental counter-parts—the notion that poetry is ennobling and leads man to truth, the vision of the poet as an illuminator who sheds light on his matter, making it brilliant, splendid, and enduring, a new sense of the importance of poetry with its heightened language to the affairs of state—these ideals acquire a new emphasis as they are embodied in the particular critical terms, metaphors, and myths of the fifteenth-century poets. In their own ways, poets who are as dif-ferent from each other as Lydgate, James I, Henryson, Dunbar, Douglas, and Hawes turn to high style as the counterpart of their visions of poetry. Conversely, the rejection of high style in the early sixteenth century marks a movement away from the conception of poetry which dominates the end of the Middle Ages.

In English literature, the shift in attitude toward poetry at the outset of the fifteenth century is first apparent in the work of John Lydgate, who has perhaps more considerable influence on the poetic practices of the period than Chaucer. In his numerous digressions about the process of writing, Lydgate defines a view of poetry, linked to that of John of Salisbury, Dante, and Boccaccio, as ennobling, a source of wisdom and virtue. In contrast to Chaucer who repeatedly questions the relation between appearance and reality, experience and authority in his art and the limitations the poet's craft, by its very nature, imposes on his effort to create a truthful vision, Lydgate neither doubts the inherent truthfulness of poetry, nor questions the poet's intentions. Rather, he envisions the poet essentially as an illuminator who uses the power of his language to shed light on his matter and make it brilliant and effective. A supreme craftsman, the poet, like the sun with its intense light, transforms common matter into works which are fairer than the ordinary and more enduring. This process of illumination, he suggests in his chapter "On Poets and Writing" in the *Fall of*

267

Princes, IV, a section which he adds to his source, has the power to dispel the darkness of man's mind and, by shedding light on the world around him, to draw him to virtue.[15] As Lydgate explains, God ordained writing to compensate for man's dullness and make the world intelligible to his infirm wit: "God sette in writyng & lettres in sentence, / Agayn the dulnesse of our infirmyte, / This world tenlumyne be crafft of elloquence" (*FP*, IV, 29–31).

The conception of the poet as an illuminator who improves and extends his matter and its manifestations in high style is suggested more fully by the terms which Lydgate coins or popularizes to define the qualities of good poetry. As I have demonstrated elsewhere, in his digressions Lydgate develops a new critical language, introducing words where none exist and assigning new meanings to terms which were found in English before his time but which were not applied to poetry.[16] Eight terms—"enlumyn," "adourne," "enbelisshe," "aureate," "goldyn," "sugrid," "rethorik," and "elloquence"—which are linked by metaphoric associations, embody the most important of his assumptions about poetry and become the standard critical language of the fifteenth century. The first of these terms, "enlumyn," which appears only once with reference to poetry in Chaucer's work, is introduced repeatedly in Lydgate's writing with a range of meanings relevant to the poetic process.[17] Most obviously, Lydgate uses "enlumyn" with the earlier meaning of "to illuminate with color or light" to emphasize the poet's power to make something illustrious, brilliant, or famous by means of his art, as in his praise of Dante in Book IX of the *Fall of Princes*: "Thou hast enlumyned Itaile & Lumbardie / With aureat dites in thi flouryng daies. . ." (*FP*, IX, 2525–26). But by developing the implicit analogy between the sun's "enlumyng" and the poet's, he extends the implications of this use of the term, linking the sun's light with the poet's beams of rhetoric and eloquence. In a second sense which is not anticipated by Chaucer, Lydgate exploits the term "enlumyn" to describe the poet's process of enriching or extending his medium, especially his effort to raise the level of his English to make it suitable for poetic endeavors. This meaning is apparent, for example, in Lydgate's repeated celebration of Chaucer as the poet who found "floures firste of rethorike / Our rude speche, only to enlumyne."[18] Finally, Lydgate exploits the term "enlumyn" to describe the poet's crucial role in clarifying or shedding light on his content as in his famous tribute to Chaucer in the *Siege of Thebes* where he applauds him for "keping in substaunce // The sentence hool / with-oute variance, // Voyding the chaf / sothly for

to seyn, // Enlumynyng / þe trewe piked greyn // Be crafty
writing. . ." (*ST*, 53-57).

While "enlumyn" and the related terms "adourne" and "en-
belissche" describe the poet's process of working on his matter,
Lydgate introduces a second group of words "aureate," "goldyn,"
and "sugrid" to represent the effect of the poet's activities. In this
usage, these words suggest the splendid nature of poetic language,
its richness, luster, and heightened effect, the qualities which set it
off from ordinary speech or writing. This meaning, for example, is
apparent in Book VIII of the *Fall of Princes* when Boccaccio praises
his master Petrarch for providing a model of good poetic style as the
"cheff exaumplaire to my gret auantage, / To refourme the rudnesse
of my stile / With aureate colours of your fressh langage" (*FP*, VIII,
79-80). On several occasions, in an even more interesting usage,
Lydgate combines "aureate" and "goldyn" with striking metaphors
from the natural world to draw attention to the uniqueness of the
poet's language, its richness, luster, visual splendor, and stylistic
perfection. By means of the metaphor "baume aureate," for example, he defines a potent analogy between the perfumed secretion
of a flower and the poet's rhetorical or poetical output which over-
whelms the reader not only by its golden appearance but by its
pleasing or intoxicating effect. Likewise, he combines the word
"goldyn" with the recurrent metaphor of "rain" or "dew," life-giving
forces which add new luster and vitality to the objects they fall
upon. This metaphor, which is quite common in Lydgate's praise of
Chaucer, refers to the distillation of poetic excellence, the golden
liquid of the poet's speech or rhetoric, which like the rain or dew in
its action, gives the poet's medium a new potency and effectiveness.

Finally, Lydgate sums up his view of good poetry by two
terms—"rethorik" and "elloquence"—which he salvages from the
pejorative meanings they had acquired in Chaucer's works.[19] In
Lydgate's writing, these terms represent the epitome of good poetry,
"souereyn style" or the way in which a writer uses language
elegantly, effectively, and appropriately. As Lydgate indicates, these
terms involve more than skillfully ornamented style or elegant
language. "Rethorik" and "elloquence" in his work generally have
the broader meaning of good writing, good speech, or noble style.
This emphasis is apparent in the following lines from the *Siege of
Thebes* when Lydgate bids the reader refer to Boccaccio for an
example of noble style: "Lok on the book / that Iohn Bochas made
// Whilom of women / with rethorikes glade // And direct be ful
souereyn style. . ." (*ST*, 3203). But more important, "rethorik" and

"elloquence" in the sense in which Lydgate defines the terms—good writing, "souereign style"—serve to illuminate the essential truth of a story. As Lydgate explains in the Prologue to the *Troy Book*, poets "Han trewly set thoruӡ diligent labour, / And enlumyned with many corious flour / Of rethorik to make vs comprehende / The trouthe of al, as it was kende/. . ." (*TB*, Prol. 217–20). Used in this way, the terms convey a different impression from what we find in Chaucer's work. While we learn to suspect the motives of the rhetoricians in the *Canterbury Tales*, in Lydgate's work, the 'rethor" is "noble" and his art is the epitome of good poetry.

Lydgate's critical vocabulary, thus, links the activities of the poet as an illuminator who sheds beams of poetic light on man's world with an ideal of high style or heightened language. The poet's "aureate," "goldyn," and "sugrid" terms distinguish his writing from all other and for Lydgate are a mark of poetic excellence. Whereas Boccaccio stresses the importance of the poet's powers of invention, Lydgate emphasizes his role as a supreme craftsman who improves and extends his matter by his "enbellishing." The good poem does not "veil" "truth in a fair and fitting garment of fiction" as Boccaccio suggests, but in Lydgate's view, it renders it glorious, illustrious, and brilliant, enabling man by "enlumining" difficult matter to apprehend its significance.

In practice, Lydgate develops the relation between high style and purpose in a variety of ways. Two examples, one from his religious lyrics and the other from his long secular narratives, indicate the range of his experimentation. The first poem, the famous "Ballade at the Reverence of Our Lady Qwene of Mercy," is at once a definition of his ideal of the religious lyric and a stunning example of its fulfillment.[20] The poem begins with a discussion of the relation between his style and his purpose as Lydgate, with an echo of the *Troilus* narrator's concluding admonition, rejects the matter and style of "olde poets," the poets of love. In stanzas 1–3, he announces his intention to "redresse" or reform his style to develop a new poetic medium capable of expressing his unsurpassed praise of Mary:

> . . . I wil now pleynly my stile redresse,
> Of on to speke at nede that will not faile:
> Allas! for dool I can nor may expresse
> His passand pris, and that is no mervaile.
> O wynd of grace, now blowe in to my saile!
> O auriat licour off Clyo, for to wryte
> Mi penne enspire, of that I wold endyte!   (8–14)

The body of the poem provides the response to Lydgate's plea, a celebration of the Virgin in a style distinct from that of the "olde poets" of stanza one. Repeatedly, Lydgate extends the Latin rhetorical traditions in which he works to create a medium which is more dazzling than any before him. His technique is to amass striking images, allusions, and epithets, to overwhelm the reader by his unusual coinages from the Latin, his elaborate aureation, his exploitation of internal rhymes, alliteration, and metrics and thus move him to awe and admiration. While he combines many of the traditional images of Mary in his tribute, he presents these images in such rapid succesion and with such elaboration of stylistic and linguistic devices that the overall effect is quite different from the passage in Alanus' *Anticlaudianus*, his immediate source.[21] The first stanza with its elaborate imagery, alliteration, repetition, and intricate pattern of sounds is typical of his treatment:

> O sterne of sternys with thi stremys clere,
>> Sterne of the see, [on] -to shipmen lyght and gyde,
> O lusty lemand, moost pleasunt to appere,
> Whos bright bemys the clowdis may not hide,
> O way of lyfe to hem þat goo or ride,
>> Haven aftyr tempest surrest as to ryve,
>> On me haue mercy for thi Ioyes fyve.   (22–28)

The effect of Lydgate's experimentation in the "Ballade at the Reverence of Our Lady" is even more pronounced when one compares his poem with Chaucer's "ABC," the most famous earlier example of this kind of celebration in English.[22] The difference between the two lyrics is not simply one of increased aureation but involves a changed conception of the role of style itself. Chaucer opens with a stately and dignified address to the Virgin, and the poem reaches a few moments of high style in Lydgate's sense, for example, in stanza 14:

> O verrey light of eyen that ben blynde,
> O verrey lust of labour and distresse,
> O tresorerre of bountee to mankynde,
> Thee whom God ches to moodir for humblesse!   (105–08)

But this is not Chaucer's main concern in the lyric. Rather, he subordinates style to his theme of Mary as man's refuge, his comfort. Lydgate, in contrast, focuses all of his effort on his medium, his attempt to create a new mode of religious praise in English. As Norton-Smith points out, to a great extent, his plot is his poetic effort, and the style he develops forms an essential part of the poem's meaning, conveying a sense of Mary's importance and invoking our admiration for her glory.[23]

The *Troy Book*, Lydgate's first substantial undertaking commissioned by Henry V, provides a large-scale example of his effort to create an elevated medium which corresponds to the noble purpose he envisions for the poet as the improver or extender of his medium. As he emphasizes in his praise of Guido delle Colonne whose version of the Troy story he follows, the poet's high style expands the significance of his story. Referring to Guido's narrative, he judges it to be the best of the Troy versions for it most effectively "enlumyneth by crafte & cadence / This noble story with many fressche colour / Of rethorik, and many rich flour / Of eloquence to make it sounde bet. . ." (Prol. 362–65).

In adapting Guido's text, Lydgate manipulates his material to produce a version of the Troy story which is even more expansive and elevated in its treatment. Although many of his changes from his source, particularly his restructuring of the narrative and his numerous additions about war, serve to accentuate the central theme of his version—the dangers of war—this thematic emphasis does not appear to have been Lydgate's main concern in reworking the Troy material. Rather, the bulk of his additions, nearly one third of the entire poem, are directed to amplifying and elevating the action, to creating a more spectacular version of the Troy story than any before him, including Chaucer's famous poem.

A good example of the effect Lydgate achieves is found in Book IV, the longest section of the poem. In this book, Lydgate introduces numerous devices to elevate his material. Most obviously, he punctuates the events with a series of eloquent set speeches, more than twenty major ones in this book alone, and a number of rhetorical laments which build in intensity to his climactic lament for the fallen Troy (IV, 6930–7108). In addition, Lydgate inserts elaborate seasonal prefaces, other descriptive passages, and eloquent sections of narrative comment and invective. In these passages, he repeatedly works to heighten the style of his descriptions, to transform the rather colorless narrative of Guido into highly charged rhetorical passages as in his climactic account of Achilles' death. Guido's version of the event is brief and matter of fact, narrated in simple, straightforward prose:

> Achilles and Antilochus were dead in the temple of Apollo, wickedly killed by Paris. Paris ordered the bodies of Achilles and Antilochus to be cast out to the crows and dogs, but by the prayers and advice of Helen they were merely cast forth

from the temple of Apollo into the square, so that they could
be seen clearly by all the Trojans. . . .[24]

Lydgate translates this passage into the elaborate rhetoric of the
Troilus epilogue, intensifies its tone, and embellishes the language of
the original with repetition, balanced phrases, word-pairing, and
more complex syntactical designs:

And afterward þe body was out drawe
Of Achille fro þe holy boundis,
And cruelly þrowen vn-to houndis,
To be deuourid in þe brode strete,
þe canel rennyng with his wawes wete—
With-oute pite or any maner routhe.
Loo! here þe ende of falshed & vntrouþe
Loo! here þe fyn of swiche trecherie,
Of fals deceit compassid by envie!
Loo! here þe knot and conclusioun,
How God quyt ay slauȝter by tresoun!
Loo! here þe guerdoun & þe final mede
Of hem þat so deliten in falsehede. . . .   (IV, 3204-16)

When effective, Lydgate's amplification and stylistic elevation
are impressive. In Book IV, his changes add a sense of grandeur to
his matter which reinforces his theme of the tragic loss brought
about by war.[25] His style enhances the splendor of what is sacrificed
by the fall of Troy—the glorious city, the noble heroes, and their
deeds and passions. But the treatment of style in the *Troy Book* also
points up the limitations of Lydgate's view of poetry. While he
conceives of the poet as an "enluminer" who improves his matter
and draws man to truth and virtue and high style as the medium
which is most appropriate to this purpose, Lydgate often is unable
to sustain the effect he initiates and to fully exploit the medium he
develops. This falling off or unevenness is typical of many of his
poems and suggests, to some extent, a disparity between his ideals
and his ability to execute them and the inherent limitations of a
vision of poetry which demands of the poet a sustained effort at
greatness. Yet even when Lydgate is not entirely successful, his
practices exert a considerable influence on the fifteenth-century
poets and often serve as a catalyst for their own more effective
experimentation.

The impact of Lydgate's views is immediately apparent in the
work of the Middle Scots poets James I, Robert Henryson, and
William Dunbar, who share with him certain conceptions of poetry
and poetic sytle which are not characteristic of Chaucer and the late

fourteenth-century poets. Dunbar, who in his lyrics makes explicit the implications of the ideals of poetry and style which Lydgate popularizes at the outset of the century, provides a particularly good example of the way in which these poets reinforce and qualify Lydgate's vision. Like Lydgate, Dunbar conceives of the poet essentially as a craftman who illuminates his matter, making it splendid and enduring. But in describing this process, he draws attention to the significance of the metaphors for the poet's craft which underlie Lydgate's terms. In his detailed treatment of the theme of poetry in the "Goldyn Targe," one of his few non-occasional poems, Dunbar defines the relation between the poet and his matter which is central to most of his other poems.[26] By exploiting the structure of the "Targe" as a triptych, he sets up an analogy between the sun and the poet, the natural landscape and the rhetorical, which extends the view of "enlumyng" suggested by Lydgate's terms. The first section of the poem, stanzas 1–5, focuses on the effect of the rising sun, "The goldin candill matutyne" (l. 4) on the landscape, emphasizing the various hues and colors created when it illuminates the meadow below. In section II, the dream, Dunbar establishes an implicit analogy between the sun's effect on nature and the poet's effect on his matter, introducing parallels between the actual landscape of stanzas 1–5 and the poetic land-scape of the vision by repeating lines from the first section in the second. The final section, the narrator's reawakening (244–79), makes the implicit parallels explicit by applying the language used to describe the sun's effects to the poet's. Although Dunbar's praise of Chaucer, Gower, and Lydgate is conventional, it is loaded with echoes of stanzas 1–5 in this new context:

> O reverend Chaucere, rose of rethoris all,
> As in oure tong ane flour imperiall,
> > That raise in Britane evir, quho redis rycht,
> Thou beris of makaris the tryumph riall;
> Thy fresch anamalit termes celicall
> > This mater coud illumynit have full brycht:
> > Was thou nought of oure Inglisch all the lycht,
> Surmounting eviry tong terrestriall,
> > Als fer as Mayis morow dois mydnychte?   (253–61)

Like the sun, which enamels the meadow with its light, Chaucer, the "lycht" of "oure Inglisch," enamels and illuminates the matter of his poetry. In a similar manner, Gower and Lydgate "ourgilt" our speech and illuminate our rude language. Without their "light," England would be bare and desolate of rhetoric and good writing:

O morall Gower, and Ludgate laureate,
Your sugurit lippis and tongis aureate,
  Bene to our eris cause of grete delyte:
Your angel mouthis most mellifulate
Oure rude langage has clere illumynate,
  And faire ourgilt our speche, that imperfyte
  Stude, or your goldyn pennis schupe to wryte;
This Ile before was bare and desolate
  Off rethorike or lusty fresch endyte.   (262–70)

Dunbar's analogy between the poet and the sun, thus, links Lydgate's critical terms to form a coherent image of the poetic act. By expanding the referent and correspondent of Lydgate's metaphor, he explains the sense in which the poet "enlumines" his matter and defines the poetic process as we witness it.

The terms "anamalit" and "ourgilt" which Dunbar adds to Lydgate's coinages, however, point up some of the ways in which his conception of poetry finally differs from Lydgate's. Both of these terms derive from the language of the enameler's craft which flourished in the late Middle Ages and are transferred for the first time by Dunbar to the poetic process.[27] "Anamalit" refers specifically to the effect achieved when semi-transparent or opaque mixtures of glass in various colors were applied to a metal surface and fused. Although enamels were executed in four or five different ways until the end of the fifteenth century, in each case, the effect depended upon a skilled arrangement of colors in perfect combination and proportion.[28] The surface which results, in contrast to the surface of a painting, is unrivaled for its hardness and its dazzling exploitation of the possibilities of color created by the interplay of light reflected and refracted by the hardened variegated glass composition. Furthermore, the enamel executed by these methods embodies an integral relationship between color and object, as the tracery or outlines engraved in the metal to hold the color provides a constant reminder of the underlying structure which the craftsman has embellished, an analogy to the relation between the occasion and the words of a poem. Often in the fifteenth century, in the last firing the entire enamel was covered or "ourgilt" with a fine layer of gold powder which gave the design added brilliance.

In applying these terms to the poetic process, Dunbar suggests the way in which the poet's illuminating creates a tightly interlocked surface of words and sounds. The good poem, like the fine enamel, is meticulously fashioned, "ourgilt" or overlaid with color to form a hard, brilliant exterior, and has a finely worked, jeweled quality that

275

is not emphasized by Lydgate's vocabulary. While the poet's enameling gives the poem a certain luster or splendor which impresses the reader, it also creates an immutable surface which survives beyond the immediate occasion of the lines. Like the enameling which enhances the structure to which it is applied, the poet's manipulation of color transforms the occasion of the poem, its underlying structure, into an event of permanence and value. The metaphor of enameling, thus, finally extends Lydgate's view of poetry by emphasizing a perfection of craft and a density or closeness of design which are not suggested by his terms.

In practice, Dunbar's conception of the poem as an enamel illuminated by the poet's "light" finds form in the pattern of tightly interlocked words and sounds which make up the surface of his poems. The difference between his techniques and Lydgate's is seen vividly in a brief comparison of their similar lyrics in praise of Mary. While Dunbar adopts the medium which Lydgate develops in his "Ballade at the Reverence of Our Lady Qwene of Mercy" in his own "Ane Ballat of Our Lady," he begins where Lydgate leaves off, making several changes to produce a much more intricate combination of words and sounds. In the first place, he extends Lydgate's ballad stanza to a more difficult twelve-line stanza of alternating long and short lines. Within this scheme, he adds a complex pattern of internal rhyme, alliteration and verbal echoing, repeating, for example, the same sounds three times in lines 1, 3, 5, 7, and 11 of each stanza. Likewise, he experiments more boldly with aureate terms, reinforcing the impact of his striking language with internal echoing and alliteration. The effect of his changes is to produce a denser and a more meticulously crafted poem:

> Hale, sterne superne! Hale, in eterne
>   In Godis sicht to schyne!
> Lucerne in derne for to discerne
>   Be glory and grace devyne;
> Hodiern, modern, semitern,
>   Angelicall regyne!
> Our tern inferne for to dispern
>   Helpe, rialest rosyne,
>   *Ave Maria, gracia plena*!
>   Haile, fresche floure femynyne!
> Yerne us, guberne, virgin matern,
>   Of reuth baith rute and ryne.   (1–12)

The tendencies apparent in Dunbar's "Ballat" are not limited to his religious poems and poems of praise, the obvious repositories of high style, but underlie many of his poems. A good example of the application of the view of poetry developed in the "Targe" in Dunbar's satires, humorous narratives, and complaints is found in the "Remonstrance to the King" (#17). In this poem, Dunbar adapts the enameled surface of the secular and religious panegyrics for the purposes of insult rather than praise. Although the colors of his poem are harsher than those of the "Ballat," the stylistic principle is the same—the creation of a surface of closely interlocked words and sounds by means of striking coinages, word-play, alliteration, internal echoing and rhyme. In the two main sections of the poem, Dunbar exploits these devices to introduce contrasting pictures of the king's two types of servants—the useful and the parasitic. Again, his style creates a verbal counterpart of the enameler's art, inscribing the object he considers in the hard surface of the poem by means of his juxtaposition of discrete and highly-colored words like the intense colors of the enamel, his dense alliteration, and his striking patterning of sounds, both within the lines and in the rhymes, which produce an intricate surface design:

> Fenyeouris, fleichouris, and flatteraris;
> Cryaris, craikaris, and clatteraris;
> Soukaris, groukaris, gledaris, gunnaris;
> Monsouris of France, gud clarat-cunnaris;
> Innopportoun askaris of Yrland kynd;
> And meit revaris, lyk out of mynd;
> Scaffaris, and scamleris in the nuke,
> And hall huntaris of draik and duik;
> Thrimlaris and thristaris, as thay war woid,
> Kokenis, and kennis na man of gude;
> Schulderaris, and schowaris, that hes no schame. . . .   (39–49)

The extreme prominence of artistry in Dunbar's poems, finally provides an important aspect of their meaning. As Fox observes, "With varying degree of validity in Dunbar's poetry, the formal manner of transmuting matter into poetry is obtrusive and more impoitant than the matter itself."[29] The matter becomes significant primarily as the poet-artisan gives it new brilliance and resiliency through his art. Dunbar's "enameling" transforms the particular fleeting occasions on which almost all of his poems rest into artefacts which are more significant and enduring.

The conceptions of poetry and the ideals of poetic style defined by Lydgate, Dunbar, and many of the early fifteenth-century poets are placed in a larger context in the poems of Gavin Douglas at the end of this period. In both the *Palice of Honour* and the *Eneados*

translation,[30] Douglas treats the recurrent fifteenth-century conceptions of poetry as an aspect of man's quest for a good life, his
struggle to attain honor and virtue in the world. The poet's effort to
illuminate his matter by means of his rhetoric and eloquence
becomes for Douglas an image of man's attempt to achieve moral
goodness and honor. The "ryall" or "knychtlyche" style which he
places above all other modes, in the broad meaning which it
acquires in his works of ideal poetic and moral style, is the verbal
counterpart of the two quests.

The relation between the poet's purpose and style and the quest
for honor and virtue is introduced in the *Palice of Honour* where it
serves as the central theme of the poem.[31] The poem defines the
redirection of the narrator as man and as poet from a state of
conflict, despair, and poetic dryness to inner harmony, a devotion to
honor, and restored poetic power. The process of the narrator's
renewal reveals an expanding vision of the purpose of poetry and a
redirection of its styles to increasingly noble ends.

Structurally, Douglas draws attention to the narrator's progress by the intricate design of the poem. In addition to the obvious
divisions into a Prologue and three books and the movement from
the Courts of Minerva, Diana, and Venus, to the Court of Poetry,
and the Palace of Honour, he introduces a series of five lais,
stylistically set off from the rest of the poem, and a corresponding
series of garden scenes which demarcate significant stages of the
narrator's journey, and, like the poemae of Boethius' *Consolation*,
epitomize the changes in vision defined by the sections of interspersed action and debate. Finally, as Miskimin demonstrates,
Douglas reinforces the poem's thematic development by a complex
numerological design of stanzas and lines based upon the medieval
concepts of musical harmony and proportion.[32]

While it is impossible to do justice to this scheme in a brief
consideration of the poem, two examples from the turning point
and the conclusion of the *Palice* reveal Douglas's emphasis. The first
scene, 772–1062, stands at the center of the work and defines the
shift in the narrator's vision from the Court of Venus to the Court of
Rhetoric. Before this point, the poet-narrator is represented in a
state of inner hell, mirrored in the barren landscape of the Prologue,
out of harmony with himself and with the world and unable to find
comfort from the traditional sources of wisdom, chastity, and love
represented by the Courts of Minerva, Diana, and Venus. Stylistically, the narrator's three lais, his opening lament for his loss of
poetic power (91–99) and his complaints against Fortune and Venus

278

LOIS EBIN

(165–92; 606–36), disturb the order around him and emphasize his lack of control over his medium as poet.

In 772–1062, Douglas defines the narrator's renewal, not through the choices afforded by the "garden of Pleasance"— wisdom, chastity, and love—but through the power of poetry, which he implies can restore man's wit and direct him to virtue. In contrast to the mutable Court of Venus, the Court of Rhetoric is described in terms of its constancy as a source of comfort and pleasure. It is the "constant ground of famous storeis sweit," the "facound well celestial," the court of "plesant steidfastnes" and "constant merines." The tuneful music it produces is linked with the celestial harmony of the spheres, and the narrator's restoration to its harmony at the end of this scene indicates allegorically his return to the larger order around him.

The shift from Venus to Calliope, likewise, marks a redirection of the narrator's purpose as poet. Like Lydgate in the "Ballet at the Reverence of Our Lady," who distinguishes his medium from that of the "olde poets," the love poets, Douglas in this scene at the center of the *Palice* develops a conception of poetry which moves beyond the narrator's earlier service to love to a devotion to honor and virtue and calls for a new relation between the poet's style and subject. The poetry envisioned in this section is a

> . . . Ioyous discipline
> Quhilk causis folk thair purpois to expres
> In ornate wise, prouokand with glaidnes
> All gentill hartis to thair lair Incline.   (846–49)

Good poetry is a combination of pleasure and effort. It inspires the expression of ideas in a special or heightened language which provokes the gentle heart or appropriate reader to its wisdom. In this link between purpose, style, and audience, Douglas's definition moves beyond the traditional combination of *dulce* and *utile* or mirth and doctrine to suggest more precisely the way in which the unique language of poetry mediates between sentence and audience and directs the reader to its meaning.

In the catalogue of Muses which follows, Douglas draws attention to the range and variety of poetic matter and styles, building up to the most noble style of all, the "kinglie stile" represented by Calliope who

> . . . of Nobil fatis hes the steir
> To write thair worschip, victorie and prowes

279

> In kinglie stile, quhilk does thair fame Incres
> Clepit in Latine Heroicus, but weir,
> Cheif of all write like as scho is Maistres.   (875–79)

This style, which celebrates the deeds of "nobill fatis" and magnifies fame, most effectively draws together worthy audience and purpose and is the epitome of good poetry. The vision ends with the narrator's fourth lai, an address to his "vnwemmit wit deliuerit of danger," which reveals his restored powers as a poet and his new-found order and harmony with the world.

The final scenes of the poem represent the fulfillment of the view of poetry which is defined at the work's center, the dedication of the narrator and his renewed poetic powers to honor, which, the allegory makes clear, is not the questionable fame of Chaucer's vision, but enduring honor based on virtue:

> . . . a thing sa precious,
> Quhairof the end is sa delicious,
> The warld can not consider quhat it is.
> It makis folk perfite and glorious,
> It causis folk ay liue in lestand blis. . . .   (1999–2004)

In the closing hymn, which the narrator writes not as the timid poet-apprentice of the vision, but as the poet who looks back in retrospect and comprehends the significance of his experience, the poem's concerns converge. The hymn, the longest and most difficult of the narrator's five lais, celebrates the "hie Honour" which is the object of his quest and the most appropriate subject for his poetry. Its style, an extension of the high style practiced by Lydgate and Dunbar, is characterized by an even more intricate arrangement of words, a difficult rhyme scheme, and increasingly intense internal echoes with two repeated sounds in each line of the first stanza, three in each line of the second, and four in each line of the last:

> Hail rois, maist chois til clois thy fois greit micht!
> Haill stone, quhilk schone vpon the throne of licht!
> Vertew, quhais trew, sweit dew ouirthrew al vice,
> Was sy, Ilk day, gar say, the way of licht.
> Amend offend, and send our end ay richt.
> Thow stant ordant, as sanct, of grant maist wise,
> Till be supplie and the hie gre of price.
> Delite the tite, me quite of site to dicht,
> For I apply, schortile, to thy deuise.   (2134–42)

Stylistically, the hymn is the culmination of the poet-narrator's journey from the poetic dryness of the first lai, to the uncontrolled complaints of the second and third lais against Fortune and Love, to the renewed poetic control in the fourth, his celebration of his revived wit, to a poetry in which his "ornate wyss" directs the audience to the celebration of honor.

In the Prologues to the thirteen books of the *Eneados*, Douglas defines a similar journey of the narrator from conflict and doubt about his craft to restored poetic ability and a redirected style and purpose. His journey as poet mirrors the larger journey of Eneas, the good man within the poem, and reveals a view of poetry similar to the ideal represented in the central scenes of the *Palice*. The first six Prologues emphasize the narrator's doubts about his undertaking in translating Virgil. As poet, he lacks skill; next to Virgil's eloquent Latin, his own native Scots is deficient, and he wonders what justification he can find for so bold a venture. Finally, he questions the value of poetry for a Christian audience. These Prologues, which progress from life on earth to a vision of afterlife, draw attention to the poet's task of celebrating "temporal blythness" without jeopardizing the eternal, in Douglas's terms, to steer the "boat" or book through the world without shipwreck.

Prologue VII, the numerical center of the work, represents a turning point for the narrator as poet just as Book VI, the center of Virgil's poem, marks a change in direction for Aeneas. After the effort of the first five books to come to terms with the worldly attachments which divert him from his quest as hero and the vision of the sixth, Aeneas proceeds toward his goal in Books VII–XII. The narrator as poet makes a corresponding, though less direct, journey in the resolution of his conflicts in the remainder of the *Eneados* Prologues. This redirection begins with Prologue VII, the winter Prologue, which like the earlier *Palice of Honour*, defines the movement from a hell-like external world, "bittir, cald, and paill," and a corresponding poetic dryness to a more beneficent landscape as a new day dawns and the narrator, "new cum furth of hell," takes pen in hand to resume his activities as poet.[33] The remaining Prologues defend the value of poetry, raising the question of its usefulness as a potential remedy for erring man, and reconsider the poet's style, sources of inspiration, subject matter, and creative process.

In these Prologues, as in the *Palice of Honour*, Douglas defines an ideal correspondence among the poet's audience, purpose, and high style. Rejecting the explicitly moral style at the outset of Prologue IX—"Eneuch of this, we nedis prech na mor" (Prol. IX, 19)—he turns to "the ryall style, clepyt heroycall" (21) as a more suitable medium for his redirected effort as poet. As in the *Palice of*

Honour, Douglas begins with a similar emphasis on this style as a vehicle of honor. "Ryall style" is "full of wirschip and nobilness" (Prol. IX, 22), void of any base or empty words. Where it does joke, it keeps to "honest wyss sportis" (24). In other words, its content is morally above reproach. From this meaning, he turns to style in the sense of literary effect and defines "ryall style" as a "high style" which avoids "all lowuss langage and lychtness" (25) and observes "bewte, sentens, and grauyte" (26). Finally, Douglas emphasizes the role which this style plays in linking the poet's audience and purpose. "The man, the sentence and the knychtlyke style" (31) should correspond if the poem is to be effective. By his use of the term style within the translation as social status or the particular combination of traits or virtues which establish a person's identity, Douglas further suggests a similar relation between a character, his "style" and his state as a man. When Aeneas makes himself known to Venus, for example, Douglas explains that he speaks in the manner in which he does not for arrogance, "bot forto schaw his style, as kyng or prince onknawin in an onkowth land. . ." (I, vi, 125 n.). As the audience is directed to the poem's meaning by its "knychtlyke style," so the style of the man suggests his significance. Douglas, thus, finally gives style a broader and more significant meaning than it had in the earlier fifteenth-century poet's works or in the *Palice of Honour*.

In the *Eneados* Prologues, Douglas introduces the high style he develops in the climactic celebration of spring in Prologue XII. While the Prologues are a virtual anthology of Scottish styles, they culminate, like the series of lais in the *Palice*, in the aureate lines of this Prologue which not only serves as a link to a single book, but also represents the completion of the entire poem as a creative act associated with the larger generative forces in the natural world. The Prologue establishes a parallel between the daily renewal of life by the sun, the seasonal revitalization of spring, signs of God's creative power, and the renewed effort of the poet-narrator. As in Dunbar's "Goldyn Targe," the poet's conspicuously crafted lines, aureate diction, and intricate design of words form the verbal counterpart of the sun's dazzling light which "enlumines" and revitalizes the natural world:

> The new cullour alychtnyng all the landis,
> Forgane thir stannyris scame the beriall strandis,
> Quhil the reflex of the diurnall bemys
> The beyn bonkis kest ful of variant glemys;
> And lusty Flora dyd hyr blomys spreid

Vnder the feit of Phebus sulʒart steid;
The swardit soyll enbroved with selcouth hewys,
Wod and forest obumbrat with thar bewys,
Quhois blisfull branschis, porturat on the grund
With schaddays schene schew rochis rubicund. . . .
(Prol. XII, 59–68)

From the winter of Prologue VII and the conflicts of the earlier prologues, we move to a vision of renewed creative power and energy and the completion of the narrator's undertaking as poet in Prologue XII. Within the translation itself, however, Douglas finds it less desireable to sustain this ideal of style. Faced with the alternative of rendering Virgil's sentence or his eloquence in shifting from one literary medium to another, he makes the choice of preserving Virgil's meaning, a decision which contrasts both with the earlier medieval practice of freely adapting the *Aeneid* and with the early Renaissance attempts to imitate Virgil's eloquence in translation.[34] In this endeavor, Douglas finally moves toward a wider range of styles and a greater variety of ways of directing the poem's new audience to its purpose than he had considered in the *Palice of Honour*.

The poetry of Stephen Hawes and of John Skelton at the outset of the sixteenth century embody, in opposite ways, a transformation of the relation between poetry and style which dominates the fifteenth century and, as such, represent both the culmination and the destruction of the ideals we have been considering. While the two poets, courtiers and rivals for preferment at the courts of Henry VII and Henry VIII, begin with the attitudes of the fifteenth-century poets, they move from these conceptions of poetry to visions which are quite alien to their English predecessors. Hawes, whom critics have almost consistently ignored, provides an important link between medieval and Renaissance poetics in his three long poems— *The Example of Virtue* (1503–04), *The Pastime of Pleasure* (1506–07), and *The Conforte of Louers* (1510)[35] A self-styled disciple of Lydgate, in his early works he retains the view of poetry as a vehicle of truth, the vision of the poet as an "enluminer" who sheds light on his matter by means of his rhetoric and eloquence, and a belief in the power of poetry with its heightened language to civilize men and bring order to the state, and, like Douglas, he places these ideals in the larger context of man's quest for honor and virtue in the world, linking the journey of the poet with that of the good man. But his perspective gradually shifts from the notion of the poet as an "enluminer" and a corresponding ideal of eloquence

283

to the poet as a prophet or *vates* and a conception of a "mysty," "clowdy," "derk" style almost entirely devoid of the features of fifteenth-century high style.

These changes are especially apparent in turning from the *Pastime* to the *Conforte*. In the *Pastime*, Hawes introduces the Lydgatian model of the poet as an illuminator who preserves man from ignorance and leads him to virtue. Like the light of the precious carbuncle, his beams of rhetoric and eloquence penetrate the darkness of man's mind:

> Carbuncles / in the most derk nyght
> Doth shyne fayre / with clere radyant beames
> Exylynge derknes / with his rayes lyght
> And so these poetes / with theyr golden streames
> Deuoyde our rudenes / with grete fyry lemes.
> (1128–32)

His language is the "golden" or "dulcet speche" which he has purified from the "language rude" and, like the words of Amphion, it civilizes and orders man:

> Before the lawe / in a tumblynge barge
> The people sayled / without parfytnes
> Throughe the world / all aboute at large
> They hadde none ordre / nor stedfastnes
> Tyll rethorycans / founde Iustyce doubtles
> Ordenynge kynges / of ryghte hye dygnyte
> Of all comyns / to haue the souerainte.... (876–82)

The poet's experience in the *Pastime* is a worldly one. He is educated through the pursuits of learning, chivalry, and love and is fashioned entirely by human means, particularly by the arts of grammar and rhetoric which comprise the major portion of his instruction in the Tower of Doctrine. The object of his quest is Pucelle, who comes to represent at once the desire of the lover, the honor of the knight, and the renown of the poet, and provides a model of human aspiration which is alluring but, as Hawes finally reveals, transitory.

In the *Conforte*, one immediately notes a changed vision. The narrator opens the Prologue with an emphasis on the difficulty of poetry and, from the outset, the surface of the poem appears to be more allusive and mysterious than the *Pastime*, characterized by riddles, complicated symbols, and difficult personal allusions. The allegory is at once more personal and internal and more universal than it is in the *Pastime* with Grand Amour presented more explicitly as the poet Hawes and as a figure for the poet in general. On one level, the *Conforte* represents a detailed allegory of Hawes's hopes for preferment at the court of Henry VII and is a defense of his practices as poet and a bid for recognition.[36] But by his imagery and allusions, Hawes links the personal plight of the poet-narrator to the experience of the poet David of *Canticles*, the divinely inspired prophet who writes sacred songs in God's praise.[37] Like David, Grand Amour presents himself as a poet alone among enemies, awaiting God's aid, firm in his devotion despite the repeated harassment of enemies who would torment him by their subtle "snares" and "traps" and tear him apart and devour him like wolves. No longer simply an "enluminer" who, in Lydgate's view, civilizes man and inspires him to virtue by the power of his words, the poet in the *Conforte* is a *vates* chosen by God, whose mission is not only political but also sacred. In contrast to the poet of the *Pastime*, he is not formed by human arts but is divinely inspired, and his words, unlike the carefully crafted language of the Scots makars, the epitome of man's artistry, are the gift of the Holy Ghost and embody God's mysteries. His poems are both prayer and promise, and as poet, he is at once a model for man in his trials and a prophet whose writing contains God's wisdom.

The conception of poetry which Hawes develops in the *Conforte* finally finds form in a stylistic solution which differs from the fifteenth-century poets' ideal of high style and "depured eloquence." In the *Conforte*, he abandons the combination of plain allegorical and rhetorical styles of the *Example* and the *Pastime* as his principal mode and introduces a medium which is a strangely discordant mixture of stylistic features from the dream vision tradition, the love allegory, the long didactic narrative, and the *Canticles*. The shifts from one style to another often are unexpected and abrupt, as in the dialogue between Grand Amour and Pucell at the end of the poem where we move from the lover's passionate complaint, to a discussion of his books, to the lady's moral instruction, to his veiled allusions to his own troubles in the style of the *Canticles*. In these passages, Hawes manipulates style to create a sense of obscurity or mystery, to form the "derk" surface which is the counterpart of his conception of the poem as prophecy which contains hidden meaning under its words. The shift from the poet as an "enluminer" or craftsman skilled in the arts of rhetoric to the poet as a divinely inspired *vates*, who turns not to high style but to a mysterious and obscure style, transforms the conception of the poem as ennobling and its heightened language as a source of truth into an ideal which is quite different from the fifteenth-century vision.

Like Hawes, Skelton begins with the fifteenth-century conception of the poet-craftsman who illuminates his matter, turning out several skillful poems—the elegies for King Edward the Fourth and Northumberland, the prayers to the Father, the Son and the Holy Ghost, and "Knowledge, Acquaintance, Resort, Favor with Grace"[38]—in a rhetorical and eloquent high style. But he moves rapidly away from this vision of poetry, questioning and finally rejecting the assumptions which underlie the fifteenth-century conceptions of poetry and the role of poetic style. While Skelton's disillusionment with the practices of his predecessors is apparent as early as 1498 in "The Bouge of Court" and is voiced explicitly c. 1508 in his parody of the effect of high style, in Jane's comic attempts at literary criticism, and in the stylistic experimentation of "Philip Sparrow," the bases for the fifteenth-century views are effectively demolished in the poems between 1521 and 1528, particularly in "Speak Parrot," "Colin Clout," "The Garland of Laurel," and "A Replication."[39] In these works, Skelton questions the ability of the heightened language of poetry to order and civilize man and lead him to truth, indeed to provide any meaningful statement or point of stability in a world marked by an increasing decay of authority. Experimenting with and rejecting both the high styles of Lydgate and his followers and the "mysty," "clowdy," and "derk" style of Hawes, Skelton searches for a new solution.

Skelton's dilemma is poignantly defined in "Speak Parrot" (1521), his most vehement attack on the ideals of the fifteenth-century poets. In this poem, he introduces as his mouthpiece the legendary Psittacus whose mythological inheritance links him both with the Ovidian parrot of Corinna, the master mimic who uncomprehendingly chronicles scraps of wisdom, stories, and events, and with the semi-divine hero of Boccaccio's *Genealogia*, the son of Deucalion, who survived the flood and saved mankind by his faith, and the grandson of Prometheus, who in old age prayed to be removed from human affairs and was transformed into the Parrot and in later tradition, placed in heaven.[40] Parrot's vacillation between these stances colors his role as poet with a troubling ambiguity. Although a "byrd of paradyse," as he reveals at the outset, he has been forced to return to the world of sixteenth-century England where he is alternately caged and pampered by "greate ladyes of estate" and prodded to "speak." He both disdains his prison and embraces it as a safe refuge from the disorder of a world which seems to invite its own destruction. Skelton taunts us with the possibilities of Parrot as satirist, seer, lover, as the Gideon of Psalm 82 who would defend Israel from the enemies that surround her, as his "own dear heart," as man's soul or better part which does not putrify. But each of these roles is rapidly undercut by Parrot's antics. As speaker, Parrot is displaced in the world of the poem, vacillating between involvement and rage at the events he witnesses and the profound detachment of his cage. Stylistically, his uneasy stance is represented by his lack of an appropriate medium. A polyglot who speaks with a smattering of different tongues, Parrot is equally uncomfortable with aureate, prophetic, and satiric modes, and has not yet found a style which would allow him to deal effectively with the world around him. Like the questor of Eliot's *Waste Land* who shores up his fragments against ruin, Parrot gathers together "shredis of sentence" from which he produces learned arguments in the poet's sacred school ("unde depromo / Dilemmata docta in paedagogio / Sacro vatum").

The dialogue between Galathea and Parrot in Part II accentuates the poet's dilemma. Refusing to accept Parrot's silence, Galathea, the object of the lover's complaint in the twelfth-century pseudo-Ovidian *Pamphilus de Amore*, demands from him a similar "moan." But, in contrast to the straightforward seduction of Pamphilus, Parrot's response is a conglomerate of stances and corresponding styles, each of which Galathea rejects as inadequate. As she bids him turn back the "shafts of fatuity" ("Psittace perge volans, fatuorum tela retundas"), to "go in haste, and reprove the evil tongues" ("I, properans Parrote, malas sic corripe linguas"), and to put aside his stylistic pretentions ("I, volitans, Parrote, tuam moderare Minervam: Vix tua percipient, qua tua teque legent"), her recurrent demand "Speak, Parrot," becomes not only a command to speak but also an urgent plea to change styles as poet and speak plainly. Parrot's final shift in style to the clear, unadorned and vigorous medium of the concluding stanzas is the tentative resolution of this poem.

Although Skelton returns to the plain style and the vision of the poet involved in the world which it implies in all but one of the poems written after "Speak, Parrot," his stylistic solution is a qualified one. Introducing an ironic mixture of styles in "The Garland of Laurel," his final long poem, he again defines the poet's dilemma in terms of a search for a suitable medium. While Fame demands that he adhere to the fifteenth-century ideals of poetic excellence and produce a quantity of aureate verse sufficient to ensure his reputation, Pallas reveals the limitations both of this stance and of his other stylistic possibilities, indeed of any solution the poet might find:

> ... if he gloryously pullishe his matter,
> Then men wyll say how he doth but flatter;
> And if so hym fortune to wryte true and plaine,
>   As sumtyme he must vyces remorde,
> Then sum wyll say he hath but lytill brayne,
>   And how his wordes with reason wyll not accorde;
>   Beware, for wrytyng remayneth of recorde;
> ·
>
> Sophisticatid craftely is many a confecture;
> Another manes mynde diffuse is to expounde;
> Yet harde is to make but sum fawt be founde.   (83–112)

But in contrast to "Speak, Parrot," Skelton's vision of his dilemma in this poem is comic. He both demonstrates his ability to fulfill the standards of Fame, by introducing eleven aureate poems of praise to the Countess of Surrey and her ladies, and rejects Fame's narrow dictates, undermining this mode with the ironic intrusion of reality. Parodying his own achievements as poet in a poem which defends his right to the garland of laurels, Skelton produces a self-advertisement which, at the same time, emphasizes the limits of his endeavor.

The development and rejection of high style in the fifteenth and early sixteenth centuries is, thus, an emblem of a changing vision of poetry and the role of the poet. While it has been convenient to consider the practices of these poets as a perversion or faulty imitation of Chaucerian innovations, the discussions of poetry within the poems themselves indicate rather that the fifteenth-century poets' high style is a conscious choice of medium and is linked to ideals and assumptions about poetry which are substantially different from those of their English predecessors. To some extent, the shift to high style at the outset of the fifteenth century may be explained in historical and social terms as a result of the restored status of English as a literary language, the encouragement provided by a new class of patrons like Humphrey of Gloucester to undertake ambitious works in the vernacular on the scale and scope of continental models, the demands of an expanding literate audience, and the shared awareness among poet, patron, and audience of an enlarged function of poetry. At the end of the century one, likewise, may link the disillusionment with high style with the obsolescence of the English which embodied it, a changed relation between poet and patron, and the increasing concern with the decay of authority in both secular and religious spheres.[41] But part of the explanation must also be sought in the self-conscious way in which, during this period, poet responds to poet in considering his own art. In the conspicuous refinement by each of the major fifteenth-century poets of the ideals popularized by Lydgate at the outset of the century many of the conceptions central to the Renaissance views of poetry emerge—the notion of the poet as *vates*, the concern with the relation between poetry and fame, the role of the poet in the world, and the renewed search for an effective poetic style. While no formal poetics appear in English until the end of the sixteenth century, the stylistic solutions of the fifteenth-century poets and their extended poems about poetry—Dunbar's "Goldyn Targe," Henryson's "Fabillis," "Douglas's *Palice of Honour* and *Eneados* Prologues, Hawes's *Pastime of Pleasure* and *Conforte of Louers*, and Skelton's "Speak, Parrot" and "Garland of Laurel" among others—provide an important, but often ignored, link between medieval and Renaissance poetics.

——— NOTES ———

[1] For examples of this view, see: George Saintsbury, "The English Chaucerians" in *Cambridge History of English Literature*, II, ed. by A. W. Ward and A. R. Waller (Cambridge, 1963), pp. 197–222; Patrick Cruttwell, "Two Scots Poets: Dunbar and Henryson" in *The Age of Chaucer*, ed. by Boris Ford (1954, repr.; Baltimore, MD, 1963), p. 176.

[2] John Burrow, *Ricardian Poetry: Chaucer, Gower, Langland, and the Gawain Poet* (New Haven, 1971), pp. 44–46; 128–29.

[3] Plato, *Republic* in *Great Dialogues of Plato*, trans. W. H. D. Rouse (New York, 1956), Book X; Aristotle, *Poetics*, trans. Ingram Bywater (New York, 1954), chap. iv.

[4] Plato, *Republic*, Book X.

[5] Aristotle, *Rhetoric*, trans. W. Rhys Roberts (New York, 1954), Book I, chap. 1.

[6] Richard A. Lanham, *The Motives of Eloquence: Literary Rhetoric in the Renaissance* (New Haven, 1976), chaps. i–ii.

[7] R. R. Bolgar, *The Classical Heritage and its Beneficiaries from the Carolingian Age to the End of the Renaissance* (New York, Evanston, & London, 1954), p. 47.

[8] Bolgar, *The Classical Heritage*, p. 51.

[9] For an informative study of these issues, see: Erich Auerbach,

Literary Language and its Public in Late Latin Antiquity and in the Middle Ages, trans. Ralph Manheim (New York, 1965).

[10]Boethius, *The Consolation of Philosophy*, trans. Richard Green (Indianapolis & New York, 1962); Bernard de Silvestris, *Commentus super sex libros Eneidos Virgilii*, ed. Julian & Elizabeth Jones (Lincoln, Nebraska, 1977); Alain de Insulis, *The Complaint of Nature*, trans. Douglas M. Moffat (New York, 1908); Jean de Meun, *The Romance of the Rose*, trans. Charles Dahlberg (Princeton, 1971); John of Salisbury, *The Metalogicon*, trans. Daniel McGarry (Berkeley, 1955); Bonaventura, *The Works of Bonaventura*, trans. José de Vinck (Patterson, N. J., 1960-70); Dante, *De vulgari eloquentia* in *The Latin Works of Dante Alighieri* (New York, 1969), pp. 3-126; *Boccaccio on Poetry*, trans. Charles G. Osgood (Indianapolis & New York, 1956). For informative analyses of medieval poetics, see: Paul Zumthor, *Langue, texts, enigme* (Paris, 1975); *Essai de poetique medievale* (Paris, 1972); *Langue et techniques poetiques a l'epoque romane (XIe-XIIIe Siècles)* (Paris, 1963).

[11]W. T. H. Jackson, *The Anatomy of Love: The Tristan of Gottfried von Strasbourg* (New York, 1971), pp. 48-63.

[12]Gottfried von Strasbourg, *Tristan*, trans. A. T. Hatto (Baltimore, 1960), p. 43.

[13]Dante, *Vita Nuova*, ed. & trans. Mark Musa (Bloomington & London, 1973), XIX.

[14]Patricia M. Kean, *Chaucer and the Making of English Poetry* (London & Boston, 1972), I, 4, 23-30.

[15]John Lydgate, *Fall of Princes* (London, 1924), IV, Prologue.

[16]"Lydgate's Views on Poetry," *AnM*, 18 (1977), 76-105.

[17]See, for example: *Life of Our Lady*, I, 58; II, 1635-36; III, 196, 583, 1029; V, 5; *Siege of Thebes*, ll. 56-57; *Temple of Glas*, l. 283; *Troy Book*, Prol. 59, 218, 362; II, 1029, 4700, 6782; Envoy, 100; *Fall of Princes*, III, 3570; IV, 31, 371; VI, 3080; VIII, 70; IX, 2525; *Life of St. Edmund*, ll. 221-22; "Exposition of the Pater Noster," l. 318; "To Mary, the Queen of Heaven," ll. 41-42.

[18]John Lydgate, *A Critical Edition of John Lydgate's Life of Our Lady*, ed. Joseph A. Lauritis (Pittsburgh, 1961), II, 1635-36.

[19]John S. P. Tatlock, *A Concordance to the Complete Works of Geoffrey Chaucer* (Gloucester, MA., 1963), p. 262.

[20]John Lydgate, *The Minor Poems of John Lydgate, Part I*, ed. Henry Noble MacCracken (London, 1911), #49, pp. 254-60.

[21]For a comparison of Lydgate's lines with the passage in the *Anticlaudianus*, see: John Norton-Smith, ed., *John Lydgate Poems* (Oxford, 1966), pp. 143-50.

[22]Geoffrey Chaucer, *The Works of Geoffrey Chaucer*, ed. F. N. Robinson, 2nd ed. (Boston, 1957), pp. 524-26.

LOIS EBIN

[23] Norton-Smith, ed., *John Lydgate Poems*, p. 144.

[24] Guido delle Colonne, *Historia destructionis Troiae*, trans. Mary Elizabeth Meek (Bloomington & London, 1974), p. 199.

[25] Derek Pearsall, *John Lydgate* (London, 1970), pp. 142-43.

[26] William Dunbar, *The Poems of William Dunbar*, ed. William MacKay Mackenzie (London, 1960), #56. All further references to Dunbar's poems will be to this edition. For a fuller discussion of the theme of poetry in the "Goldyn Targe," see: Ebin, "The Theme of Poetry in Dunbar's 'Goldyn Targe,'" *ChauR*, 7 (1972), 147–59. For useful critical considerations of the "Goldyn Targe," see: Denton Fox, "Dunbar's *The Golden Targe*," *ELH*, 26 (1959), 311–34; John Leyerle, "The Two Voices of William Dunbar," *UTQ*, 31 (1962), 316–38; Isabel Hyde, "Poetic Imagery: A Point of Comparison between Henryson and Dunbar," *SSL*, 2 (1965), 183–97; _____, "Primary Sources and Associations of Dunbar's Aureate Imagery," *MLR*, 51 (1956), 481–92; Tom Scott, *A Critical Exposition of the Poems* (Edinburgh & London, 1966), pp. 40–46; Roderick J. Lyall, "Moral Allegory in Dunbar's 'Goldyn Targe,'" *SSL*, 11 (1973), 47–66; Walter Scheps, "*The Goldyn Targe*: Dunbar's Comic Psychomachia," *PLL*, 11 (1975), 339–56. For an examination of the relation of Dunbar's poetry to the tradition of aureate diction, see: John Cooper Mendenhall, *Aureate Terms: A Study in the Literary Diction of the Fifteenth Century* (Lancaster, PA, 1919); Hyde, "Primary Sources and Associations of Dunbar's Aureate Imagery," 418–92; John A. Conley, "Four Studies in Aureate Terms," Diss. Stanford 1956.

[27] According to dictionary evidence, Dunbar is the first to apply these terms to the poetic process. *MED*, s.v. *enamelen*, v. and s.v. *ouergilden*, v.; *OED*, s.v. *enamel*, v., and *enameled*, ppl.a.

[28] For useful descriptions of the process of enameling in the Middle Ages, see: Mary Chamot, *English Medieval Enamels* (London, 1930); Philippe Burty, *Les émaux cloisonnés anciens et moderns* (Paris, 1868); Lewis Foremann Day, *Enameling, A Comparative Account of the Development and Practice of the Art* (London, 1907); Marie Madeline S. Gauthier, *Émaux limousins champlevés des XIIe, XIIIe, & XIVe siècles* (Paris, 1950); Louis Elie Millenet, *Enameling on Metal, A Practical Manual on Enameling and Painting on Enamel*, trans. H. de Koningh (London, 1947); Victoria and Albert Museum, South Kensington, *A Picture Book of Medieval Enamels* (London, 1927); Walters Art Gallery, Baltimore, *Catalogue of the Painted Enamels of the Renaissance*, ed. Philippe Verdier (Baltimore, 1967); Isa Barsali Belli, *European Enamels*, trans. R. Rudorff (London, 1969)

[29] Fox, "Dunbar's *The Goldyn Targe*," 331–32. For other studies of Dunbar's technical virtuosity, see: Florence Ridley, "The Prosodiac Irony of William Dunbar," paper presented in the Special Session, "Scots Literature and Language," Modern Language Association Meeting, New

York, Dec. 27, 1976; Hyde, "Poetic Imagery: A Point of Comparison between Henryson and Dunbar," 183–97; _____, "Primary Sources and Associations of Dunbar's Aureate Imagery," 481–92; Edwin Morgan, "Dunbar and the Language of Poetry," *EIC*, 2 (1952), 138–58; Priscilla Bawcutt, "Aspects of Dunbar's Imagery" in *Chaucer and Middle English Studies*, ed. Beryl Rowland (Kent, OH, 1974), pp. 190–200; Wilhelm F. H. Nicolaisen, "Line and Sentence in Dunbar's Poetry" in *Bards and Makaris*, ed. A. Aitken, M. McDiarmid, D. Thomson (Glasgow, 1977), pp. 41–52.

[30]Gavin Douglas, *The Shorter Poems of Gavin Douglas*, ed. Priscilla J. Bawcutt (Edinburgh & London, 1967). All subsequent references to the *Palice of Honour* will be to the Edinburgh text printed in this edition. _____, *Virgil's Aeneid*, ed. David F. C. Coldwell (Edinburgh & London, 1964). All references to the *Eneados* will be to this text.

[31]For a consideration of the *Palice of Honour* as a poem about poetry, see: Gerald B. Kinneavy, "The Poet in *The Palice of Honour*," *ChauR*, 3 (1969), 280–303.

[32]Alice Miskimin, "The Design of Douglas's *Palice of Honour*," *Acts du 2ᵉ Colloque de Langue et de Litterature Ecossaises (Moyen Age et Renaissance)* (Strasbourg, France, 1978), pp. 396–408.

[33]For a revaluation of this prologue, see: Penelope Schott Starkey, "Gavin Douglas's *Eneados*: Dilemmas in the Nature Prologues," SSL, 11 (1973), 82–98. For useful studies of the nature prologues, see: Charles R. Blyth, "Gavin Douglas' Prologues of Natural Description," *PQ*, 49 (1970), 164–77; Priscilla Bawcutt, *Gavin Douglas: A Critical Study* (Edinburgh, 1976), pp. 164–91.

[34]For a fuller discussion of Douglas's departure from the methods of the medieval and early Renaissance translators of the *Aeneid*, see: Charles R. Blyth, "The 'Kynchtlyke Style': A Study of Gavin Douglas's *Aeneid*," Diss. Harvard 1963, pp. 65–130.

[35]Stephen Hawes, *The Example of Virtue* in *Stephen Hawes: Minor Poems*, ed. Florence Gluck and Alice Morgan (London, 1974), pp. 1–71; *The Pastime of Pleasure*, ed. William E. Mead (London, 1928); *The Conforte of Louers* in *Stephen Hawes: Minor Poems*, pp. 93–122.

[36]For a detailed account of this allegory, see: Gluck and Morgan, *Stephen Hawes: Minor Poems*, pp. 152–62.

[37]For a useful discussion of the figure of David in the Middle Ages and early Renaissance, see: Edward Alberic Gosselin, *The King's Progress to Jerusalem: Some Interpretations of David during the Reformation Period and their Medieval Background* (Malibu, CA, 1976).

[38]John Skelton, *The Poetical Works of John Skelton*, ed. Alexander Dyce (London, 1843), I, 1–14; 25–26; 139–40. All further references to Skelton's poems will be to this edition.

[39]Dyce, ed., *The Poetical Works of John Skelton*, I, 206–24, 311–427; II, 1–25.

⁴⁰For a consideration of the traditions which Parrot inherits, see: William Nelson, *John Skelton, Laureate* (1939, repr.; New York, 1964), pp. 182–83; A. R. Heiserman, *Skelton and Satire'* (Chicago, 1961), pp. 126–89. Note also F. W. Brownlow's interesting suggestion ("The Boke Compiled by Maister Skelton, Poet Laureate, called Speake Parrot," *ELR*, 1 [1972], 3–26) that the figure of Parrot is influenced by Lydgate's *The Churl and the Bird* and the later alchemical interpretations of this poem.

⁴¹For a useful survey of these developments, see: Derek Pearsall, *Old English and Middle English Poetry* (London, 1977), pp. 189–283.